Beckett at 100

Beckett at 100

Revolving It All

Edited by

Linda Ben-Zvi *and* Angela Moorjani

OXFORD

UNIVERSITY PRESS

2008

Oxford University Press, Inc., publishes works that further
Oxford University's objective of excellence
in research, scholarship, and education.

Oxford   New York
Auckland   Cape Town   Dar es Salaam   Hong Kong   Karachi
Kuala Lumpur   Madrid   Melbourne   Mexico City   Nairobi
New Delhi   Shanghai   Taipei   Toronto

With offices in
Argentina   Austria   Brazil   Chile   Czech Republic   France   Greece
Guatemala   Hungary   Italy   Japan   Poland   Portugal   Singapore
South Korea   Switzerland   Thailand   Turkey   Ukraine   Vietnam

Copyright © 2008 by Oxford University Press, Inc.

Published by Oxford University Press, Inc.
198 Madison Avenue, New York, New York 10016

www.oup.com

Oxford is a registered trademark of Oxford University Press

Library of Congress Cataloging-in-Publication Data
Beckett at 100 : revolving it all / edited by Linda Ben-Zvi and Angela Moorjani.
    p. cm.
Includes index.
ISBN 978-0-19-532547-8; 978-0-19-532548-5 (pbk.)
1. Beckett, Samuel, 1906–1989—Criticism and interpretation. I. Ben-Zvi, Linda. II. Moorjani, Angela
PR6003.E282Z5716 2007
848'.91409—dc22   2007011366

9 8 7 6 5 4 3 2 1

Printed in the United States of America
on acid-free paper

For Ruby Cohn

Contents

Contributors

H. PORTER ABBOTT is professor emeritus of English at the University of California, Santa Barbara. He has written numerous articles and two books on Beckett, most recently *Beckett Writing Beckett: The Author in the Autograph*. In 2002, he published *The Cambridge Introduction to Narrative* and is currently preparing a second edition.

LINDA BEN-ZVI is professor of theater studies, Tel Aviv University, where she edits *Assaph: Studies in Theatre*. She is currently serving a second term as president of the Samuel Beckett Society, and since 1996 she has headed the Beckett Working Group of the International Federation of Theatre Research. Her Beckett books include *Samuel Beckett, Women in Beckett*, and *Drawing on Beckett*. Her biography of the American playwright Susan Glaspell, *Susan Glaspell: Her Life and Times*, won the George Freedley Special Jury Prize of the Theatre Library Association of America in 2006.

HERBERT BLAU is currently Byron W. and Alice L. Lockwood Professor of the Humanities at the University of Washington. He has also had a parallel career in the theater, as cofounder and codirector of the Actors' Workshop of San Francisco, then codirector of the Repertory Theater of Lincoln Center in New York, and as artistic director of the experimental group KRAKEN. His most recent books are *The Dubious Spectacle: Extremities of Theater, 1976–2000; Nothing in Itself: Complexions of Fashion;* and *Sails of the Herring Fleet: Essays on Beckett*. He is currently working on *As If: An Autobiography*.

ENOCH BRATER is the Kenneth T. Rowe Collegiate Professor of Dramatic Literature and professor of English and theater at the University of Michigan. His studies of Beckett and other modern and contemporary playwrights have been translated into Japanese, Spanish, French, Portuguese, Polish, and Italian and have been published in book form and journals and periodicals, including the *Nation, American Theatre,* and the *New Republic.* His Beckett studies include *Beyond Minimalism: Beckett's Late Style in the Theater; The Drama in the Text: Beckett's Late Fiction; Why Beckett; The Essential Samuel Beckett; The Theatrical Gamut: Notes for a Post-Beckettian Stage;* and *Beckett at 80/Beckett in Context.*

MARY BRYDEN is professor of French studies at the University of Reading, where she has served in the past as codirector of the Beckett International Foundation. Her previous post was as a professor of European literature at Cardiff University. A recent president of the Samuel Beckett Society, she has been a Visiting Fellow at Magdalen College Oxford and an Andrew W. Mellon Foundation Fellow at Harry Ransom Humanities Research Center, University of Texas at Austin. Her authored or edited books include *Women in Samuel Beckett's Prose and Drama: Her Own Other; Samuel Beckett and the Idea of God; Samuel Beckett and Music; Deleuze and Religion;* and *Gilles Deleuze: Travels in Literature.*

JULIE CAMPBELL, lecturer in literature and drama at the University of Southampton, UK, has written widely on Samuel Beckett's fiction and drama. Recent publications include " 'There is no more . . .': Cultural Memory in *Endgame*," and "The Entrapment of the Female Body in Beckett's Plays in Relation to Jung's Third Tavistock Lecture," in *Historicizing Beckett/Issues of Performance,* vol. 15 of *Samuel Beckett Today/Aujourd'hui.*

IRIT DEGANI-RAZ lectures in the Multidisciplinary Program of the Arts, Tel Aviv University. Her doctorate from the Cohen Center for the Philosophy and History of Science and Ideas, Tel Aviv University, was on the topic "Theatrical Possible Worlds" and examined logic and uncertainty in Beckett's works as a case study of a general theory of theater. Her recent major publications include "Beckett's Worlds as Thought Experiments," in *Drawing on Beckett*; "Possible Worlds and the Concept of 'Reference' in the Semiotics of Theatre," *Semiotica* 147.1/4; and "Theatrical Fictional Worlds, Counterfactuals, and Scientific Thought Experiments," *Semiotica* 157.1/4.

ELIN DIAMOND is professor of English at Rutgers University. She is the author of *Unmaking Mimesis: Essays on Feminism and Theater* and *Pinter's Comic Play* and editor of *Performance and Cultural Politics.* Her essays on drama, performance, and feminist theory have appeared in *Theatre Journal, ELH, Discourse, TDR, Modern Drama, Kenyon Review, Art and Cinema,*

Maska, Cahiers Renaud-Barrault, and numerous anthologies in the United States, Europe, and India. She is currently at work on a book on modernism and performance and is coeditor of the forthcoming *Cambridge Companion to Caryl Churchill.*

MATTHIJS ENGELBERTS is based at the University of Amsterdam, where he is a member of the Amsterdam School for Cultural Analysis. His current research is centered on the relations between different media in the arts. Among his publications are eight edited or coedited volumes of the annual bilingual review *Samuel Beckett Today/Aujourd'hui (SBT/A)*; articles on Beckett, Tardieu, Duras, Molière, surrealist theater, and theater sports; and *Défis du récit scénique* on the relation between narrative and theater, mainly in Beckett. He has been a member of the editorial board of *SBT/A* since its inception.

PETER GIDAL is an experimental filmmaker and writer on aesthetics. His 16mm films include *Volcano, No Night No Day, Assumption, Flare Out, Guilt,* and the earlier *Room Film 1973, Up-Side Down Feature,* and *Clouds.* His books include *Materialist Film*; *Andy Warhol: Films and Paintings*; and *Understanding Beckett: Monologue and Gesture.* He lives and works in London.

S. E. GONTARSKI is Sarah Herndon Professor of English at Florida State University, where he is general editor of the *Journal of Beckett Studies,* Journal of Beckett Studies Books, and Journal of Beckett Studies E-books. He has edited *Samuel Beckett: The Complete Short Prose, 1928–1989;* and *Endgame* and *The Shorter Plays,* volumes 2 and 4 of The Theatrical Notebooks of Samuel Beckett series. Recent books include *The Grove Companion to Samuel Beckett* and *The Faber Companion to Samuel Beckett,* both written with C. J. Ackerley, and *Beckett after Beckett,* coedited with Anthony Uhlmann. He is currently editing *The Blackwell Companion to Samuel Beckett.*

DAVID HOUSTON JONES, lecturer in French at the University of Exeter, UK, completed a Ph.D. on Samuel Beckett and Jean Genet at the University of Cambridge and subsequently taught at the University of Paris VIII (St. Denis), St. John's College, Oxford, and the University of Bristol. His publications include *The Body Abject: Self and Text in Jean Genet and Samuel Beckett*; *Jean Genet: "Journal du voleur"*; and a critical edition of François Tanazacq, *La suprême abjection de la passion du Christ.*

JAMES KNOWLSON is emeritus professor of French at the University of Reading, where he established the Beckett Archive, now the Beckett International Foundation, and founded the *Journal of Beckett Studies.* He wrote a biography of Beckett, *Damned to Fame: The Life of Samuel Beckett,* and is the author or editor of ten other books on Beckett. The general editor of The Theatrical Notebooks of Samuel Beckett, he edited *Krapp's Last Tape* and coedited *Waiting for Godot* for that four-volume series. Most recently, he published *Images of Beckett* (with John Haynes) and *Beckett Remembering Remembering Beckett* (with Elizabeth Knowlson).

CATHERINE LAWS is associate director of music at Dartington College of Arts, UK, and a pianist specializing in contemporary music. Much of her research focuses on the musical quality of Beckett's work, composers' responses to his texts, and related issues in the relationship between music, language, and meaning. She has published a range of articles on these topics and is currently completing a book on Beckett and music. Other research interests include the relationship between postmodern theory and contemporary musicology, contemporary music performance practice, and gender and music.

CARLA LOCATELLI, professor of theory and comparative literature and vice-rector for international relations and research at the University of Trento, Italy, is also associated on a visiting basis with the English department at the University of Pennsylvania. She is the author or editor of fourteen books, including *Unwording the World: Beckett's Prose Works after the Nobel Prize.* She has published more than 150 articles and contributions to volumes, many of which relate to the Beckett canon.

ANNA MCMULLAN is chair in drama at Queens University Belfast, Northern Ireland. She is author of *Theatre on Trial: The Later Drama of Samuel Beckett* and numerous articles on Beckett in collections such as *Palgrave Advances in Samuel Beckett Studies, Samuel Beckett: A Casebook,* and *The Cambridge Companion to Samuel Beckett. Performing Embodiment in Samuel Beckett's Theatre and Media Plays* will be published by Routledge in 2007.

ANGELA MOORJANI is professor emerita of modern languages and linguistics (French) at the University of Maryland–UMBC. Her poststructural study, *Abysmal Games in the Novels of Samuel Beckett,* and, more recently, *The Aesthetics of Loss and Lessness* and *Beyond Fetishism* reflect on the aesthetic and ethical effects of melancholy in literature and the arts. Coeditor of several collections of articles on Beckett, she serves on the editorial board of *Samuel Beckett Today/Aujourd'hui*. Her recent essays investigate gaze deixis, cultural ghosts, and multitiered effects in Beckett.

NAOYA MORI is professor of English at Kobe Women's University, Japan. He is a coeditor of *Beckett Taizen (Beckett A to Z)*, and a cotranslator of James Knowlson's *Damned to Fame* into Japanese. Among his recent essays focusing on Beckett and philosophy, specifically Leibniz's monadology, are "Beckett's Windows and 'the Windowless Self,'" in *Samuel Beckett Today/Aujourd'hui* 14, and "Korogaru Ishi no Mita Yume" ("The Dream a Rolling Stone Dreamt"), in *Samuel Beckett no Vision to Undo* (*Samuel Beckett's Vision and Movement*).

MINAKO OKAMURO, professor of theater and film arts at Waseda University, Tokyo, coedited *Beckett Taizen* (*All about Beckett*). She has published a number of articles in Japanese on Beckett and recently translated *Endgame* into Japanese. Her essays in English include "Alchemical Dances in Beckett and Yeats," *Samuel Beckett Today/Aujourd'hui* 14, and "The Cartesian Egg: Alchemical Images in Beckett's Early Writings," *Journal of Beckett Studies* 9.2. She was the general director of the 2006 International Samuel Beckett Symposium in Tokyo: "Borderless Beckett," held at Waseda University.

ANTONIA RODRÍGUEZ-GAGO is profesora titular of English literature at the University Autónoma of Madrid, Spain, where she teaches English Renaissance and Jacobean drama and contemporary Anglo-American theater. *Rockaby, Ohio Impromptu,* and *Catastrophe* were premiered in Spain in 1985 using her authorized translations. She is currently preparing the fifth edition of her annotated bilingual edition of *Happy Days*. Her recent Beckett essays include "Translating and Adapting *Company* for the Screen," in *Samuel Beckett Today/Aujourd'hui* 11; "Beckett's Performances in Spain," published in Italian translation in *Drammaturgia: Beckett in Scena*; and "Memory (and Forgetting) in Beckett's Late Women's Plays," in *Drawing on Beckett*.

JÜRGEN SIESS retired recently as professor of comparative literature from the University of Caen, France. His principal fields of research are correspondence, theater, eighteenth-century fiction, and intercultural communication, with his work on Beckett focusing mainly on the theater and other media. Among his recent publications are the edited and coedited volumes: *Rilke, images de la ville, figures de l'artiste*; *Qu'est-ce que la tolérance? Perspectives sur Voltaire*; SEMEN 20—*Le rapport de places dans l'épistolaire*; *L'épistolaire au féminin*; and the essay "The Actor's Body and Institutional Tensions: From *Act without Words I* to *Not I*," in *Drawing on Beckett*.

MARIKO HORI TANAKA, professor at Aoyama Gakuin University, Japan, has published on British and American theater. Her articles on Beckett include "Special Features of Beckett Performances in Japan," in *Beckett On and On...*; "The Legacy of Beckett in Contemporary Japanese Theatre," in *Drawing on Beckett*; "Postmodern Stagings of *Waiting for Godot*" and "Elements of Haiku in Beckett," in *Samuel Beckett Today/Aujourd'hui* 6 and 11; and "'Hidden Voices' in Samuel Beckett's Late Work," in *The Harp*, the International Association for the Study of Irish Literature, Japan Bulletin. She has also coedited *Beckett Taizen* and cotranslated James Knowlson's *Damned to Fame* into Japanese.

HERSH ZEIFMAN, professor of English and drama at York University, Toronto, has published widely on contemporary British and American drama. Formerly a script reader for London's National Theatre, coeditor of the journal *Modern Drama,* and president of the Samuel Beckett Society, he is the coeditor of *Contemporary British Drama* and the editor of *David Hare: A Casebook*.

Beckett at 100

Introduction

LINDA BEN-ZVI

S AMUEL JOHNSON, in making the claim for the greatness of Shakespeare, argued that "a test of literary merit" can be determined by whether a writer has "outlived his century" (qtd. in Quinault 304). If any proof were needed for the greatness of Samuel Beckett, the 2006 outpouring of events around the world marking the centenary of his birth—stage and media performances; conferences and lectures; new editions of his writings; gala concerts; and art, film, and photography exhibits—indicate that he too has "outlived his century."

"I am not sure what a centenarian Samuel Beckett would have made of these effusions in the country of his birth," his nephew and executor Edward Beckett wrote in the official catalogue for the Dublin festival, alluding to his uncle's well-known dislike of any celebrations in his name, "but I am proud to witness what his country is making of him" (2). Unlike James Joyce, whom his biographer Richard Ellmann claims, "thought about his centenary long before it occurred to his readers to do so" (par. 1), Beckett tried assiduously to avoid such occasions. In response to one planned in Paris to mark his seventy-fifth birthday, he confided to his friend and scenic designer Jocelyn Herbert: "I dread the year now upon us and all the fuss in store for me here, as if it were my centenary. I'll make myself scare while it lasts, where I don't know. Perhaps the great Wall of China, crouch behind it till the coast is clear" (qtd. in Knowlson 671). "Damned to fame," he jotted in his notebook at the time, the phrase his biographer James Knowlson chose as the title of his book. Yet, even China—a country still primarily wedded to Ibsen and O'Neill realism and which officially ignores its own

Beckett-influenced, Nobel Prize–winning writer Gao Xingjian[1]—would have provided little anonymity in 2006, given the considerable number of Beckett events held there.[2]

While the centenary frenzy might have troubled Beckett, it has served a purpose. It has brought new audiences and readers to his writing; it has also provided opportunities for scholars and theater practitioners to rethink traditional readings, theories, and stagings of his works; consider new contexts and approaches for future research and productions; and generally reassess Beckett's place in his own century and his legacy to the postmillennial world. The purpose of this collection—the first to be published after the centenary year—is to offer a wide range of essays reflecting these directions and illustrating what contemporary scholarship is "making of" Beckett and his writing 100 years after his birth and 19 years after his death.

The majority of the essays were first presented at Trinity College Dublin, Beckett's alma mater, in the Samuel Beckett Working Group symposium, which served as the academic component of the Dublin centenary celebration in April 2006. Thirty-eight participants from fourteen countries gave papers; of those, fourteen are published here, along with eight others, most by previous Working Group members.[3] We have divided them into three broad categories: Thinking through Beckett, Shifting Perspectives, and Echoing Beckett. Like most of Beckett's plays, in this book too images precede words. The book opens with experimental filmmaker and scholar Peter Gidal's selection of stills from his *Room Film 1973* whose "ill-seen" fragments resonate with Beckett's attacks on the authority of eye and "I." And James Knowlson offers never-before-published descriptions excerpted from Beckett's 1936–1937 Germany travel diary, with permission from the Beckett Estate.

These selections and the essays that follow are dedicated to Ruby Cohn, charter member of the Working Group and the most consistent and influential voice in Beckett scholarship from its inception. Ruby published her first Beckett essay in 1959, undeterred by an editor who informed her, "We like your criticism, but we don't feel your author merits publishing space" (*Canon* 1); and for nearly 50 years she has been illustrating the "merits" of "her author." Her meticulous scholarship laid the foundations of Beckett studies; her lucid writing, elegant and always to the point, nourished it; and her great generosity of spirit provided the model for the collegiality that has developed among Beckett scholars. All those who study Beckett are familiar with her work. Most in the field know her personally. Some have maintained friendships with her that go back decades—mine thirty years. Angela Moorjani tells of hoarding Ruby moments ever since Édouard Morot-Sir invited Beckett scholars to muse over his "art of rhetoric" two years before Beckett's seventieth birthday. For us Ruby is more than a respected critic; she is our intellectual conscience, our ideal reader. I remember my Colorado colleague Rubin Rabinovitz—a fine scholar whose early, tragic death impoverished our field—telling me that when he wrote on Beckett, he wrote for one person: Ruby Cohn. I knew exactly what he meant. To write "for Ruby" means to write clearly, without cant or pomposity, and, most important, to be faithful to Beckett's work, no matter from what critical direction you approach it.

Revolving It All, the subtitle of this book, relates to Cohn's work. The phrase is taken from *Footfalls,* where it is descriptive of the central image of that play, the "revolving walker," herself a semblance of those continuously revolving, mutable characters, places, and themes that pervade Beckett's writing and evade fixity. These tenacious traces of presence, desiccated though they may be, are still attached to the physical world of bodies, things, and places, whether unnamed, variously named, or misnamed. Cohn described this condition in the first lines of her first Beckett study, *Samuel Beckett: The Comic Gamut* (1962):

> On Samuel Beckett's planet, matter is minimal, physiography and physiology barely support life. The air is exceedingly thin, and the light exceedingly dim. But all the cluttered complexity of our own planet is required to educate the taste that can savor the unique comic flavor of Beckett's creation. Our world, "so various, so beautiful, so new," so stingily admitted to Beckett's work, is nevertheless the essential background for appreciation of that work. (3)

Her own work on Beckett over the years has consistently focused on the here and now of the texts, and the theatereality—her coined word (*Just Play* 30–31)—of his stage world, a practice shaped by what she admits is "my habitual search for meaning" (*Canon* 383) and sustained by her abiding excitement about theater, "the most perishable of goods" (*Modern Shakespeare* 393). In criticism never cut to fit the particular fashion of the time, she has elucidated the links between Beckett's writing and lived experience, between the challenging complexities of the plays, fiction, and poetry and the complexities of modern life that gave rise to them and continue to shape the powerful and personal reactions of readers, audiences, and critics over time. Cohn's title for her reading of the Beckett oeuvre, *A Beckett Canon,* reflects her awareness that every reading is *a* reading not *the* reading, hers "personal, after long immersion" (2).

On the first page of that book she declares, "I flaunt the label that has sometimes been scornfully affixed to me—humanist" (1). After a period in which some theoretical approaches have omitted lived experience from the parameters of their discussions, a growing number of centenary studies seem to have come back to Cohn and her basic starting point, paraphrased by Steven Connor in a lecture at the 2006 Tokyo symposium: "the un-encompassibility of the here and now, that is possible of access only in the here and now" (5), this presentment of presence the locus of Beckett's writing, no matter how "parched, patched, [and] penurious" (7) it may be. "In such a world that's all I can manage, more than I could," Beckett told Alan Schneider (qtd. in Harmon 24); and "in such a world" palpable, present, but ultimately unknowable, unnamable, and unencompassible, Cohn's criticism, like Beckett's writing, is grounded. So too in different ways, are the essays that follow.

Despite a personal predilection toward explication, I forgo the extensive parsing that is part of traditional introductions to essay collections. The subtlety and complexity of the essays, their arguments, language, and style—what has always marked the best of Beckett criticism—are lost in paraphrase. What I do want to point out, however, are some emerging themes and approaches that run through a number of these centenary studies. I will begin by using a technique William Saroyan employed in his sleeve note review for the recording of the Broadway premiere of *Waiting for Godot,* unearthed and discussed by Mary Bryden in her essay: mentioning what is not included as a way of pointing to what is. In these essays there are no comprehensive readings of the Beckett canon or even one specific work, as might be expected given the centenary opportunity for account-taking. Nobel Prize–winning novelist J. M. Coetzee, whose doctoral dissertation was on Beckett's early fiction, chose as the title for his public lecture at the Tokyo conference "Eight Ways of Looking at Samuel Beckett," each way a discrete form and approach, the aggregate producing multivocality much like Beckett's with no attempt to impose thematic unity.

If there is no "clear autobahn through Beckett's works"—as poet Paul Muldoon admitted at the end of his lecture at the Dublin conference in which he attempted to explicate references in *Watt* in order to arrive at a unified reading of the novel—some routes earlier traveled are no longer being taken. For example, feminist readings have either run their course or are so self-evident that they need not be pursued. The same goes for studies of the body; to use Beckett's words, there is "not another crumb of carrion left" (*Ill Seen* 59), at least concerning descriptions of Beckett's decrepits. Readings exclusively based on specific poststructuralist thinkers have become rarer as their works become successfully incorporated into broader readings, as illustrated in a number of studies that follow.

Those are some of the subjects not included. The major trends emerging from the centenary and presented in this book can be divided roughly into five categories that generally traverse the book's tripartite division.

1. Historicizing and Particularizing

One striking trend is the acceleration in the number of studies that have looked at Beckett's works through multifocal lenses correcting for the historical as well as the metaphysical or universal. In his personal, powerful essay Herbert Blau notes the "political immediacy" he found in the Beckett plays he directed in the 1960s—more political than those of Brecht—and argues their relevance to our contemporary world that has learned nothing from the past. Blau, David Houston Jones, Anna McMullan, and Mariko Hori Tanaka all point to concrete images related to Beckett's experiences in World War II and the Holocaust, which some earlier critics tended to universalize or overlook: the barbed wire that encircles the Krap apartment and the family's indifference to it in *Eleutheria;* the corpses and skeletons in the "charnel-house!" of *Waiting for Godot;* the stink of death hovering over *Endgame;* and those unnamed but ubiquitous torturers and tortures that run through the entire canon.[4] As Blau argues, while Beckett's people curse their birth, their words also point to Beckett's "undeluded awareness of those corporeal bodies out there, or once there, but incinerated, or buried too, some of them, not where death came with birth, but where, dead, yes dead, imagine, they've never yet been found, or in a mass grave, among the multitudinous dead" (48). An important intertext for connecting the ontological and the historical, Jones and Hori Tanaka suggest, is

Remnants of Auschwitz, Giorgio Agamben's exploration of the possibilities of testimony after the Holocaust, in which he argues that only the absent, silent dead, the corpses, or those living-dead—the *Muselmann* of the concentration camps—can testify, speaking "only on the basis of the impossibility of speaking" (164), an awareness that lies at the heart of Beckett's work[5] and is reflected, Jones indicates, in Beckett's linguistic displacements and the multiple naming that point to the impossibility of ever claiming the subject position. In a variation of the argument, Carla Locatelli suggests that a chain of images, rather than names, can be substituted for agency, as illustrated in *Krapp's Last Tape* and *Not I,* reflective of both the impossibility of autobiography and the desire for it by audiences and readers who assign agency to Beckett as unitary author of his work in order to assuage their own sense of lost subjectivity in the contemporary world.

2. Contesting Isms

If Beckett's writings can be historicized and particularized as well as universalized, then the question arises: where is he—and who is he—when he is home? McMullan calls his writing exilic, marked by an alterity that denies fixed classification of any kind, such as the recent Irish trend toward Hibernianization of Beckett and his works, a process she claims exchanges one "we" for another, and which Beckett warned against in "The Capital of the Ruins." On the other hand, Jürgen Siess argues that in cultivating the stance, or *posture,* of outsider and decentered writer, Beckett was paradoxically looking for an entry into the Parisian literary field he found when he arrived there in the late 1930s.

Nationalism, like any other ism or defining belief system, was anathema to Beckett; therefore, as Porter Abbott suggests, he repeatedly denied that he was a philosopher, since "the philosopher's trade [...] is to make a system with noncontradictory parts" (85), whereas art, Beckett understood, was predicated on "letting go," renouncing control of any sort. That is not to deny the part that philosophy has played in Beckett's writing. Over the years, numerous studies have explored the subject. In this current collection, Stan Gontarski suggests the importance of the theories of Henri Bergson, whom Beckett discussed in his 1931 lectures on modern literature at Trinity College; and Naoya Mori probes Gottfried Wilhelm Leibniz's theories of motion that he argues parallel those employed by Beckett.

3. Coupling the Arts

The relation between Beckett's works and other art forms has gained critical attention in recent years, prompted by the biography of James Knowlson and studies such as Lois Oppenheim on art and Catherine Laws on music. Almost every centenary event included exhibits of paintings influencing or influenced by Beckett; concerts featuring the works of composers who set music to Beckett texts, including Morton Feldman, Philip Glass, Heinz Holliger, Earl Kim, György Kurtág, and Marcel Mihalovici; and tapes of Beckett's film, radio, and television productions. In this collection, Laws's essay typifies this interdisciplinary approach, detailing the ways in which the techniques of Beckett, Feldman, and Jasper Johns have points of complementarity, indicated by their similar nonreferential frames of reference. Beckett's fascination with music's simultaneities and his dazzling blend of artistic allusions—from ancient Egypt's underworld to Adam Elsheimer's boundless space—are the focus of Angela Moorjani's essay on the multi-tiered and destabilizing effects of *Play.* Two essays discuss Beckett's work related to film and television: Matthijs Engelberts's study suggesting the importance of film criticism, particularly the writing of Rudolph Arnheim, on Beckett's *Film;* and my essay reading selected Beckett television plays through the theories of media guru Marshall McLuhan, a new name in Beckett studies, whose own writing references Beckett.

4. Selecting a Text for the Times

Critics in specific periods have tended to focus on certain Beckett writings that most directly illustrate contemporary concerns. In the 1960s and 1970s in drama it was *Waiting for Godot* or *Endgame;* in the 1980s *Happy Days* or *Not I;* in this decade, judging from these centenary essays and other recent research, it is *Krapp's Last Tape.*[6] Carla Locatelli, Enoch Brater, Irit Degani-Raz, and Antonia Rodríguez-Gago all discuss it. Brater elucidates Beckett's strain of romanticism, most powerfully and evocatively evidenced in Krapp's recorded memory of the girl in the punt. Degani-Raz argues that

Beckett's use of the tape recorder can be understood as a modern reversal of the myth of Telephus—what wounds can heal—since rather than "healing human longing for a paradise that has been lost" by preserving memories, it actually distorts and corrupts, illustrating the destructive aspects of technology in the process (191). Rodríguez-Gago focuses on the performative construction of Krapp as both speaker and listener, interacting with the mechanical recorder, a theme Locatelli also explores, describing both the contrapuntal discrepancies between speaking and listening to oneself speak and the "arbitrary and fragmented nature of self-portraiture based on memory, especially when played ironically against willed intention" (73).

5. Tracing Influences and Impacts

Beckett's influence on other playwrights and novelists, and theirs on him, has been a constant theme over the years. The centenary studies in this collection, however, rather than confining themselves to delineating specific, shared similarities, tend to show the complexities, challenges, and dangers of literary legacies as well as benefits. Julie Campbell's essay on Paul Auster's debt to Beckett highlights the burden and anxiety of influence Auster felt and his means of overcoming it.[7] Mariko Hori Tanaka adds Japanese post–World War II playwright Minoru Betsuyaku to the list of followers, illustrating the ways in which his post-Hiroshima plays are inspired by Beckett's images of pain and torture, just as Pinter's plays are as well. Mary Bryden pairs Beckett with William Saroyan, pointing to their surprising thematic connections, despite stylistic and linguistic differences, while Elin Diamond, although not suggesting influence, suggests the ways in which Caryl Churchill's plays, like Beckett's, create strong emotional responses despite the spareness of the texts. Beckett's own debt to Yeats has often been discussed, but in her essay Minako Okamuro cites the ways in which the poet's interest in the occult influenced Beckett's *...but the clouds...* and *Words and Music,* as did Yeats's romanticism, a topic also taken up by Brater in his essay.

The final essay of the collection, by Hersh Zeifman, stands alone. It illustrates how Samuel Beckett, as well as *Waiting for Godot,* has become a cultural icon, and how the creator and his creations are being absorbed into popular culture around the world. To illustrate the tendency, Zeifman offers examples of Beckett citings in a number of recent plays: Justin Fleming's *Burnt Piano* (1999), Sean Dixon's *Sam's Last Dance* (1997), and Michael Hastings's *Calico*

(2004). What Fleming's work points to, and Zeifman underlines, is that "the only Beckett that truly exists for us is the one we create by responding to his work" (318). What has most strongly emerged from Beckett's centenary year and is reflected in the essays in this book is how rich, powerful, and varied these responses continue to be as we move into Beckett's second century.

Notes

1. Gao Xingjian's 1983 play *The Bus Stop* has obvious parallels to *Waiting for Godot,* in its ironic, yet politically charged, tale of people waiting ten years for the right bus to arrive.

2. Beckett events in China included a workshop held at the Central Academy of Drama in Beijing led by Dublin director Sarah Jane Scaife; a festival of his short plays presented in Shanghai; and two versions of *Waiting for Godot,* one in Chinese opera style, the other the celebrated Dublin Gate Theatre production, directed by Walter Asmus, which had sold-out runs in both Shanghai and Beijing.

3. An additional group of essays from the Dublin Working Group will appear in *Samuel Beckett Today/Aujourd'hui (SBT/A)* 18 (forthcoming 2007).

4. In addition to Beckett biographies, a number of works have explored the subject of Beckett and World War II and the Holocaust. See, for example, Blackman, Lamont, Moorjani, Perloff, and Uhlmann.

5. Russell Smith also reads Beckett through Agamben in his essay in *Samuel Beckett Today/Aujourd'hui (SBT/A)* 18 (forthcoming, 2007).

6. The 2005 Beckett Working Group also chose *Krapp's Last Tape* for its central text. The members, writing about the work, found that they had barely uncovered its possibilities.

7. Auster was not alone; Jonathan Kalb's article querying twelve American playwrights about the influence of Beckett clearly shows this anxiety. David Mamet, for example, refused to respond, remarking only, "He was a great kisser," while Tony Kushner, after calling Beckett "that matzo of a playwright," as opposed to himself, more the lasagna type, spoke seriously of the influence, "so powerful that it threatened paralysis for a playwright [...] because his voice is so overwhelmingly persuasive and influential." See also Auster's and Edward Albee's comments in *Beckett Remembering/Remembering Beckett* (Knowlson and Knowlson 229–34), which discuss the dangers that Beckett's bogey creates.

Works Cited

Agamben, Giorgio. *Remnants of Auschwitz: The Witness and the Archive.* Trans. Daniel Heller-Roazen. New York: Zone Books, 1999.

Beckett, Edward. "A Message from Edward Beckett." *Beckett Centenary Festival: A Commemorative Programme.* Dublin: Department of Arts, Sport, and Tourism, 2006. 2.

Beckett, Samuel. *The Collected Shorter Plays.* New York: Grove, 1984.

———. *Ill Seen Ill Said.* New York: Grove, 1981.

Blackman, Jackie. "Beckett Judaizing Beckett: 'a Jew from Greenland' in Paris." (Forthcoming in SBT/A 18, 2007).

Coetzee, J. M. "Eight Ways of Looking at Samuel Beckett." Borderless Beckett Symposium, Tokyo, 30 Sept. 2006. (Forthcoming in *Borderless Beckett*, vol. 19 of SBT/A, 2008.)

Cohn, Ruby. *A Beckett Canon.* Ann Arbor: University of Michigan Press, 2001.

———. *Just Play.* Princeton, NJ: Princeton University Press, 1980.

———. *Modern Shakespeare's Offshoots.* Princeton, NJ: Princeton University Press, 1976.

———. *Samuel Beckett: The Comic Gamut.* New Brunswick, NJ: Rutgers University Press, 1962.

Connor, Steven. "'On such and such a day... in such a world': Beckett's Radical Finitude." Borderless Beckett Symposium, Tokyo, 1 Oct. 2006. 7 July 2007. <http://www.bbk.ac.uk/english/skc/finitude/finitude.pdf>. (Forthcoming in *Borderless Beckett*, vol. 19 of *SBT/A*, 2008.)

Ellmann, Richard. "Joyce at 100." *New York Review of Books* 18 Nov. 1982. 7 July 2007 <http://www.nybooks.com/articles/6404>

Gao, Xingjian. *The Bus Stop.* Trans. Kimberly Besio. *Theatre and Society: An Anthology of Contemporary Chinese Drama.* Ed. Haiping Yan. New York: Sharpe, 1998.

Harmon, Maurice, ed. *No Author Better Served: The Correspondence of Samuel Beckett and Alan Schneider.* Cambridge, MA: Harvard University Press, 1998.

Kalb, Jonathan. "You Must Go On after Beckett. I Can't Go On after Beckett. Go On." *New York Times* 26 Mar. 2006: Arts Sec., 4.

Knowlson, James. *Damned to Fame: The Life of Samuel Beckett.* London: Bloomsbury, 1996.

Knowlson, James, and Elizabeth Knowlson, eds. *Beckett Remembering/Remembering Beckett.* London: Bloomsbury, 2006.

Lamont, Rosette. "Samuel Beckett's Wandering Jew." *Reflections of the Holocaust in Art and Literature.* Ed. Randolph L. Braham. Boulder, CO: Social Science Monographs, 1990. 35–53.

Moorjani, Angela. "Diogenes Lampoons Alexandre Kojève: Cultural Ghosts in Beckett's Early French Plays." *Drawing on Beckett.* Ed. Linda Ben-Zvi. Tel Aviv: Assaph Books, 2003. 69–88.

Muldoon, Paul. "Watt Ho: On Being Taken Aback by *Watt*." Beckett Centenary Symposium. Trinity College Dublin. 7 Apr. 2006.

Perloff, Marjorie. "'In Love with Hiding': Samuel Beckett's War." *Iowa Review* 35 (2005): 76–103.

Quinault, Roland. "The Cult of the Century, 1784–1914." *Historical Research* 71 (1998): 303–23.

Uhlmann, Anthony. *Beckett and Poststructuralism.* Cambridge: Cambridge University Press, 1999.

Images

FOR RUBY COHN

Still for Ruby

PETER GIDAL

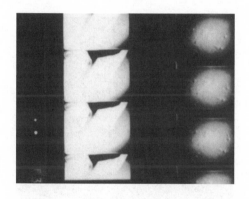

from *Room Film 1973*

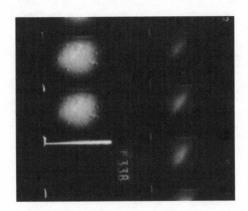

16   For Ruby Cohn

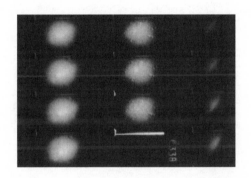

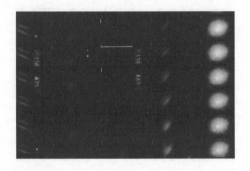

18   For Ruby Cohn

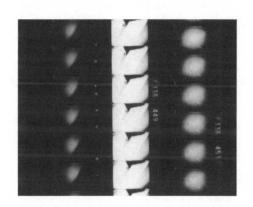

20   For Ruby Cohn

Beckett the Tourist

Bamberg and Würzburg

JAMES KNOWLSON

IN THE COURSE of a six-month-long stay in Germany in 1936–1937, Samuel Beckett spent the final week of February 1937 in the beautiful, small Mainfranken towns of Bamberg and Würzburg. His earlier, much lengthier stays in the larger cities of Hamburg, Berlin, and Dresden had often been busy and social. To his own great surprise, he had managed to establish contact there with several groups of people, mostly artists, art collectors, dealers, or booksellers. This happened because one acquaintance would introduce him to another, who would then pass him on to another.[1]

By contrast, during his stays of only a few days in Bamberg and Würzburg, he found himself alone, like any other foreign tourist traveling on his own, dependent for any company on casual meetings in hotels, cafés, restaurants, or public buildings. While he was in the two towns, he bought (and studied avidly) various books and guides to the cathedrals, churches, and public buildings, often seeking out the most recondite details concerning the architecture, the statuary, and the paintings. And every night, just as he had done throughout the whole of his stay in Germany, he confided his impressions on what he had seen during the day to a voluminous travel diary. He had been in the country since the beginning of October and had already reached volume five. In these diary entries he reveals far more about himself and his attitudes toward art and sculpture than he does anywhere else in his writings, except perhaps for his postwar letters to his art-critic friend Georges Duthuit.

For Beckett, solitariness combined with unfamiliarity to confer a strange sense of wonderment on what for local residents were very commonplace events or sights. Certain visual scenes caught his eye and appealed to his writer's sensibility. In Bamberg, for instance, he spotted "a little girl whipping at [a] top that will not stand up on [a] spinner, unlike little boy yesterday curling his lash round."[2] At the Concordiabrunnen, he noticed an "old woman filling [a] huge pitcher with straps" with water from the fountain.[3] Crossing a little bridge over the Regnitz, he registered how the water was "dead calm on one side and a boiling fury on [the] other, lovely brown, grey, yellow view back downstream,"[4] and, from the main Obere Brücke, he recorded how the water goes "out of light into darkness."[5] Approaching Bamberg Cathedral's imposing east front, he felt "the east towers falling on top of me as the clouds drift behind them *away* from me."[6] A few days later, as he was wandering around Würzburg, he looked down the steep slopes of the vineyards to watch "the women below toiling down through the vines with hods full of fresh earth, depositing, and toiling back for a refill, from the only man with them. They stand patiently till it is their turn, then he shovels the clay into hod[s] on their backs" (see figure 1).[7]

It was, of course, winter at the time of his visits, and the weather was mostly atrocious during his stays both in Bamberg and Würzburg. His trip out into the country from Bamberg to Banz, for instance, and his long trek on from there to the pilgrimage church of Vierzehnheiligen took place in

FIGURE I. Marienberg, vineyards, and bridge over the Main, Würzburg.

an unpleasant mixture of fog, snow, sleet, and pouring rain. On several other occasions in the towns, too, he got soaked through to the skin. Yet he displayed a quite extraordinary resilience and a determination not to allow the bad weather to stop him visiting the buildings that he had been told in Dresden should on no account be missed.

Architecture, Art, and Erudition

Bamberg

While he was in Bamberg, Beckett spent a lot of his time in its imposing cathedral ("4 towered double choired Romanesque and transitional, with 18th century spires"),[8] returning there on several separate occasions. A fascinating passage in his diary in which he sets down his reactions to the celebrated Fürstentor, the north entrance door to the cathedral, brings together both his keen interest in history and his wide knowledge of the history of art:

> Whole feeling stiller and transcendentaler than in Naumburg or even Freiberg. Which does not necessarily involve a lesser naturalism (Stephen, Adam and Eve and the last apostel [apostle] at extreme right of Fürstentor), but tends to selection of ideal attitude. The damned and saved in Last Judgment are naturalized almost to caricature, especially among former [i.e., the damned] figures of miser and Emperor. And yet the Naumburger figures and the best of the Meissen belong to an utterly different vision, a gulf apart from this, almost the difference between Giotto and Masaccio, because Beato Angelico kommt gar nicht in Frage [i.e., does not come into it]. [...] Interior proportions practically identical with those of Naumburg, but again more exalted.[9]

In the diary account of his thoughts in front of one statue or group of statues or another, he revealed his artistic preferences as well as the idiosyncratic nature of his judgments. The *Bamberger Reiter* (Bamberg Horseman), the most famous of all the statues in the cathedral, seemed to him, for example, "somehow disappointing, too much of an idea (chivalrous Treu[e] [loyalty]) and hardly so superbly lonely and remote as Stauss found him."[10] (Stauss was someone whom Beckett had met in Dresden who, while showing him an illustrated book on Bamberg, had enthused about these aspects of the *Reiter.*) There were, however, a number of other statues in the cathedral that appealed more directly to Beckett's aesthetic sense and even his sense of humor. "The Elisabeth wonderful," he wrote, "in fact whole Visitation group, with incredible grinning angel very close to the Stephen of Adamstor" (see figure 2).[11] Reading an article by Karl Giebert in the *Bamberger Volksblatt,* which spoke of the "brutal" juxtaposition around one pillar of the statues of Elizabeth, Mary, and the Laughing Angel, he commented, "God grant that there were more such 'brutalities' in art."[12] The two celebrated statues of Ecclesia and Synagogue were, he felt, "still and withdrawn to the point of petrification. (Petrified statue

FIGURE 2. Elizabeth, *The Visitation,* Bamberg Cathedral.

is good.) Annunciation wonderfully gentle and tender with intent angel almost on tiptoe and right hand in caressing gesture."[13] And, after another visit, he wrote in his diary that he was "disappointed that I can't keep a laughing angel in an Annunciation."[14]

Beckett's daylong excursion from Bamberg to the church at Banz and then to the Vierzehnheiligen (Fourteen Saints Basilica) elicited some of his most revealing remarks. The Vierzehnheiligen was, he wrote, "Open. Cooler, calmer, infinitely nobler than Banz. Extraordinary ground plan (voir en regard [= see opposite, where he had sketched a little plan of the shape of the church]), i.e. essentially the beam [of the cross] one large and two small ovals and the arms two circles. A pot bellied bacchanalian Christ Crucified."[15] Of the altar pictures by Palme in the church, he noted, "Religious feeling gloriously absent, the Virgin a more or less naked nymph, saints shepherds and shepherdesses."[16] In 1445 and 1446, a herdsman resting on the spot had experienced a vision of the Christ child, seeing him surrounded by the fourteen saints revered in the region for their protection against the plague and other diseases. When Vierzehnheiligen was constructed—and it is the most famous example of rococo church architecture by Balthasar Neumann in Germany—it became (and still is today) a revered, much frequented place of pilgrimage. The oval belly of the nave was, wrote Beckett, "occupied by the huge Gnadenaltar [mercy altar] with the saintly 14, crowned by the child Jesus in glory with a red cross on his bosom, with at his feet in bowl relics of the 14. Through glass door E [East] end visible the naked earth where the Vision took place. Of figures St Vitus with cock and St Margaret with dragon on string especially charming."[17] What is perhaps most significant here is that Beckett's interest in the details of the legend dominated his skepticism and his distrust of tales of miracles. One is reminded of a remark that he made much later in conversation with Colin Duckworth when, speaking of *Waiting for Godot,* he said, "Christianity is a mythology with which I am perfectly familiar. So naturally I use it."[18]

The next day, Beckett walked "in the icy cold" around the art gallery of Bamberg's Neue Residenz.[19] To his great annoyance, he was escorted all the time by a guide who, for some reason, was determined not to leave him to look at the pictures at his leisure. He found the entire collection very disappointing: "nothing much," he wrote.[20] Later, in his diary, he listed (as he usually did) most of what he had seen but, apart from a few words of identification or description, such as "*Pieter Jan[s]z v. Quast* (1606–47). Man shitting with another looking on; tiny," he commented on only a few paintings: the four small Peter Breughel the Younger's ("a cut above Velvet [Breughel]," he wrote) and Marinus von Reymerswaele's *St. Jerome* ("Excellent").[21]

The following day, he was much more impressed by the neighboring Staatsbibliothek, where he saw one of only two copies of the Alcuin Bible in existence (the other, sometimes known as the Bible of Charlemagne, being in the British Museum), "the 10th century Reichenau Apocalypse with 57 superb miniatures, as fresh as though done yesterday," and Henry the Second and Cunégonde's prayer books, "including a missal with wonderful ivory boards."[22] Somewhat surprisingly in view of a debate about the possible impact on Beckett of the Albrecht Dürer engraving of *Melencolia,* he notes only that he has seen some "original Dürer copper prints (inc. Melancholy, Reiter, Tod u.[und] Teufel [Death and the Devil], St. Jerome, Virgin and Child) and Holbein and Dürer etc."[23] The diary does at least establish, however, that Beckett had personally seen some of these celebrated and potentially influential engravings, "in the flesh" as it were, at an early stage of his career as a writer.

Beckett's social contacts in Bamberg were almost inevitably casual, except for his encounter with the tailor/guide Arnold Mrowietz from whom he ordered a "midnight blue" suit and met up with later in his trip in different towns to have fittings. It was his meeting with Mrowietz that elicited the delightful distinction between "being done" (when you realize that you are being conned) and "being done in the eye" (when you are unaware of it), as well as an even more profound insight into his own nature when he wrote, "curious that I can so court a person that essentially I shudder away from. My need of the sick and evil."[24]

Würzburg

There were brief flurries of snow as Beckett walked briskly around the town of Würzburg and, for much of the time, he was once again frozen to the bone. He stayed at the Weisses Lamm hotel (now the Wiener Café Lammle) in the Marienplatz—recommended by Mrowietz and also by a man he had met in the train on the way from Bamberg—in what he described as "a stinking little room" for 4.95 marks.[25] Yet, in spite of the bitter cold, he was waiting eagerly at the entrance of the Residenz as soon as it opened the next morning and (with a German couple and a little Chinese tourist) was escorted around by an official guide, again much too hastily for Beckett, who wanted to linger to savor the splendors of the palace. The previous evening, he had purchased Professor Fritz Knapp's very scholarly book *Mainfranken: Bamberg. Würzburg. Aschaffenburg* (1928), which he read avidly at night and over breakfast. So before his visit he was already familiar with some of the architecture of the town and the history of the Residenz. As an admirer of the rococo rather than the baroque,[26] he was most impressed by both the scale and the ornamentation of Balthasar Neumann's building and by Giovanni Battista Tiepolo's huge, magnificent frescoes. In his diary, he enthused that Tiepolo's staircase paintings (figure 3) were full of "light and sky and sense of unlimited space. The rococo liquidation of architectural limits," while he described the ceiling of the Kaisersaal (Emperor's Hall) as a "radiant vibration."[27]

FIGURE 3. Giovanni Battista Tiepolo, *Allegory of the Planets and Continents*, 1750–1753, fresco, Residenz, Würzburg.

Many years later, Beckett was to draw on his memories of Würzburg and its imposing Residenz in his novel *Malone Dies,* when he wrote: "And if I ever succeed in breathing my last it will not be in the street, or in a hospital, but here, in the midst of my possessions, beside this window that sometimes looks as if it were painted on the wall, like Tiepolo's ceiling at Würzburg, what a tourist I must have been, I even remember the diaeresis, if it is one."[28]

But Beckett's visit was not confined to the celebrated Residenz. The same afternoon, he walked round the Fränkisches Luitpold-Museum (situated in 1937 close to the Residenz in a building destroyed in the bombings of World War II), which contained many of the exhibits now displayed in the Mainfränkisches Museum in the Marienberg fortress. His main purpose there was to look (with exceptional curiosity) at the museum's outstanding collection of wood and stone carvings by Tilman Riemenschneider for which Würzburg is so famous. The items in the museum were, he wrote, "miserably presented" and "horribly straggling." There was also no heating in the building at the time and a minimum of labeling.[29] Yet, in spite of these inadequacies, he found the Adam carving in the Adam and Eve pair of statues, formerly from the south door of the Marienkapelle, "exquisite." In the Marienkapelle itself, he saw more of Riemenschneider carvings, some of which (notably the statue of Konrad von Schönborn "awkward in armour, with copious hair like the Adam") he found "rather sentimental (as Riemenschneider tends mostly to be)."[30]

Crossing the "lyrical Main," he wandered next into the Burkardkirche, where he commented on the "violent contrast of Romanesque flat-roofed Basilica with Stützenwechsel [alternating round columns and square pillars] and late Gothic choir" and picked out an "excellent 14th century high-relief crucifixion," praising it as "free and passionate."[31]

The next day, after leaving the Weisses Lamm, he went on to the Neumünster-Kirche, wandering out of the north transept into the pleasant little "Lusam-Gärtlein" where the Minnesinger poet Walther von der Vogelweide is said to be buried. Some of Beckett's early poems, particularly "Da tagte es," reveal the influence of Walther's *alba,* and the great German lyric poet makes an appearance, first in the novella *Le calmant,* then in his novel *Molloy,* and finally, for a third and last time, in his last prose work, *Stirrings Still:* "To this end for want of a stone on which to sit like Walther and cross his legs the best he could do was stop dead and stand stock still."[32]

As in Bamberg, Würzburg's cathedral contained a number of medieval statues to which Beckett felt himself instinctively drawn, as he had been earlier to the figure of the older Elizabeth. Indeed, more clearly than anywhere else in the German diaries, his comments on the statues sculpted by the man known as the "Wolfskehlmeister," so named because he had carved the stone statue of Bishop Otto von Wolfskehl, revealed how he recognized in the work of others certain key affinities with his *own* world. Beckett described the medieval master sculptor as "a Master of the senile and [the] collapsed," commenting, "Another man for me," and told himself: "Remember: WOLFSKEHLMEISTER."[33] Later, he wrote, "Quantities of admirable semi-free sculpture, of which I take notice only of *Otto von Wolfskehl,* collapsed and hopelessly humble representation by the master of that name, with great affinities with 2 Bamberg Bishops" (see figure 4).[34]

By 1937, after writing the then unpublished *Dream of Fair to Middling Women, More Pricks than Kicks,* the poems of *Echo's Bones and Other Precipitates,* and the novel *Murphy* (finished in the early summer before he left for Germany), he already had a very clear perception of what his own vision involved, recognizing that certain figures who were created by others would be perfectly at home in his literary universe. This perception reached forward also to his later postwar work, when figures of "the senile and the collapsed" were to become even more regular denizens of Beckett's

FIGURE 4. Wolfskehlmeister, tomb figure (close-up) of Bishop von Hohenlohe, fourteenth century, Bamberg Cathedral.

world. As I have argued briefly elsewhere,[35] these examples of what may be described as "self-recognition" are significant when we come to address questions of artistic influence on the writer. Of course, as with any other author, Beckett is not immune to influence. Yet, more often, he appears to be either recognizing elements of himself and his artistic world in the work of others (painters and sculptors, as well as writers) or simply appropriating allied features that he finds there before making them totally his own.

He left the town of Würzburg with a wealth of memories. Some of these were personal. In a draper's shop there, for instance, he bought his mother a gray, artificial silk handkerchief and posted it to her for her birthday on the first of March.[36] On the same day, he learned that one of the best of the Franken wines, the Würzburger Leisten Riesling, was produced on the slopes facing Würzburg. To celebrate this discovery, when he arrived in Nuremberg that evening, he sought out and drank half a bottle of the 1935 vintage in the Julius-Spital.[37] (In spite of his reputation for asceticism, even as a young man, Beckett had developed a taste for fine wines whenever he could afford to buy them.) Above all, however, it was his memories of Tiepolo's ceilings, the statues of the "Wolfskehlmeister," and the poems of Walther von der Vogelweide that were to echo so vividly later in his mind and transform this brief yet intense and sharply focused sojourn in Bamberg and Würzburg into a source of inspiration worthy of the attention of Beckett scholars.

Notes

This account of Beckett's visits to Bamberg and Würzburg in 1937, which is based on a study of his unpublished diaries, was especially written in 2006 to honor Ruby Cohn. All quotations from the German Diaries are published with the agreement of Edward Beckett and the Beckett Estate.

1. These lengthier stays in Hamburg, Berlin, Dresden, and, later, Munich as described by Beckett in his German Diaries, are discussed in "Germany: The Unknown Diaries 1936–37," *Damned to Fame: The Life of Samuel Beckett,* by James Knowlson (London: Bloomsbury; New York: Simon, 1996; reissued in the United States in 2004 by Grove Atlantic).

2. German Diaries (six notebooks), no ms. number assigned, Reading University Library, Reading, vol. 5, 20 Feb. 1937. After first citation here, volume 5 of the German Diaries will be referred to as GD5, followed by the day and month only for the extract. All diary entries cited are dated from 20 Feb. to 26 Feb. 1937.

3. GD5, 20 Feb.

4. GD5, 21 Feb.

5. GD5, 20 Feb.

6. GD5, 20 Feb.

7. GD5, 26 Feb.

8. GD5, 20 Feb.

9. GD5, 20 Feb.

10. GD5, 20 Feb.

11. GD5, 20 Feb.

12. GD5, 24 Feb.

13. GD5, 20 Feb.

14. GD5, 23 Feb.

15. GD5, 22 Feb.

16. GD5, 22 Feb.

17. GD5, 22 Feb.

18. Colin Duckworth, *Angels of Darkness: Dramatic Effect in Beckett and Ionesco* (London: Allen 1974) 18.

19. GD5, 23 Feb.

20. GD5, 23 Feb.

21. All these quotations are from GD5, 23 Feb.

22. GD5, 23 Feb.

23. GD5, 23 Feb.

24. GD5, 23 Feb. For a fuller account of this encounter with the Bamberg tailor/guide, see *Damned to Fame* 254–55 (Bloomsbury ed.), 236–37 (Simon ed.).

25. GD5, 24 Feb.

26. "How is it then that I am as much for Romanesque as against Gothic as I am for Rococo as against barock?" Beckett asked himself in his diary (GD5, 25 Feb.).

27. GD5, 25 Feb.

28. Samuel Beckett, *Malone Dies* (London, Calder, 1958) 62.

29. GD5, 25 Feb.

30. GD5, 25 Feb.

31. GD5, 25 Feb.

32. Samuel Beckett, *Stirrings Still*, illus. Louis le Brocquy (New York: Blue Moon, 1988) no pagination.

33. GD5, 25 Feb.

34. GD5, 25 Feb.

35. James Knowlson, "Beckett's First Encounters with Modern German (and Irish) Art," *Samuel Beckett: A Passion for Painting*, ed. Fionnuala Croke (Dublin: National Gallery of Ireland, 2006) 61–74.

36. GD5, 26 Feb.

37. "Drink half a Bock[s]beutel [a squat, spherical bottle used for Franken wine] most excellent Würzburger Leisten Riesling 1935, come from the slope below Marienburg [Marienberg] where I watched the old women toiling" (GD5, 26 Feb.).

Part I

THINKING THROUGH BECKETT

Apnea and True Illusion

Breath(less) in Beckett

HERBERT BLAU

Astride of a grave and a difficult birth. Down in the hole,
lingeringly, the grave-digger puts on the forceps.
We have time to grow old. The air is full of our cries.

And, even now, unrelieved by his winning a Nobel Prize, some of us still
hear them—although sometimes we're not sure whose cries they are.

Preface

Years ago I published a book called Blooded Thought, *the title of which came
out of a line by the poet Wallace Stevens: "An abstraction blooded, as a man by
thought." Actually, some of that blood rushed to the head when I was first directing Beckett's plays—in San Francisco, more than half a century ago—and
would often speak to the actors in a Beckettian way, my words inseparable
from his words, as a way of thinking through, or by means of, what it is that
he thought. I've written several essays in the past in which I was thinking thus,
and there are passages here in which I'll be doing the same. If, then, in reading
what I've written, I sometimes indicate quotations and sometimes (or mostly)
don't—though I think you'll know when he's speaking—it's because I'm trying
to convey in the moment what he thought as I think it. I should say that one
of the things confirmed by Beckett every time I read him is that it's precisely*

where thought escapes me, at the selvedge or circuitous limit of thought, that it may, tautologically, turn back upon itself, which is what keeps it going, to be thought all over again—this time, to begin with, in even more personal terms.

About those personal terms, I've had reason to be especially self-conscious, because I've been reading through a long correspondence with Ruby Cohn, who has known my work in the theater, and a good deal about my life, since we first met as colleagues at San Francisco State. That was shortly after she edited the Samuel Beckett Issue of Perspective, *in 1959, which pretty much gathered together the few scholars in the United States who knew anything about Beckett then. Several times in her letters, after some achievement or calamity, or change of course in my career, Ruby would say, you ought to write your autobiography. But when I was staying with her not long ago in San Francisco, and made some remark about the one I'm actually writing—and for which I was reading those letters—Ruby said in her characteristic way, about the inarguably self-evident, "What are you doing that for, you're always writing autobiography."*

Maybe so. But if it does get personal here, that may be partly due to where I am at the moment in the superfetation of memory, As If: An Autobiography, not far now from my first meeting with Beckett, whom I knew for many years, having met him some months before Ruby published the issue of Perspective. *As for the present essay, with its opening and shutting on me as in the shifting spotlights of Play, its title picks up on a psychic condition long ago known by Beckett, affecting much of his life, and pervading all he has written—not perhaps the sort of thing you want to remember in celebration, but then, remembering Beckett, how could you forget.*

The epigraph that follows the title is from Waiting for Godot. *It's probably quite familiar.*

S OME YEARS AGO, that time, I was having a late lunch with my son Dick and his partner, Jane, fair food, good conversation, when I had a vague sense of their staring at me, and looking puzzled at each other, as I kept on talking, of I know not what, just talking and talking, with no sense of what I was talking about, or for that matter, who I was, at what turned out to be some logorrhea of incoherence, or a regressively aging "dehiscence," a word used by Beckett for coherence gone to pieces, but otherwise made familiar through the Oedipal fractures in the mirror stage of Lacan, with its drama of a specular ego, and the mirage of identity, still haunting the personal pronoun, I, not I, as we'll certainly see in Beckett, brought on by some primal

FIGURE I. Beatrice Manley as Winnie, in *Happy Days*, directed by Lee Breuer, designed by Robert LaVigne, the Actor's Workshop of San Francisco, 1961. Photograph by Chic Lloyd.

discord, and subsequent paranoia, at "a real *specific prematurity of birth....*"[1] When they took me to the emergency room, babbling into a murmur, "infant languors in the end sheets," as in one of the *Texts for Nothing*,[2] as if falling out of a dream, it was diagnosed as a transient ischemic attack, or momentary stroke; yet since I was not unable to talk, speech not blurred or impeded, but rather accelerated, as from the Mouth of *Not I*, "...but the brain still...still...in a way,"[3] it was more like a kind of psychogenic amnesia, what they call a "fugue state," or dissociative identity disorder. If there was anything polyphonic in what I was saying, or somehow contrapuntal—"From the word go. The word begone."[4]—I have no idea, but from what I later heard from Dick and Jane, relieved when I came to myself, not I, my self, whatever that may be, "Thought of nothing?...Forgotten nothing?...You're all right now, eh?"[5] I was indeed saying things over and over, to some indeterminate other, by way of anxious others, who could hardly decipher anything in the disjointed repetitions.

"We have time to grow old." But as you get older, and memory fails you, forgetting a name or a face—or, as with me, more frequently now in a class, you suddenly lose the lines of a poem long known by heart—it's hard not to think of Alzheimer's, from the complications of which my brother recently died, the last time I saw him not knowing who I was. The fugue state, however, was apparently nothing like that, and for all the repeats within it, they say it happens only once. But if I somehow came to myself, it must be "painful to be no longer oneself, even more painful if possible," as Beckett wrote in *First Love*, "than when one is. For when one is one knows what to do to be less so, whereas when one is not one is any old one irredeemably" (*Prose* 31). Still, depend upon age to keep you guessing at the edge of consciousness, or for that matter, deep down, in the identity disorder of the unconsciousness of sleep—"But deep in what sleep, deep in what sleep already?" as Hamm says in *Endgame*—where even dream isn't, at least for me, what it used to be. And here Hamm elides with Hamlet, when he says, "O God, I could be bounded in a nutshell and count myself a king of infinite space, were it not that I have bad dreams" (*Hamlet* 2.2.251–52)—in which, if our little lives are rounded with a sleep, it's far from infinite space, or even as he waits to be whistled, staring at the wall, the "Nice dimensions, nice proportions" of Clov's sequestered kitchen, "ten feet by ten feet by ten feet" (*Endgame* 2); indeed, in a nutshell, or, as from the Book of Revelations, the length and breadth and height of it, Clov's occluded cube, or the root of it in the psyche, my dreaming's claustrophobic. For in rather distressing, anamorphic, eye-opening ways, I'm crawling through a tunnel, a shaft, or drainpipe, or in a cramped elevator, or with a pounding heart in a windowless room, or smothered under a blanket, legs drawn under, as if curled up still in a womb, that "god-forsaken hole" (*Not I* 216), or "some old grave I can't tear myself away from,"[7] then suddenly I'm awake, panicked, wanting to speak but unable, or ready to wawl and cry, as if I'd just been born, if not birth the death of me, as now and again in Beckett, terribly short of breath.

Which turns out to be the title of his shortest play, *Breath*, about thirty-seven seconds on stage: inspiration, expiration, with those "instant[s] of recorded vagitus," a wail or cry of distress, birthright, death rite, out of this world, or in, with the stage directions insisting that the "two cries be identical, switching on and off strictly synchronized light and breath" (*Plays* 211), all timed exactly, all time, no time, through the final silence, no light, no cry, no breath, an eternity, that time, no more than five seconds. Over the asphyxiating sensation, however, I had no such control, nor did Beckett, actually, in the panic of similar seizures, for him lifelong, and as he has described it—once in a conversation, suddenly stuttering, when he was writing *Comment c'est*—even more severe. They call it sleep apnea, a blockage of air in the windpipe, which at its worst seems to be caused by the nervous system's not getting an expected signal from the brain, which otherwise never stops, what leaves you breathless in Beckett. It's as if he'd transposed the nocturnal attacks, the fear, the blood pressure rising until it was about to burst, or the terror of expectation, the waiting, for the imminent suffocation, heart racing, audible thumping, to the debraining volatility of his most compulsive texts. Or to see it another way, it's as if the specific prematurity could only become a subject, as through the mirror stage, by finding itself in words, but in the insurgency there (in the Imaginary, not the Symbolic, but headlong toward the Real), spastic, aphasic, the rush of words or "sudden flashes," the elliptical "vain reasonings" (*Not I* 217), with "the whole brain begging...something begging in the brain...begging the mouth to stop," but no stopping, the buzzing, "the brain...flickering away on its own," like mine in the ischemic attack, "now this...this...quicker and quicker...the words...the brain," as if brainless, "flickering away like mad"—and even when it wasn't happening "this other awful thought" (219–22), some whisper in your head, "Isn't that what you said?...The whisper...The odd word" (*Eh Joe* 204), that it might be happening again, with "the words [...] everywhere, inside me, outside me, [...] impossible to stop, I'm in words, made of words, others' words, what others," as with Dick and Jane that day, "the place too, the air, the walls, the floor, the ceiling, all words, the whole world is here with me,"[8] and then again the breathing stops.

Is it mere coincidence that these sensations of apnea appear to have increased, with the memory of amnesia, as I was thinking of Beckett again, as if his own history of tormented sleep, palpitations, spasms, suffocations, and memories of forgetting, or the always egregious aggregate of those he'd rather forget—not only sebaceous cysts on the anus, eczema, or herpes on the face, but a life before birth, which he always claimed to remember, his own stifling fetal existence, "curled up worm in slime,"[9] the intrauterine position, trapped there, imprisoned, crying out to escape, nobody hearing, nobody listening—were responsible for my symptoms? As for his symptoms, they appeared to be, as in *The Unnamable,* the identity disorder of a nonidentity, or equivocal dubious being, referred to as I, that most pernicious pronoun in the semiosis of Beckett, *I,* not me, "it is not about me" (*Unnamable* 3), as it appears to be in *Endgame,* when Hamm removes the handkerchief from his face and announces, "Me—(*he yawns*)—to play" (2), in the objective case. But in the preamble to *The Unnamable* that never comes to an end, perhaps because it never begins, the "affirmations and negations invalidated as uttered, or sooner or later" (3), always return to the "I, of whom I know nothing. I know my eyes are open because of the tears that pour from them unceasingly. I know I am seated, my hands on my knees, because of the pressure against my rump, against the soles of my feet, against the palms of my hands, against my knees." But what is this pressure, that retrograde pressure, in which the hypertensive body may not, with tears flowing, really be sure which end is up? "I don't know. My spine is not supported. I mention these details to make sure I am not lying on my back, my legs raised and bent, my eyes closed" (22)—darkling there, forgotten, as if abandoned before birth.

If there's long been, not only in the theater, but in my writings on Beckett too, that virtual habit of thinking *through* him, his words my words, or by means of the aporias in his own afflicted thought, ephectic, solipsistic, and even masochistic, that occurs by something more than the self-commiserating solace of sympathetic identification. What drew me to Beckett to begin with, from the "Nothing to be done," the line that launches the waiting for the absence known as Godot, to the traumatizing mathematics in his shorter plays and prose, was an activating *exactitude* about an encrypted void, what otherwise seemed hopeless, or what if you really engaged it, through the temptations to laugh it off, what Beckett himself provoked (but mostly overdone now in stagings of his plays), was really unnerving too. That is, it was still disoriented, even desperate, for all the going "On!" as when Pozzo takes off with Lucky,[10] to those late "Variations on a 'Still' Point," "he having been dreamt away [letting] himself be dreamt away,"[11] over the abyssal depths, "Whence when back no knowing where no telling where been how long how it was."[12] There is always that impasse in Beckett, whether waiting, going or coming, the hopeless detour of an incessant impasse, where you try to go on and you can't go on, and the talking seems to continue, call it the babble or drivel, "that's what hell will be like" (96), says Henry, in the long opening monologue of the radio play *Embers,* which also begins with "On. [...] On!" (93), which "always went on for ever" (94), like the stories he told himself, "Stories, stories, years and years of stories, till the need came on me, for someone, to be with me, anyone" (95), but Ada? hellish, a conversation with Ada, "that was something, [...] small chat to the babbling of Lethe about the good old days when we wished we were dead" (96).

One might say, not only with Pozzo's coming and going, or the stories, stories, that Beckett gets a lot of mileage out of the vicissitudes of despair, and when the measures are taken, the astringent mathematics, with the abyss more or less at a parodistic distance. So with *Rough for Theatre I*, when B in his wheelchair asks the blind fiddler A, "why don't you let yourself die?" and A says he's thought of it, whereupon B says in irritation, "But you don't do it!" To which A replies, and with some violence when B pursues it, "I am not unhappy enough!" (*Plays* 69). Now I grant you, that "Nothing is funnier than unhappiness.... Yes, yes, it's the most comical thing in the world," as Nell says in her ashbin, before she's pushed down with no pulse, and the lid closed again, "we laugh, we laugh," but then, "like the funny story we have heard too often, we still find it funny, but we don't laugh anymore" (*Endgame* 19).

And so it must have been for Beckett, at the extremities of despair, in letting you see what you wouldn't, sometimes manic obsessively, if the exactitude weren't *exacting*, like the nothing to be done that had to be *done*, to become the nothing that *is*, which would be the merest nothing, without a psychic cost, inscribed on the body as well. And it could be, like the "fibrous degeneration" in his play *Catastrophe* (*Plays* 298), felt at considerable cost. One of the tumescent or edemic conditions from which Beckett himself suffered—a thickening of deep tissue that passes from palm to fingers, causing the hands to claw—it was inflicted on the character P, the barefoot protagonist up on a plinth who seems nothing more than a prop—fists clenched, face down, black wide-brimmed hat, black gown, not hooded or veiled, but like the now-notorious figure at Abu Ghraib, up on a pedestal too, with electric wires attached to his hands. With D, the director as chief sadist, the torture is a performance, or the performance tortuous, prepared by precise instructions to A, the more than willing female assistant, with a "craze for explicitation! Every i dotted to death!" (299), every element carefully staged, but as if for a Broadway audience, or the French boulevards, in the composition of pain.

Elsewhere it might be diagrammed or timed down to the second, or as in the play *Play*, with "faces lost to age" (*Plays* 147), up to their necks in the urns, not "just...play" (153), but "all out, all the pain" (148), with a direction to "REPEAT" (160), the repetition for confirmation like an experiment in a lab. For there is in Beckett, with his own explicitation, a microphysics of misery or, as he once said about Proust, a "science of affliction,"[13] in which at some self-punitive molecular extremity, or ineluctable non sequitur rage, there's a desire for atomization, as with Mrs. Rooney in *All That Fall*, "never tranquil," laughing wildly, "oh to be in atoms, in atoms! (*Frenziedly.*) ATOMS!" (*Plays* 17)—in the annihilating wish of despair, subtextually, subatomically, an apotheosis of dehiscence. Now, there's not only a science here, with those words behaving like quarks, a Beckettian string theory, but also an aesthetic: in the birth that is the death of him, as it happens again, "no difficulty there," there happens to be an exception, "imagination not dead yet, yes, dead, good, imagination dead imagine"[14]—which, imagine, puts the burden on you, and yes, dead, good, if you ever had imagination, the question is whether you can, including, from "a thousand little signs too long to imagine, [...] the infinitesimal shudder instantaneously suppressed" (*Imagination* 185).

Meanwhile, with a philosophical disposition that Beckett often denied (or was disturbed by in others when applied to his work), there is an epistemology, too, in the tormented susurrus or superfetation of words, that "sudden urge...to tell," get it all out, if not a confessional, "nearest lavatory...start pouring it out...steady stream...mad stuff...half the vowels wrong...no one could follow" (*Not I* 222). I mean the whole heartbreaking excremental glut, "That's right, wordshit, bury me, avalanche" (*Text* 9 137), if not then silence, words unspoken, errors acknowledged, knowledge unknowing, "Thoughts, no, not thoughts," rather "profounds of mind. Buried in who knows what profounds of mind. Or mindlessness"[15]—which, with no relief, deep in what sleep already, brain still going, dream-thought, you have to bring to mind. There is, of course, the minimalist side of Beckett, the parsimonious aesthetic, the "mere-most minimum,"[16] of those claustral plays and prose, where "Words are few. Dying too" (*Monologue* 265). But when it comes to thinking the worst, ill seen ill said, who was saying it better, what where, and who would have thought that in the "accusative [of] inexistence," along with a rush of amnesia, "no notion who it was saying what you were saying," there is also a "grand apnoea" (*Text* 8 134), taking your breath away—what signal from the brain, what particle physics, *apnea with a grandeur?* "whose skull you were clapped up in" (*That Time* 231), where else would you find that but Beckett?

"Can there be misery—" says Hamm, yawning, "—loftier than mine? No doubt? Formerly. But now?" (*Endgame* 2). "What remains of all that misery?" says Krapp (*Plays* 58), playing and replaying his tapes, as if it were desired. "Be again, be again. (*Pause.*) All that old misery. (*Pause.*) Once wasn't enough for you" (63). Better if only remembered, since more than enough of it now, including the telling and retelling of what forever escapes you because you can never forget, "those things you kept making up to keep the void out just another of those old tales to keep the void from pouring in on you the shroud" (*That Time* 230). Nothing personal, of course, or merely personal, never mind the shrouding, the mess is universal, or as with Krapp, every new retrospect, moving between the two, the mess and those other "Moments. Her moments, my moments," even "The dog's moments. (*Pause.*) [...] he took it in his mouth, gently, gently. A small, old, black, hard, solid rubber ball" (*Krapp* 60), what he might have kept, something solid in his life, but he gave it to the dog. As for the mess, "Everything there, everything on this old muckball, all the light and dark and famine and feasting of... (*hesitates*)... the ages! (*In a shout.*) Yes! (*Pause*)," even the drifting pleasure, "among the flags and stuck" (62–63), gently up and down with her, be again, be again, some old chance of happiness, what all told, rewound on spools, he "revelled in the word [...] Spooool!" (62), you'd still rather forget. And what is it there in *Breath,* that mimicry of a play, with its two vagital cries, what is it being remembered, except remembered being, being bygone, if it ever was, always nostalgia for it, or something more than being, with nothing there on stage, except a litter of rubbish, as if some token of the ruins of history, which gives another dimension to the birth astride of a grave.

"Know minimum," wrote Beckett, in *Worstward Ho* (91), but at mere-most minimum that pitiful rubbish was proleptic about what, ideologically, we've since encountered in critical theory, most specifically through Walter Benjamin in his "Theses on the Philosophy of History." For it suggests the wreckage of time accumulating before the "Angelus Novus," as described by Benjamin in a painting by Paul Klee. Wings outspread, caught up in a violent storm from Paradise, the Angel is being blown backward into the future, facing the catastrophe of the past, the debris growing skyward before him,[17] from which Beckett might have gathered the litter, as a kind of bricolage, scraps and tatters from those ruins of time, "no verticals, all scattered and lying" (*Breath* 211), not flat-out, but at minima, if not Benjamin's "chips of Messianic time" ("Theses" 265), an ideographic suggestion of the Beckettian view of history. Thus it is that the rubbish on stage might also be a corrective to what Theodor Adorno wrote, in an essay on *Endgame,* with profounds of mind (and the philosophical disposition, to which, when they met, Beckett more than objected),[18] about the play not meaning anything becoming the only meaning, and with that certain certitudes about Beckett's indifference to history.

As if he were giving another contour to his well-known assertion that there could be no poetry after Auschwitz, Adorno insisted that Beckett actually excluded history, because "it itself has dehydrated the power of consciousness to think history," dessicating as well "the power of remembrance."[19] For the most part rigorous in its focus on Beckett, there is in the essay a passing vengeance on "totalitarians like Lukács," still serving their Stalinist bosses, while despising the decadence that, from Baudelairean disgust to existential nausea, the "nausea of satiation," won't follow the party line ("Trying to Understand" 11). Yet, in countering Lukács's judgment of Beckett as irresponsibly nihilistic and politically irrelevant, with a "subjectivist ontology" that becomes "the excavated index of degenerate art because of its worldlessness and infantility" (15), Adorno is nevertheless still selling him short, because he doesn't think that Beckett has much to say about politics either. Overtly, to be sure, no politics on stage, in any usual way, nor even as it turned up in the theater of the absurd—with which, misleadingly, in Martin Esslin's eponymous book, Beckett was identified. But in the past I've made the case that when his plays first appeared on the scene, particularly in San Francisco, where various events ignited the dissidence of the sixties, they had more political immediacy than the plays of Bertolt Brecht, which I had also directed—and this despite Beckett's denial, though he served in the French Resistance, of bearing "political witness," to use Adorno's term (15).

"Yes, no more denials, all is false," but the fact is—and "dupes" we may be, "dupes of every time and tense, until it's done, all past and done" (*Text 4* 109)—that Beckett, like some of his characters, or not quite characters, for all the lapsing remembrance, fact, I say, and not factitiously, never seems to forget, like the voices of *That Time* or the Mother in *Footfalls* or, back in the time of the waiting, in the frenzy of Lucky's speech, from the existence as uttered forth of a personal God through the death of Bishop Berkeley to the skulls in Connemara, never mind all the tennis or the quaquaquaqua, or paying attention to it, the skulls the skulls, as to some cacophonic sounding of the calamity of Western culture, echoed by Clov in *Endgame,* but anally, acidically, parsing the horrors out, the inexplicable punishment, zero out the window, the hollow in the wall, since he remembers everything, so appalling he wants it finished, "it must be nearly finished," even his walk impeded, that "*stiff, staggering walk,*" with a sort of raging measure, six steps, three steps, one step, brief laughs (1), why should he move at all? *how* can he move at all? as if he had to will it, in a vertigo of stasis, thus the stiffness, movement spastic, so much history on the brain. As for the subjectivity in Beckett, sure it's ontological, and no mere "subject position" (defined by race, class, gender, ethnicity), as in cultural studies today; and so far as there is, with imagination dead imagine, anything like the vision that came from imagination, maybe only "The semblance. Faint, though by no means invisible in a certain light,"[20] it is no mere social construction. It may resemble, however, the semblance, more than faintly in a certain light, those sublimates of material life-process, what Marx speaks of as phantoms of the brain—or be haunted there, as with Marx himself, for all he tried to dispel it, by the future of illusion in the catastrophe of the past, about which one may say (and I've said it, taking a cue from the later Freud, what accounts for his tragic view in *Civilization and Its Discontents*) there is no other future.

So much, for the illusory moment, of what Beckett saw of the semblance. There was a time, there was a time, in his earliest story *Assumption,* where he sublimated, in the anguish of a young man struggling to be an artist, his own pretentious doubts and grievances "with the vulgar, uncultivated, terribly clear and personal ideas of the unread intelligenzia" (*Prose* 3), who'd never understand his desire, inherited from German Romanticism, for "a wild rebellious surge" that, aspiring "violently towards realization in sound," would restore the "inexplicable bombshell perfection" that came with Promethean fire. What he wanted—perhaps to offset that other anguish, the palpitating terror, the rush of blood in the body that kept him breathless at night—was another pain, "the pain of Beauty" (4), which has been dismissed since deconstruction, along with Vision and Imagination, especially when the words are capitalized, as transcendental signifiers. But in the 1950s, before that critique occurred, Beckett asked in a text for nothing, with nothing like Promethean fire (and the usual absence of the question mark), "And beauty, strength, intelligence"—of which he wrote in the same light as the semblance, or "a kind of light, sufficient to see by"—simply more of the same? "the latest, daily, action, poetry, all one price for one and all"? Now the words embarrass him, they always did, but even more, the mind slow, the words slow, the subject there dying in an unpredicated clutter. "If only it could be wiped from knowledge. To have suffered under that miserable light, what a blunder" (*Text* 2 106).

But with Beckett you never know, for in all "times and tenses," he's surely blundered worse, like giving himself up "for dead all over the place," only to find that there's "nothing like breathing your last to put new life in you"—with, of course, the mutterings undiminished, "the same old stories, the same old questions and answers" (*Text* 1 102–03), but the same plus one, and therefore not the Same—as Nietzsche declared, speaking of beauty, strength, intelligence, about the Eternal Return. Be eternity what it may, "now here, what now here, one enormous second, as in Paradise" (*Text* 2 106), within a page or so of the shorter prose it's possible to move, with nuances of disdain for each nuance, from desolation to nostalgia to transcendental longing, for the outside prospect of some otherness there, or maybe there on the inside, "other others, invisible" (106), or from whatever it was in the semblance to thoughts in a dry season, not quite like T. S. Eliot's (whom Beckett early admired), not quite the wasteland either, but on a Sunday morning, with no paradise to be lost.

"Dry, it's possible, or wet, or slime, as before matter took ill." And then the familiar sensation, with slime, if that, the originary trace, as when he was still unborn, some continuity with the womb. "Is this stuff air that permits you to suffocate still, almost audibly at times, it's possible, a kind of air," says the voice of a text for nothing, turning to "one more memory, one last memory, it may help, to abort again." But will memory never cease, for that aborting again suggests what Beckett apparently said about himself to the psychoanalyst Wilfred Bion, about an inadequate parturition, still unborn when he was born, and out of breath, repeatedly. As for the dry season, however, there were signs of renewal there, and if not Eternal, "it was none the less the return, to what no matter, the return, unscathed, always a matter for wonder. What happened? Is that the question? An encounter? Bang! No." No Big Bang either, nor creation myth that day, yet if something more than a semblance, nothing more than "a glow, red, afar, at night, in winter, that's worth having, that must have been worth having" (*Text* 2 107–08).

Sometimes you can maybe see it, sometimes you have to listen, and keep what you hear in mind. "A voice comes to one in the dark. Imagine." After that opening line, from *Company,* triple space, section break, aporetic silence. For the sake of imagining. "To one on his back in the dark. This he can tell by the pressure on his hind parts [. . .]," the pronoun *This* confounding, *what* can he tell? *that* he is in the dark? or that the voice comes? and how do the hind parts certify that? or, if it is the voice, by virtue of this or that, what exactly can he tell of it, or being in the dark itself, "by how the dark changes when he shuts his eyes and again when he opens them again"? Whatever we imagine, he, whoever he is, "must acknowledge the truth of what is said. But by far the greater part of what is said cannot be verified."[21] Which is, of course, the way with Beckett. "For why or? Why in another dark or in the same? And whose voice is asking this? Who asks, Whose voice is asking this?" (*Company* 16). Of course, we'll never know, but whatever is there to know or, as here, "a certain mental activity" (7), high order, low order, or crawling "the mute count. Grain by grain in the mind," as at the beginning of *Endgame,* with the fugal desire to be finished, Clov's "impossible heap," but the mute count not so punishing, nor those grains so metaphysical, the futile desire to be finished, though of that we can't be sure, in the arithmetical introspection. "One two three four one. Knee hand knee hand two. One foot. Till say after five he falls. Then sooner or later on from nought anew. One two three four one" (36). I could go on, but I won't go on. I'll keep him company.

Whatever it is that, "with no dead end for his pains," might set his mind in motion, his mind, mine, the mind needs company, "what if not sound [...], Sight? The temptation is strong to decree there is nothing to see. But too late for the moment. For he sees a change of dark when he opens or shuts his eyes." And let there be light, the faintest light, should they happen to be open, "no longer perceived than the time it takes the lid to fall," the seeing unseeing, and so with taste or touch, "The thrust of the ground against his bones. All the way from calcaneum to philo-progenitiveness," ever failing, failing better, a consensus of the senses, "Smell? His own?" or "a rat long dead. Or some other carrion. Yet to be imagined" (37). Or maybe a sixth sense, or as if evolution were reversed, crawling, eyelids stirring, "till the last thump" (29), stirring still, if not "pure reason," an awakening dehiscence, *le dérèglement des sens* (Beckett had lectured on Rimbaud), and it will be, you can be sure, as Artaud said of the naked, sonorous realization of the essential theater, "as localized and as precise as the circulation of the blood in the arteries or," in the impeccably ordered disorder that is a compulsion in Beckett, "the apparently chaotic development of dream images in the brain"—what in his manifesto for the Theater of Cruelty, Artaud called "true illusion."[22] And while there's a far cry between them—not only Artaud's actor signaling through the flames, whom Beckett would never direct—there is in both a rigorous intellectuality and, as Artaud saw it in the Balinese theater, a "mathematical meticulousness" to the "inexhaustible mental ratiocination, like a mind ceaselessly taking its bearings in the maze of its unconscious."[23] As for what they take to be "the truthful precipitates of dreams"

(Artaud, "Manifesto" 92), for the ratiocinative Beckett the precipitations are endless, "what vicissitudes within what changelessness" (*Text* 9 137), yet if "Never but in passing dream the passing hour long short,"[24] there remains for him the semblance, shrouded perhaps, and obscured by history—returning to which, as to the dreamscape of a nightmare, there was surely much to remember, word unspoken, but Auschwitz there, and a century of rational slaughter, or promiscuous devastation, the Holocaust, Dresden, Hiroshima, and beyond the Gulag, genocides yet to come; in short, a real theater of cruelty.

In this regard, speak as we wish, through the fetishism of writing in theory, of the text as body in the body of the text—and Beckett's writing may be the exemplary model of that—I'm speaking now of his undeluded awareness of those corporeal bodies out there, or once there, but incinerated, or buried too, some of them, not where death came with birth, but where, dead, yes dead, imagine, they've never yet been found, or in a mass grave, among the multitudinous dead. "Dying on. No more no less. No. Less. Less to die. Ever less" (*Monologue* 266), because so many wantonly dead, though in the dialectic of Beckett, if less is not more, "Lessness" (the title of one of his stories) is no less than never(the)less. Which, for all the syncopated changes, ever more, ever less, are no mere contradictions, though sometimes too they come, as in sundry stage directions, with the rage I mentioned before, if not an eruptive virulence, then caustically ironic, seething, barely contained. Thus, when Hamm moves from his taunting scorn for Clov's stinking to "The whole place stinks of corpses," and Clov deflates it or maybe trumps it with "The whole universe" (46), that may seem a Beckettian joke, as it may with the tramps in *Godot*, when to somehow reduce the misery, they think they are maybe thinking, and suddenly realize, even "in no danger of ever thinking any more," that "What is terrible is to *have* thought," which leads to the question that, however we screen it out, is always subliminally there: "Where are all these corpses from?" And then, though they may be putting on the audience, as from the edge of the stage, caught up in specularity, looking at those looking, at a presumably safe distance, the spectators in their dark: "A charnel-house! A charnel-house!" (41).

If not writing for the dead, as Heiner Müller claimed to be doing— with his usual mordancy, because the dead are in the majority, and it's properly democratic to write for the majority—Beckett did say, even as his plays were being canonized, that he was writing into a void. And that goes, in its incriminating alienation, far beyond the Brechtian judgment of the bourgeois audience, not to mention the universe, or with atrocities unending on a global scale, the world as we know it today: not only the spectacle of televised terrorism and the war against it, with the actualities unseen, suicide bombings, death squads, beheadings, as well as the fallout killings and scandals that, with the "doctrine of distinction" and collateral damage, are the coefficient of invasive democracy, but also the widespread torture of massive poverty, tribal murders, sectarian cleansing, ears cut off, toes cut off, janjaweed rapes, then zina (women punished for fornication), forced migration, labor camps, smuggling of the unnamable, not only drugs and teenage girls, but an international trade of prostituted children, and then those other diseases, yard-long Guinea worms in slime, AIDS, blinding trachoma, and other abysmal plagues. Now, it would seem that this is not the kind of thing, for all his laughable lists at which you couldn't quite laugh, that Beckett would catalogue. And there is certainly substance to the view that "the focus of injustice in Beckett is almost never local, civil, or social, but cosmic, the injustice of having been born [...]."[25] But if his work didn't seem to draw upon what, page by miserable page, shows up every morning in my reading of the *New York Times,* beside larger and larger ads for Tourneau watches, Gucci bags, or Ferragamo shoes, he was very well aware, too, of what—as he read of it in *Le Monde* or *Libération* (which he *did* read, a French newspaper, though rumor was that he didn't)—you can hardly bear to read. When Clov said, "The whole universe," that was not merely cosmic, and Beckett knew very well, as Clov said at the wall, through the subjective ontology of that claustrophobic space, "Beyond is the ... other hell" (26), and if that still sounds cosmic, "Outside of here it's death" (70)—which is something other than the death of him, something more brutally lethal, the untold numbers dead, not in a text, no text for nothing, but in the brutal material world.

"There's something dripping in my head. (*Pause.*) A heart, a heart in my head," says Hamm, in what would seem the introjected extremity of his solipsistic mode (*Endgame* 18), but as Clov has his telescope, the magnifier, to liven up the deadliness, there is in Hamm's heart and head, "*With prophetic relish,*" another magnitude, where "there'll be no wall anymore," and if not infinite space, Hamletic, "Infinite emptiness," which "all the resurrected dead of all the ages wouldn't fill," and if that, in Hamm, still sounds magniloquent, what he goes on to say would be merely vapid if there wasn't in Beckett himself some unapocalyptic sense of the unresurrected dead or the universe of suffering, the unconsoled reality of it, that Hamm takes upon himself: "Yes, one day you'll know what it is, you'll be like me, except that you won't have anyone with you, because you won't have pity on anyone and because there won't be anyone left to have pity on" (36). No doubt, as formerly, the outburst will be deflated and, what a pity, it seems walled in again, the pity, "But you," and this comes at the end of the play, "you ought to know what the earth is like, nowadays" (83). No more no less (see figure 2).

And I knew him well enough to know that no more no less was, in his "poor mind,"[26] with all the brilliance of it, the equilibration of human misery with something like infinite pain, which he could also parody, mixing the personal with the abstract, as in *Rough for Theatre II*, when A and B are summing up the reasons to let the suicidal figure jump: "Work, family, third fatherland, cunt, finances, art and nature, heart and conscience, health, housing conditions, God and man, so many disasters" (*Plays* 78).

FIGURE 2. Robert Symonds as Hamm and Tom Rosqui as Clov, in *Endgame*, directed by Herbert Blau, designed by Robert LaVigne, the Actor's Workshop of San Francisco, 1959. Photograph by Chic Lloyd.

If there seems no measure here, of what comes together in pain, from the personal to the political, from the aesthetic to social disasters, there is in the story "Enough," where the focus is personal and the voice is that of a woman, whose mental calculations or "flight into arithmetic" are not unlike Beckett's, who could be more than uneasy about it: "The art of combining," she says, "is not my fault. It's a curse from above. For the rest I would suggest not guilty" (*Prose* 187–88).

Which, peace to Sam Beckett, is at best a guilty plea, or like one of his "Faux Départs" (from a novel called *Fancy Dying*), maybe a false start, or pretext for starting again, "talking to himself the last person. / Saying, Now where is he, no, Now he is here,"[27] and in the Grand Apnea, the elision of texts as I think them, "what...who?...no!...she!..." who, as the words pour out of the Mouth, that sliver of body on stage, with a silent Auditor there, whose sex is undeterminable, comes "...out...into this world...this world," out "before her time," but is it out of, or into, that "godforsaken hole," where she "found herself in the dark...and if not exactly...insentient...insentient," remembers the fetal position, as Beckett remembered it, or something much like it—what it was "she did not know...what position she was in...imagine!"—maybe because that's the place, if it was, where you take on the suffering, for what you can't forget. And it starts all over again, "but the brain—what?" the words coming on like mad, from the first awful thought to another, each "dismissed as foolish," like being punished for her sins, "as she suddenly realized...gradually realized...she was not suffering...imagine!...not suffering!...," but with no steady state in Beckett, or on the Möbius strip of misery, or just short on a sigmoid curve, "unless of course she was...*meant* to be suffering...ha!...*thought* to be suffering..." (*Not I* 216–17), as if thinking itself were the sin, nothing more terrible than to *have* thought, that for the anxious moment, and then again a "sudden flash...very foolish really but—...what?" we'll take a Beckettian (*Pause*), as from the causal of the fugal or, there again (*Pause*), for all the truthful precipitates, the substance of a bad dream, but good or bad, "revolving it all?" and "Where it began. (*Pause.*) It all began," the absurdity of it, that *It*, "It all. (*Pause.*) It all" (*Footfalls* 243, 240), never it all but the semblance, the shadow of true illusion, or maybe a *faux départ*, another false start, taking thought, last thought, perhaps the thought that's lasting, damn that sin! another way of thinking—and even when breathless, the pity of it, the pity, the revolving never stops.

But wait, wait! in all the despair, is there anything like hope, even if true, something more to that illusion? You can be sure there's a text for that. "A pity hope is dead. No." Yet, now and again, with the same old cries, or moans and groans, from the cradle to the grave, even down there when the grave-digger put on the forceps, "How one hoped above, on and off. With what diversity" (*Text* 2 108). Diversity? Well, it's not exactly affirmative action, but speaking of moans and groans, even short of breath, the cost of inspiration, why is it that the work of Beckett, woeful, mournful, impossibly painful, or simply ready, as in *Rockaby*, to say, "fuck life" (*Plays* 282), is more enlivening than other things we encounter with a more sanguine, less grievous, funny not funny, funereal view of it all? One two three four one. "Better hope deferred than none. Up to a point. Till the heart starts to sicken. Company too up to a point. Better a sick heart than none. Till it starts to break." Now, take a breath. "For the time being leave it at that" (*Company* 18).

Notes

This essay was a Distinguished Lecture for the Beckett Centennial, at the Graduate Center for Study of Drama, the University of Toronto, 7 April 2006. It was subsequently published in a special issue of *Modern Drama* 49.4 (Winter 2006). The preface here is slightly revised.

1. Jacques Lacan, *Écrits: A Selection,* trans. Alan Sheridan (New York: Norton, 1977) 4.

2. *Texts for Nothing 13, The Complete Shorter Prose, 1929–1989,* ed. and intro. S. E. Gontarski (New York: Grove, 1995) 154; abbreviated as *Prose*. After first citation here, selections from this volume will be referred to only by their titles, sometimes abbreviated, as with *Text* (and number) for *Texts for Nothing*.

3. *Not I,* in *Collected Shorter Plays* (New York: Grove, 1984) 217; abbreviated as *Plays*. After first reference to a play here, or in the text, only its title will be given, sometimes abbreviated.

4. *A Piece of Monologue, Plays* 269.

5. *Eh Joe, Plays* 202.

6. *Endgame* (New York: Grove, 1958) 53.

7. *Embers, Plays* 98.

8. *The Unnamable* (New York: Grove, 1958) 139.

9. *That Time, Plays* 230.

10. According to Beckett, the last word of his father on his deathbed, passed on to Pozzo, as he leaves the stage with Lucky, in *Waiting for Godot* (57).

11. "Sounds," Appendix I: "Variations on a 'Still' Point," *Prose* 267.

12. "Still 3," Appendix I, *Prose* 269.

13. *Proust* (New York: Grove, n.d.) 4.

14. *Imagination Dead Imagine, Prose* 182.

15. *Ohio Impromptu, Plays* 288.

16. *Worstward Ho, Nohow On: Three Novels by Samuel Beckett,* intro. S. E. Gontarski (New York: Grove, 1996) 91; the other two novels are *Company* and *Ill Seen Ill Said.*

17. Walter Benjamin, "Theses on the Philosophy of History," *Illuminations,* ed. and intro. Hannah Arendt, trans. Harry Zohn (New York: Harcourt, 1968) 259.

18. About Beckett's disdain for Adorno, see James Knowlson, *Damned to Fame: The Life of Samuel Beckett* (New York: Simon, 1996) 428.

19. Theodor W. Adorno, "Trying to Understand *Endgame,*" *Samuel Beckett's* Endgame, ed. and intro. Harold Bloom (New York: Chelsea House, 1988).

20. *Footfalls, Plays* 242.

21. *Company, Nohow On* 3.

22. Antonin Artaud, "The Theater of Cruelty (First Manifesto)," *The Theater and Its Double,* trans. Mary Caroline Richards (New York: Grove, 1958) 92.

23. Artaud, "On Balinese Theater," *Theater and Its Double* 57, 63.

24. *Lessness, Prose* 200.

25. S. E. Gontarski, introduction to *Prose* xxiii.

26. *Footfalls, Plays* 240.

27. Appendix II: "Faux Départs," *Prose* 272.

From Contumacy to Shame

Reading Beckett's Testimonies with Agamben

DAVID HOUSTON JONES

WHAT INTERESTS GIORGIO Agamben above all in his groundbreaking account of testimony in *Remnants of Auschwitz* is the juxtaposition of the sayable and the unsayable, and in particular the inscription of the unsayable within the sayable: "in opposition to the *archive,* which designates the system of relations between the unsaid and the said, we give the name *testimony* to the system of relations between the inside and outside of *langue,* between the sayable and the unsayable in every language" (145).[1] His response to the argument that Auschwitz is an "unspeakable" event is to claim that testimony persists, but in a form that is inevitably marked by its own impossibility. Drawing upon Primo Levi and François Lyotard, Agamben maintains that only those who died in the camps could be valid witnesses; their testimony therefore cannot be articulated. What is notable here is that testimony is not simply canceled but lives on in residual form in the very fact of its cancellation. The emblem of testimony is the figure of the *Muselmann,* the prisoner who has given up and in whom the life of "relation" has already been extinguished. His testimony cannot be voiced but exists within Agamben's work as a haunting presence, signaled by its own avowed impossibility.

The resonances of such a haunting presence within Beckett's work are manifold. The paradoxical figure of unspeakability, encapsulated in the famous "expression that there is nothing to express" (Beckett, *Three Dialogues* 139), becomes the guiding principle of Beckett's later work beginning with the trilogy. It attains perhaps its most concentrated form in

Texts for Nothing and *The Unnamable:* the subject and condition of the narrative is the impossible predicament inhabited by the narrator, "this unnamable thing that I name" (Beckett, *Text 6* 34).[2] As a result, it is not only impossible to determine the narrator's identity, but his existence appears to be expressly denied by the narrative that he is in the process of producing. *The Unnamable* evokes the "silence" in which "you must go on, I can't go on, I'll go on" (382), while *Texts for Nothing* begins with what appears to be a retrospective account of the same predicament: "Suddenly, no, at last, long last, I couldn't any more, I couldn't go on" (*Text 1* 77). In both cases, untenable narrative positions are persistently aligned with uncontextualized images of wounding and trauma, and the narrative voice is drawn into equivocal substitutions and heteronymy (multiple names referring to a single subject). In Agamben, meanwhile, survivor testimony can only bear witness to a missing testimony, that of those who died: "no one can bear witness from the inside of death, and there is no voice for the disappearance of voice" (34). In what follows, I examine the problematic viewpoint in *The Unnamable* and *Texts for Nothing* alongside the "lacuna" of testimony in Agamben's account. Since Beckett's texts are accompanied by unsituated references to shame and violence, their resonance is both thematic and epistemological.

Narrating Shame

Just as Beckett's narratives issue from their own impossibility (owing to the failure, absence, or death of the narrator), the witness's account is always a substitute for a narrative that does not exist; survivors "bear witness to a missing testimony" (Agamben, *Remnants* 34). To become authentic that account must somehow give voice to the nonlanguage of the lacuna, reduce itself, as in the Unnamable's abdications of narrative authority, to nonlanguage: "If I could speak and yet say nothing, really nothing?" (*Unnamable* 277). The complex of suffering and memory in *Texts for Nothing,* meanwhile, reads as a striking enactment of the central dilemma of *Remnants of Auschwitz.*

The origin of the narrative voice is so ruthlessly and explicitly problematized that the *Texts* have been read as compressed "meditations on linguistic mediation" (Wolosky 220). Having agonized over its uncertain origin throughout ("who's speaking?" 59), the speaker's voice is, by *Text* 12, intermittently overcome by that of the unnamed "other" who plays on the margins of the narrative throughout:

> Who's this speaking in me, and who's this disowning me, as though I had taken his place, usurped his life, that old shame that kept me from living, the shame of my living that kept me from living. [...] Will they succeed in slipping me into him, the memory and dream of me, into him still living, amn't I there already, wasn't I always there, like a stain of remorse, is that my night and contumacy, in the dungeons of this moribund, and from now till he dies my last chance to have been, and who is this raving now, pah there are voices everywhere, ears everywhere, one who speaks saying, without ceasing to speak, Who's speaking?, and one who hears, mute, uncomprehending, far from all. (59)[3]

The relation between the two voices is at once symbiotic and antagonistic, and turns on the impossibility of verifying which (if either) corresponds to a living being. While the speaker ponders his "last chance to have been," an existence made posthumous in the moment of its announcement, the conditions of its being are simultaneously thrown into doubt. Not only is the window of opportunity impossibly small (the other is already "moribund"), but the narrator's activity is equated with the paradoxical performative "it's me in him remembering." The discursive marker appears to transplant the voice into the body of the other, momentarily fusing with it before admitting, "Oh I know, it's not me, not yet, it's a veteran." The dawning sense of an event to be witnessed ("a winter night, without moon or stars"), together with a survivor to bear witness to it, is preempted by the violent rejection of the speaker that follows his usurpation of the other's position ("disowning me, as though I had taken his place"). A voice preemptively canceling the existence of the other and remaining only in ventriloquized form is uncomfortably reminiscent of the problematic situation with which Agamben is concerned in chapter 3 of *Remnants of Auschwitz*.

Like the speaker of *Text* 12, the subject of testimony in *Remnants of Auschwitz* is both constituted and destroyed in the annihilating experience of shame: "in shame, the subject [...] has no other content than its own desubjectification; it becomes witness to its own disorder, its own oblivion as a subject" (106). Such is precisely the condition of the Beckettian speaker, who lives through the shameful and disabling taking the place of the other, "the shame of my living that kept me from living" (*Text* 12 59). The radical self-dispossession undergone by the speaker here uncannily anticipates that of the subject in Agamben, so that the underlying discursive structure of *Texts for Nothing* can be rethought as an oblique and impersonal version of testimony. Not only are atrocious past events periodically glimpsed in the narrative—"bodies everywhere" (*Text* 12 59); "a head strewn with arms laid down and corpses fighting fresh" (*Text* 4 23)—but the sense of a testimony by proxy is increasingly strongly felt: "it's me in him remembering" (*Text* 12 58). The logic of the narrative situation now becomes increasingly fraught: because of the large number of references in the third person, the ventriloquized presentation of a dead protagonist seems increasingly likely. The difficulty, however, lies in the explicit thematization of voice ("who says this, saying it's me?" [*Text* 4 22]), leaving the marker "it's" suspended between the fictive reality and the moment of enunciation.

The speaker's presence within the other is simultaneously figured in terms of "contumacy," and therefore is a slippery and indeterminate form of absence. Rather than describing the fact of being absent, contumacy is concerned with the inferred meaning of that absence. To be "put in contumacy," in legal terms, is to be judged to have committed an act of "wilful disobedience to the summons or order of a court" (*Oxford English Dictionary* 856): one's absence from court is deemed to signify resistance to the juridical regime represented by it. Like the dead prisoner who haunts the survivor in Agamben, the dead protagonist of *Texts for Nothing* persists within the living as an inescapable blind spot, violating the textual regime in which he is supposed to participate. Not only does the speaker bear witness to his own desubjectification, but he narrates "in absentia," by means and by virtue of that desubjectification.

Heteronymy

The narrator's attempts to speak of himself in *Text* 4 are again so comprehensively absorbed by the other, "the same old stranger as ever, for whom alone accusative I exist" that the inquiry "who would I be, if I could be" (22) rapidly gives way to the anguished "if at least he would dignify me with the third person" (23). The self-abnegating state of shame proves to be allied with another of the key figures of Agamben's discourse: heteronymy. This notion is understood here in the sense of characters and fictional authors functioning as alter egos of the author or narrator: the multiple names are seen as referring to a single subject.[4] The equivocation which lies at the heart of *Texts for Nothing* between "I" and "he" is consequently manifested as an evacuation of the self into a series of secondary identities drawn from other parts of the Beckett corpus, in this case those of Molloy and Malone, "those mere mortals, happy mortals" (23).

Rather than providing any prospect of escape from the speaker's imprisonment, the heteronomy of *Text* 4 articulates an anxiety over identity and difference that is one of the key structures of the text. While the narrator cannot remain within the bracket of the "I," instead becoming "accusative" in the very act of speaking, the movement by which alternative identities are assumed is equally precarious. It is in this context that Simon Critchley persuasively aligns the leaching out of the Beckettian utterance from one pronoun to another with Blanchot's idea of the neuter and of an impersonal form of speech: "I do not speak, it speaks" (Critchley 128).[5] The central move in *The Unnamable,* for Critchley, is of an attempted transition from the first to the third person, and for this reason he is able to propose Beckett's *Not I* as "a distilled redrafting of *The Unnamable*" (128). What is certain is that the "I" of *Texts for Nothing* cannot be properly confined within the limits set out for it in the narrative, and intersects and periodically fuses with the "he" which designates the impossible other. It is precisely the "shifting value of pronouns and other deictics" (O'Donovan 169) that, in Patrick O'Donovan's account, shapes the text and orchestrates its disorientating engagement with the processes of reading.[6]

Such a wholesale undermining of the building blocks of discourse recalls Agamben's arguments on shame, and in particular the bizarre figure of "homopseudonymy," which he derives from the novelist Giorgio Manganelli and defines as "using a pseudonym that is in every respect identical to one's own name" (Agamben, *Remnants* 130). The example that Agamben gives concerns friends of the author figure within the fictive reality of Manganelli's text: the books that they report having seen in bookstore windows, signed in the name of the author figure, are completely unknown to him. This fictional incident, for Agamben, proves to be an extreme and peculiar example of heteronymy, or "our non-coincidence with ourselves" (130). While heteronymy and homopseudonymy appear diametrically opposed, each in fact attests to language's dramatic failure to capture the self. In Agamben's example, nonidentity is expressed not by the divergence between the speaker's "proper" name and the substitute identities foisted upon him, but in terms of an ontological clash: the non-identity of the name and the book which its bearer is considered to have written.

This nonrecognition of the self in the real (in which the books are produced) highlights the ontological unease inherent in Beckett's use of heteronymy. The appeal to Molloy and Malone in *Texts for Nothing* is followed by the anguished "What am I doing, talking, having my figments talk, it can only be me" (*Text* 4 24). These are imposed identities, like those evoked by the speaker's "keepers"—"it's they murmur my name, speak to me of me" (*Text* 5 29)—and which, in John Pilling's analysis, represent the fundamental violence of *Texts for Nothing*: "so tenacious are these aggressive phantoms in their quest to provide the 'I' with a self ('They want to create me,' [*Text* 5 30]), that the speaker can only resign himself to being tormented by them permanently" (Knowlson and Pilling 50). The Unnamable, meanwhile, perhaps represents a still more extreme form of this ontological torture and can speak only as the latest in a long line of substitutes or avatars. His narrative reaches us only through his abortive assumption of their identities: "Malone is there. Of his mortal liveliness little trace remains" (268); all, it appears increasingly, are earlier incarnations, "delegates" (272), of the Unnamable itself. The tone of jocular self-loathing in which the realization is voiced resonates with the shattering experience of shame and loss of selfhood which, for Agamben, underpins survivor accounts: "*the subject of testimony is the one who bears witness to a desubjectification*" (120–21; emphasis in original).

In this version of testimony, to bear witness is to fracture one's own subject position, to inscribe one's subjectivity with that of the absent, voiceless other. If to bear witness is to enter into the all-consuming "zone of indistinction" (120) that lies at the heart of *Remnants of Auschwitz,* the Unnamable's rebirth in an endless series of "vice-existers" (289) conflates physical and ontological wounding: "mutilate, mutilate, and perhaps some day, fifteen generations hence, you'll succeed in beginning to look like yourself" (289). It is increasingly clear that there is a form of concentrationary violence in the identifications themselves, what Leo Bersani calls the "brilliantly simple device of making the Unnamable the victim of a conspiracy to force him just to live. His persecutors want him to be a man, to be born. They give him roles to play (which nicely accounts for the Beckett œuvre), but he has resisted being identified with them (which dismisses the Beckett œuvre)" (Bersani 324).

The narrator, in fact, has already fantasized about freeing himself definitively from the surrogate identities forced upon him, in a conflictual passage in which the specters of testimony and shame again raise their heads: "All these Murphys, Molloys and Malones do not fool me. They have made me waste my time, suffer for nothing [...]. I thought I was right in enlisting these sufferers of my pains. I was wrong. They never suffered my pains, their pains are nothing, compared to mine, a mere tittle of mine, the tittle I thought I could put from me, in order to witness it" (278). Although the heteronyms are the invention of the speaker and adopted by him in order to express his pain, that pain proves to be exacerbated by, if not caused by, this very trick. Realizing its failure, the narrator angrily demands, "give me back the pains I lent them and vanish, from my life, my memory, my terrors and shames" (278). Shame, then, is the privileged figure of this deposition, associated with the desire "to witness it" and giving rise to an identification that is, in Agamben's terms, both "absolutely foreign and perfectly intimate" (*Remnants* 131).[7]

Heteronomy and Biopolitical Discourse

A movement of repudiation characterizes Beckettian heteronymy: not only does the speaker refuse to be "fooled" by the Murphys, Molloys, and Malones that populate his speech, but he periodically casts off the names that have been imposed upon him, facetiously abandoning the name Basil in favor of Mahood (283) and, finally, Worm: "if I am not yet Worm, I shall be when I cease to be Mahood, plop" (310). Worm, for Critchley, has a special status, representing the problematic possibility of survival or of death: "Worm is that which somehow *remains,* he is a remainder, what Blanchot calls 'une survivance' (312), outside of life and the possibility of death" (Critchley 123).[8] Worm, then, resonates with the figure at the heart of Agamben's account of testimony: the *Muselmann,* the prisoner who, in an extreme of suffering, has gone beyond the sphere of human interaction, and who no longer rejects the labels attached to him. Heteronymy is an essential part of Agamben's account of the concentrationary universe, as the prisoner is assigned a set of biopolitical identities that are continually exchanged until a final point is reached:

The non-Aryan passes into the Jew, the Jew into the deportee (*umgesiedelt, ausgesiedelt*), the deportee into the prisoner (*Häftling*), until biopolitical caesuras reach their final limit in the camp. This limit is the *Muselmann.* At the point in which the *Häftling* becomes a *Muselmann,* the biopolitics of racism so to speak transcends race, penetrating into a threshold in which it is no longer possible to establish caesuras. Here the wavering link between people and population is definitively broken, and we witness the emergence of something like an absolute biopolitical substance that cannot be assigned to a particular bearer or subject, or be divided by another caesura. (85)

The *Muselmann,* the prisoner who has given up and effectively relinquished the "life of relation" that defines him as human, represents the end point in the process, a point at which no further roles can be forced upon him. This "absolute biopolitical substance" is not simply an extreme of physical degradation and psychological breakdown, but the permanent contamination of the human with the nonhuman which the *Muselmann* represents, and which is uncannily anticipated in Beckett: "Pupil Mahood, repeat after me, Man is a higher mammal, I couldn't" (*Unnamable* 309–10). At this point in the narrative, humanity is no longer distinct from animal life (or "bare life," in Agamben's term) and the only residual meaning that it retains is as the plaything of a malevolent god: "The essential is to go on squirming forever at the end of the line, as long as there are waters and banks and ravening in heaven a sporting God to plague his creature, per pro his chosen shits" (311). The narrative is rapidly becoming a continuum of suffering, in which the master-slave dialectic maps directly onto ontological hierarchies. As Gary Adelman claims in *Naming Beckett's Unnamable,* "control—sadistic violation—is a primal law of creation" (107–08). While Adelman specifically (although briefly) compares the narrator of *The Unnamable* to the *Muselmann* (81), elsewhere he speculates that "in *Texts,* the writer's imagination continuously reanimates itself under the stimulation of self-torture"; meanwhile, "the spur to creativity expands to include the torture of others" (107).[9]

Such a view of the creative process as essentially sadistic sheds considerable light on the sardonic commentary that accompanies the Unnamable's physical transformations. A series of "vice-existers" are foisted upon him, as well as a sinister form of medical experimentation in which his body is remodeled in forms designed to create ever-greater suffering: "Let's try him this time with a hairless wedge-head, he might fancy that, that kind of talk. With the solitary leg in the middle, that might appeal to him" (289). The physical suffering that runs through *The Unnamable* here reaches a peak, and the next bodily modification brings with it an explicit inquiry into the limits of the human: "They could clap an artificial anus in the hollow of my hand and still I wouldn't be there, alive with their life, not far short of a man, just barely a man, sufficiently a man to have hopes one day of being one, my avatars behind me" (289).

The nightmare vision of suffering presented here produces further insights into the relevance of Agamben's larger inquiry into modern biopolitics of which his theory of testimony is a part. What Agamben calls "bare life" is "included in politics in the form of the exception, that is, as something that is included solely through an exclusion" (*Homo Sacer* 11). Like the juridical concept of "life unworthy to be lived" invented in Nazi Germany, the Unnamable's biological existence is entirely determined and controlled by the technology of his tormentors, and his identity is defined solely within the sphere of their atrocious whims.[10] The constant reimagining of his body is merely the arena in which their desires are played out, and the status of its owner as a human being is invoked only in order to foreground the nature of the suffering he experiences.

The subject position occupied by the narrator is once more crucially ambiguous: the "not far short of a man" segment is in fact prefaced by the claim "still I wouldn't be there, alive with their life," suggesting a residual form of resistance to the prosthetic identities and bodies which he is forced to occupy. The addition of "I wouldn't be there" spells out the Unnamable's predicament: it serves to include the subject in the form of an exclusion, adding epistemological torture to the physical torments that surround it. Like the ambivalent "it's me in him remembering" in *Text* 12 (58), *The Unnamable* becomes a narrative of exception, in which bare, biological life is included only in its capacity to be excluded from the realm of the living. The tortured, sadistically imagined body offers the dubious possibility "to know it's life still, a form of life, ordained to end" (*Text* 6 34) while perpetually occupying the appalling interval preceding the end, "hugging the slaughter-house walls" (*Unnamable* 289), "without the strength to end or the courage to continue" (Beckett, "The End" 95).

Narrating Testimony

The narrative situation in both *Texts for Nothing* and *The Unnamable* is avowedly untenable, situating expression within an impossible dual viewpoint that is never satisfactorily resolved: "he thinks because words fail him he's on his way to my speechlessness" (*Text* 4 22). In Agamben, the corresponding position, sharply recalling the confrontation of language with the "unfathomable abysses of silence" that surround it in Beckett (qtd. in Harvey 434), is that of the narrative of the witness who cannot speak, or the poet who situates himself within a dead language: "This is why what is borne witness to cannot already be language or writing. It can only be something to which no one has borne witness. And this is the sound that arises from the lacuna, the nonlanguage that one speaks when one is alone, the nonlanguage to which language answers, in which language is born" (*Remnants* 38).

The pivotal question is the nature and status of the resulting testimony, its undecidable and impersonal form. To what, finally, does such a language bear witness? The answer lies in the impossible encounter of living and dead witnesses that dominates *Remnants of Auschwitz* and that models the indeterminate relationship of the archive and testimony. The rigorously implosive subject positions of Beckett's work thus anticipate recent theorizations of testimony and of the archive, creating echoes of the atrocities of the camps and of the epistemological problems of survivor testimony. These problems are paradoxically amplified by the refusal to concretize subliminal references to atrocity:

> To what does such a language bear witness? To something—a fact or an event, a memory or a hope, a delight or an agony—that could be registered in the *corpus* of what has already been said? Or to enunciation, which, in the archive, attests to the irreducibility of saying to the said? It bears witness to neither one nor the other. What cannot be stated, what cannot be archived is the language in which the author succeeds in bearing witness to his incapacity to speak. In this language, a language that survives the subjects who spoke it coincides with a speaker who remains beyond it. (Agamben, *Remnants* 161–62)

The resulting enigma is at once discursive and ethical: just as Agamben's work brings into play the pressing question of the status of testimony by proxy, *The Unnamable* and *Texts for Nothing* leave behind them an unresolved tension between narrator and reader. In Agamben's case, the question is actualized in the final section of *Remnants of Auschwitz,* which is devoted to the transcription of survivors' accounts of their own experiences as *Muselmänner,* prefaced by the paradoxical formula "I was a *Muselmann*" (166–71).[11] The problem, of course, is that the *Muselmann* by definition cannot speak: these survivors' accounts (rare examples of prisoners who survived the state that Agamben and Levi describe) can function only by substituting the voice of the survivor for that of the *Muselmann.*

To do so, though, is a highly ambivalent gesture: to speak *for* the *Muselmann* may be to impose a foreign discursive structure, may be simply to put the words of the living into the mouths of the dead. The ethical consequences of such a move are complex, as is indicated in Thomas Trezise's more general analysis of the ethical problems of survivor testimony: "to remain true to those who perished by speaking *for* them, and especially to do so in the first person, was in a sense to betray them, if only because it required availing oneself of the very speech that they themselves had been forever denied" (61). Agamben's defense is the argument that he pursues throughout *Remnants of Auschwitz,* that testimony necessarily undermines the subject position of the witness and underwrites it with a desubjectification: "Testimony is thus strictly unassignable; it cannot be attributed either to the survivor, who speaks of experiences which are not his own, or to the *Muselmann,* who does not speak at all" (Davis 85).[12] The cleft within subjectivity, a deep-seated nonidentity within the self like the paralysis of shame, allows Agamben to make this extraordinary gesture, paradoxically deriving a forceful argument from the radical disempowerment of the *Muselmann:* as Colin Davis argues, "the position from which Agamben speaks and writes turns out to be more secure than that of his other desubjectified subjects" (87).

Can such a problematic, finally, be applied (or reapplied) to Beckett? The acts of creation by which the Unnamable and his avatars come into being, as we have seen, are frequently imbued with sadism, with the desire to bring into being a form of life that is synonymous with suffering. The argument that Adelman extrapolates from this is that *literary* creation and, therefore, the narrator's stance toward the reader are sadistic. While such a possibility is undoubtedly left open in the complex engagement with discourse and with reading in *Texts* and in *The Unnamable,* to equate Beckett's "syntax of weakness" (qtd. in Harvey 435) with an act of violence is surely to underestimate its subtlety and discursive impact. The deliberate disabling of operative structures seen in these works reads rather as the converse of Agamben's forceful (contumacious?) argument, as an enactment of the disempowerment that lies at the heart of testimony and by which testimony is obliquely, but so empathetically, invoked. While the atrocities of these two texts are never brought directly into view, they lurk on the margins of reading like a half-forgotten memory, like an utterance which is never quite finished and which (like Agamben's archive) can never finally be consigned to the repertoire of the said.

Notes

1. Agamben's discussion of testimony in *Remnants of Auschwitz* is inextricably bound up with the Foucauldian notion of the archive, "the positive dimension that corresponds to the plane of enunciation, 'the general system of the formation and transformation of statements'" (Foucault, *Archaeology* 130, qtd. in Agamben, *Remnants* 143). While Agamben's understanding of the archive is refined in the course of the book, the idea of a "set of rules which at a given period and for a given society define [...] the limits and forms of the sayable" (Foucault, *Discipline* 59) remains crucial.

2. Selections from *Texts for Nothing* are referred to by the abbreviated title *Text* (and number) followed by page number.

3. All references in this excerpt and in the paragraph in which it is embedded are to *Text* 12 (58–59).

4. The key reference point (specifically drawn upon by Agamben) is Fernando Pessoa; for a philosophical reading of Pessoa's heteronyms, see Badiou (36–45).

5. See also Hill's important earlier comments on the neuter in Beckett.

6. In this context, see also Moorjani (29–37), in particular the analysis of a "polyphonic interaction among three agencies at different psychic levels" at the opening of *Texts for Nothing* (Moorjani 32).

7. David Watson, in an analysis of *The Unnamable,* uncovers a strikingly similar structure: "I reject my own voice as other, I am elsewhere; in doing so I adopt the other's voice as my own" (Watson 51–52).

8. Blanchot's reference to "une survivance parlante" has particular resonance in the present context, his analysis of the Beckettian voice creating further echoes of the idea of survivor testimony. See Blanchot (259).

9. While Adelman's suggestion on *The Unnamable* is fascinating, it is not developed, and there is no consideration of Agamben in *Naming Beckett's Unnamable.*

10. See Agamben, *Homo Sacer* (in particular 138–42).

11. The accounts are taken from Ryn and Klodzinski's study *An der Grenze zwischen Leben und Tod. Eine Studie über die Erscheinug des "Muselmanns" im Konzentrazionslager,* a key reference point in *Remnants of Auschwitz.*

12. The problem of the narrative voice in Agamben's own project is at the heart of Davis's searching critique. For further engagements with the question of viewpoint

and survivor testimony, see also La Capra, *History and Memory* (11) and, specifically on Agamben and the *Muselmann,* La Capra, *History in Transit* (144–94).

Works Cited

Adelman, Gary. *Naming Beckett's Unnamable.* Lewisburg, PA: Bucknell University Press, 2004.

Agamben, Giorgio. *Homo Sacer: Sovereign Power and Bare Life.* Trans. Daniel Heller-Roazen. Stanford, CA: Stanford University Press, 1998.

———. *Remnants of Auschwitz: The Witness and the Archive.* Trans. Daniel Heller-Roazen. New York: Zone Books, 1999.

Badiou, Alain. *Handbook of Inaesthetics.* Trans. Alberto Toscano. Stanford, CA: Stanford University Press, 2005.

Beckett, Samuel. "The End." *No's Knife: Collected Shorter Prose 1945–1966.* London: Calder, 1967.

———. *Texts for Nothing.* London: Calder, 1999.

———. *Three Dialogues with Georges Duthuit. Disjecta: Miscellaneous Writings and a Dramatic Fragment.* Ed. Ruby Cohn. London: Calder, 1983.

———. *The Unnamable. The Beckett Trilogy.* London: Picador, 1979.

Bersani, Leo. *Balzac to Beckett: Center and Circumference in French Fiction.* New York: Oxford University Press, 1970.

Blanchot, Maurice. *Le Livre à venir.* Paris: Gallimard, 1959.

Critchley, Simon. "Who Speaks in the Work of Samuel Beckett?" *Yale French Studies* 93 (1998): 114–30.

Davis, Colin. "Can the Dead Speak to Us? De Man, Levinas and Agamben." *Culture, Theory and Critique* 45 (2004): 77–89.

Foucault, Michel. *The Archaeology of Knowledge.* Trans. A. M. Sheridan Smith. New York: Pantheon, 1972.

———. *Discipline and Punish.* Trans. Alan Sheridan. Harmondsworth: Penguin, 1979.

———. *The Discourse on Language.* Trans. A. M. Sheridan Smith. New York: Pantheon, 1972.

Harvey, Lawrence E. *Samuel Beckett: Poet and Critic.* Princeton, NJ: Princeton University Press, 1970.

Hill, Leslie. *Beckett's Fiction: In Different Words.* Cambridge: Cambridge University Press, 1990.

Knowlson, James, and John Pilling. *Frescoes of the Skull: The Later Prose and Drama of Samuel Beckett.* London: Calder, 1979.

La Capra, Dominick. *History and Memory after Auschwitz.* Ithaca, NY: Cornell University Press, 1998.

———. *History in Transit: Experience, Identity, Cultural Theory.* Ithaca, NY: Cornell University Press, 2004.

Moorjani, Angela. *Beyond Fetishism and Other Excursions in Psychopragmatics.* Houndmills, UK: Macmillan, 2000.

O'Donovan, Patrick. "Beckett's Happy Few." *Zeitschrift für Französische Sprache und Literatur* 100 (1990): 168–79.

Oxford English Dictionary. Ed. J. A. Simpson and E. S. C. Weiner. 2nd ed. Vol. 3. Oxford: Clarendon, 1989.

Trezise, Thomas. "Unspeakable." *Yale Journal of Criticism* 14 (2001): 39–66.

Watson, David. *Paradox and Desire in Samuel Beckett's Fiction.* Basingstoke, UK: Macmillan, 1991.

Wolosky, Shira. "The Negative Way Negated: Samuel Beckett's *Texts for Nothing.*" *New Literary History* 22 (1991): 213–30.

Projections

Beckett's *Krapp's Last Tape* and *Not I* as Autobiographies

CARLA LOCATELLI

> *Total object, complete with missing parts, instead of partial object. Question of degree.*
>
> —S. Beckett

> *Of these neither, and both at once*
>
> —W. Wordsworth

THE WORLDWIDE CELEBRATIONS of an empirical author usually identified as the flesh-and-blood Samuel Barclay Beckett—born in Cooldrinagh, Ireland, in 1906—bring to the fore concerns about the auto-biographical aspects of his work.[1] Beckett's centenary prompts me to reflect on the status of autobiography in the Beckett canon within a framework that builds on the latest epistemological considerations about autobio-graphical reading and honors the antilyrical stakes set forth in Beckett's works.

The literary corpus that we call Beckett calls for poststructuralist thinking on autobiography in a unique and unprecedented way. In this essay, I use this thinking as scaffolding to explore two Beckett plays—one from the fifties (*Krapp's Last Tape*, 1958) and one from the seventies (*Not I*, 1972)—as autobiographies. Because lack of space prevents me from extending my hermeneutical inquiry to still other Beckettian texts, it is helpful to recall Alan Schneider's words about the representative nature of Beckett's works: "every line of Beckett's contains the whole of Beckett. Every piece of Beckett's says what every other piece says in a different way" (17).

Imaging and Imagining the Author

After decades of structuralist and poststructuralist critical studies, it is common knowledge that Beckett shares a radical linguistic skepticism with more recent poststructuralist thought concerning the notions of *reference* and *naming* while, at the same time, resisting hasty dogmas that would proclaim the full disappearance of the author.[2] The latter perspective is possibly less evident today, as various announcements of the death of the author seem to have silenced anxieties about history and rhetoric (usually at the cost of abolishing history). In my view, however, the deconstructive notions of "distance" and "trace" (voiced first in existentialist criticism) continue to be significant in the discussion of the concept of authorship and autobiography in Beckett.[3] In this relation, the complexity of the issue of the (im)personality of writing can be summed up by a passage from *Not I:* "...realized...words were coming...a voice she did not recognize...at first...so long since it had sounded...then finally had to admit...could be none other...than her own..." (379).

Further, Oswald Ducrot's definition of the referential paradox is useful for our understanding of both authorship and autobiography: "precisely because a word *demands* to be related to a real external to it, it forbids the thinking of this real as different from the image of it it conveys" (706; my translation). On this ground, that is, precisely because, culturally, an author's name demands to be related to an empirical author, I emphasize the fact that it forbids thinking of this author as different from the image the author's name conveys. The issue is relevant in the context of a study of the autobiographical Beckett, since the question can shift from asking, "What is the name that conveys the image?" to asking, "What is the image that conveys the name (as a referent)?" and also, "Could there be more than one image?" and even, "Could the text be that image?"

Referential Collaboration and Projective Reading

In recent times, the most radical and persistent interrogation of the epistemological value of mimesis has been voiced by Paul de Man: he has argued for the notion of "autobiography as de-facement" and has highlighted the idea that autobiography is not a literary genre but rather "a figure of reading or of understanding that occurs, to some degree, in all texts" (70). As a matter of fact, de Man indicates that "any book with a readable title page is, to some extent, autobiographical" (67) and that "the autobiographical moment happens as an alignment between the two subjects involved in the process of reading in which they determine each other by mutual reflexive substitution" (70). These lucid statements inspire my approach to the issues relating Beckett to autobiography.

Jacques Derrida's assertion that "it is the ear of the other that signs" parallels and complements de Man's notion of autobiography as alignment "between the two subjects involved in the process of reading" (70). As Derrida explains, "the signature becomes effective—performed and performing—not at the moment it apparently takes place, but only later, when ears will have managed to receive the message. In some way the signature will take place on the addressee's side, that is, on the side of him or her whose ear will be keen enough to hear my name, for example, or to understand my signature, that with which I sign" (*Ear* 50). It is interesting to note that for Derrida either the name or the signature as figures (although they are semiotically heterogeneous) may be referentially effective. Why is this so? Is it because it makes no difference from the point of view of referential performance? If this is the case, hermeneutical possibilities for reading autobiographically could also be taken to exceed the mere name or signature of the author, and, therefore I suggest that an entire text could be taken as an autobiographical figure. In other words, I can read a text as the pseudoreferent of an author, not so much because of some distinctive stylistic features, that is, not because of what de Man calls "a genetic causality" (69), but because I relate the name of the author (on the first page) to the text, seeing them as coexisting patterns of figuration, as correlated figures of self-portraiture, and of autobiographical understanding. This is what directs my autobiographical reading of *Krapp* and *Not I*.

As we have seen, both de Man and Derrida agree on the idea that it is "reading autobiographically" that produces the autobiographical texts.

Readers decide to read autobiographically when they cast into narration a self that is simultaneously uttering and self-narrating. In both *Krapp* and *Not I,* the concurrent utterance and narration of the self, which make up the thematic and performative kernel of the plays, actually challenge the "one" and the "self" of the presumed "oneself." This fragmentation shows that autobiographical narrative and identity can only come about as the result of the decision that determines a reading. So, given that it is only a reading that determines the subject as an autobiographical subject, we could ask (again) if this subject can be determined only by *the figure* of a proper name (or signature) or by some other correlated figure (possibly such as a text), a figure capable of producing a singular subjective reference by way of the reader's decision.

Producing the Subject beyond the Textual Object

Problems with reading *Krapp's Last Tape* and *Not I* autobiographically would arise if one took a structuralist approach, which basically thinks of the author only as an implied author, that is, as a modeling function of the text, or if one chose a traditional autobiographical approach, which would base the meaning of the text on the "life of the author." A post-structuralist reading, however, could situate an autobiographical nonmimetic Beckett in *Krapp's Last Tape* and *Not I,* two texts that, in my view, struggle, the one with putting together an identity through prosthetic memory, and the other with self-portraiture through repetition and citation of the discursive process of identity work.[4]

If, as de Man and Derrida assert, reading autobiographically produces autobiographical texts, then the kind of reading that is performed—its structure and economies and teleologies—determines the kind of "hermeneutical object" that Beckett's autobiography becomes. In short, the autobiographical object produced depends on how the following questions are addressed:

1. Do we decide (or not) to read a Beckett text autobiographically? (Notice that to call it "Beckettian" is already to project an identity on it.)
2. Who do we (want to) read into a text? A subject? An implied and/or an empirical author? An autobiographical function? All of these?

In this context, it is worth noticing that a poststructuralist autobiographical reading can produce the referential identity of an *I* by way of a *not I* owing to the acknowledged negativity inherent in the sign. A *not I* can represent the unavoidable autobiographical distances between author (implied and empirical) and self that are—however—reciprocally determined. Specifically, the autobiographical question posed by the autobiographical reader would then be: "Who names the *not I?*" It must be an *I* who knows there is no way of naming himself/herself, and who is therefore characterized, in a note preceding the script of Beckett's *Not I,* by the "vehement refusal to relinquish third person" (375). If the reader poses this particular question for Beckett's play ("who names the *not I*"?), he or she can produce the reading of an autobiographical text in which the referent of that unstable *I* can shift from this (non)character to an implied author, and from it to the proper name Beckett. The play's failed enunciator, who paradoxically refuses the first person, could then be read as Beckett, the Beckett returning to a typical Beckett-the-writer obsession in a typical Beckettian voice.

Specifically, in highlighting the simultaneous obligation and impossibility of self-representation, *Not I* can be read autobiographically as Beckett-the-writer's failure and obligation of representing his *I.* The "reflexive substitution" (de Man 70) succeeds then as a result of the reader reading Beckett's (im)possible autobiography into the text.[5]

The Mimetic Fallacy and the Narrating Self

Because there is no way of verifying the factual content in a narrative text (is it fiction? is it fact?), de Man and Derrida locate the moment of autobiographical productivity in reading, rather than in mimesis (as it is traditionally understood). In this nonmimetic sense, I can read Beckett into *Krapp,* and I can read Beckett into *Not I,* especially in the guise of Beckett-the-writer who knows that he cannot relinquish the third person once his self comes to writing.

If we imagine the possibility that it is the figure (such as the name or the signature Beckett) that determines the referent (and not the other way around, as it is traditionally believed in defining autobiography), then we also have to admit assigning reference can be divorced from the mimetic imperative of distinguishing fact from fiction: "It appears, then, that the distinction between fiction and autobiography is not an either/or polarity but that it is undecidable" (de Man 70). This undecidability points to the fact that "what is at stake is not only the distance that shelters the author of autobiography from his experience but the possible convergence of aesthetics and of history" (de Man 67).

The deconstruction of the mimetic fallacy reinforces the evidence of the insurmountable distance between *I* and *self.* Indeed, the poststructuralist characterizations of self-expression, which deny the self authenticity and immediacy, emphasize both its dispersion and the fact that to speak is always already to speak of a self. In other words, there is no access to utterance without a subjective trace. *Not I* develops this idea by showing a subject that strenuously resists narcissistic self-identity: the image of the self is precisely an image, even when it is taken for the self, and yet this image is the only way in which one can speak of, and eventually identify, oneself: "yes... the tongue in the mouth... all those contortions without which... no speech possible... and yet in the ordinary way... not felt at all... so intent one is... on what one is saying... *the whole being... hanging on its words...* so that not only she had... had she... not only had she... to give up... admit hers alone... her voice alone..." (379; emphasis added).

The subjective gap is also conceptualized in *Krapp's Last Tape,* and it is arguably the play's most powerful theme. At the performative level, the impossible coincidence of *self* and *I* is evident in the contrapuntal discrepancy between speaking and listening to oneself speak. Additionally, the intermittent and random nature of recording one's experience shows the arbitrary and fragmented nature of self-portraiture based on memory, especially when played ironically against willed intention: "Just been listening to that stupid bastard I took myself for thirty years ago, hard to believe I was ever as bad as that. Thank God that's all done with anyway. [*Pause.*] The eyes she had! [*Broods, realizes he is recording silence, switches off broods. Finally.*] Everything there, everything, all the—[*Realizes this is not being recorded, switches on.*] Everything there, everything on this old muckball, all the light and dark and famine and feasting of... [*hesitates*]... the ages! [*In a shout.*] Yes! [*Pause.*] Let that go! Jesus! Take his mind off his homework!" (222). Krapp is a character stubbornly engaged in self-definition, but bound to be exhausted by this "homework" and ridiculed for trying it, still, at the end of his life, when it becomes clear that the best he can do is to go on taking himself for someone like him.

To the hopeless attempts of closing up the gap between *I* and a retrospective self must be added the impossibility of recording the facts of a life as mnemonic traces on which the autobiographical task, as traditionally understood, depends. Remembering is destined to fail, unless—perhaps—one is willing to subtract the continuity of identity as the desired outcome of autobiographical narrative. But in that case the failure of self-representation is repeated in the failure of narrative. Whereas self-narration is usually expected to determine the construction of identity, Beckett in *Krapp* questions this warrant. *Not I* further widens the distance between self-narration and identity by focusing on the gap between the enunciating subject and the enunciated subject and the uncertainty about who is saying what to whom. The recurrence of "…what?…who?…no!…she!" challenges the very notion of subjectivity in language. The issue is also exemplified in the interrogation of the very possibility of autobiographical recording: "now this…something she had to tell…could that be it?…something that would tell…how it was…how she—…what?…had been?…yes…something that would tell how it had been…how she had lived…lived on and on…" (381).

Subverting the Convergence of *Auto-bio-graphy*

The radical poststructuralist transformation of the notions of subjectivity and writing, as evident in the thinking about allegory and performance, literality and tropology, encompasses a resistance to and a subversion of the metaphysical *convergence* of *autos, bios,* and *graphein* that was taken for granted in traditional definitions of auto-bio-graphy.[6] In a poststructuralist world, "all of the three semiosic 'factors-conditions' of *auto-bio-graphy* (i.e., self, life and writing) are still objects of a theoretical discussion, but much more distinctly, i.e., as working at various levels (levels which are conceptually and phenomenologically different), and not converging, but actually displacing the metaphysical component of each" (Locatelli, "Is S/he" 4).[7]

Not I radicalizes the deconstruction of the auto-bio-graphical convergence, through the pervasiveness of the "refusal to relinquish third person" (375). *Krapp* voices a similar deconstructive attitude by way of deriding the romantic fantasy of remembering the self, since Krapp finds himself only as a residuum of vanishing selves. The fantasy of self-expression, as the gathering of the pieces of the self, is ridiculed most in the *crap* metaphor, which is the most obvious image of disintegration, rather than accumulation. Once the self is "processed," and once it is constructed in writing, it is always already expelled, so that it is never "there," never really somewhere, in one place. The subject in search of self-expression finds its self-portrait in the signifier "Krapp," an *omen nomen* showing that the interpretive level of this reference reverberates, from the semantic level to the discursive level, and onto the level of writing, in a radical self-ironic game ridiculing the excremental nature of the autobiographical author-writer.

In fact, the obsessive archive which is produced by the drive to capture the self, and which somehow certifies one's own existence, indicates the failure to which writing itself is destined. This constraint of writing calls for a clear-cut "desistance" of the type Beckett admired in Bram van Velde, who, he writes, "is the first to desist from this estheticized automatism, the first to admit that to be an artist is to fail, as no other dare fail [...]" ("Three Dialogues" 145). Beyond the aestheticized automatism of autobiography as a traditional literary genre, one can perceive the mimetic lie of self-expression.

Therefore, "fidelity to failure" is the logical consequence of the impossibility of self-expression, an expression that inevitably "expels" the *I* but does not "express" it. The expressive act has no available terms, except for the ones that speak the *I* in an expelled form. In short, Beckett's scorn makes of ex-pression an excremental ex-pulsion, and a failed aestheticized automatism of the author's autobiographical project.

The *Angustia* of Autobiographical Understanding

From my discussion it follows that autobiography as an object of critical thought can be conceptualized in different ways. The more traditional conceptions tend to emphasize documentary "truth"; other approaches valorize the *angustia* of writing. In using this Latin term, which conveys both "constraint" and "anguish," Derrida draws attention to the nonempirical dimension of the constriction intrinsic to writing. He explains: "If the anguish of writing is not and must not be a determined pathos, it is because this anguish is not an empirical modification or state of the writer, but is the responsibility of *angustia:* the necessarily restricted passageway of speech against which all possible meanings push each other, preventing each other's emergence" ("Force" 9).

In *Not I* the obsessive recurrence of the interrogative pronouns of identification ("what?..who?...no!...she!...") and of apparently contradictory confessions illustrates well the *angustia* of writing and thus of the autobiographical understanding: "imagine!.. no idea what she was saying!..till she began trying to...delude herself...it was not hers at all...not her voice at all," soon followed by, "so that not only she had...had she...not only had she...to give up...admit hers alone...her voice alone" (379). One can deny the subjective trace of one's utterance, and "delude herself" about not having a subjective voice, but—in the end—she must admit that speaking is irreducibly a speaking of, and by, someone.

In "Homage to Jack B. Yeats," Beckett describes a "high solitary art uniquely self-pervaded, one with its wellhead in a hiddenmost of spirit [...]," and he asserts, "The artist who stakes his being is from nowhere, has no kith" (149). The oxymoron of autobiography as defacement could not be more clearly underscored than by the figure of the artist who simultaneously "stakes his being" and "is from nowhere." This is the *angustia* of writing: that is, not the correlative of an expressive frustration, but rather the mark of the inevitable impersonality of uttering the self in narrations where the multiplicity of images that the self can take must be submitted to linguistic constraints and discursive protocols of self-portraiture.

The process of thinking in *Not I* is presented as irreducibly tropological and therefore as incapable of constructing an *I:* "try something else...think of something else [...] not that either...all right...something else again...so on...hit on it in the end...think everything keep on long enough [...] what?...not that either?...nothing to do with that either?...nothing she could think?...all right...nothing she could tell..." (382). Thought does have content, and no matter how hard we try to empty our mind of it, when we reflect profoundly on our thinking, it proves to be a stream of figures of which, in the end, we can only say, "not that either." Thus, the self is caught, both fixed and trapped, in its performance of talk; the *I* is simultaneously lost and found in the ongoing production of thoughts and in a necessarily restrained writing, which cannot include "all possible meanings" of the self.

In returning now to the status of autobiography and the constraints of reference, Beckett progressively prompts his readers throughout his work not only to question the obligation to make sense but also to put in doubt the dubious belief that a referent can be successfully assigned to a unified meaning including all the semantic outcomes the referent could take.

In de Man's words, Beckett would seem to resist this mimetic imperative that produces amnesia about discarded alternative meanings, and thus he would also dispute the illusion that the empirical author can be found in a proper name. Instead, Beckett can be said to stage for his audience, "the specular moment that is part of all understanding [and that] reveals the tropological structure that underlies all cognitions, including knowledge of self" (de Man 71). Once again, the figurative nature of knowledge and self-knowledge emerges in Beckett in ways that both perform the erosion of metaphoric stratifications and, at the same time, denounce the insufficiency of singular meanings produced in writing. To put it simply, Beckett shows us that we are always and simultaneously saying too much and not enough. This is the phenomenological and epistemological *angustia* of writing.

As for the autobiographical reader, at this point of exhaustion, the question can be raised: "Why do we want to read someone into a text?" A plausible Beckettian answer seems to be: "because there is no chance of doing otherwise." We are caught in "the specular moment that is part of all understanding." As Beckett would phrase it in *Not I*, "...and can't stop...no stopping it..." (380). In short, the name of Beckett is everywhere and nowhere, once writing occurs. Inscribed in Mouth, "[s/he] who but a moment before...but a moment!...could not make a sound...no sound of any kind...now can't stop...imagine!...can't stop the stream" (380). The text can neither stop nor be stopped, nor can the autobiographical reading of an author into the text with a "readable title page."

I would like to understand this highly problematic (de)construction of a self, or a subject, and/or an author as an "autobiographical word-function." Although partly dependent on the materiality of a text and its discursive structure, this word-function is not totally determined by them; as a consequence, it cannot be delimited by haphazard autobiographical projections. Nor would such a function leave room for idealistic illusions of self-expression in language or readings derived from an abstract metalanguage.

The Reader's Need to Project and the Text's Desire

To conclude, I would like to comment briefly on the provocative nature of those Beckett texts that, anticipating the desires readers project, resist them by mirroring them to the audience in the form of an endless questioning. Many lucid productions of Beckett's plays, since the 1980s and early 1990s, have valorized the issue of the fractured subject, but, unfortunately, this concern with the complexities of subjectivity and identity was often culturally received as a mere symptom of the personal struggle of the flesh-and-blood Beckett coming to terms with his own existential malaise. On the contrary, I think what is most relevant is the fact that in representing the failure of a unified subject, Beckett was reflecting back to his spectators the voyeuristic dimension of their *pathos:* either compassion and pain (as in *Not I*) or pathetic rage (as in *Krapp's Last Tape*). Beckett's grim tongue-in-cheek humor was probably addressing the facile projections of his (autobiographical) readers and spectators.

Roland Barthes has cogently illustrated the desire of the reader, while referring to the projective mechanism generated by texts: the text desires a reader who desires an author. The author is thus the result of the wish of the reader, who creates him or her, by way of his understanding:

> The text chooses me, by a whole disposition of invisible screens, selective baffles: vocabulary, references, readability, etc.; and lost in the midst of a text (not *behind* it, like a *deus ex machina*) there is always the other, the author.
>
> As institution the author is dead [...] but in the text, in a way, *I desire* the author: I need his figure (which is neither his representation nor his projection), as he needs mine. (Barthes 27)

The reader's desire of the author is the author's desire of the reader, with no concession to mimetic representation or to willed, intentional projections.

However, the reader's projections—endless and circular, pervasive and elusive, biographical and autobiographical, and ambivalently (im)personal—are constantly evoked in Beckett. So, Beckett's work, like Barthes's, is perhaps the most seductive account of the hermeneutical cycle produced by a skeptical writer in search of an autobiographical reader.

Notes

1. The use of the proper name in this essay does not indicate an empirical subject but refers to the referential identity produced by a textual corpus (often *read* in search of an empirical author).

2. On the issue of naming and reference in autobiography, see Locatelli, "Osservazioni sullo statuto dell'autobiografia," 341–51.

3. See Caselli for recent work that addresses the issue of authorship, albeit in a context focalized on intertextuality.

4. *Not I* can be seen as a sequel to *Krapp,* in the sense that it coalesces random fragments of narration into a possibly identifying discourse, but reducing the stronger mimetic components of Krapp's narrative.

5. Among the most relevant discussions of the thematics of identity work and linguistic self-expression in Beckett, see Angela Moorjani, *The Aesthetics of Loss and Lessness* (ch. 11 and 12) and *Beyond Fetishism and Other Excursions in Psychopragmatics* (ch. 3 and 5).

6. I have discussed this point at length in Locatelli, "Passaggi obbligati," 151–96.

7. See also Locatelli, "Figures of Displacement and Displacement of Figures," 11–22.

Works Cited

Barthes, Roland. *The Pleasure of the Text.* Trans. Richard Miller. New York: Farrar, 1975.

Beckett, Samuel. "Homage to Jack B. Yeats." Cohn 149.

———. *Krapp's Last Tape. The Complete Dramatic Works.* London: Faber, 1986. 213–23.

———. *Not I. The Complete Dramatic Works.* London: Faber, 1986. 373–83.

———. "Three Dialogues." Cohn 138–45.

Caselli, Daniela. *Beckett's Dantes: Intertextuality in the Fiction and Criticism.* Manchester: Manchester University Press, 2005.

Cohn, Ruby, ed. *Disjecta: Miscellaneous Writings and a Dramatic Fragment.* By Samuel Beckett. New York: Grove, 1984.

de Man, Paul. "Autobiography as Defacement." *The Rhetoric of Romanticism.* New York: Columbia University Press, 1984. 67–81.

Derrida, Jacques. *The Ear of the Other: Otobiography, Transference, Translation.* Ed. Claude Levesque and Christie McDonald. New York: Schocken, 1985.

———. "Force and Signification." *Writing and Difference.* Trans. Alan Bass. London: Routledge, 1978. 3–30.

Ducrot, Oswald. "Referente." *Enciclopedia Einaudi.* Vol. 11. Turin: Einaudi, 1980.

Locatelli, Carla. "Figures of Displacement and Displacement of Figures: The Play of Autobiography in V. Woolf's *Moments of Being.*" *La tipografia nel salotto: saggi su Virginia Woolf.* Ed. Oriana Palusci. Turin: Tirrenia Stampatori, 1999. 11–22.

———. "Is S/he My Gaze? (Feminist) Possibilities for Autobiographical Co(n)texts." *L'impulso autobiografico.* Ed. Michele Bottalico and Maria Teresa Chialant. Naples: Liguori, 2005. 3–21.

———. "Osservazioni sullo statuto dell'autobiografia nel pensiero della modernità" ("Observations on the Status of Autobiography in Contemporary Thought"). *Autobiografia e filosofia.* Ed. Nestore Pirillo. Rome: Edizioni di storia e letteratura, 2002. 341–51.

———. "Passaggi obbligati: la differenza (auto)biografica come politica co(n)testuale" ("Obligatory Passages: (Auto)biographical Difference as Co(n)textual Politics"). *Co(n)testi. Implicazioni testuali,* Ed. C. Locatelli. Trento: University of Trento Press, 2000. 151–96.

Moorjani, Angela. *The Aesthetics of Loss and Lessness.* New York: St. Martin's, 1992.

———. *Beyond Fetishism and Other Excursions in Psychopragmatics.* New York: St. Martin's, 2000.

Schneider, Alan. "Alan Schneider Directs *Rockaby.*" *Directing Beckett.* Ed. Lois Oppenheim. Ann Arbor: University of Michigan Press, 1997. 13–19.

"I Am Not a Philosopher"

H. PORTER ABBOTT

T HE QUESTION I am addressing in this essay does not have to do with
Beckett's extensive and deeply engaged reading of philosophy. And
only by indirection does it have to do with the multitude of philosophical
issues that are at stake in his work and that were clearly inflected by his
reading. This is ground that has been covered so extensively and so ably
by others that I have little chance of improving on their insights. What I
want to get at here is why Beckett, despite his absorption in philosophy,
should have insisted so emphatically that he was "not a philosopher," as
he famously told Tom Driver (23). Why should this have been a matter of
such urgency for him?

One answer, on the personal level, is that it comes out of Beckett's fear
of appropriation—the same that was aroused by Deirdre Bair's unauthor-
ized biography. I have argued at some length that a complement of this
fear was the positive autographical enterprise of his work, the vitality of
which lies in an art of surprising escapes from the nets of biography (*Beckett
Writing Beckett*). The moral equivalent of this orientation toward his writing is thematized everywhere in motifs of appropriation and enslavement
that have been richly discussed in the length and breadth of Beckett criticism, if not necessarily in the terms that I proposed. So it is no stretch
to include in this take on Beckett's aesthetic a resistance to philosophical
mastery as well, especially when reading philosophically means a happy
matching of fictional content to philosophical idea, with its implicit rel-
egation of fiction to a second-order discipline in which philosophy is the
master and fiction the handmaiden. As a critical practice, this is often interpretation by circularity: finding in the text what is already known in the
abstract. There are many instances of this kind of reading in Lance St. John

Butler's nonetheless enduringly useful *Samuel Beckett and the Meaning of Being:* Hamm in the bunker as the "Being-in" of *Dasein* (18), the problem of Watt's pot as a case of slippage from *Zuhanden* to *Vorhanden* (20), Malone's room as "Heideggerian space" (22). One is tempted to put this problem of philosophical appropriation in Heideggerian terms: that the "they" (*Mann*) who daily appropriate *Dasein,* keeping it from authenticity, would include those Heideggerians who would apply this distinction to Beckett. But even this paradox goes too far. There are many references to "they" in Beckett, intermittently attendant, residing vaguely above his narrators. But to absorb these hypotheticals into a working binary of a philosophical system, even at the expense of that system, is itself an appropriation of Beckett's text. Thus, by logical extension, Beckett's desire not to be classified as a philosopher would be a desire not to be classified as one who would do unto others what he so strenuously wished not to be done unto himself. This would be consistent with his generosity of spirit.

A different class of philosophically oriented Beckett scholars have generally avoided the more overt kinds of philosophical appropriation by examining Beckett, in Richard Begam's words, as he relates "not to a set of philosophers but to a philosophical problem." This Beckett is no handmaiden of philosophy but a serious "philosophical writer" in his own right, doing original philosophical work. For Begam, it is important, then, to find out "where Beckett stands on one of the defining questions" of philosophy ("whether it is possible to establish a discourse that stands outside all other discourses, and therefore escapes what Rorty calls contingency" 12–13). But if I am right, Beckett would still reject the description "philosophical writer" and with it the idea of "taking a stand," however infirm the nonfoundation on which he took it. Among this generation, perhaps the one who has most directly addressed the incompatibility of Beckett and philosophy has been Simon Critchley. In his essay "Know Happiness—on Beckett," Critchley argues that the "writings of Samuel Beckett seem to be particularly, perhaps uniquely, resistant to philosophical interpretation" (165). Critchley builds on contentions about Beckett by other philosophers (Adorno, Derrida, Cavell), arguing that Beckett displaces meaning itself by undoing its language. But Critchley's own language curiously restores Beckett to the status of hardworking philosopher that Begam admires. Beckett does philosophical work, "debating the meaning of meaning" (178), and by this work he arrives at a stand. The stand may be nowhere, afloat in a vacuum, but it is nonetheless definable in terms of where it is not.

Please don't get me wrong. I believe Begam and Critchley, like many other Beckett scholars who have adopted a philosophical approach (Lance Butler, Angela Moorjani, David Hesla, Steven Connor, Jean-Michel Rabaté, Leslie Hill, Linda Ben-Zvi, Thomas Trezise, P. J. Murphy, Marjorie Perloff, Dan Katz, Martha Nussbaum, Anthony Uhlmann, the whole smorgasbord of essayists in Richard Lane's excellent anthology, *Beckett and Philosophy*, plus some actual philosophers themselves, like Adorno, Badieu, and Cavell), do valuable, provocative work. They help us think about Beckett. But they do not help us understand why it was so important for Beckett that he not be considered a philosopher—why he so emphatically repudiated the label. As I argued earlier, a strong case can be made that philosophy in Beckett's eyes could be classified among the range of efforts to exert mastery over others for which he had so strong a moral and personal repugnance. But I think the problem with *being* a philosopher goes deeper than this. It is not simply the moral threat of such mastery that is the problem but the broader threat to artistic success that is inherent in the attitude of mastery. This deep incompatibility of art and philosophical mastery connects with the centrality of the themes of failure and incompetence in Beckett's aesthetic. "Fail better" is a great joke, but it is also no joke. And part of the reason it is no joke—let me put this strongly for the purposes of argument—is because Beckett expresses here not simply his aesthetic but an absolute of aesthetic practice. In other words, the deep difference between what Beckett does as an artist and what philosophers do as philosophers is fail. I have to walk especially carefully here because, among artists, Beckett has seemed so unique in his embrace of incompetence. Failure seems not so much essential art as quintessential Beckett. Indeed, Beckett stressed how different he was in this regard from traditional artists, and certainly from the masters of high modernism, and quite specifically from the master he trained with, James Joyce.[1]

But if the terms "failure" and "incompetence" are read as the relinquishing of power and control, then they can be seen as forceful expressions of one of the commonest tropes in the discourse of writers about their art: that is, that as they write, characters and plot are not so much made as discovered, their characters seeming to have an existence independent of the author's own will and the events of the plot seeming to emerge in often surprising succession. "Guess what Flem Snopes did last night!" as Faulkner told his friend Phil Stone. Repeatedly, the lesson for the artist has been to restrain the urge to dominate. As John Fowles put it, "It is only when our characters and events begin to disobey us that they begin to live" (81). E. M. Forster referred to this as the "mutiny" of the created, "that wonderful thing, a character running away with you" (28). In his 2005 Nobel Prize acceptance speech, Harold Pinter stated that in writing he starts with the barest seed, an image or word, but that soon he has on his hands characters who are "people with will and an individual sensibility of their own, made out of component parts you are unable to change, manipulate or distort" (qtd. in Lyall A3). Fowles, Forster, and Pinter are just three of many modern writers who have featured this vital powerlessness of the artist. The Turkish novelist Orhan Pamuk, in his novel *Snow*, tracks the magical emergence of nineteen poems that come to the poet Ka during three days snowbound in the city of Kars:

> Ka heard the call from deep inside him: the call he heard only in moments of inspiration, the only sound that could ever make him happy, the sound of his muse. For the first time in four years, a poem was coming to him; although he had yet to hear the words, he knew it was already written; even as it waited in its hiding place, it radiated the power and beauty of destiny. Ka's heart rejoiced.[...] [He] wrote out the poem as it came to him, word by word. It was like copying down a poem someone was whispering in his ear. [...] He carried on his writing, hardly pausing at all, leaving spaces only here and there for the words he had not quite heard, until he had written thirty-four lines. (86–87)

The locus classicus for Ka's thrilling experience is Coleridge's "Kubla Khan," which according to the poet he wrote as if on dictation and which, once interrupted, he could not regain by any exertion of the will. But what Coleridge showcased in "Kubla Khan" is in turn simply one instance in a tradition that is at least as ancient as the concept of the muse, invoked earlier by Pamuk. In this understanding of the creative act, the fickle muse may or may not visit the poet, but without her nothing of any value will be written. "When your daemon is in charge do not try to think consciously.[...] Drift, wait, and obey."[2] In this regard, poetry and fiction are forms of what is called "emergent behavior." They come into being not from the top down but from the bottom up—not, in other words, from the exertion of control or the imposition of design but from the chemistry of local interactions out of which form emerges. This oversimplifies, of course. What emerges is continually inflected by what has already emerged, and then subject to broader inflections as the artist revises. Few poets are as blessed as Coleridge was when he wrote "Kubla Khan," and even in this landmark case there is evidence that the poem as published is not quite what it was when Coleridge transcribed his dream.[3]

So, though we are talking about the writing of poetry and fiction as a process that depends on a lack of centralized control, that is, a freedom from top-down management, there is control in the form of feedback loops that contribute their own shaping influence to the process of emergence.[4] Revision, it must be stressed, is only the outer layer of such feedback, most of which operates with the same unconscious swiftness as emergence itself. This added complexity distinguishes the productivity of art from forms of emergent behavior in which the productivity is predictable within narrow limits (termite mounds, flocking birds) or shapelessly anarchic (traffic jams, the World Wide Web). But it may be very close to the neurology of thought itself. The mechanics of cognition is a subject about which there is much controversy and much that is still mysterious. But the work of Marvin Minsky, Gerald Edelman, and others strongly suggests that there is neither a blueprint in our brains nor any single entity fabricating and directing our thoughts, but instead billions of local neurological interactions, the results of which are only imperfectly predictable from one moment to the next.

But then, to get back to my main theme, isn't this what happens in the minds of philosophers as well as poets? Don't their ideas "come to them" in the same way as the ideas of poets and novelists? And the answer is yes. The difference, I want to argue, lies in the distance that is sought and maintained from the conditions of such productivity. It is a difference in comfort level. The philosopher's trade, after all, is to make a system with noncontradictory parts. And even where contradictory parts and ambiguities are necessary, the effort is to bring them in turn into a larger tent of belonging by metasystematic moves. This is true, I would argue, even in such recent proponents of a necessary systematic inconclusion as Wittgenstein and the very different Derrida. It is the life and breath of Western philosophy, however tentative or troubled or doomed, to create a discursive architecture robust enough that its terms and distinctions prevail, traveling from the philosopher through time and space in a proliferation of application. So though the philosopher, as a human being, necessarily depends on the emergent productivity of thought, and even, like Heidegger, may feature philosophical pursuit as a process that only stops with death ("An on-the-way in the field of paths for the changing questioning of the manifold question of Being"),[5] the process is given direction and purpose by residing within a system. Named and situated, such concepts as Heidegger's "Being-free-for" and "Being-towards" and Being as "possibility" are domesticated and to that degree exclude freedom and possibility. The terms "possibility" and "freedom" themselves become containers in the sense of holding and restricting. Only thus are they available for repeated use.

On this view, the artist, or at least the one whose work comes alive, must take up a position closer to the bottom than to the top, closer to where the work is emerging. It takes talent, certainly, but also courage to let go like this. And the result is not always an entirely happy one, as Pirandello complained repeatedly. In J. M. Coetzee's recent novel *Slow Man,* the failure to control one's creation is more a curse than a blessing. Eighty pages into the novel, Coetzee's surrogate novelist, Elizabeth Costello, enters the diegesis to confront her disappointing protagonist. She urges him with only mild success to follow her cues, if only to liven the plot and get things over and done with. Stuck with this character, the book lumbers along with blatant reflexivity, as if to tell the whole world of its author's misfortune. But that Coetzee should still choose to publish this refractory novel is, I think, some indication of the importance he gave to the aesthetic issue of the necessary limitations on an author's power to control the children whom she or he has brought into whatever fictive world.

"A voice comes to one in the dark. Imagine" (*Nohow On* 3). Richard Begam has written eloquently on the ways in which the opening line of *Company* and other representations and activations of the voice in Beckett bear out Derrida's argument that writing precedes speaking in the sense that it writes large the condition of speech as "contaminated with the contingency of language" (16–17). Derrida's notorious overstatement (we did in fact speak long before anyone picked up a stylus) was a rhetorical liberty taken on behalf of a truth that appears demonstrable: that neither speech nor writing is "originary" in the sense of giving unmediated access to whatever is "prelinguistic," nor is one of these media closer than the other (so the word "precedes" is also a rhetorical overstatement). In this way, Derrida sought to overthrow a mystical privileging of the spoken word, the voice, that was as old as Plato and as recent as much twentieth-century phenomenology. And this I think is a position that we can all (or many of us) go along with.

Beckett certainly could, or at least his narrators could, complaining as they do with such frequency that they have "no words but the words of others" (*Unnamable* 314). So if Beckett can be said to "privilege" the voice, as when he has the Unnamable say that "it's entirely a matter of voices, no other metaphor is appropriate" (325), he too is writing/speaking figuratively, as did Derrida, though crucially, I want to argue, in service to a different idea.

"A voice comes to one in the dark." Whether one is speaking or writing, this is what happens: something comes to one. Let's call it a voice, since no other metaphor is appropriate. It says "Imagine," and promptly an image comes to one in the dark, an image of "one on his back in the dark." It emerges. A moment ago it wasn't here; now it is. It could have been male or female, it could have been standing, sitting, kneeling, crawling, rolling, but this one is male and, at the moment, he lies on his back. So, the image freighted in the voice not only comes to one but is unprecedented in the sense that one doesn't know what it is going to be until it arrives: "Did I say I catch flies? I snap them up, clack! Does this mean I still have my teeth? To have lost one's limbs and preserved one's dentition, what a mockery!" (*Unnamable* 332). As Michael Gazzaniga writes in *The Mind's Past*, "the brain gets things done before we know about it" (75). It goes about its business, as it were, in the dark, and then something comes to one. It may be a word or an image or something else, but since it appears to be transmitted, let's call it a voice. To privilege the word "voice" in this way, then, is not to privilege speaking over writing, since both come to one equally out of the dark. Rather, it is to train one's attention on the moment of emergence: "I say it as I hear it" (*How It Is* 7). And whether there is *an* origin to what one hears in the dark or a multiplicity of origin or something else again entirely different, the mystery of how the unprecedented comes into being is still there, and it's a pretty exotic mystery at that.

But there's another justification for the word "voice" in this context. This has to do not so much with the idea of origin or origins as it does with that of original and originality, at least as these terms have been used since the late eighteenth century—not, that is, as the beginning or the first (as in "original sin") but as unique or, to use the term I have been featuring, unprecedented. So that when the Unnamable cries out, "I'm all these words, all these strangers, this dust of words, with no ground for their settling, no sky for their dispersing, coming together to say, fleeing one another to say, that I am they" (*Unnamable* 386), he may be lamenting the condition that Derrida describes, imprisoned in the words of strangers, but the words of his lament nonetheless bear the imprint of his creator's originality. Though the words were all swarming long before Beckett came into the world, it is fair to say that no one ever put them together in this way. And they are, moreover, put together in a way that is powerfully consistent with the equally unprecedented prose that both precedes and succeeds them. There is, in other words, a distinctive *voice* here, making its own music in the silence of print.

The difference between having a voice and not having one is the difference between creation and production or, as I have argued elsewhere, between allusion and intertextuality ("Extratextual Intelligence"). Everything we say is intertextual. There is no escaping this condition just as there is no escaping the priority of language to one's use of it. But to allude is to make intertextuality work for you. When you allude, language does your bidding, obeys your will, even as you remain in the dark about the meaning of such words as "you," "your," and "will." But—and here's the clincher and the return once more to my main theme—you only get to your voice, that is, to your originality and what you might call the product of your will, by letting go.

> I began again. But little by little with a different aim, no longer in order to succeed, but in order to fail. Nuance. What I sought, when I struggled out of my hole, then aloft through the stinging air towards an inaccessible boon, was the rapture of vertigo, the letting go, the fall, the gulf, the relapse to darkness, to nothingness, to earnestness, to home, to him waiting for me always, who needed me and whom I needed, who took me in his arms and told me to stay with him always, who gave me his place and watched over me, who suffered every time I left him, whom I have often made suffer and seldom contented, whom I have never seen. (*Malone* 195)

In this riff on failure, on letting go, on returning to darkness and nothingness there is the Bible, Milton, the Tractarians, melodrama, and much else in the way of allusion, all singing together for the first time from a score that no one else could write. This is no mere intertextuality. We recognize the voice in the art, and vital to that recognition is its originality, the way in which it takes the old and makes it new.

People have seen in this oft-cited passage from *Malone Dies* an autobiographical reference to the "revelation" Beckett claimed to have had in 1945, which told him that his art depended on the awareness "of my own folly [...] that my own way was in impoverishment, in lack of knowledge and in taking away." In his remarks on this moment to James Knowlson, Beckett contrasted his own way with Joyce's greater exertion of top-down control over his art (qtd. in Knowlson 319). Yet there are signs that what he called, deferentially, "his own way," was an attitude that he not only admired in the art of others but also considered the heart of the artistic enterprise. Four years after the revelation in his mother's room, Beckett would argue that failure was the lifeblood of the art of painting and that "the history of painting [...] is the history of its attempts to escape from this sense of failure." What has hindered the artist all this time has been fear. For "to be an artist is to fail, as no other dare fail" (Beckett and Duthuit 21). It must have taken enormous courage for Beckett, the control freak, notorious for his determination to maintain his authority over the products of his pen, paradoxically to practice an art that depends on the willing loss of control. But the man who directed plays, who tried to intervene when people broke his rules, who denied permissions for adaptations, was not the same man who wrote. The writer was of necessity "like a mole in a mole-hill,"[6] tunneling away with no idea of where he was going or for how long. "I am constantly working in the dark," he told Alec Reid (53). The darkness in which his work was conceived was the condition of its emergence. And on those rare occasions when he broke this rule, as I think he did in *Film*, the laborious machinery of the art creaks and groans under the weight of its idea—"*Esse est percipi.* [...] Search of non-being in flight from extraneous perception breaking down in inescapability of self-perception" (11).[7]

For Beckett—at the far end of the romantic fascination with spontaneous utterance—the darkness in which he works is not a sign of, but a safeguard against, the mystique of unity. Here, again, I want to be careful. As art, Beckett's works often achieve an exquisite unity of effect that is comparable to what one finds in music. So, as an artist, Beckett revises no less perhaps than any other, shaping and polishing from the top down. But he does so with care to avoid higher order strategies of containment that interfere with the vitality of incompletion. To be recognizable, to have your own signature, as Beckett so emphatically does, can't be taken as a presumption of wholeness. All one can presume from the singularity of Beckett's genius, on this issue as on all philosophical issues running through his work, is ignorance. Butler sees a kind of tragedy in "Beckett's dreadful struggles for unity" and contrasts them with the hopefulness of Heidegger: "In Heidegger this unity is held out as a possibility—it can grasp itself as a whole that exists between thrownness and death. In Beckett this 'loyalty of existence to its own Self' is never achieved" (69). But I think it is a mistake to transpose Heidegger's "struggles" to Beckett. Heidegger insisted on unity. This in turn governs, I think, the idea of the fragment in Heidegger. As a romantic trace, the valuation of the fragment is itself a valuation of unity. The fragment, after all, is a fragment of something to which it belongs. It testifies to a wholeness. *Being and Time,* itself, has this romantic aura—it is a self-declared fragment that, as such, acquires a certain indemnity from philosophical critique. But fragments in Beckett take apart this tradition, declaring the absence of any grounds on which to infer an invisible unity to which they belong. There is no unobserved or unobservable whole, which might confer a kind of validation—as if to say, given world enough and time, all this stuff, ourselves included, would be seen to hold together. For Beckett, this would be simply a relocation of philosophical mastery to another sphere, and he would have no part of it. In his "autobiographical" masterpiece of fragments, *Company,* the last word is "Alone." And if you can see or hear in this word, as many have, the words "all one," the important point is that these are not the words that Beckett wrote.

"A voice comes to one in the dark. Imagine." Sometimes I like to read "Imagine" in this instance as "Imagine that!" One need not, in fact I would argue one must not, apply any metaphysical preconceptions to appreciate what an amazing thing it is that a voice should come to one in the dark. "[I]n the dead of t'other night," he wrote Nancy Cunard, "got a nice gruesome idea full of cartwheels and dragging feet and puffing and panting which may or may not lead to something" (qtd. in Knowlson 385). This visitation from out of the dark did lead to something, and the result was a play, *All That Fall,* written specifically, in Beckett's words, to "come out of the dark" (qtd. in Knowlson 501). From the war years on, Beckett stayed as close as he could to this fecund darkness where words "somehow from some soft of mind they ooze. From it in it ooze" (*Nohow On* 107). And in the course of this work the sheer productivity of the dark became a theme, laced everywhere with the frustration of meaning that only grows the closer you get. There is much to wonder at here—beginning with the sheer ontological excess of a voice that will not stop with its stories and people and questions and answers. "Ah this blind voice, and these moments of held breath when all listen wildly, and the voice that begins to fumble again, without knowing what it's looking for, and again the tiny silence, and the listening again, for what, no one knows, a sign of life perhaps..." (*Unnamable* 372).

Notes

1. To Israel Shenker (1). See also Beckett and Duthuit.

2. A newspaper clipping found in the songwriter Harold Arlen's journal (Lahr 90).

3. "In a note to an autograph copy of *Kubla Khan* that came to public notice only in 1934, Coleridge himself made a less sensational claim than in his published note" (Schneider 533n.).

4. My terminology here comes from recent work on emergent systems. See especially Clark, Johnson, and Resnick.

5. Dorothea Frede's translation, cited by Barfield as "Heidegger's final comment for his intended collected works" (Barfield 66).

6. "Je suis comme une taupe dans une taupinière" (qtd. in Juliet 19).

7. In his screenplay, Beckett tried to hedge this aesthetic bet with a disclaimer that followed: "No truth value attaches to above, regarded as of merely structural and dramatic convenience" (11). But there is nothing in the film to mute what you might call, adapting Barthes, the truth effect of this convenience.

Works Cited

Abbott, H. Porter. *Beckett Writing Beckett: The Author in the Autograph.* Ithaca, NY: Cornell University Press, 1996.

———. "Extratextual Intelligence." *New Literary History* 28 (1997): 811–20.

Barfield, Steve. "Beckett and Heidegger." Lane 154–65.

Beckett, Samuel. *Film.* New York: Grove, 1969.

———. *How It Is.* New York: Grove, 1964.

———. *Malone Dies. Three Novels* 179–288.

———. *Nohow On.* New York: Grove, 1996.

———. *Three Novels.* New York: Grove, 1965.

———. *The Unnamable. Three Novels* 291–414.

Beckett, Samuel, and Georges Duthuit. "Three Dialogues." *Samuel Beckett: A Collection of Critical Essays.* Ed. Martin Esslin. Englewood Cliffs, NJ: Prentice-Hall, 1965. 16–22.

Begam, Richard. "Beckett and Postfoundationalism, or, How Fundamental Are Those Fundamental Sounds?" Lane 11–39.

Butler, Lance St. John. *Samuel Beckett and the Meaning of Being: A Study in Ontological Parable.* London: Macmillan, 1984.

Clark, Andy. *Being There: Putting Brain, Body, and World Together Again.* Cambridge, MA: MIT Press, 1997.

Coetzee, J. M. *Slow Man.* New York: Viking, 2005.

Critchley, Simon. "Know Happiness—on Beckett." *Very Little . . . Almost Nothing.* London: Routledge, 1997. 165–207.

Driver, Tom. "Beckett by the Madeleine." *Columbia University Forum* 4 (1961): 21–25.

Forster, E. M. "E. M. Forster." *Writers at Work: The Paris Review Interviews.* Ed. Malcolm Cowley. New York: Viking, 1959. 23–35.

Fowles, John. *The French Lieutenant's Woman.* New York: New American Library, 1969.

Gazzaniga, Michael S. *The Mind's Past.* Berkeley: University of California Press, 1998.

Johnson, Steven. *Emergence: The Connected Lives of Ants, Brains, Cities, and Software.* New York: Simon, 2001.

Juliet, Charles. *Rencontre avec Samuel Beckett.* [Montpellier]: Fata Morgana, 1986.

Knowlson, James. *Damned to Fame: The Life of Samuel Beckett.* New York: Simon, 1996.

Lahr, John. "Come Rain or Shine: The Bittersweet Life of Harold Arlen." *New Yorker* 19 Sept. 2005: 88–94.

Lane, Richard, ed. *Beckett and Philosophy.* Houndmills, UK: Palgrave, 2002.

Lyall, Sarah. "Playwright Takes a Prize and a Jab at U.S." *New York Times* 8 Dec. 2005: A3

Pamuk, Orhan. *Snow.* Trans. Maureen Freely. New York: Vintage, 2004.

Reid, Alec. *All I Can Manage, More Than I Could.* Dublin: Dolmen, 1968.

Resnick, Michael. *Turtles, Termites, and Traffic Jams: Explorations in Massively Parallel Microworlds.* Cambridge, MA: MIT Press, 1994.

Schneider, Elizabeth, ed. *Selected Poetry and Prose.* By Samuel Taylor Coleridge. New York: Holt, 1961.

Shenker, Israel. "Moody Man of Letters." *New York Times* 6 May 1956, sec. 2: 1, 3.

Recovering Beckett's Bergsonism

S. E. GONTARSKI

> *Now, if some bold novelist, tearing aside the cleverly*
> *woven curtain of our conventional ego, shows us under this*
> *appearance of logic a fundamental absurdity, under this*
> *juxtaposition of simple states an infinite permeation of a*
> *thousand different impressions which have already ceased*
> *to exist the instant they are named, we commend him for*
> *having known us better than we know ourselves. This is not*
> *the case, however, and the very fact that he spreads out our*
> *feelings in a homogeneous time, and expresses its elements*
> *by words, shows that he in his turn is only offering us its*
> *shadow....*
>
> —Henri Bergson, *Time and Free Will*

> *Wearying soon of this he dropped his head on his arms in*
> *the midst of the chessmen, which scattered with a terrible*
> *noise. Mr. Endon's finery persisted for a little in an after-*
> *image scarcely inferior to the original. Then this also faded*
> *and Murphy began to see nothing, that colourlessness which*
> *is such a rare postnatal treat, being the absence (to abuse a*
> *nice distinction) not of* percipere *but of* percipi.
>
> —Samuel Beckett, *Murphy*

IN HIS 1966 critique of Henri Bergson, which he calls *Bergsonism* (trans. 1988), Gilles Deleuze focuses on intuition as *the* method in Bergson's overall philosophical project, a rethinking of metaphysics in terms of duration (*durée*), that is, time as opposed to space. "Intuition is neither a feeling, an inspiration, nor a disorderly sympathy, but a fully developed method," notes Deleuze, "one of the most fully developed methods in philosophy. It has strict rules, constituting that which Bergson calls 'precision' in philosophy," and the method already assumes, and perhaps subsumes, duration (13). Elizabeth Grosz picks up the analysis in her lecture "Bergson, Deleuze and Becoming," where she notes:

> Intuition is, for Bergson, a relatively rare but ever-productive force in the history of philosophy: it occurs only when old and familiar methods by which intelligence seeks to address the present and the new exhaust themselves and provide only generalizations rather than a concept uniquely suited to its object. [...] intuition is an emergent and imprecise movement of simplicity that erupts by negating the old, resisting the temptations of intellect to understand the new in terms of the language and concepts of the old (and thus the durational in terms of the spatial). This eruption of intuition, as rare as it is, marks the history of philosophy, much as Kuhn [*The Structure of Scientific Revolutions* 1970] understands that the paradigm shift continually marks and remakes the history of science. (7–8)

In Bergson's restatement of what might be called Cartesian dualism, the brain, especially if conceived as the seat of, or reservoir for, memory is part of the spatialization of time, since it is connected to the machinery of the body; and perception, as opposed to the perceiver him- or herself, is the process of connection between the inner and the outer, material world. The interaction of the perceiver and the perceived may have been a central tenet for Beckett's thought, what he often called rapport or relation,[1] and which he overtly associated with Berkeley's *esse est percipi,* but, thus stated, it is a false question for Bergson, as is the central Cartesian equation "Cogito ergo sum," since the spacialized "I" of the conclusion is already posited, *ipse dixit,* as a premise. Thought, on the other hand, is another matter— or, rather, something *other,* since it is not matter at all, not a spacialized entity but what Bergson calls pure *durée,* the discussion of which must be segmented and extended to be examined and represented. That representation falsifies life's flow, *durée,* as it is segmented and brought into the realm of space, and so representation is always already doomed to failure for Bergson (and, finally, for Beckett as well). As Bergson summarizes the issue at the opening of *Time and Free Will,* his 1889 treatise on *The Immediate Data of Consciousness,* as his original title of the work proclaims, language itself is a major part of the philosophical confusion:

> Language requires us to establish between our ideas the same sharp and precise distinctions, the same discontinuity, as between material objects. [...] But it may be asked whether the insurmountable difficulties presented by certain philosophical problems do not arise from our placing side by side phenomena which do not occupy space, and whether, by merely getting rid of the clumsy symbols round which we are fighting, we might not bring the fight to an end. (xix)

Beckett summarizes the idea in his 1931 lectures on the modern novel as Bergson's "idea of inadequacy of the *word* to translate impressions registered by instinct" (qtd. in Burrows 9); and again, in his analysis of Gide and Dostoyevsky, Beckett notes, "Bergson denied value of language to translate impression" (qtd. in Burrows 17).

The issue is thus most often, for Bergson, "a confusion of duration with extensity, of succession with simultaneity, of quality with quantity" (*T&FW* xx); these are the three antinomies or binaries at the heart of the Bergsonian enterprise and the source of most philosophical confusion. Pure *durée* is unrepresentable, ineffable, and constitutes for Bergson (and Beckett) a central metaphysical, ontological, existential, and so literary problem, the attempt to "eff" the ineffable, to represent, and so segment and spatialize, the flow of being. As Bergson describes it, duration "is the form which the succession of our conscious states assumes when our ego lets itself *live,* when it refrains from separating its present state from its former states [...]. We can thus conceive of succession without distinction, and think of it as a mutual penetration, an interconnection and organization of elements, each one of which represents the whole, and cannot be distinguished or isolated from it except by abstract thought" (*T&FW* 100–01). The struggle, or in Beckett's case the imperative, to represent it, to present its flow satisfactorily, wholly, accurately is foredoomed to failure but is, nonetheless, the driving élan of Beckettian men and women (or of the Beckettian narrator), the impossible figures who inhabit Beckett's art, and the unavoidable consequence of being. If duration is accessible at all, it is so through what Bergson, whom Beckett has called "a philosophical visionary," discovers as his discourse on method intuition, which he opposed to the scientific, quotidian functioning of mind. Beckett reviewed these issues for his class at Trinity College during Michaelmas 1931, where he distinguished between "Bergsonian conception of intelligence & intuition"; "B's [Bergson, but "B" might equally signify Beckett as well] intuition *is* highest intelligence—*l'intelligence personnelle*"; on the other hand, "*fonctionnement de l'esprit* [that is, function of mind] = lowest form of intelligence, mind doing twice work" (qtd. in Burrows 9),[2] Beckett here reiterating Bergson's insistence on the irreconcilability of intelligence and intuition. As part of his definition of postnaturalism, what we might today simply call modernism, Beckett told his class that "intuition can obtain a total vision that intelligence can't." Intelligence can "apprehend the passage of time but not [the] present moment" (qtd. in Burrows 7). In student Rachel Burrows's notes, from which these observations are taken, she is for a time confused about whether Beckett's comments apply to Proust or Bergson, attributing them first in her notebook to "Bergson," then having doubts and scratching that out to replace it with "Proust," then again scratching out "Proust" to reassert "Bergs" (8). Beckett further relates Bergson's "method" to "la vision intuitive" of Rimbaud. Against the "order" of romanticism and naturalism, Beckett posited an "artistic disorder," its method Bergson's intuition and "la vision intuitive" of Rimbaud (7). For much of his lecture Beckett cites Julien Benda's 1927 work *La trahison des clercs* (*The Treason of Intellectuals* [or of the man of letters, perhaps]) on Bergson favorably (8);[3] "B's intuition is heightened intelligence," according to Burrows's notes, what Beckett called "'l'intelligence personnelle,'" and he reminds his pupils of "Bergs. contempt for mechanical intelligence" (Burrows 19–21).

Beckett's preoccupation with time, "that double-headed monster of damnation and salvation" that he announces at the opening of his antiacademic manifesto on Marcel Proust, is indeed an equation "never simple," in part because his monograph is as much a critique of Proust's Proust—Henri Bergson (and some Nietzsche)—as of Proust himself. The Bergson connection to his *Proust* is not often acknowledged by Beckett and so has remained underexplored by his critics; the sole mention in the Knowlson biography, for example, is Beckett's letter to Thomas McGreevy of 24 February 1931, where he associated the juvenile prank, *Le Kid*, with Corneille and Bergson (126). Beckett took pains to separate Bergson from Proust in class that same year, noting that the latter was "detached from the

Bergsonian conception of time but interested in this opposition—instinct and [or, versus] conscious intelligence. Bergson insists on absolute time: Proust denies it. For Proust it's a function of too many things—local but not absolute reality" (qtd. in Burrows 9). But Proustian time and its corollaries, memory and habit, overlap Bergsonian time, or duration, and both offer critiques of (or even solutions to) Cartesian duality. But Beckett seems to misconstrue here what he calls Bergson's sense of both "absolute time" and "absolute reality." In *Creative Evolution* (1911), Bergson certainly seems less than absolutist about time, noting that those who posit what he calls "radical mechanism"—a problem about which Beckett complains as well in his Proust monograph and in his first novel, *Dream of Fair to Middling Women*—postulate a time "complete in eternity, and in which the apparent duration of things expresses merely the infirmity of a mind that cannot know everything at once," or in Beckett's terms, "We cannot know and cannot be known" (*Proust* 49). "But duration," Bergson continues, "is something very different from this for our consciousness, for that which is most indisputable in our experience. We perceive duration as a stream against which we cannot go. It is the foundation of our being, and, as we feel, the very substance of the world in which we live" (*CE* 45). And Bergson repeatedly acknowledges "a cardinal difference between *concrete* time [. . .] and that *abstract* time which enters into our speculations on artificial systems" (*CE* 25.)

Admittedly, Beckett could and would find much to resist in Bergson, or at least to feel ambivalent about, especially Bergson's mysticism, its corollary the *élan vital,* and Bergson's insistence on a total vision, mystically achieved through intuition, if at all. In his summary of *Bergsonism,* Deleuze focuses on the idea of the "certainty" of the whole (or hole?) to which mysticism (or intuition) offers access, which in some regards is Bergson's resolution to Cartesian dualism:

> The great souls—to a greater extent than philosophers—are those of artists and mystics (at least those of a Christian mysticism that Bergson describes as being completely superabundant activity, action, creation). At the limit it is the mystic who plays with the whole of creation, who invents an expression of it, whose adequacy increases with its dynamism. Servant of an open and finite God (such are the characteristics of the *Élan Vital*), the mystical soul actively plays the whole of the universe [what Bergson calls "the real

whole" (*CE* 36)], and reproduces the opening of a Whole in which there is nothing to see or to contemplate. [...] Everything happens as if that which remained indeterminate in philosophical intuition gained a new kind of determination in mystical intuition—as though the properly philosophical "probability" extended itself into mystical certainty. (Deleuze 112)

There may be precious little "mystical certainty" in Beckett, but, as Bergson makes clear in *Creative Evolution,* the *élan vital,* the "'vital principle' may indeed not explain much, but it is at least a sort of label affixed to our ignorance, so as to remind us of this occasionally" (*CE* 48). It is decidedly opposed to teleology, or what Bergson calls "mechanism." What Deleuze sees as certainty, another name for which is evolution, or *durée* itself, moreover, is a process of perpetual becoming. If the whole represents a continuity, it is a "Continuity of change, preservation of the past in the present, real duration—the living being seems, then, to share these attributes with consciousness. Can we go further and say that life, like conscious activity, is invention, is unceasing creation?" (Deleuze 27).

Beckett's reading of Proust, and more broadly his critique of music, is, of course, decidedly, avowedly mystical. As he concludes his monograph on Proust, he notes:

Schopenhauer rejects the Leibnitzian view of music as "occult arithmetic," and in his aesthetics separates it from the other arts, which can only produce the Idea with its other concomitant phenomena, whereas music is the Idea itself [that is, *durée*], unaware of the world of phenomena, existing ideally outside the universe, apprehended not in Space but in Time only, and consequently untouched by the teleological hypothesis. This essential quality of music is distorted by the listener who, being an impure subject, insists on giving a figure [extensity, spatialization] to that which is ideal and invisible [the seamless simultaneity that is *durée*], on incarnating the Idea in what he conceives to be an appropriate paradigm. (70–71)

The passage does indeed summarize Schopenhauer, but it is a gloss on Bergsonian *durée* as well, the art corrupted by the subject's struggles to extend into space that which is pure, seamless, temporal simultaneity. The final apprehension of music, the highest in the hierarchy of the arts, is thus mystical.

Proust (1931), moreover, articulates the distinction between voluntary and involuntary memory; the latter restores the past object and reveals the real (55). The past is thus contemporaneous with the present, the smell of the perfume "new precisely because already experienced" (*Proust* 55). Beckett thus describes Proust's *méthode,* but it is unalloyed Bergsonism as well. As Beckett lays out the argument in *Proust,* voluntary memory is rejected as "the application of a concordance to the Old Testament of the individual" (19). Linked with Habit as "attributes of the Time cancer" (7), voluntary memory presents the past in monochrome, like "turning the leaves of an album of photographs" (19), with no interest in "the mysterious element of inattention that colours our most commonplace experiences" (19). Murphy's attempt to reconstitute the image of his father (251), for example, is an allegory of its failings. Involuntary memory, on the other hand, is "an unruly magician and will not be importuned" (20); Proust's book is a monument to its action. The madeleine episode in particular conjures a childhood world that "comes out of a teapot" (21); it offers the only possible "accidental and fugitive salvation" (22). Beckett calls it a "mystic experience," the factor that resolves the Proustian equation. If *by accident* (emphasis in original), by "some miracle of analogy" (54), the impression of a past sensation recurs as an immediate stimulus, then the "total past sensation, not its echo nor its copy but the sensation itself" (54), rushes in to (re-)create the experience, whole and real, apparently, and thus overcome the gulf between past and present, symbol and substance, perception and remembering, ideal and real. Such moments are real without being actual, ideal without being abstract (*Le temps retrouvé* 2: 872), and decidedly of a piece with what we might call Bergsonian material metaphysics.

A summary of Proust's self-consciousness, Beckett's critique serves as a gloss on Bergson as well, who, in *Matter and Memory* (1896, trans. 1911), particularly in its justly famous opening chapter, discussed the differences between what he called "cerebral memory" (that is, "voluntary memory") and "pure recollection" (or "involuntary memory"). Like Proust (but unlike Descartes in this respect), Bergson claimed that all of a human's experience is retained by one or another of the memories. Cerebral, or voluntary, memory is tied to the body and is thus the record of habitual actions; pure recollection, on the other hand, cannot be accessed at or by will. It reveals itself through the accidents of living.

For Bergson, it is memory that permits the existence of consciousness, which, in turn, supports the idea of self, but in a state of constant
becoming. The self is itself memory, and is thus experienced as a spatialized
break in the flow of *durée,* which at each moment, at each instant presents a new image of self to consciousness. But even involuntary memory,
or pure recollection, corrupts for Bergson, for it too is an extension, a
spatialization of life's flow, time, *durée.* What is perceived thus is a static,
spatialized *image* of life's flow, further removed from *durée* by attempts to
represent it in language, an agent of habit. At best one can experience, and
so represent, images of not *durée* itself, or because of the temporal delays of
consciousness, afterimages of *durée,* the ghosts of *durée.* As Bergson notes
in *Matter and Memory,* "The moment of which I am speaking is already far
from me [...]. The physical state, then, that I call my 'present,' must be
both a perception of the immediate past and a determination of the immediate future" (138). That perception then itself is thus always late, belated,
its image always and only an afterimage:

> Every *active* perception truly involves a *reflection* [...] that is to
> say the projection, outside ourselves, of an actively created image,
> identical with, or similar to, the object on which it comes to mould
> itself. If, after having gazed at an object, we turn our eyes abruptly
> away, we obtain an "afterimage" of it: Must we not suppose that
> this image existed already while we were looking? [The originary
> image, if such there were, is thus already an afterimage.] [...] Any
> memory-image that is capable of interpreting our perception in-
> serts itself so thoroughly into it that we are no longer able to discern
> what is memory and what is perception (*M&M* 102–03).[4]

Cognitive scientists like Antonio Damasio have confirmed Bergson's
intuitions. As Damasio suggests in *Descartes' Error,* "Present continuously
becomes the past and by the time we take stock of it we are in another
present, consumed with planning for the future, which we do on step-
ping stones of the past. The present is never here. We are hopelessly late
for consciousness" (240). As Bergson puts it early in *Matter and Memory:*
"However brief we suppose any perception to be, it always occupies a
certain duration, and involves, consequently, an effort of memory, which
prolongs, one into another, the plurality of the moment" (34); and again,

"the process of perception consists in an exteriorization of internal states" (52); and yet again, "We assert, at the outset, that if there be memory, that is, survival of past images, these images must constantly mingle with our perception of the present and may even take its place" (66). We have to remind ourselves reading Bergson that he is actually not glossing individual works of Beckett, in this case, perhaps, "La falaise" ("The Cliff"), say.

For a time Beckett accepted this sense of involuntary memory, or pure recollection, as epiphanic. His metaphor of the vase and the paradox of a perfume that is new because already experienced (*Proust* 55) imply a validation of the Proustian and Bergsonian experience (see also the poem "Rue de Vaugirard"). But the unity of the self with its past implied in the acceptance of involuntary memory is parodied as early as *Dream of Fair to Middling Women* where the only unity is *involuntary* (132); the hawthorn (1) and verbena (128) irreverently gloss the Proustian moment, and the ending parodies Joyce's "The Dead." Beckett's work is marked by an increasing distrust of epiphanic moments, perhaps not the psychological experience but its lasting significance. Arsene tries to define the mystical sense of something that slips; and Watt has residual memories of flowering currant; but the ineffable experience remains fugitive for both. In *Words and Music,* Croak is enthralled by a face in the ashes, while texts as distant as "Enueg II" and "Old Earth" share a motif of the sky suddenly turning to faces, underlining the persistence of involuntary memory throughout Beckett's oeuvre. But whatever unity exists between perceived image, memory, and past is as accidental as the coincidence of dampers, hammers, and strings in Mr. Watt's Piano, the attempted "chooning" of which is the mission of "the Galls father and son" (*Watt* 70). This "incident of note" is one of the defining moments in Watt's stay with Mr. Knott and exemplifies Watt's failure of memory, the failure to connect experience with memory, in decidedly Bergsonian terms. In *Matter and Memory,* Bergson details the dialectic between memory and perception: "these two contrary hypotheses, the first identifying the elements of perception with the elements of memory, the second distinguishing among them, are of such a nature that each sends us back to the other without allowing us to rest in either" (127). Bergson's analysis here not only serves as anticipation of Beckett's shortest poemlike prose work, "Neither," but outlines Watt's final demise, his inability to accept "the simple games that time plays with space," or that memory (time) plays with perception (space). Bergson's metaphor for the machinery of this connection in "the cerebral centers" is the keyboard, the piano:

> This organ is constructed precisely with a view to allowing the plurality of simultaneous excitants to impress it in a certain order and in a certain way [as in a chord, say], by distributing themselves, all at one time, over selected portions of its surface. It is like an immense keyboard, on which the external object executes at once its harmony of a thousand notes, thus calling forth in a definite order, and at a single moment, a great multitude of elementary sensations corresponding to all the points of the sensory center that are concerned. (128)

Since memories are not stored or deposited in any sort of receptacle in the brain or anywhere else for Bergson (or for contemporary philosophers of cognition like Steven Pinker and Antonio Damasio as well), but remain part of a constant process of distribution, electronic and chemical, the machinery, the perpetual correspondence of memory, sensation, and stimulus, is paramount to its adequate functioning, and for Watt that machinery has broken down. For Bergson, memories exist as images, and in this case he is discussing particularly "auditory images," music, perhaps, the "region of images, if it exists, can only be a keyboard of this nature" (129), he reminds us. "[T]he auditory image called back by memory," notes Bergson, "must set in motion the same nervous elements as the first perception and that recollection must thus change gradually into perception" (129). Watt's recitation of the word "pot" is the novel's central example of the dislocation of that machinery; or as Bergson puts the matter, "The strings are still there, and to the influence of external sounds they still vibrate; it is the internal keyboard which is lacking" (129), as it is in Mr. Knott's establishment. When Bergson changes his metaphor, he moves to the image of a circle: "Our distinct perception is really comparable to a *closed circle,* in which the perception-image, going toward the mind, and the memory-image, launched into space, careen the one behind the other" (103; emphasis added). Bergson may finally reject the linear implications in "the one behind the other," but he retains the metaphor-image of the circle for his qualification: "Reflective perception is a circuit, in which all the elements, including the perceived object itself, hold each other in a state of mutual tension as in an electrical circuit, so that no disturbance starting from the object can stop on its way and remain in the depths of the mind: it must always find its way back to the object from where it proceeds" (104). Such circuitry is short-circuited for Watt, the image of pot never returning to "the object from where it proceeds"; the circuit, like the painting in Erskine's bedroom, remains broken, the hammers (almost) never corresponding to the strings of Watt's (or Knott's) keyboard.

If we examine *Waiting for Godot* as a memory play, or at least as an exploration or taxonomy of the ways that memory systems break down, we are again led to consider the neurological implications of the process. Didi and Gogo cannot re-call, that is, cannot call to mind, the exact details of their appointment with Godot, and Pozzo's sensory systems begin to break down as well; he is blind, after all, apparently a neurological problem, in act 2, and he cannot remember his previous meeting with Didi and Gogo, which occurred, apparently (if the text can be trusted), the preceding day. Such vagaries or failures of memory remind us of the imagery used by contemporary analysts of memory (all in the wake of Bergson, whose influences they only scantly acknowledge, unfortunately). Damasio notes that "whenever we recall a given object, or face, or scene, we do not get an exact reproduction but rather an *interpretation,* a newly constructed version of the original" (100); and he continues, "a dispositional representation for the face of Aunt Maggie [...] contains not her face as such, but rather the firing patterns which trigger the momentary reconstruction of an approximate representation [...]" (102). In *Waiting for Godot* (and in much of Beckett's work, for that matter), something seems to have gone awry with the "firing patterns." Furthermore, none of the characters seems able to recognize the hopelessness of their situation, which condition may be a form of anosognosia, the "inability to acknowledge disease in one-self" (for examples see Damasio 62). One of the play's most enigmatic moments, when all four characters collapse and cannot rise, may be most explicable as another, simultaneous in this case, memory or neurological lapse, a failure to remember the system or the habit of locomotion. As they consciously try to remember how to get up, voluntary or habitual memory fails, their final success a matter of *inattention,* that is, a return to the habit of movement. Bergson describes the link between memory and action: "Pure memories, as they become actual, tend to bring about, within the body, all corresponding sensations. But these virtual sensations themselves, in order to become real, must tend to urge the body to action and to impress upon it those movements and attitudes of which they are the habitual antecedent" (130). What may break down for the four principles of *Waiting for Godot* is, at least sporadically, the habit of memory, or the memory of habit, most dramatically with Didi and Gogo's immobility at the end of both acts: "They do not move." Their mobility, their ability to act in general, seems to have been (at least sporadically) short-circuited.

All this is not to suggest that Beckett created his art with Bergson spread on the table before him, but that his study of Bergson, if only for his preparation for teaching his Trinity students, remained with him as a ghost, an afterimage that informed much of his work for the remainder of his career. Bergson's study of memory and his emphasis on what I have earlier called his material metaphysics seem perfectly consonant with Beckett and Proust's "ideal real," which Beckett considered "the essential, the extratemporal" (*Proust* 56). One of Hamm's epiphanies, "I was never there" (*Endgame* 74), moreover, suggests what is perhaps the most fundamental of Bergson's and Beckett's principles of life and art, that we engage the world solely on the level of image, the direct, actual world unknowable and inaccessible. The afterimage comes up in part 3 of *Footfalls,* as May, who may only be narrated and hence an image, narrates a semblance of what is on stage and calls attention to her apparitional, ghostly state. May's anagrammatic other, the semblance Amy, replies to her mother, Mrs. Winter, about attendance at Evensong: "I observed nothing of any kind, strange or otherwise. I saw nothing, heard nothing, of any kind. I was not there" (243). The short fourth act of *Footfalls,* the final ten seconds with "No trace of May," is a crucial reminder that May was always already "not there," or there only as a "trace," an image or afterimage.[5]

The depth of Beckett's debt to Bergsonism needs to be reserved for a fuller study, but at the very least it seems clear that Beckett seems to have answered Bergson's 1889 challenge for, "some bold novelist, tearing aside the cleverly woven curtain of our conventional ego, shows us under this appearance of logic a fundamental absurdity, under this juxtaposition of simple states an infinite permeation of a thousand different impressions which have already ceased to exist the instant they are named" (*T&FW* 133–34).

Notes

1. See Beckett's "Three Dialogues" (144) and "Letter to Georges Duthuit" 9–10 Mar. 1949 (20).

2. Rachel (Dobbin) Burrows's notebook to lectures given by Samuel Beckett at Trinity College in 1931 explicitly indicate Beckett's strong knowledge of Bergson. What currently

exists in the Trinity College Dublin archives are two reproductions, the notebook itself having been lost since the death of Burrows in 1987. See also Gontarski, McMillan, and Fehsenfeld.

3. Benda was a leading opponent of Bergson and what he saw as a resurgence of romanticism. In his review in the *New Republic* (12 Dec. 1928), T. S. Eliot noted that Benda is in search of the man of letters who is detached from passions of class, race, nation, and party, but that "half of the most excitable authors of our time, in France at least, have been Bergsonians," and Bergson, for Eliot, was a clear example of the "pure" philosopher detached from politics.

4. Bergson goes on here to discuss the Külpe school and the Würzburg school usually called "the School of imageless thought" from its contention that "states of awareness have no sensory content, representation, or image" (Ackerley and Gontarski 306). For Bergson here, "The experiments of Münsterberg and of Külpe leave no doubt as to this latter point: any memory-image that is capable of interpreting our actual perception inserts itself so thoroughly into it that we are no longer able to discern what is perception and what is memory" (*M&M* 103). One of its followers, by the by, was Henry J. Watt (1879–1925). For the Külpe school in Beckett, see *Murphy* (80).

5. See Bergson's opening to *Matter and Memory,* for instance: "Matter, in our view, is an aggregate of 'images.' And by 'image' we mean a certain existence which is more than that which the idealists call a *representation,* but less than that which the realist calls a *thing*—an existence placed half-way between the 'thing' and the 'representation.' [...] the object exists in itself, and, on the other hand, the object is, in itself, pictorial, as we perceive it: the image it is, but a self-existing image" (99–100).

Works Cited

Ackerley, C. J., and S. E. Gontarski. *The Faber Companion to Samuel Beckett: A Reader's Guide to His Works, Life, and Thought.* London: Faber, 2006.

Beckett, Samuel. *Dream of Fair to Middling Women.* Ed. Eoin O'Brien and Edith Fournier. New York: Arcade, 1993.

———. *Endgame.* New York: Grove, 1958.

———. *Footfalls. The Complete Dramatic Works.* London: Faber, 1986.

———. "Letter to Georges Duthuit." 9–10 Mar. 1949. Gontarski and Uhlmann 18–21.

———. *Murphy.* New York: Grove, 1957.

———. *Proust.* New York: Grove, [1957].

———. "Three Dialogues with George Duthuit." *Disjecta: Miscellaneous Writings and a Dramatic Fragment by Samuel Beckett.* Ed. Ruby Cohn. New York: Grove, 1984. 138–45.

———. *Watt.* New York: Grove, 1959.

Bergson, Henri. *Creative Evolution.* 1911. Trans. Arthur Mitchell. New York: Modern Library, 1944. (Abbreviated *CE.*)

———. *Matter and Memory.* 1896. Trans. Nancy Margaret Paul and W. Scott Palmer. New York: Zone Books, 1991. Rpt. of 5th ed. 1908. (Abbreviated *M&M.*)

———. *Time and Free Will: An Essay on the Immediate Data of Consciousness.* 1889. Trans. F. L. Pogson. Mineola, NY: Dover, 2001. Rpt. 3rd ed. 1913. (Abbreviated *T&FW.*)

Burrows, Rachel. Ms. notebook. Microfilm 60 and misc. photocopy 166. Trinity College Dublin.

Damasio, Antonio R. *Descartes' Error: Emotion, Reason and the Human Brain.* New York: Avon, 1994.

Deleuze, Gilles. *Bergsonism.* Trans. Hugh Tomlinson and Barbara Habberjam. New York: Zone Books, 1988.

Gontarski, S. E., Dougald McMillan, and Martha Fehsenfeld. "Interview with Rachel Burroughs." *Journal of Beckett Studies* 11–12 (1988): 1–15.

Gontarski, S. E., and Anthony Uhlmann, eds. *Beckett after Beckett.* Gainesville: University Press of Florida, 2006.

Grosz, Elizabeth. "Bergson, Deleuze and Becoming." *Parallax* 35 (April–June 2005): 4–13. Another version of the material appears in her "Deleuze, Bergson, and the Virtual." *Time Travels: Feminism, Nature, Power.* Durham, NC: Duke University Press, 2005. 93–112.

Knowlson, James. *Damned to Fame: The Life of Samuel Beckett.* New York: Simon, 1996.

Proust, Marcel. *Le temps retrouvé.* 1927. 2 parts. Vol. 8 of *À la recherche du temps perdu.* 8 vols. Paris: Gallimard-NRF, 1919–27.

"No Body Is at Rest"

The Legacy of Leibniz's *Force* in Beckett's Oeuvre

NAOYA MORI

"Keep Moving"

SAMUEL BECKETT PORTRAYS a ubiquitous *force* that drives things and beings into endless motion. Although critics have commented on the extensive interplay between the static and dynamic in his works, the relation of Beckett's ubiquitous force to Leibniz's monadic force has yet to be explored. Because these tensions are central to Beckett's thought, I argue in this essay that Leibniz's ideas on dynamics offer a useful pathway into the Beckett canon.

That nothing remains unchanged may remind us of Heraclitus's famous aphorism, "Everything is in flux," or Geulincx's principle of *mundus est corpus in motu* (the world is a body in motion; qtd. in Ackerley and Gontarski 314), both possible sources of Beckett's hidden dynamics. However, in my view, a different source can serve to explain the dynamic motion of Beckett's protagonists, particularly Murphy's. The "Whoroscope Notebook" contains an intriguing note: "Dynamist ethic of X. Keep moving the only virtue" (Ms. 3000). We know that Beckett used the term "X" to denote the protagonist who was later to become Murphy. In other words, Beckett put the label of "dynamist" on his protagonist before giving him a name, indicating that "keep moving" is X's quintessential quality. Generally speaking, the impetus to move on is Beckett's maxim throughout his career, from his 1933 poem "Serena III" that ends with the refrain "keep on the move" (*SB* 4: 28), to his 1987 short poem "Brief Dream," in which a dreamer accepts that the end of his life is nothing but another transition

(Ms. 2934). I consider that the virtue of continually moving should be regarded as a kind of Beckettian code of ethics, as it were, encompassing more often than not the Leibnizian monadic drive that urges Murphy to set out on the job path and to rock himself in his rocking chair.

As Chris Ackerley observes, "What emerges from Beckett's anthill of motion and extension is the image of Murphy as a monad" (*Demented* xxiii). Beckett himself discloses that the "dynamist" X is an incarnation of the German philosopher Gottfried Wilhelm Leibniz (1646–1716). By adding the following passage to his translation of *Murphy* into French, he reveals that Murphy's garret is a palimpsest of Leibniz's *mansarde* in Hanover: "Murphy avait occupé à Hanovre, assez longtemps pour faire l'expérience de tous ses avantages, une mansarde dans la belle maison renaissance de la Schmiedestrasse où avait vécu, mais surtout où était mort, Gottfried Wilhelm Leibniz" (Murphy had occupied a garret in Hanover, long enough to experiences all its advantages, in the beautiful Renaissance house on Schmiedestrasse, where Gottfried Wilhelm Leibniz had lived, and, more important, had died; 119). Christopher Ricks marvels at this addition by the author-translator: "An unexpected arrival, there in the French: Leibniz of all people, along with the house [...]" (160). However, Leibniz is not "born anew" (160) in the French translation, as Ricks suggests, but latently and unshakably exists in the original English *Murphy.*

In *Murphy*, Beckett clearly alludes to the windowless monad in his depiction of the garret's viewless "small frosted skylight" (*SB* 1: 98). According to Leibniz, the monad is a single substance, derived from the Greek word *monas,* meaning "one" or "unity." The metaphor of the windowless monad derives from Leibniz's *Monadology:* "Monads have no windows through which anything could enter or depart" (*PPL* 643). Yet the concept of the windowless monad is ambiguous in many ways, thereby producing several paradoxes. The inside/outside and closed/openness paradox of the monad is especially important in our context. In a letter to Antoine Arnauld, dated 14 July 1686, Leibniz writes: "each individual substance [monad] or complete being is a world apart, independent of every other thing except God" (*PPL* 337).[1]

On the other hand, Leibniz states in *Principes de la nature et de la grace fondés en raison* (*Principles of Nature and Grace Founded on Reason*) that "chaque Monade est un miroir vivant, ou doué d'action interne, representatif de l'univers, suivant son point de veue, et aussi reglé que l'univers luy même" (each monad is a living mirror, or a mirror endowed with inner activity, representative of the universe according to its point of view and regulated as completely as is the universe itself; G 6: 599, *PPL* 637; spelling as in the original).

Deleuze expresses the paradox in these words: "The monad is the autonomy of the inside, an inside without an outside. It has as its correlative the independence of the façade, an outside without an inside" (28). Leibniz maintains in the *Monadology* that, despite its closed structure, the monad is essentially open to the universe through its internal principles of *perception* and *appetition* (*PPL* 644). From the "small frosted skylight" of Murphy's garret to the last window of *Stirrings Still*, Beckett's strange windows are best described by the dualities of the monad (Mori 360–61). As correlative examples, Beckett explains that both Murphy's suit of clothes and mind are "windowless," for the former is "entirely nonporous" (*SB* 1: 46), and the latter is "hermetically closed to the universe without" (1: 67). In a word, Murphy is a self-complete monad in whom the Leibnizian "virtual or actual" dynamics prevail in the deepest zone of his mind (1: 67–68). "The third, the dark," Beckett writes, "was a flux of forms, a perpetual coming together and falling asunder of forms. [...] Here there was nothing but commotion and the pure forms of commotion" (*SB* 1: 70). In his later writing Beckett is to cherish this image of a state of flux in chaos, that is, the image of a monadic limbo as his innermost vision.

Why Leibniz, however? Where is Descartes? Hugh Kenner's view on Beckett's departure from Descartes, as summarized by David Pattie, may be helpful here: "a developing Cartesian split between the mind and body was central to the development of Beckett's work: as Beckett progressed, the divisions between mind and body became greater" (113). Chris Ackerley and Stanley Gontarski follow Kenner's views in asserting, "*Murphy* has been aptly described as a 'Cartesian catastrophe,' the protagonist unable to reconcile this dualism" (134). In retrospect, such a view has lasted since Samuel Mintz's first ascription of *Murphy* to Cartesian philosophy (157). It turns out, however, that Beckett bluntly negates Cartesian dualism in the novel. When Neary says to Murphy, "I should say your conarium has shrunk to nothing" (*SB* 1: 6), Beckett dislocates the Cartesian dualism once and for all by removing its symbolic organ from Murphy. According to Descartes's hypothesis, the *conarium,* or pineal gland, unites the two substances of body and mind. Therefore, like Leibniz himself, Murphy, the "dynamist" X, has moved beyond the mind-body dualism of Descartes to a position in which both are analyzed into elementary motions.

In the Labyrinth of the Continuum

"The *Monadology,* itself, written when Leibniz was almost 70," Nicholas Rescher states, "was, as it were, a last-minute attempt to provide a systematic sketch of his overall system" (5). In fact, Leibniz started writing the essay during his visit to Vienna in the summer of 1714, when he was about to turn sixty-eight on 1 July. He completed the essay later in the year after returning to his room on Schmiedestrasse, where he had settled in 1676 in the service of the Hanoverian Brunswick dukes, and where he remained until he died in 1716, as Beckett reminds us in the French *Murphy.* The *Monadology* is a condensed manifestation of the principles of his philosophy. Most likely written in less than six months, it took more than forty-five years for Leibniz to develop and integrate his thoughts into a concise system. Consequently, to understand the depth of his theory, we need to go back to Leibniz's earlier essays, to the nascent state of the *Monadology.* The year 1671 was a pivotal point for Leibniz, aged twenty-four, for he wrote two essays on motion (the *Hypothesis physica nova*) that served as the foundation of his system. Leibniz sought to establish the fundamental connection between dynamics and metaphysics. To achieve this purpose, he had to resolve the problem of infinity. He referred to this problem as "the labyrinth of metaphysics." The young Leibniz declared, "Unless we enter into this labyrinth, we cannot penetrate into the nature of motion itself" (qtd. in Aiton 68). To construct a theory of motion meant revealing the composition of the continuum, or, as Aiton summarizes Leibniz's view: "space cannot be simply an aggregate of points nor time an aggregate of instants" (68).

The labyrinth of the continuum is a paradox that stands for both the infinite divisibility of space and the endless evasiveness of its parts, which Descartes called "the indefinite" so that he might not enter the labyrinth. It has a long history dating to Zeno's paradoxes in ancient Greece to which Beckett alludes in *Endgame:* "Moment upon moment, pattering down, like the millet grains of...(*he hesitates*)...that old Greek, and all life long you wait for that to mount up to a life" (*SB* 3: 142–43). Leibniz never accepted Descartes's explanation that "the indefinite division is beyond the grasp of our finite minds,"[2] arguing that "the indefinite of Descartes is not in the thing but in the thinker" (*PPL* 139). Leibniz captures the indefinite under the law of continuity, claiming that "motion is continuous or not interrupted by little intervals of rest" (*PPL* 140). Then, in a letter to Antoine Arnauld, written in early November 1671, he postulates on the basis of his discovery, "corpus quiescens nullum esse" (no body is at rest; G 1: 71).

One breakthrough by Leibniz was his revolutionary concept of the unextended monads. In Cartesian philosophy, the body is defined as an "extension" and is synonymous with "space." Leibniz's view of unextended monads posits that space and body are distinct and that the body alone is no longer a substance. This is how Leibniz departs from Descartes's dualism of body and mind, and consequently poses a great challenge to Newtonian physics. For Leibniz, unlike Newton, neither space nor time is an entity. According to E. J. Aiton, "Geometrical points, considered as parts of space with zero magnitude, do not exist. In order, therefore, to define the beginning and end of a given space or body, these unextended geometrical points must be invested with some kind of reality. It was this problem that eventually led Leibniz to his metaphysical theory in which the real continuum was constructed from the unextended monads" (33). This demonstration of the unextended monads is but a hypothetical necessity.

Beyond his departure from Descartes, however, Leibniz held an even more powerful idea: the dynamic concept of *conatus,* or force, acquired from Thomas Hobbes. In a letter to Hobbes, dated 13–22 July 1670, Leibniz wrote: "*Conatus* is the beginning of motion, and therefore the beginning of existence in the place into which the body is striving" (*PPL* 107). With this concept of *conatus,* Leibniz dismantled Cartesian dualism, establishing the law of conservation of force, and arriving finally at the concept of the unextended, indestructible monad, or force.[3] Although Descartes begins the first chapter of his *Discours de la méthode* with "Le bon sens est la chose du monde la mieux partagée" (Good sense is the best distributed thing in the world; 44), thereby setting the groundwork for, as his subtitle states, his "method of rightly conducting one's reason and seeking truth in the sciences," good sense may not be able to accept Leibniz's premise that substance can exist without occupying any space.[4] Leibniz, in contrast, recognizes the necessity of questing for what we call today the realm of the unconscious, noting that innumerable things are taking place in nature behind and beyond our senses and our "good sense." Therefore, he advocates another revolutionary concept, the *petites perceptions*: "We have an infinity of little perceptions which we are incapable of distinguishing" (*PPL* 557).

Beckett's application of the principle is found, for instance, when Clov repeats, "Something is taking its course" (*SB* 3: 100, 114), and when Hamm says, "Something dripping in my head, ever since the fontanelles" (*SB* 3: 127). In Gontarski's judicious gloss, "Clov senses the almost imperceptible change, the single grain 'needed to make the heap—the last straw'" (47). The parallel between Leibniz's "labyrinth of the continuum" and Beckett's theme of "the last straw," specifically found in *Endgame,* is significant. In a letter to de Volder, dated 30 June 1704, Leibniz writes: "However, properly speaking, matter isn't composed of constitutive unities, but results from them, since matter, that is, extended [*massa*] is only a phenomenon grounded in things, like a rainbow or a parhelion, and all reality belongs only to *unities.* Thus, phenomena can always be divided into lesser phenomena [...] and we will never arrive at the least phenomena. *Substantial unities aren't really parts,* but the foundations of phenomena" (*Philosophical Essays* 179; emphasis added). Leibniz proclaims that his exploration in the labyrinth of the continuum is not meant to capture the lesser parts of matter but rather unextended substantial unities that are the foundations of bodies. Thus Leibniz's quest for the labyrinth of the continuum leads him to discover the unextended monad. If Beckett's quest for the "last straw" in *Endgame* parallels Leibniz's quest for the monad, what emerges from the endless game of Hamm and Clov would not be another straw but unextended substantial unities—that is, force—represented by their stasis/movement dynamics.

"No Body Is at Rest"

A number of scholars have remarked upon Beckett's peculiar interest in the dynamics of motion. In his analysis of *Whoroscope*'s "That's not moving, that's *moving*" (*SB* 4: 3), Lawrence Harvey argues for "the idea of simultaneous motion and immobility" (14–15).[5] The static/dynamic duality found in Beckett's first published book is remarkably expressed in *Molloy.* Molloy, who keeps on moving—on foot, on crutches, by bicycle, on his knees and belly—talks about his movement in the forest:

> For standing there is no rest, nor sitting either. And there are men
> who move about sitting, and even kneeling, hauling themselves to
> right and left, forward and backward, with the help of hooks. But

he who moves this way, crawling on his belly, like a reptile, no sooner comes to rest than he begins to rest, and even the very movement is a kind of rest, compared to other movements, I mean those that have worn me out. And in this way I moved onward in the forest, slowly, but with a certain regularity, and I covered my fifteen paces, day in, day out, without killing myself. (*SB* 2: 84)[6]

For Molloy, there is no clear distinction between movement and rest. Movement is a kind of rest, and rest is a kind of movement, thus indicating another parallel between Beckett and Leibniz. While Descartes defines rest as an absence of motion, and sees rest and motion as opposites, Leibniz never admits absence of motion in a body. With the law of continuity, Leibniz succeeds in defining stasis as an infinitesimally small movement, and movement as an infinitesimally big slowness.[7] That is to say, the law of continuity opens up a new horizon for Leibniz in which the correspondence of opposites is in perspective. Beckett's application of this principle to Molloy's movement is funny, if obvious. In discussing Beckett's late plays, Ruby Cohn notes that "Beckett comes close to painting still lives in movement" (31). Drawing on this observation, Mary Bryden refers to the "co-occurrence of movement and stasis" in Beckett's writings as "the dynamic still," concluding, "for Beckett, movement is never definitely halted" ("Beckett" 182, 190).[8]

It is apparent, then, that Beckett attached considerable importance to the static/dynamic duality of movement, but the connection to Leibniz's system is more difficult to uncover. Harvey considers "the idea of simultaneous motion and immobility" in connection with Descartes's metaphor of a sailor on a moving vessel (14–15). Cohn's focus is on Beckett's late plays, and Bryden compares Beckett's "dynamic still" to Pascal and Deleuze, not Leibniz. In effect, they are commenting indirectly on the legacy of Leibniz's force without relating it to his system. However, those who do, hear the echoes of his principle "no body is at rest" ringing throughout Beckett's oeuvre—particularly in the title of his last prose, *Stirrings Still.*

Beckett's *Petites Perceptions*

According to Leibniz's *Principes de la nature et de la grace* (§6), "tout va à l'infini dans la nature" (everything in nature proceeds to infinity; G 6: 601,

PPL 638). The concept of infinity pervades Leibniz's system, including his ideas on nature and cosmology as well as his ontological and epistemological principles. Accordingly, no matter how determinedly modest Beckett's applications of Leibniz's principles may be and no matter how invisible the Leibnizian substratum, more often than not, Beckett's novels and plays draw our attention to the concept of infinity in nature:

> HAMM: Nature has forgotten us.
> CLOV: There's no more nature.
> HAMM: No more nature! You exaggerate.
> CLOV: In the vicinity.
> HAMM: But we breathe, we change! We lose our hair, our teeth! Our bloom! Our ideals!
> CLOV: Then she hasn't forgotten us. (*SB* 3: 99)

Despite Hamm and Clov's claim that nature is scarcely perceptible, one of Beckett's typescripts for *Fin de partie* alludes to Leibniz's maxim on infinity in nature. According to the typescript, Hamm says, "La Nature...la Nature...voyons...abhorre le vide [...]. Abhorre le vide...ne fait pas de sauts" (Nature...Nature...no doubt...abhors the void [...]. Abhors the void...takes no leaps). Nothing echoes Leibniz's principle of the law of continuity more than "La Nature ne fait pas de sauts" (Nature takes no leaps).[9] But Beckett revised it into "La nature nous a oubliés" (Nature has forgotten us; *Théâtre* 1: 152.), erasing a marker of Leibniz from the published text. Again, the manuscripts of *Stirrings Still* reveal Beckett's similar tendency to hide Leibniz's influence in the creative process of this work. For example, Beckett changes "So dark in *his windowless self* that no knowing whether day or night" in a draft (Ms. 2935/1; emphasis added) into "One night or day" in the published text (*SB* 4: 487).

Even more significant of Leibniz's influence than the manuscript evidence is Beckett's constant and calculated use of Leibniz's principles of dynamics. The multilayered interplay of static/dynamic is found throughout Beckett's oeuvre. Winnie, buried up to her waist in the mound, exemplifies the significance of the tensions between the static and the dynamic. Like a trapped bird, she is wedged between the two opposing forces. Her buried part represents immobility, and her exposed part mobility. The Vladimir-Estragon couple is in a state of stagnancy in relation to the Pozzo-Lucky couple. The latter find themselves in a relentless movement of time, as is obvious in Pozzo's statement in act 2: "one day he went dumb, one day I went blind, one day we'll go deaf, one day we were born, one day we shall die, the same day, the same second" (*SB* 3: 82). In comparison, the Vladimir-Estragon couple find themselves unchanged, as if time stopped, as Estragon complains in act 1: "They [Pozzo and Lucky] all change. Only we can't" (*SB* 3: 41). The contrast, therefore, highlights two kinds of dynamics in *Waiting for Godot*—active and static—yet, on a different scale, each individual appears to have a different dynamic; Vladimir moves restlessly, while Estragon prefers to sit and sleep on a stone. It is on this individual scale that one of Beckett's theater notebooks shows the importance of these two kinds of dynamics in the play: "Thus establish at [the] outset 2 caged dynamics, E. [Estragon] sluggish, V. [Vladimir] restless. + perpetual separation and reunion of V/E" (qtd. in McMillan and Knowlson 185–87). Beckett's intention of giving each character a distinctive dynamic is evident. Thus "their perpetual separation and reunion" express a mixture of the two opposing dynamics.

Nevertheless, what really counts for Beckett is neither the superficial active force nor the static force, but the single ubiquitous force into which both of them finally and relentlessly converge. The latent force seldom appears on the surface of Beckett's works, and yet one may perceive the moment it does in the "frozen postures" and "frozen tableaux" of *Waiting for Godot* (see Haynes and Knowlson 126–27). The play's closing tableaux provide a good example. Act 1 ends with Vladimir's words, "Yes, let's go," followed by the stage directions, "*They do not move.*" Act 2 ends identically, but with Estragon repeating the words (*SB* 3: 47, 87). Words and bodies cancel their impetus with each other, but something emerges from this scene. Their "frozen postures" do not imply that they are in a complete stasis. Instead, they evoke a striking image of striving toward a change. The frozen tableaux are, I believe, intended by Beckett to generate a dramatic and startling moment, like a Joycean epiphany, when the reader-audience has flashes of insight that nobody remains still. Significantly, "Beckett knew perfectly well," writes James Knowlson, "that a flesh-and-blood actor is not, and never can be, a wholly static or still-life image" (Haynes and Knowlson 127). Accordingly, the audience will see in the "frozen tableaux" the imperceptible movements of the flesh. To borrow from Knowlson again, "in even the stillest of postures, eyes blink, lips quiver, hands tremble" (127). Leibniz's principles of "no body is at rest" and *petites perceptions* thus offer useful avenues into the Beckett œuvre.

Vis Viva (Living Force)

Speaking of Jack B. Yeats's art, Beckett wrote to Georges Duthuit: "Ce n'est donc pas avec moi qu'on puisse parler art et ce n'est pas là-dessus que je risque d'exprimer autre chose que mes propres hantises" (So you can't talk art with me; all I risk expressing when I speak about it are my own obsessions; qtd. in Knowlson 268). Likewise, Beckett's essay on the painting of Bram van Velde offers an intriguing instance in which it is possible to comprehend how the Leibnizian dynamics deeply resides in Beckett's aesthetics:

> Comment parler de ces couleurs qui respirent, halètent? De *cette stase grouillante?* De ce monde sans poids, sans force, sans ombre? Ici tout bouge, nage, fuit, revient, se défait, se refait. Tout cesse, sans cesse. On dirait l'insurrection des molécules, l'intérieur d'une pierre un millième de seconde avant qu'elle ne se désagrège.
> What can we say about these breathing, panting colors? *This wriggling stasis?* This weightless, forceless, shadowless world? Everything here is moving, swimming, fleeing, turning back, undoing, and redoing itself. Everything is coming to an end endlessly. It is like an insurrection of molecules, the inside of a stone a millisecond before it disintegrates. (*Le monde* 35; emphasis added)

Here all the colors keep dancing in a high-entropy state of disorder. This quantum limbolike commotion reminds us of the image of a monadic limbo in the third zone of Murphy's mind. Specifically interesting is the phrase "cette stase grouillante" (this wriggling stasis), which explains the hidden dynamics of what Ruby Cohn calls "still lives in movement" or Bryden's "the dynamic still" on a microscopic level. Furthermore, a close reading of this phrase leads us, more significantly, to its Leibnizian-theoretical basis. Comparing it to the internal stirrings of a stone at rest, and in contrast to Descartes's definition of the body as extension, Beckett perceives in the stone something other than extension, that is, *conatus,* or force, described, as we have seen, in Leibniz's letter to Hobbes as "the beginning of motion, and therefore the beginning of existence in the place into which the body is striving." This stone is almost a living creature. Actually, in his essay *Specimen Dynamicum* (1695), Leibniz calls this force *vis viva* (living force; *PPL* 438). Beckett has never been closer to Leibniz, not only in Beckett's vitalistic grip of "living force" but also in his use of the *petites perceptions* in the analysis. Remember, for Descartes, "a millisecond" means "the indefinite," since it goes far "beyond the grasp of our finite minds."[10] For Leibniz, regardless of the infinite divisibility of time and space, the essence of substance—that is, force—remains unchanged. Leibniz goes so far as to say that "there is nothing real in motion itself except that momentaneous state which must consist of *a force striving toward change*" (*PPL* 436; emphasis added). To Beckett's eyes, the stone is precisely "a force striving toward change," and thus, in this sense, there is little difference between the stone at rest and Vladimir-Estragon in their frozen postures, since they are also enduring internal stirrings. Beckett's vision is therefore based squarely on Leibniz's principle of the dynamics of motion.

Finally, it may be useful to examine the image of the monadic limbo reappearing in Beckett's letter to MacGreevy, dated 30 August 1937, in which Beckett refers to his own commotion of mind: "The real consciousness is the chaos, a grey commotion of mind, with no premises or conclusions or problems or solutions or cases or judgements. I lie for days on the floor, or in the woods, accompanied and unaccompanied, in a coenaesthesic of mind, a fullness of mental self-aesthesia that is entirely useless. The monad without the conflict, lightless and darkless" (qtd. in Knowlson 269). Again, this passage echoes the language Beckett uses about the third zone of Murphy's mind, as Knowlson points out, "reminiscent of Murphy's lowest zone of mind" (269). Leibniz is no longer an unexpected arrival.

Notes

I thank the editors for their help with this essay, and Angela Moorjani for her assistance with the translations from the French.

1. It was not until 1696 that Leibniz began to use the term "monad." Until then, he used various terms to express the concept of the monad: "the individual substance," "the substantial form," *vis activa* (active force); "substantial unity," *entelecheia* (entelechy), and so on.

2. Descartes states, "That it is not needful to enter into disputes regarding *the infinite*, but merely to hold all that in which we can find no limits as *indefinite*, such as the extension

of the world, the divisibility of the parts of matter, the number of the stars, etc." (*Principles* 2: §24; emphasis added).

3. Daniel Garber writes, "Basic to Descartes' physics was the principle of the conservation of quantity of motion. According to Descartes' physics, God sustains the universe from moment to moment and, in doing so, preserves the same quantity of motion in the world as a whole as measured by the size times the speed of each of the bodies in the world" (Jolley 309–11). What counts for Leibniz, however, is not the conservation of quantity of motion, but the conservation of *force* that is indestructible and unextended. Thus, Leibniz establishes a formula: that which is conserved is mv^2.

4. Leibniz's assertion that the body is nothing but phenomena and that its essence is indestructible, unextended force was nothing but a fantasy to his contemporaries. It was not until Einstein published his groundbreaking theory in 1905 that Leibniz's law of conservation of force was recognized for its historical significance. As we know, matter (mass) and energy are interchangeable according to Einstein's celebrated formula $e = mc^2$.

5. In the line, Beckett caricatures an instance of relativity given by Descartes: "a person seated in a vessel, which is setting sail, thinks he is in motion if he look to the shore that he has left, and consider it as fixed; but not if he regard the ship itself, among the parts of which he preserves always the same situation" (Descartes, *Principles* 2: §24).

6. Michael Mooney aptly remarks on "Molloy's inability to travel in a 'straight line,'" regarding this "a deliberate obfuscation which means to clarify Descartes's methodology!" (51). Still, he fails to detect that Leibniz's law of motion is hidden in the passage.

7. In *Theodicy*, Leibniz writes: "In virtue of this law [the law of continuity], one must be able to regard rest as a movement vanishing after having continually diminished [...]" (333–34).

8. Bryden also makes a similar point in her essay "Nomads and Statues": "Stirrings to stir, stirrings to stay: each inhabits the other in cycles of regret and indecision throughout Beckett's writing" (36).

9. I owe this manuscript evidence to Yoshiyuki Inoue, whose paper "Beckett and Pascal," written in Japanese, first pointed out that Beckett cites Leibniz's "La Nature ne fait pas de sauts" in the corrected typescript for *Fin de partie*, no. 1, leaf 9, Ohio State University (111).

10. It is probable that Beckett is quoting from Henri Bergson's *Matter and Memory*: "Now the smallest interval of empty time which we can detect equals, according to Exner, 0.002 seconds; and it is even doubtful whether we can perceive in succession several intervals as short as this" (205). If 0.002 seconds, that is, two milliseconds, is the limit of our perception, "a millisecond" is barely perceptible.

Works Cited

Ackerley, C. J. *Demented Particulars: The Annotated "Murphy."* Tallahassee, FL: Journal of Beckett Studies Books, 1998.

Ackerley, C. J., and S. E. Gontarski. *The Grove Companion to Samuel Beckett.* New York: Grove, 2004.

Aiton E. J. *Leibniz: A Biography.* Boston: Hilger, 1985.

Beckett, Samuel. "Brief Dream." Ms. 2934. Reading University Library, England.

———. *Le monde et le pantalon suivi de Peintres de l'empêchement.* Paris: Minuit, 1990.

———. *Murphy.* Paris: Minuit, 1965.

———. *Samuel Beckett: The Grove Centenary Edition.* Ed. Paul Auster. 4 vols. New York: Grove, 2006. (Abbreviated *SB*.)

———. *Stirrings Still,* Mss. 2933 and 2935/1. Reading University Library, England.

———. *Théâtre* 1. Paris: Minuit, 1971.

———. "Whoroscope Notebook." Ms. 3000. Reading University Library, England.

Bergson, Henri. *Matter and Memory.* Trans. Nancy Margaret Paul and W. Scott Palmer. New York: Zone, 1991.

Bryden, Mary. "Beckett and the Dynamic Still." *After Beckett/D'après Beckett.* Vol. 14 of *SBT/A.* Ed. Anthony Uhlmann, Sjef Houpermans, and Bruno Clément. Amsterdam: Rodopi, 2004. 179–92.

———. "Nomads and Statues: Beckett's Staged Movement." *Drawing on Beckett.* Ed. Linda Ben-Zvi. Tel Aviv: Assaph, 2003. 35–46.

Cohn, Ruby. *Just Play: Beckett's Theater.* Princeton, NJ: Princeton University Press, 1980.

Deleuze, Gilles. *The Fold: Leibniz and the Baroque.* Trans. Tom Conley. Minneapolis: University of Minnesota Press, 1988.

Descartes, René. *Discours de la méthode.* Paris: Vrin, 1966.

———. *A Discourse on Method, Meditations on the First Philosophy, Principles of Philosophy.* 1912. Trans. John Veitch. London: Dent, 1992.

Gontarski, S. E., ed. *The Theatrical Notebooks of Samuel Beckett: Endgame.* London: Faber, 1992.

Harvey, Lawrence E. *Samuel Beckett: Poet and Critic.* Princeton, NJ: Princeton University Press, 1970.

Haynes, John, and James Knowlson. *Images of Beckett.* Cambridge: Cambridge University Press, 2003.

Inoue, Yoshiyuki. "Beketto to Pasukaru—Beketto no *Shobu no Owari* ni okeru Kyojin Shisetsu/Rogoku/Fune no Naibu" ("Beckett and Pascal: Asylum, Prison, and the Inside of a Ship in Beckett's *Fin de partie*"). *Hannan Ronshu: Journal of the Humanities and Natural Sciences* 30 (1995): 99–115.

Jolley, Nicholas, ed. *The Cambridge Companion to Leibniz.* New York: Cambridge University Press, 1995.

Knowlson, James. *Damned to Fame: The Life of Samuel Beckett.* London: Bloomsbury, 1996.

Leibniz, G. W. *Philosophical Essays.* Ed. and trans. Roger Ariew and Daniel Garber. Indianapolis: Hackett, 1989.

———. *Philosophical Papers and Letters.* Ed. Leroy E. Loemker. 2nd ed. Dordrecht: Kluwer Academic, 1989. (Abbreviated *PPL*.)

————. *Die Philosophischen Schriften von G. W. Leibniz.* Ed. C. J. Gerhardt. 7 vols. Hildesheim: Olms, 1875–90. (Abbreviated G [Gerhardt].)

————. *Theodicy: Essays on the Goodness of God, the Freedom of Man, and the Origin of Evil.* Trans E. M. Huggard. La Salle, IL: Open Court, 1985.

McMillan, Dougald, and James Knowlson, eds. *The Theatrical Notebooks of Samuel Beckett: Waiting for Godot.* London: Faber, 1993.

Mintz, I. Samuel. "Beckett's *Murphy:* A 'Cartesian' Novel." *Perspective* 11 (1959): 156–65.

Mooney, Michael. "*Molloy,* Part 1: Beckett's Discourse on Method." *Journal of Beckett Studies* 3 (1978): 40–55.

Mori, Naoya. "Beckett's Windows and 'the Windowless Self.'" *After Beckett/D'après Beckett.* Vol. 14 of *SBT/A.* Ed. Anthony Uhlmann, Sjef Houpermans, and Bruno Clément. Amsterdam: Rodopi, 2004. 357–70.

Pattie, David. *Samuel Beckett.* London: Routledge, 2000.

Rescher, Nicholas. *G. W. Leibniz's Monadology: An Edition for Students.* Pittsburgh, PA: University of Pittsburgh Press, 1991.

Ricks, Christopher. *Beckett's Dying Words.* Oxford: Oxford University Press, 1993.

Part II

SHIFTING PERSPECTIVES

SHIFTING PERSPECTIVES

"Just Looking"

Ne(i)ther-World Icons, Elsheimer Nocturnes, and Other Simultaneities in Beckett's *Play*

ANGELA MOORJANI

> *Two things fill the mind with ever new and increasing admiration and awe, the oftener and the more steadily we reflect on them: the starry heavens above and the moral law within.*
>
> —Immanuel Kant

> *The stars are undoubtedly superb . . .*
>
> —Sigmund Freud as quoted by Samuel Beckett

THE PLEASURES (if not the rapture) of vertigo are felt by many readers plunging into Beckett's contrapuntal and paradoxical texts. Aware of the effects that encourage superimposed readings, some commentators nevertheless downplay those that are in a different domain from their own, the political seemingly disqualifying the psychoanalytical, or the inquiry into the medium ruling out the mythical or ontological, or the other way around. The number of indirect effects that Beckett interweaves into his texts makes me suspect, however, that he was reviving the ancient fourfold method, if with the ironic intent of upending it. This method practiced by the ancient Egyptians, adopted for biblical exegesis, and recommended by Dante for his *Commedia* involves multi-tiered interpretations for the same sign or text, beginning with the literal or historical. Focusing from textual form to superimposed strata that stretch from the innermost unconscious to the outermost historical and cosmic realities, we find an interlocking structure, with each level echoing the other, but endlessly and paradoxically.

Simultaneities

Fourfold exegesis anticipates the pragmatic insight that the interpretation of signs depends in part on the inner and outer context that receivers bring to the interaction, thereby turning it into an unlimited process. Beckett, though, while engaging us in this process, also found ways of turning it against us. Thus one of his preferred oppositional devices is contrapuntal irony understood in the pragmatic sense as the echoing of an utterance while simultaneously disowning it. In Peter Gidal's apt words, "Meaning is unmade as it is made" (162).

Multivocal and discordant, Beckett's procedures for placing sense *en abyme* suggest parallels with modernist, posttonal and poststructural polyphonies (with nods to Arnold Schoenberg, Mikhail Bakhtin, Sergei Eisenstein, Roland Barthes, and others). As we know, Beckett was fond of musical parallels, noting in his German Diaries on 26 March 1937: "dissonance [...] has become principle" and "literature can no more escape from chronologies to simultaneities" than "the human voice can sing chords." He then adds his sudden realization that Joyce's *Work in Progress* is "the heroic attempt to make literature accomplish what belongs to music—the miteinander [togetherness] + the simultaneous" (qtd. in Nixon 31). Beckett was to compose such simultaneous fiction himself beginning with the *mise en abyme* structure of *Watt,* thus making "literature accomplish what belongs to music." Reading his fiction and theater contrapuntally has always had its rewards.[1]

In drawing on the fourfold method for *Play* (translated into French as *Comédie* and into Italian as, yes, *Commedia*), one could situate the spotlight on four simultaneous planes, while keeping in mind the instability of each: (1) on the literal level, it is a mechanical spotlight; (2) on the social level, it functions as a tormentor; (3) on the psychic plane, it calls to mind a self-observing eye/I, and (4) in the anagogical realm of myth or religion, it conjures up a diabolical or divine creator-judge. In reversing perspective, one could place the psychic text first, seeing in the other enfolded meanings extensions of its obsessions, but the psychic script is in turn rooted in and reinforced by the other three, whether in the sense of the controlling role of media, hierarchical social structures, or belief systems. In any case, except for the literal sense, with which the others are entangled in what Ruby Cohn aptly calls "theatereality" (*Just Play* 28), meanings are toyed with and undone in the interest of the "integrity of incoherence" that Beckett, as a young academic at Trinity College Dublin, prized in André Gide's novels (qtd. in Burrows 14),

Such four-part exegesis aligns Beckett's drama *simultaneously* with meta-theater (the stage-as-stage), with a *theatrum mundi* (the world-as-stage, the stage-as-world), a *theatrum mentis* (the psyche-as stage, the stage-as-psyche), and with a *theatrum dei* or a "divine comedy," (the other-world-as-stage, the stage-as-the-other-world), all of which fade into the enfolding dark and silence of the deserted stage. And where is the "truth" of the text? Surely, it is a matter of "just play," with the stage a transitional playground (in the Winnicottian sense) where multiple levels intersect in a space in between theatereality, social reality, and the imaginary, if not to say the hallucinatory, and where the coming and going in and out of the dark endlessly repeat.[2]

To appreciate *Play*, Ruby Cohn remarks, it has to be seen, listened to, and read (*Canon* 282). In my discussion of the play's contrapuntal and iconographical embeddings, I will therefore refer not only to the play in performance, which Beckett divided into Chorus, Narration, and Meditation (Esslin 44), but also to the written text, and the brilliant Karmitz-Beckett translation of *Comédie* into film.

Literally, as Beckett exegetes have seen, the spotlight functions as the mechanical means of bringing the urn figures into view for the spectators. Without the light, there is no visible play. A similar literalness is at work in Beckett's *Film* (whose generic and punning title evokes the more or less contemporaneous *Play*), in which the camera-eye fulfills the function of enforced filmic visibility. As often noted, both camera-eye and spot-eye, moreover, closely involve the spectators whose vision is anchored to theirs. The resistance to the light and to the camera-eye that the protagonists of *Play* and *Film* display serves to interrogate the power of the spectators' gaze as structured through the technology of each medium.

Thereby, we have crossed over into the *theatrum mundi* that echoes on *Play*'s diegetic level the onstage distaste of pursuit by the punishing spot-eye. In the Narration, the wife (w 1) tells of having the husband (m)

who is involved with another woman (w 2) followed by a private eye, a "bloodhound" in the text, a cliché of boulevard farce resonating with the spot-eye's role. The cruelty of the gaze, too, is a refrain within the trio's fictions, so that, not unlike the threesome in Jean-Paul Sartre's *Huis clos,* each of the three can be taken to be the others' tormentor. Each woman finds the other common and physically repulsive in comparison to herself: "Pudding face, puffy, spots, blubber mouth, jowls, no neck [...]," w 1 opines about w 2, whereas m exclaims, "God what vermin women" (*Play* 150–51). Only the women, never the man, are the objects of the disdainful gaze and death threats of the other two. m's comment, "We had fun trying to work this out" (150), suggests that the readers or spectators are likewise to interrogate the Narration's gender disparity, especially contradicted as it is by the stage image: "faces so lost to age and aspect as to seem almost part of urns" (147). The *nouveau théâtre* tableau of the three ungendered, disembodied, and depersonalized urn figures, immobilized side by side, delivering their rapid and inexpressive recitativo, contrasts with their gendered physicality, their middle-class way of life, and the frantic activity required by their triangular scheming in the Narration's clichéd parody of soap opera melodramas or French boulevard farce. In analyzing brilliantly such contrasting stage-text counterpoint as the suggestive parallels between the adultery story and the stage story of the light's actions, Paul Lawley maintains that each situation points ultimately to this life, not the next, and confines the figures to a "parody of being" ("Beckett's" 28–41). I, however, argue for the simultaneity of the here and there and nowhere, of the now and then and never, of this life and the before- and afterlife in *Play* and throughout Beckett's oeuvre.[3]

Here we cross over into the third level of the *theatrum mentis,* the one portrayed in the Meditation part of the play. Each of the three urn-bound figures is unaware that they are confined side by side, sharing the "hellish half-light" of self-torture in the guise of the mechanical spotlight turned inquisitorial eye. This mechanical eye, without a mind, as m specifies, is the play's most important protagonist (Beckett qtd. in Karmitz 73). And like the camera-eye of *Film,* the spot-eye can be taken as a double of the figures, a part of themselves projected outward and turned into a "bizarre object" (in the Bionien sense) that mirrors to them from the outside the inner censoring agency, call it conscience or superego.[4] The three monologues are thus (pace Gidal) internal dialogues after all (as self-persuasion has been taken to be from Plato to C. S. Peirce and Bakhtin), addressed as they are to this bizarre double that responds nonverbally as a split-off eye or I.[5]

There is, however, nothing stable or univocal about the relationship pitting the trio against their tormentor. In envisaging a repeat that expresses "a slight weakening" of both the questioning light and the responding voices, Beckett adds, "The inquirer (light) begins to emerge as no less a victim of his inquiry than they [...]" (Letter to George Devine 112). In reversing perspective, the spotlight from tormentor becomes the tormented (see also Lawley, "Beckett's" 39). On the level of the theater of the mind, in which the spotlight is a projection of the figures, "he" is as much their object from one perspective as they are his from another. Beckett's often commented-on oppressor-victim reversals not only preclude anchoring in any fixed perspective in his fiction and theater but also suggest the instability of power, which exists to be resisted and toppled.

But the meanings the textual effects tempt us into giving the spotlight do not end here. Beckett, it would seem, was much taken with Freud's claim that beliefs in a divine being are extensions of our parental imagos (Freud, *New Introductory Lectures* 163), for he has time and again parodied this particular psychic projection in his cosmic Knotts, Youdis, Lousses, and other tyrannical figures associated with fire power, light, and vision. Thus in *Film* the print of "God the Father" and the photograph of the "mother-God" (Beckett's characterization qtd. in Harmon 159), each with severe eyes, are ripped into pieces by the protagonist in his frantic flight from being perceived. Such an escape, too, is the wish of the three inurned figures of *Play*, who yearn for the total darkness, silence, peace, and rest of oblivion. And now we have crossed over into the otherworldly stage, where the spotlight takes on shadings of a judge in the netherworld.

Bounded Boundlessness 1: Icons of the Egyptian Netherworld

The diabolical light (a visual pun on Lucifer?), recollections of a former life, "sins" mirrored in their punishment, the questionable role of pity, along with the hope for mercy evoke a blend of Dante's hellish and purgatorial visions. Yet the stage image of the three urns, encircled in darkness, echoes a still older mythic netherworld. I have in mind ancient Egypt's cult of the dead, envisioned in terms of the cycles of death and resurrection of the diurnal and nocturnal sun gods Ra and Osiris. Often alluded to by modernist writers and artists, Osiris's journey evoked for them their own plumbing of the depths. No doubt Beckett's familiarity with ancient Egyptian rituals and beliefs was further informed by the psychoanalytic literature he read and the museums he visited.[6] It was while absorbed in a small Egyptian exhibit in Lyon that it came to me that Beckett mingled, if rather sardonically, artifacts of the Egyptian passage to the afterlife with Dante's *Commedia* in fashioning *Play*'s underworld tableau. And, as we know, he joined other modernists in identifying generativity with the ancients' before- and afterlife.

The trio's musings about life in the sun and Hamm's figurative description of the end of day in his chronicle, "the sun was sinking down into the...down among the dead" (*Endgame* 51), which M echoes in his question to the light "Why go down" (155), recall Ra's daily trajectory, but it is in particular the nocturnal sun god Osiris's death, dismemberment, descent into the netherworld, and rebirth that evoke both a journey from death to the afterlife and the descent into psychic depths of the creative process. Divinity of the underworld and of regeneration, Osiris adds to these functions the role of judge of the dead. For the ancient Egyptians, the defense of justice was the prerogative of the Sacred Eye that they associated with light and the surveillance of the smallest details (Jacq 127–39). Anticipating Berkeley, they imagined a divine perceiving eye that assures being to all that is, and as Freud was to do, they gave a watchful eye the role of an observer split off from their moral conscience whose surveillance is without pity and whose projection into the religious, social, and political realms Michel Foucault was to probe with such acumen. "Just looking," is M's punning taunt to the spotlight-cum-netherworld-judge (157). As we know, Beckett quotes the various functions of the power gaze obsessively throughout his theater, more often than not in the form of an inquisitor that seeks to shine light on what others would prefer to keep in the dark, beginning with the Glazier of *Eleutheria,* continuing with the spotlight character of *Play,* and ending with Bam of *What Where.*

Death for the ancient Egyptians was not a finality but a passage that, following Osiris's example, leads from ritual dismemberment and embalming to judgment in the underworld. (M: "Down, all going down, into the dark [...] I was right, after all, thank God, when first this change" [152]). Part of the ritual preparation for judgment consisted in removing organs from the body and placing them in canopic jars whose contents were under the protection of the four sons of the rising sun god Horus. These divinities' falcon, jackal, baboon, and human heads are depicted on the jars' lids (see figure 1). Would any Beckettian coming upon an exhibition of these funerary jars not think of the urn heads of *Play?* The canopic jars, some of which reach the height of three feet that Beckett specifies for his urns, accompanied the mummified body wrapped in layers of linen and placed in coffins (Hornung and Bryan xii). And invaluable for the successful outcome of judgment was the *Book of Exit from the Light,* known to us as the *Book of the Dead,* with its magical words to persuade the underworld judge (w 1: "So it must be something I have to say" [153]).

In the Egyptian imaginary, the dead identified with Osiris undergo a period of second gestation enveloped in a "skin of resurrection," both embryonic sack and shroud, to effect the passage to the afterlife (Jacq 156). The coffins containing the wrapped mummies or the funerary jars thus combine womb and tomb in one container (Rank 150), and indeed Beckett in the first five of the twelve typescript drafts of the play envisaged his three figures encased in oblong boxes before deciding on the urns (Bryden et al., 75–76). Either form

FIGURE 1. Canopic jars, Egypt, Late Period, Dynasty 26, 664–525 B.C., travertine, 45.3 by 18.6 cm., © The Cleveland Museum of Art, The Charles W. Harkness Endowment Fund 1921.1018.

of second gestation resonates with Beckett's imaginary blending of death and birth into a pregnant darkness from which visions fade in and out.

Although I have mostly concentrated on the polyphonic relation between the spotlight and the protagonists, the impression the urns make on viewers of the play are just as likely to result in simultaneous glimmerings of meaning. I have emphasized four tiers associated with ancient methods, Dante, and four-part counterpoint; but who is to say that there are only four or always the same four? Still, if we stay with four for the moment, then viewed as stage props, the urns imprison the actors' bodies, depriving them of movement and expressiveness. While paying attention to the diegesis, viewers are more likely to see them as funerary urns or as the solitary confinement to which the adulterous trio has been condemned. From the point of view of *theatrum mentis*, the urns suggest Beckett's obsessively repeated trope of gestation in the mind blending womb and tomb into one, which resonates in turn with the otherworldly sense of ritual jars required for passage to another world. Each reading is partial, reverberating contrapuntally with the other levels, and unstable, as any meanings we project into the text are both solicited by it and put in doubt.

Bounded Boundlessness 2: Elsheimer Nocturnes

The "all dark, all still" obliteration (*Play* 147) with which Beckettian figures play their obsessive *fort-da* games of come and go became the dramatic frame for his plays in the late fifties and early sixties. In *Play* (written 1961–1963), "*The curtain rises on a stage in almost complete darkness*" (147), and at the end there is a blackout held five seconds before the curtain falls. Beckett transferred this scenic device to *Film* (1964), directed by Alan Schneider, and to *Comédie* (1966), directed by Marin Karmitz, both with Beckett's active participation. Each film begins and ends with a black or a nearly black screen (Schneider qtd. in Harmon 160; Karmitz 74). In *Comédie*, the establishing shot is of nothing on an almost black screen, then the urn figures become visible in the distance, individualized by the light beam as they come progressively closer, until at the end of the repeat they recede into the distance in a breathtaking zoom to dissolve into blackness. The role of the light beam in bringing the screen to visibility for the viewers parallels the material role of the spotlight on the stage. Additionally, on first seeing this film, shortly after it was made, and then again in 2000, after it was rediscovered, I had the impression of the urn-enveloped figures reduced to three points of light in the distance, where they shimmer like dim stars on the firmament before fading into the darkness. It is an unforgettably powerful image of the play with come and go that Beckett never tired of repeating in work after work.

Katharine Worth identifies the cosmic space that I experienced in the filmed *Comédie* with all the scenic spaces Beckett envisaged for his plays, "where we find ourselves," she writes, "in the Maeterlinckian phrase, face to face with 'the vast unknown that surrounds us'" (22). Worth hypothesizes that Beckett may well have been echoing Maeterlinck's devices for conferring cosmic significance to his stage spaces, although she points out that the two paintings that inspired the stage image of *Waiting for Godot*—Jack Yeats's *Two Travellers* and Caspar David Friedrich's *Two Men Contemplating the Moon*—similarly evoke a sense of the vastness of space (28).

For *Play*, a much earlier painting than those quoted in *Godot* come to mind, one long celebrated for its depiction of limitless space. The renowned and often imitated nightscape *The Flight into Egypt* (1609) by Adam Elsheimer (Frankfurt 1578–Rome 1610) is one Beckett would have read about in R. H. Wilenski's book on Dutch painting, on which he took thirty-five pages of notes in the early 1930s. In a 1935 letter to Tom Mac-Greevy he terms one of Elsheimer's paintings "exquisite," and he was to admire *The Flight into Egypt* at Munich's Alte Pinakothek in 1937 (Haynes and Knowlson 79–80). For Wilenski, Elsheimer influenced Rembrandt and other artists to conceive of and portray the universe as boundless in time and space (100). Elsheimer's sky, Wilenski writes, is "no longer a backcloth but a symbol for boundless space" (68).

Coincidentally, just in time for the Beckett centenary, the Alte Pinakothek organized a brilliant exhibition around Elsheimer's *Flight into Egypt*. Working with astronomers, the curators of the show learned that Elsheimer's depiction of innumerable individual stars making up the Milky Way as well as the craterlike shadows that he shows on his moonscape point to the use of the newly discovered telescope with the help of which Galileo was about to reinforce awareness of the universe's vastness (Baumstark). Beckett's admiration for the Elsheimer painting may well have to do in part with the forlornness of the figures in the limitless dark only intermittently pierced by points of light, bringing to mind Hamm's description of himself as "a speck in the void, in the dark, for ever" (*Endgame* 36). As Beckett told Gottfried Büttner, "Since Galileo made the earth into a speck of dust in a vast universe [...], we live in the desolation [lostness] of our time ("in der Verlorenheit unserer Zeit," in Beckett's German) (qtd. in Büttner 115).

Beckett's apprehensive approach to boundlessness echoes many a philosophical response in the wake of Galileo, including Pascal's famous terror at the eternal silence of an infinite universe and the Kantian and then Schopenhauerian boundless sublime: "A mere speck in the universe" is Kant's version of human *Verlorenheit* (desolation) in the conclusion of his *Critique of Practical Reason* (1788). Beckett was aware as well of Kant's often quoted words from the conclusion of the same work: "Two things fill the mind with ever new and increasing admiration and awe [...] *the starry heavens above and the moral law within*" (360–61; emphasis in original). On reading Freud's comment in the *New Introductory Lectures on Psychoanalysis* (1933) on Kant's famous pronouncement to the effect that "a pious man might well be tempted to honour these two things [the starry heavens and the moral law] as the masterpieces of creation" (61), Beckett copied Freud's witty rejoinder into his notes of the 1930s: "The stars are unquestionably superb . . ." (Beckett, "Id" 160).[7] From *Play*, it is apparent that Beckett did not disagree with Freud's judgment that "as regards conscience God has done an uneven and careless piece of work" (*New Introductory Lectures* 61).

Elsheimer's portrayal of the Flight motif, which he integrated into a nocturnal landscape, shows the overall darkness pierced by the illuminated night sky, the diagonal spray of the Milky Way, and the moon low on the horizon reflected in water (on the right side of the painting), a lighting effect echoed on the left side by a bonfire tended by shepherds palely reflected in water and spewing fiery sparks up in the direction of the stars. Centered between these light sources, the fleeing family, depicted against a dark cluster of trees, is heading left in the direction of the shepherds counter the diagonals of the Milky Way and trees descending left to right. The three faces are partially illuminated by a torch in Joseph's left hand; in his right hand, he holds a twig or a reed for the child to play with (see figure 2). Although written in reference to a different painting that has since been reassigned to a follower of Elsheimer, Wilenski's words about the artist's contrapuntal use of light and darkness are apropos: "we have here an attitude of mind reacting emotionally, not only to the idea of an escape from defined darkness into infinite light, but also to the idea of an escape from defined light into darkness and mystery" (69).

FIGURE 2. Adam Elsheimer, *The Flight into Egypt*, 1609, oil on copper, Bayerische Staatsgemäldesammlungen, Alte Pinakothek Munich.

Beckett cites the mood of the Elsheimer nocturne in *Molloy*, in which the eponymous self-narrator compares his writing in his mother's room to a cycle "of flight and bivouac, in an Egypt without bounds, without infant, without mother" (66). In the meeting with the shepherd repeated contrapuntally in both parts of the novel, Molloy comes upon him in the morning after having spent the night in a ditch, imagining behind closed lids "the little night and its little lights" which he associates with fire fed "by filth and martyrs" (28). When Moran comes upon the shepherd at night, he perceives him as a figure of refuge as are the shepherds encamped around their bonfire in Elsheimer's painting, as well as the shepherds sheltering the Holy Family at rest in Rembrandt's quotation of Elsheimer's nocturne in the National Gallery of Ireland, Dublin. Rembrandt's Elsheimer-inspired rendition of *Rest on the Flight to Egypt* (1647), too, is known to be among Beckett's favorites (Haynes and Knowlson 59). In Beckett's novel, in contrast to Molloy's inner vision of "the little night"—more psychical underworld than moral law—the self-narrating Moran describes the starry heavens (note the painterly language): "I distinguished at last, at the limit of the plain, a dim glow, the sum of countless points of light blurred by the distance, I thought of Juno's milk. It lay like a faint splash on the sharp dark sweep of the horizon" (159). Beckett would appear to be alluding to more than one iconographical source here: Elsheimer's starry night and possibly Jacopo Tintoretto's *The Origin of the Milky Way* (circa 1575) in The National Gallery, London or Peter Paul Ruben's painting by the same title in the Prado, both depicting spurts of Juno's milk turning into stars.[8] By means of such "imaginative blending" (Haynes and Knowlson 71), Beckett transfers the night atmosphere and feelings of cosmic space, of desolation and refuge from the paintings to the meeting with the shepherd by his double persona Molloy-Moran.

In reference to lighting effects, Knowlson mentions Beckett's interest in "spotlight painting" and his adoption of old master chiaroscuro effects in his theatrical images of heads emerging out of darkness (Haynes and Knowlson 77–80). This interest was stimulated by Wilenski's discussion of "spot-light effects," that is, "the exploitation of effects of concentrated or artificial light" (61) in works by Raphael and Caravaggio whose popularity spread throughout Europe with the night pictures of painters working in Italy in the early seventeenth century: the Dutch Gerrit van Honthorst, the French Georges de la Tour, and, of course, the German Elsheimer, spotlighting the three faces with the light emanating from Joseph's torch. Wilensky writes somewhat disapprovingly that this manner culminated in Rembrandt's at times "theatrical" spotlighting of his sitters' heads against darkness, preferring Rembrandt's chiaroscuro paintings, in which light and shade dissolve into each other endlessly (101–02).

In returning now to Beckett's theater, we find that in *Play,* Beckett merges the "theatrical" spotlighting of the three faces and the chiaroscuro boundless-ness by specifying, "The best background [for the urns] is that which best suggests empty unlit space" (qtd. in Harmon 145). And, in the fourfold man-ner, the fade-ins and dissolves of Beckett's stage sets in and out of darkness suggest beyond their literal theatrical sense, outer and inner space, stretching from the boundlessness of cosmic space and time to an inner endlessness of mind, and in *Play,* as we have seen, implying the mythic passage from one world to the next. "Light, w 1, w 2, and m belong to the same separate world," Beckett wrote to Alan Schneider (qtd. in Harmon 145).

Beckett, of course, was not the first to reimagine for the stage the at-mospheric or mood-setting lighting effects that Wilenski discusses in painting. He inherited from the symbolists and other early modernists a rejection of naturalistic settings and use of lighting choreography that aspires to parallel pictorial and musical effects. And yet, perhaps partly on the basis of his keen awareness of pictorial and filmic lighting techniques, Beckett was able to radicalize their use beyond that of his predecessors and contemporaries, whether by means of the aggressive spotlighting or the diffuse chiaroscuro or the enfolding darkness.

Although I have lingered on the stage darkness, seconded by echoing pictorial nocturnes, that is, as you would guess, not the entire picture. Indeed, in an instance of stage-text counterpoint, the intermittent darkness of the stage image is in conflict with the offstage sun-drenched daylight to which the urn figures repeatedly refer. At the same time, readers of the text are most likely aware of the polyphony of w 1's comments about the darkness, which are, however, difficult to catch in delivery: "Yes, strange, darkness best, and the darker the worse, till all dark, then all well, [. . .] all dark, all still, all over, wiped out—" (147). The words she uses for her own situation evoke the various degrees of darkness of the stage image and most likely the spectators' wish to have it "all over" with. Similarly, w 2 echoes the spectators' feelings of being kept in the dark: "To say I am not disappointed, no, I am. I had anticipated something better. [. . .] Less confusing" (152). Yet, paradoxically, if the figures wish for darkness, they also dread it: "Am I as much as . . . being seen?" (157) is the man's last utterance before the repeat. It appears, then, as if the trio is losing faith in the capacity of this bizarre object to be anything but an on-again, off-again mechanical device of light torture. Thus it gives them a taste of the pleasure of darkness and silence, only to interrupt it with beams of light, and conversely, it cuts off their attempts to "bring it up" into the light by plunging them into darkness. m's hiccups comically literalize the bringing up for which he has to ask his "pardons." Neither for the urn figures nor for the spectators is there any settling into the dark of unknowing, the dark of oblivion, or the light of knowing, the light of visibility that ties them to being. Instead, one and the other are in conflict, without resolution.

Beckett's dramatic texts destabilize spectatorship by means of their contrapuntal paradoxes and "integrity of incoherence." They leave us divided between seeing and unseeing, meaning and meaninglessness, light and dark, akin to *Play*'s urn figures bounded paradoxically in boundlessness. But, simultaneously, echoing now my words about Beckett's fiction in *Abysmal Games,* I find that in playfully and contrapuntally embedding cultural texts or ghosts into his plays, he moves us to suspect their power to make us see clearly what is not clear and their power to blind us to the darkness waiting to be explored.

Notes

1. While revising the present centenary essay written in honor of Ruby Cohn, it was a pleasure to run across Beckett's diary entry for the first time. It took me back to my *Abysmal Games,* of which Ruby was one of the first readers, and in which I made much of Beckettian "dissonance" in my contrapuntal (nonlinear/abysmal) readings of the fiction beginning with *Murphy* (22–67). After completing this essay I reread, after many years, Beckett's "Dante... Bruno. Vico.. Joyce" (1929). To my astonishment, I found that Beckett had applied to Joyce's *Work in Progress* a fourfold method that he relates to Vico's "four human institutions—Providence counting as one!" (23; exclamation mark in the original). As I argue in this essay, what Beckett terms Joyce's "endless" variations on "such interior intertwining" (22) were to become one of his own hidden structural devices. Beckett's own "reverberations" and "reapplications" are, as he maintains for Joyce, "without [...] the faintest explicit illustration" (20).

2. For Donald W. Winnicott, a child's potential for play and later cultural productivity depend on an "intermediate playground" mediating between a "me" and a "not-me" and a dreamlike inner world and a socially shared outer world (47–52, 100). See also Julie Campbell's essay in this volume.

3. In drawing attention to counterpoint in *Play,* Rosemary Pountney sees Beckett adopting some of the stylized features of Noh drama via W. B. Yeats, in particular, *Play's* "dialogue counterpointed by linked opening, central, and closing choruses" (28). Pountney points out the similarity of situation in *Play* and in Yeats's *Purgatory* and *The Dreaming of the Bones,* in which "spirits are trapped and compelled to relive their unhappy experience, like a record stuck in a groove" (29). In Noh drama, Yeats, and Beckett, life and afterlife intermingle.

4. In a page of notes dating from 1933–1935, Beckett quotes Freud's view on a projected superego: "delusions of observation of certain psychotics, whose observing function (superego) has become sharply separated from the ego & projected into external reality" (Beckett, "Id" 160). Wilfred R. Bion similarly postulates that the self attempts to rid itself of split-off eye/I fragments by expelling them into an external object. This object, let us say a spotlight (or a piece of furniture), is transformed into a "bizarre object" that encapsulates the projected eye fragments and looks menacingly at the expelling personality (47–50).

5. A similar split-off function for the Auditor of *Not I* was postulated by Hersh Zeifman (qtd. in Lawley, "Counterpoint" 408).

6. Cf. Rank (150–53). The underworld "sun-ship" Rank mentions (151) is echoed in *Play's* "little dinghy, on the river" (156). On Beckett's museum visits and readings, see Nixon (49) and Knowlson (170–72).

7. Freud's German reads, "Die Gestirne sind gewiß großartig" (*Neue Folge* 67). Beckett, however, appears to have taken his notes on the 1933 English translation by W. J. H. Sprott shortly after it was published. The impression Freud's aside made on Beckett is apparent from his quoting it in the 1949 *Three Dialogues* as "*the stars are undoubtedly superb*" (141; emphasis in original; see also Engelberts et al. 158, 161).

8. The comparison to the Milky Way is more direct (if less iconographical) in the French: "Ça tenait de la galaxie" (*Molloy* 247).

Works Cited

Baumstark, Reinhold, ed. *Von neuen Sternen: Adam Elsheimers "Flucht nach Ägypten."* Munich: Pinakothek-DuMont, 2005.

Beckett, Samuel. "Dante...Bruno. Vico..Joyce." Cohn, *Disjecta* 19–33.

———. *Endgame.* New York: Grove, 1958.

———. "Id, Ego & Superego." Notes on *The New Introductory Lectures.* By Sigmund Freud. 1933. Ms. 10971/7. Trinity College Dublin. Rpt. in Engelberts et al. 160.

———. Letter to George Devine. 9 Mar. 1964. Cohn, *Disjecta* 111–12.

———. *Molloy.* Paris: Minuit, 1951.

———. *Molloy. Three Novels.* New York: Grove, 1955.

———. *Play. Collected Shorter Plays.* New York: Grove, 1984. 145–60.

———. *Three Dialogues.* Cohn, *Disjecta* 138–45.

Bion, Wilfred R. *Second Thoughts: Selected Papers on Psycho-analysis.* New York: Aronson, 1967.

Bryden, Mary, Julian Garforth, and Peter Mills, eds. *Beckett at Reading: Catalogue of the Beckett Manuscript Collection at the University of Reading.* Reading, UK: Whiteknights Press and Beckett International Foundation, 1998.

Burrows, Rachel. Interview with S. E. Gontarski, Martha Fehsenfeld, and Dougald McMillan. Dublin, Bloomsday, 1982. *Journal of Beckett Studies* 11/12 (1989): 6–15.

Büttner, Gottfried. "Schopenhauer's Recommendations to Beckett." *Samuel Beckett: Endlessness in the Year 2000.* Vol. 11 of *SBT/A.* Ed. Angela Moorjani and Carola Veit. Amsterdam: Rodopi, 2001. 114–22.

Cohn, Ruby. *A Beckett Canon.* Ann Arbor: University of Michigan Press, 2005.

———, ed. *Disjecta: Miscellaneous Writings and a Dramatic Fragment.* New York: Grove, 1984.

———. *Just Play: Beckett's Theater.* Princeton, NJ: Princeton University Press, 1980.

Engelberts, Matthijs, Everett Frost, with Jane Maxwell, eds. *Notes Diverse[s] Holo.* Vol. 16 of *SBT/A.* Amsterdam: Rodopi, 2006.

Esslin, Martin. "Samuel Beckett and the Art of Broadcasting." *Encounter* Sept. 1975: 38–46.

Freud, Sigmund. *Neue Folge der Vorlesungen zur Einführung in die Psychanalyse. Gesammelte Werke.* Ed. Anna Freud et al. Vol. 15. Frankfurt am Main: S. Fischer, 1990.

———. *New Introductory Lectures on Psycho-analysis*. 1933. *The Standard Edition of the Complete Psychological Works*. Ed. and trans. James Strachey. Vol. 22. London: Hogarth, 1964. 3–182.

Gidal, Peter. *Understanding Beckett: A Study of Monologue and Gesture*. 1986. London: Macmillan, 1988.

Harmon, Maurice, ed. *No Author Better Served: The Correspondence of Samuel Beckett and Alan Schneider*. Cambridge, MA: Harvard University Press, 1998.

Haynes, John, and James Knowlson. *Images of Beckett*. Cambridge: Cambridge University Press, 2003.

Hornung, Erik, and Betsy M. Bryan. Prologue. *The Quest for Immortality: Treasures of Ancient Egypt*. Ed. E. Hornung and B. Bryan. Washington, DC: National Gallery of Art, 2002. xi-xiv.

Jacq, Christian. *Pouvoir et sagesse selon l'Égypte ancienne*. Paris: XO Éditions, 2003.

Kant, Immanuel. *Critique of Practical Reason*. 1788. Trans. Thomas Kingsmill Abbott. Vol. 42, Great Books of the Western World. Ed. Maynard Hutchins. Chicago: Encyclopedia Britannica, 1952.

Karmitz, Marin. Interview with Elisabeth Lebovici. *Comédie*. By Marin Karmitz and Samuel Beckett. Paris: Éditions du Regard, 2001. 70–76.

Knowlson, James. *Damned to Fame: The Life of Samuel Beckett*. New York: Simon, 1996.

Lawley, Paul. "Beckett's Dramatic Counterpoint: A Reading of *Play*." *Journal of Beckett Studies* 9 (1984): 25–41.

———. "Counterpoint, Absence and the Medium in Beckett's *Not I*." *Modern Drama* 26 (1983): 407–14.

Moorjani, Angela. *Abysmal Games in the Novels of Samuel Beckett*. Chapel Hill: University of North Carolina Press, 1982.

Nixon, Mark. "Becketts *German Diaries* der Deutschlandreise 1936/37." Trans. Sabine Klewe. *Der unbekannte Beckett: Samuel Beckett und die deutsche Kultur*. Ed. Therese Fischer-Seidel and Marion Fries-Dieckmann. Frankfurt: Suhrkamp, 2005. 21–63.

Pountney, Rosemary. *Theatre of Shadows: Samuel Beckett's Drama 1956–1976*. Gerrards Cross, UK: Colin Smythe, 1998.

Rank, Otto. *The Trauma of Birth*. 1924. New York: Brunner, 1957.

Wilenski, Reginald H. *Dutch Painting*. New York: Beechhurst, 1955. Rev. ed. of *Introduction to Dutch Painting*. 1929.

Winnicott, Donald W. *Playing and Reality*. 1971. New York: Routledge, 1989.

Worth, Katharine. *Samuel Beckett's Theatre: Life Journeys*. Oxford: Oxford University Press, 1999.

Beckett's Romanticism

ENOCH BRATER

i.

THE BECKETT CENTENARY offers us the rare opportunity to consider not only the richness of his literary legacy but also the dynamics of the daunting critical response to his work. As the present volume illustrates, that work itself has proved to be remarkably resilient, surviving at long last the onslaught of the new critics with their careful and ingenious close readings; the ambitious poststructuralists who followed in their wake; scrupulous biographers and others much less so; intertextualists, postmodernists, formalists, feminists; historicists both old and new; as well as other well-trained theorists inspired by nothing less than wholesale deconstruction (a note of caution here: even a bold thinker like Herbert Blau wondered if it was finally possible to deconstruct Beckett,[1] the Frenchified Irishman posing as some sort of Jacques Derrida *avant la lettre*—or more likely, especially to my way of thinking, it's the other way around). As a result of so much attention from the academic community, what Ruby Cohn aptly calls "*a* Beckett canon"[2] (her emphasis as well as mine) has been no stranger to the critical gamut—and, especially in a landmark year like 2006, that is indeed "to put it mildly."[3] But in this essay my thoughts turn back to an event that took place a quarter of a century ago, the symposium entitled "Samuel Beckett: Humanistic Perspectives" organized by Morris Beja, S. E. Gontarski, and Pierre Astier at Ohio State University in Columbus in May 1981.

I do so not only for reasons of purposeful nostalgia, a yearning to be back where several of the essayists whose work appears in this collection once were (ah "...Once!..."),[4] but rather to emphasize what academic conferences, when they work, do best: offer us a forum for the exchange of ideas, as well as a site to introduce new approaches we might not have considered in precisely the same way before. What better way to find an antidote for "habit" as "a great deadener."[5] And as often happens at such venues, some of the most fruitful discussions take place not in formal sessions but casually and spontaneously, around a dinner table.

I recall one evening in particular: surrounded by Martin Esslin, Edith Kern, Rubin Rabinovitz, Porter Abbott, and Hersh Zeifman, among a few others, I ventured something about "Beckett's romanticism." I had been thinking about the recently published *Company*, the subject of my lecture earlier that same day;[6] *Rockaby*, whose premiere I saw in Buffalo a month before; and the just-performed *Ohio Impromptu*, which the playwright wrote especially for the occasion. Reluctant at the time to dig in my heels—my idea at the time was merely impressionistic—I remained unusually quiet when I was soundly called to task for such a "soft," "sentimental"—even "grotesque"—map of misreading.

I wondered then. And I wonder even more so twenty-five years later.

As we now recognize, Beckett's fiction and drama are susceptible, of course, to a variety of discourses, and to an even richer ensemble of moods and sometimes surprising textures. Not one of them seems to me more definitive than some others; his text takes wing only when we surrender ourselves to the reverie of holding as many of them in our head at the same time. It is rather like reading Chekhov. And in this "case nought,"[7] the humbler the critic is, the better.

Beckett's earliest confrontations with his own romantic impulse, for example, are the center of considerable disruption and unease as they display the adamancy of a beginner. There's an awful lot of textual anxiety. And here parody, though clearly a mask, serves him well. Not for the young author of "Walking Out," one of the short stories published in *More Pricks than Kicks*, the tempting delusions of "The Lake Isle of Innisfree" by "the Nobel Yeats";[8] even in the 1938 *Murphy*, far "less Wordsworthy," escape means "chaos" and "superfine chaos" means "gas."[9] Such strategic diversions continue even in the trilogy, and most notably in *Molloy*, where Gaber/Youdi's flamboyant colonization of "life" as "a thing of beauty and a joy forever" is the vain subject of comic deflation, though piercing all the same: "Do you think he meant human life?"[10] Such a corrupt figuration of "Endymion," turned as it is on its head, is not, however, necessarily absolute; something—a part—of the youthful Keats remains. That "trace," too long ignored, according to C. J. Ackerley and S. E. Gontarski, is beginning to show signs of a remarkable resilience. And as Philip Laubach-Kiani argues, that romantic discourse is very much a part of what makes "Beckett the [quintessential] 'European.'" Yet how Beckett liberates himself from parody to confront his own "profounds of mind" is a story still waiting to be told.[11]

ii.

Beckett's fiction might seem at first glance an odd place to look for this transformation. Yet even in the pre-trilogy fiction that depends very much on where one is looking and what one is looking for. The brashly overwritten *Dream of Fair to Middling Women,* always on the verge of being toppled by the sheer weight of its allusive name-dropping, and the far more austere *More Pricks than Kicks* that follows appear to have left romanticism at least one century behind. *Murphy,* too, has its broken-down heart located elsewhere: it is hard to find transcendence in scenes set in seedy West Brompton or the lavatory of the Irish Abbey Theatre, Oscar Wilde notwithstanding. But *Watt,* the novel Beckett wrote in Roussillon in the south of France when he was hiding out from the Nazis, is another matter. This four-part invention, part Faulkner, part New Testament, turns narrative certainty on its head as its central figure, the "long wet dream with the hat and bags,"[12] is on a futile journey to find nothing less than "home." Postmodern nostalgia is surely one way to account for this.[13] But even Beckett's nuances have nuances: *isn't it romantic?* Molloy's quest may be similarly motivated and similarly imperiled; only in his case he ends up in a ditch.

Beckett's trilogy fiction, *Molloy, Malone Dies,* and *The Unnamable,* is determined, however, to take us elsewhere. Part of the intrigue of this fascinating enterprise lies in the way Beckett's storytellers work overtime (and over time) to find an authentic narrative voice—and he, that is Beckett, along with them. Even a half century or so after its composition it is still difficult for anyone seriously concerned with writing not to be impressed by the trilogy's remarkable achievement. Considerations of form, not the least of which is the form of the novel itself, become part of the breathless storytelling: in the beginning, as in the anxious middle and the richly symphonic end, is, as it always already was, the word. "You must go on, I can't go on, I'll go on," *The Unnamable*'s long-awaited terminus ad quem, [14] celebrates nothing so much as itself: the word—so to speak—given ample material flesh. Such romanticization of the word, and what it can be made to do on its busy journey to nowhere *in particular,* in this sense rivals Ulysses 1 (Homer) and *Ulysses* 2 (Joyce); it makes us think even more so of the heady triumphalism in "Ulysses" 3 (Tennyson): "to strive, to seek, to find, and not to yield."[15]

Tim Parks is quite right when he says that throughout Beckett's writing, despite the pyrotechnics, and most especially so in the trilogy, "we come across passages of haunting descriptive power in which we cannot help feeling the author has a considerable emotional investment."[16] "What tenderness in these little words, what savagery."[17] That emotional investment will take on a surprising romantic complexion in a second trilogy that begins with the composition of *Company.* In this eloquent work non-linearity is made linear as the malleability of time is as much a character as any other. Past and present frame each other, and each literally contextualizes the other. A voice comes to one in the dark, to one, moreover, on his back in the dark; and as it does so it gathers up fragments of memory with a force so strong that it seems that almost everything else might be annihilated.

Such determination to recapture the past, and to lyricize it this time so confidently in prose, demonstrates just how far Beckett's fiction has traveled from the posturing of its early beginnings. In this regard the trilogy that begins with *Molloy* and ends with *The Unnamable* serves a mediating function as a sort of clearinghouse for narrative bric-a-brac, "a little yes, a little no, enough to exterminate a regiment of dragoons" (20). It offers us, of course, many other things as well, including the opportunity to see how a moment from the past is shaped into words that will be before long reconfigured and reimagined in *Company:*

One day we were walking along the road, up a hill of extraordinary steepness, near home I imagine; my memory is full of steep hills, I get them confused. The sky is further away than you think, is it not, mama? It was without malice. I was simply thinking of all the leagues that separated me from it. She replied, to me her son, It is precisely as far away as it appears to be. She was right. But at the time I was aghast. I can still see the spot, opposite Tyler's gate. A market-gardener, he had only one eye and wore side-whiskers.[18]

The highly evocative passage from *Malone Dies* is quickly contaminated when a very different rhetoric uneasily but abruptly intrudes: "That's the idea, rattle on," as though the text needed to remind itself that it better not go too far in this direction. The beast, however, is not quite so easily tamed, for in Malone's very next line, "You could see the sea, the islands, the head-lands, the isthmuses, the coast stretching away to north and south and the crooked moles of the harbor." Embarrassed, perhaps, this self-censorer tries again: "My mother? Perhaps it was just another story, told me by some one who found it funny. The stories I was told, at one time! And all funny, not one not funny. In any case here I am back in the shit" (98).

By the time Beckett's mature fiction revisits the same moment some two decades later in *Company,* intercalations like this one have been care-fully erased. More secure in itself, the voice no longer needs or desires self-pity or self-laceration. What emerges in the process is a kind of ultimate liberation, a freedom to encounter the past without shying away from ro-mantic implications. The child is the father of man, *tout court.* And the text, reinvented, now speaks "voice verbatim,"[19] all gimmicks gone:

> You make ground in silence hand in hand through the warm still summer air. It is late afternoon and after some hundred paces the sun appears above the crest of the rise. Looking up at the blue sky and then at your mother's face you break the silence asking her if it is not in reality much more distant than it appears. The sky that is. The blue sky. Receiving no answer you mentally reframe your question and some hundred paces later look up at her face again and ask her if it does not appear much less distant than in reality it is. For some reason you could never fathom this question must have angered her exceedingly. For she shook off your little hand and made you a cutting retort you have never forgotten.[20]

Close readers of *Company* will be sure to notice how Beckett gives an easy rhythm to the voice of memory and a far more circumspect one to the voice of reason, then lets the two play off one another in vigorous counterpoint. That second voice, always commenting in "the state of faint uncertainty," edits and revises itself as it goes along, playing its assigned role as "Devised deviser devising it all for company" (11, 64). The voice of memory, on the other hand, displays no such trepidation:

> You stand on the tip of the high board. High above the sea. In it your father's upturned face. Upturned to you. You look down to the loved trusted face. He calls to you to jump. He calls, Be a brave boy. The red round face. The thick moustache. The greying hair. The swell sways it under and sways it up again. The far call again. Be a brave boy. Many eyes upon you. From the water and from the bathing place. (23–24)

Yet readers of Beckett's late fiction should not necessarily assume that the same elements on display in *Company* are the ones to be found with the same level of coordination in the works that follow. Beckett's romanticism, if it exists at all, is in every case nothing if not case specific. *Ill Seen Ill Said* and *Worstward Ho* are poised, moreover, in very different directions; and romantic elements will be far more difficult to pinpoint and specify. The former, for example, configures a highly suggestive landscape of mystery in which the individual remains isolated before the vastness of a cold and uncomprehending universe, as though the pathetic fallacy were rendered this time as truly pathetic. And though this might be read as a *Wuthering Heights* redux, 100,000 years later, nature itself, while not quite dead, appears both unresponsive and indifferent to "the farrago from eye to mind."[21] The situation is even more bleak in the ninety-seven paragraphs that constitute *Worstward Ho,* "Said nohow on." Here there is no meaning, at least none that can be found in any easily defined way; significance, yes—affects, authority, mystery, all singular and all unchanging. "A pox on void."[22]

iii.

Beckett's romanticism follows a very different trajectory in the theater. When, in *Krapp's Last Tape,* a machine invades his stage scenography, the same texture can be viewed from a slightly different angle; and this time, once again, the "angle" is no longer one of complete "immunity."[23] Still reluctant to give up on parody, even at times farce—this old drunk goes to Vespers and falls off a pew; he tells Fanny, that "bony old ghost of a whore," that he had "been saving up for her" all his life—Beckett's "Magee Monologue" nevertheless presupposes a world where nature, for one, has not necessarily "forgotten us." Consider, for a moment, one of this play's most famous passages:

> I said again I thought it was hopeless and no good going on, and she agreed, without opening her eyes. (*Pause.*) I asked her to look at me and after a few moments—(*pause*)—after a few moments she did, but the eyes just slits, because of the glare. I bent over her to get them in the shadow and they opened. (*Pause. Low.*) Let me in. (*Pause*). We drifted in among the flags and stuck. The way they went down, sighing before the stem! (*Pause.*) I lay down across her with my face in her breasts and my hand on her. We lay there without moving. But under us all moved, and moved us, gently, up and down, and from side to side.[24]

Just where, exactly, did that come from? Certainly not from the same place where the thirty-nine-year-old Krapp we hear on the same tape, "box...three...spool...five," concocted his pretentious Byronic "vision": that formulaic "crest of the wave" takes place in a dark landscape replete with "great granite rocks," "the foam flying up," and is illuminated by the perilous beam of a faraway "lighthouse"—not surprisingly, the most heroically romantic of isolated structures. So much "storm" and so much stress! The image is—how shall I put it?—a bit tired and, on Beckett's part, deliberately designed to be trite, a sure recipe for any author's *not* "getting known." No wonder Krapp has sold so few books.

James Knowlson, Beckett's most reliable biographer, has nonetheless linked Krapp's "vision at last" to the author's own moment of awareness, one that took place in his mother's room during one of his periodic visits to his family in Ireland.[25] Yet however much this fact satisfies a need to "historicize" Beckett's recognition that "darkness" would become the true inspiration for his work, such information tells us very little about what actually happens in the play, where that "moment" is transferred to the ferry wharf at Dun Laoghaire. When Krapp listens to himself on the tape he made almost thirty years before, almost as though the past was pausing on its way toward oblivion, his attitude is anything but honorific; and Beckett, moreover, is not Krapp.

Defying time, but soon undone by it, Krapp keeps winding his tape back, and back again, to the lyrical passage on the punt quoted at some length earlier in this essay. He approaches this set piece almost as he might another character; and Beckett allows him to do so in a profoundly literary manner. Through the will and force of his own subjectivity, Krapp yearns to be in silent dialogue with it again, to hear from it once more, and then again once more. As do we, the members of this play's captive audience. Each time the act of listening, both Krapp's but ours as well, is effectively called into question.[26] Frozen, so to speak, on magnetic recording tape (despite my questionable metaphor), the lines are always the same; yet as the tape winds backward, then forward, then backward once again, we hear them as different ("We know it by heart," as a later text will have it, "and yet the pang is ever new").[27] Such secure placement and *replacement* and *displacement* in the text—these lines will prepare us, too, for the play's closure—guarantee their privileged position in the emerging soundscape, making a much-used term like "overdetermined" seem like an understatement.

Certainly the image of a love long lost is one of the more familiar tropes of a heterosexual, male-centered romantic fantasy; only in death can the female figure live fully. Yeats, in particular, can be spectacular on this point, as Beckett well knew when he relied on "The Tower" for the controlling metaphor he used with so much dramatic authority in . . . *but the clouds*. . . . Here is Yeats:

> Does the imagination dwell the most
> Upon a woman won or a woman lost?
> If on the lost, admit you turned aside
> From a great labyrinth out of pride,
> Cowardice, some silly over-subtle thought
> Or anything called conscience once;
> And that if memory recur, the sun's
> Under eclipse and the day blotted out.[28]

Krapp's "woman lost," like Yeats's, never stood much of a chance anyway, reduced as she is in both cases to mythic figuration, objectification, and invention—one more "dark lady," one more "belle dame sans merci," one more Mona Lisa smile (in Beckett's . . . *but the clouds* . . . she's reduced to a mere scrim). Her image is, nonetheless, all that "remains of all [Krapp's] misery": "A girl in a shabby green coat, on a railway-station platform." Well, and something else too, perhaps, despite the narcissism and the arrogant masculinist egocentricity: the ingenuity and genuine grandeur of haunting lines that finally put to rest what has been shown to be in performance a truly compelling drama.

> Here I end this reel. Box—(*pause*)—three, spool—(*pause*)—five. (*Pause.*) Perhaps my best years are gone. When there was a chance of happiness. But I wouldn't want them back. Not with the fire in me now. No, I wouldn't want them back.

> Krapp motionless staring before him. The tape runs on in silence.

> CURTAIN (28)

Why does this ending work as forcefully on us as it does? Perhaps because in this play Krapp, the so-called hero, is its self-inflicted victim; he is also an ambiguous figure who sits apart from the action, thinking about it. Isolated and alone, and with the requisite hint of dementia vying with moments of heartrending lucidity, he is sometimes grandly stoical, at other moments far less so. Forcing himself to remember, to remember—to memorialize and reimagine a past that can be brought back only in words—he is simultaneously wistful and forgetful. And in this troubled and willful blurring of time present and time past, his participation in the drama, oddly enough, is anything but tentative.

Beckett's deliberate staging of a man with a recording machine allows him to exploit the rich dynamics of a highly efficient framing device. Crude by today's supremacist standards of electronic intervention (even the cassettes Beckett later uses in his television play *Ghost Trio* are now horribly out of date), Krapp's bulky tape recorder is nonetheless an effective instrument for keeping romanticism in check. The machine, clumsy player that it is, is also the stage prop that ironizes and particularizes it. Without its inspired intrusions, its nerve-wrenching switching on and off, its cruel and fateful midsentence rewindings—grinding away so harshly at "lies like truth"[29]—even the erotic evocation of the girl in the punt might be rendered as agonizingly absurd. For by the time Beckett comes along, his late-modernist audience is no longer willing to take such "splendour in the grass" raw.[30] Postmodernist before it was quite ready to call itself *post-*, Beckett finds in Krapp's machine, awkward though it may be, the potential to give technology a human face—and a tender one at that—where we may have least expected to find it. And as he does so he discovers his principal means to rechannel and reposition a romantic impulse that is anything but sentimental.

That is making a rather large claim for Beckett, but the proof of it will come in the late, great works he designed for the stage and the mechanical media. In complex dramas like *That Time, Footfalls,* and *Rockaby,* Beckett displays just how much he has learned about "the sound of the human voice" and "its power to evoke an entire world."[31] He did so before, in the radio play *All That Fall,* but it is not until *Krapp's Last Tape* that the recorded voice and the seated figure of the actor on stage develop such a convincing pas de deux. Part of the affective nature of this elegant duet depends on the coordination of technology with live stage action, without which the dramatic tension cannot take place. In the plays for television that date from the same general period, that tension and that conflict will become even more vigorous and precise. Working with expert technicians like Jim Lewis, first at the BBC and later at Süddeutscher Rundfunk (SDR),[32] Beckett showed himself to be a sensitive collaborator, especially when questions of rhythm, harmony, color (or its conspicuous absence), atmosphere, and the structure and spirit of the piece demanded a heightened sense of the camera's vulnerability to the coordination of recorded sound with light, movement, and meaning. What emerges, especially in highly lyricized pieces like *Nacht und Träume, ... but the clouds...,* and *Ghost Trio,* is nothing less than the evocation of intensely realized romantic images, all the more compelling because of their technological discipline and proficiency. Nor is that steady reliance on (in this case) televisual machinery absent from the eye and ear of the viewer: "Mine is a faint voice. Kindly tune accordingly. [...] Having seen that specimen of floor you have seen," rectangularly, "it all."[33]

Much of what I am trying to argue in this essay will depend, as we might expect, on the instance of performance, how directors and especially actors respond to Beckett and to Beckett's intrusive but intuitive romanticism. "Play the line" is a mantra always worth repeating when staging such complicated texts; but what to do with that line when it has, at times, a decidedly romantic edge? How it works and why it works—and *if* it works—will only come through in the theater. Those competing moments of pathos (or is it simultaneously bathos?), for instance, box three, spool five's "Her moments, my moments. [...] The dog's moments," only serve to render that romantic impulse even more cauterizing, as Krapp-at-sixty-nine, "all to end," learns at his peril. "This is what we call making an exit."[34]

Beckett actors have responded to this challenge differently: Pat Magee, for whom the piece was written, with a baritone of verbal nuance; a burly Jack MacGowran with sweaty determination; the great Canadian player Donald Davies with enviable understanding of the work's opposing moods and alternating inflections; a thin, pale, gaunt, and frail-seeming John Hurt, by holding the illusion of vexed interiority confronting the tragedy of failing memory on a darkened stage; Hume Cronyn by allowing silence to have its persuasive say; and Pierre Chabert, who appreciated the rich pun on the play's French title, *La dernière bande,* by emphasizing the translation's other double entendres. (I omit Giancarlo Canteruccio's 1996 rendering of *L'ultimo nastro di Krapp* featuring two desks and two Krapps at the Teatro Krypton in Scandicci, but share with the reader of this essay my confusion by citing Malone's response to Sucky Moll's earrings: "Why two Christs?" implying that one was more than enough—besides, as "the reader will remember," Christ was in her mouth.)[35]

Beckett's romanticism may be, as these strong actors might be the first to recognize, just a lot of crap (with a small *c*); but, as their expert illumination of the multiple dramas in the text seems to indicate, it is also a great deal of Krapp (in this case with a very big *K*): that seedy old figure of a drunk whose tense interactions with magnetic recording tape have the potential to disarm us so unexpectedly—so poignantly, too, just as Beckett's fiction has done—in this solo performance event (not so solo after all) we consider perhaps too prosaically as *Krapp's Last Tape.*

In the Beckett canon, as drama and fiction unfold, they energize and illuminate one another; and those "traces blurs signs"[36] of a not always latent romanticism are yet one more way in which they seek so passionately—so convincingly, too—to do so.

Notes

1. See Herbert Blau, *Sails of the Herring Fleet: Essays on Beckett* (Ann Arbor: University of Michigan Press, 2000).

2. Ruby Cohn, *A Beckett Canon* (Ann Arbor: University of Michigan Press, 2001).

3. Samuel Beckett, *Footfalls, The Collected Shorter Plays of Samuel Beckett* (New York: Grove, 1984) 243; abbreviated as *Plays.*

4. Samuel Beckett, *Endgame* (New York: Grove, 1958) 17.

5. Samuel Beckett, *Waiting for Godot* (New York: Grove, 1954) 58b.

6. See Enoch Brater, "The *Company* Beckett Keeps: The Shape of Memory and One Fablist's Decay of Lying," *Samuel Beckett: Humanistic Perspectives,* ed. Morris Beja, S. E. Gontarski, and Pierre Astier (Columbus: Ohio State University Press, 1983) 157–71.

7. Samuel Beckett, *. . . but the clouds . . . , Plays* 261.

8. Samuel Beckett, "Walking Out," *More Pricks than Kicks* (London: Calder, 1970) 114.

9. Samuel Beckett, *Murphy* (New York, Grove, 1957) 8, 20, 106.

10. Samuel Beckett, *Molloy* (New York: Grove, 1955) 226.

11. See C. J. Ackerley and S. E. Gontarski, *The Grove Companion to Samuel Beckett* (New York: Grove, 2004) 487; and Philip Laubach-Kiani, "'I Close My Eyes and Try and Imagine Them': Romantic Discourse Formations in *Krapp's Last Tape,*" *Beckett the European,* ed. Dirk Van Hulle (Tallahassee, FL: Journal of Beckett Studies Books, 2005) 125–36. For "profounds of mind," see Samuel Beckett, *Ohio Impromptu, Plays* 288.

12. Samuel Beckett, *Watt* (New York: Grove, 1959) 246.

13. For useful discussions relating to this point, see Eyal Amiran, *Wandering and Home: Beckett's Metaphysical Narrative* (University Park: Pennsylvania State University Press, 1993); and Richard Begam, *Samuel Beckett and the End of Modernity* (Stanford, CA: Stanford University Press, 1996).

14. Samuel Beckett, *The Unnamable* (New York: Grove, 1958) 179.

15. See the last line of Alfred Tennyson's "Ulysses" (1833) in *Major British Writers,* ed. G. B. Harrison, vol. 2 (New York: Harcourt, 1959) 395.

16. See Tim Parks, "Beckett: Still Stirring," *New York Review of Books* 13 July 2006: 24.

17. Beckett, *Molloy* 112.

18. Samuel Beckett, *Malone Dies* (New York: Grove, 1956) 98.

19. On the question of the "voice verbatim," see Charles Krance, ed., *Samuel Beckett's "Company/Compagnie" and "A Piece of Monologue/Solo": A Bilingual Variorum Edition* (New York: Garland, 1993) 189–94.

20. Samuel Beckett, *Company* (London: Calder, 1980) 12–13.

21. Samuel Beckett, *Ill Seen Ill Said* (New York: Grove, 1981) 40.

22. Samuel Beckett, *Worstward Ho* (New York: Grove, 1983) 43, 47.

23. Samuel Beckett, *Film, Plays* 169.

24. Samuel Beckett, *"Krapp's Last Tape" and Other Dramatic Pieces* (New York: Grove, 1958) 22–23, 27.

25. James Knowlson, *Damned to Fame: The Life of Samuel Beckett* (New York: Simon, 1996) 318–19.

26. See Bernard Beckerman, "Beckett and the Act of Listening," *Beckett at 80/Beckett in Context,* ed. Enoch Brater (New York: Oxford University Press, 1986) 149–67.

27. Samuel Beckett, *Rough for Radio II, Plays* 115.

28. W. B. Yeats, "The Tower," *The Collected Poems of W. B. Yeats*, ed. Peter Allt and Russell K. Alspach (New York: Macmillan, 1966) 195.

29. William Shakespeare, *Macbeth* V.v.43.

30. See William Wordsworth, "Ode: Intimations of Immortality from Recollections of Early Childhood," *English Romantic Writers,* ed. David Perkins (New York: Harcourt, 1967) 282.

31. See Alan Schneider, *Entrances: An American Director's Journey* (New York: Viking, 1986) 269.

32. See Enoch Brater, *Beyond Minimalism: Beckett's Late Style in the Theater* (New York: Oxford University Press, 1987) 107, 109, 160–64.

33. Samuel Beckett, *Ghost Trio, Plays* 248.

34. See Samuel Beckett, "Stirrings Still," *Samuel Beckett: The Complete Short Prose, 1929–1989,* ed. S. E. Gontarski (New York: Grove, 1995) 265; and *Endgame* 81.

35. *Malone Dies* 93; and *Footfalls, Plays* 242.

36. Samuel Beckett, "Ping," *Complete Short Prose* 193.

Film and *Film*

Beckett and Early Film Theory

MATTHIJS ENGELBERTS

ECKETT AND CINEMA: the topic means paying close attention to his *Film*, a work whose very title indicates reflexivity. Beckett's well-known 1963 screenplay and the somewhat less well-known 1964 film (directed by Alan Schneider and starring the nearly seventy-year-old Buster Keaton) have been extensively commented on—for instance, by Gilles Deleuze, who in his famous *Cinema 1,* so admirably steeped in film history, applies an analysis to *Film* that allows him to state: "the directions and the schemas that [Beckett] gives himself, and the moments that he distinguishes in his film, only go half-way towards disclosing his intention" (67). After this very masterful lesson—Deleuze disclosing a writer's true "intention"!—he analyzes *Film* using his theoretical framework ("action-image," "perception-image," "affection-image").[1] To be sure; but it is worthwhile to reposition—and at the outset—*Film* in the theoretical context that gave birth to it. This theory is obviously in the first place Berkeley's philosophy, given the epigraph *Esse est percipi* the film project borrowed from the Irish philosopher and on which the majority of commentaries focus. But there is another philosophy that marks the only cinematographic work published by Beckett: the philosophy of film or, more specifically, the first theories of cinema that tried to transform this technical intruder into an art worthy to hold its own against the other muses—or to surpass them, if we are to believe Eisenstein, who refers to "art in the specific example of its highest form—film" (*Film Form* 48). Unlike what one might be tempted to believe, however, the writings of Eisenstein do not seem to constitute the primary groundwork of *Film*. I believe Beckett's scenario can be situated above all as a sequel to early modernist film theory *in general,* as represented by Rudolf Arnheim, for instance, in his book *Film als Kunst,* first published in Germany in 1932. An English translation appeared in 1933 under the title *Film,* which is no doubt the edition Beckett read in the thirties.

My purpose is to show, to the extent possible, to what degree *Film*—both Beckett's scenario and the 1964 film he helped shape—is a continuation of the modernist theory of cinema that was formulated in different countries at the end of the 1920s and the beginning of the 1930s, and of which Arnheim is a representative figure. There is more to consider than the obvious facts that *Film* is an—almost—silent movie starring an actor known from the silent era and that the action takes place around 1929. The relationship between Beckett's *Film* and early cinema theory has not been examined in any precise manner in spite of the valuable commentaries of critics who have drawn attention to Beckett's reading in the area of film theory,[2] and in spite of Jay Leyda's discovery of the letter Beckett wrote to Eisenstein in 1936 requesting admission to the Moscow State School of Cinematography (Leyda 59).

Silent Film in Black and White

In 1936, more than twenty-five years before writing his only cinematographic scenario, Beckett is reading books and articles on cinema written by the Soviet directors Vsevolod Pudovkin and Sergei Eisenstein and the theorist of German origin Rudolf Arnheim. In January of that year he writes in a letter to Thomas MacGreevy: "I borrowed a lot of works on cinema [. . .]: Pudovkin, Arnheim & back numbers of Close Up with stuff by Eisenstein. How I would like to go to Moscow and work under Eisenstein for a year."[3] Around a week later we find a theory that is surprisingly advanced for someone who is just beginning to study cinema, even if the individual in question has already formed a desire to pursue his studies under Eisenstein:

> What I would like to learn under a person like Pudovkin is how to handle a camera, the higher lines of the editing bench, and so on [. . .]. It is interesting that *Becky Sharp* in colour, which I think had a long run in London, was a complete flop here and was taken off at the Savoy after three days and not transferred to any other

house. That does not encourage any hope that the industrial film will become so completely naturalistic in stereoscopic colour and gramophonic sound, that a backwater may be created for the two-dimensional silent film that had barely emerged from its rudiments when it was swamped. Then there would be two separate things and no question of a fight between them or rather of a rout.[4]

In this characteristic passage, Beckett is expressing a desire for the existence of two genres of film (an improbable situation, according to his judgment based on the short run of a single film in Dublin), or rather two wholly different cinematographies. One would be realistic to the utmost degree, thanks to technical advances that would permit the addition of sound to image and render the image in stereoscopic color. This kind of cinema, inevitably "industrial" because of the technology necessary to make it possible, would dominate the cinematic landscape. But there would also be a second genre of cinema, silent and monoscopic; without explicitly saying so, the letter suggests that this nonindustrial, nonrealistic genre would give cinema the chance to become something more than commercial and realistic entertainment.

This idea was far from unusual in the thirties. In his book *Film als Kunst,* Arnheim devotes the beginning of the fourth and final section to the issue of the introduction of sound to cinema, a subject he often discussed. Here are his opening lines:

> The technical development of the motion picture will soon carry the mechanical imitation of nature to an extreme. The addition of sound was the first obvious step in this direction. The [...] best film artists [...] were engaged in working out an explicit and pure style of silent film, using its restrictions to transform the peep show into an art. The introduction of sound film smashed many of the forms that the film artists were using in favor of the inartistic demand for the greatest possible "naturalness" [...]. The development of the silent film was arrested possibly forever when it had hardly begun to produce good results; but it has left us with a few splendidly mature films. (154/283)[5]

Beckett, for his part, tried in 1963 to redirect this technical and artistic evolution by proposing a new kind of film that was very consciously *silent*—along the lines called for by Arnheim, to which Beckett had probably already adhered in 1936 when he read *Film* in the first English translation.

Let us recall briefly why Arnheim and other authors of the 1920s and 1930s are opposed to the introduction of sound. For Arnheim, cinema is an art because it is *not* a mechanical production of reality: "Art begins where mechanical reproduction leaves off" (57/69). From this point of view, the fact that the screen is a flat surface, and thus does not permit the same effects of depth that three-dimensional space provides, and the fact that the field is restricted by the lens of the camera (as compared with the eye) are to the advantage of cinematographic art. Since reality is subjected to the space-time continuum, the leaps in time and space that montage allows are yet another pillar of the aesthetic character of cinema for Arnheim. Further, the absence of color in black-and-white cinema benefits cinema as *art,* as does the absence of sound, with Arnheim emphasizing early in his book "the potentialities of silent film, even since the introduction of sound" (33/38). For Arnheim, cinema is above all a *visual* art, the result of the artistic use of a new medium that consists of image and movement captured by the camera and projected on the big screen. In short, he insists on an art *in general* that does not merely reproduce reality, and he defends a *cinematographic art* that by its specifically visual nature sets itself apart from the word-based literary and dramatic arts. From this point of view, the danger sound poses for cinema is that it threatens the specificity of cinematographic art, for example, by reducing cinema to a technique for recording theatrical works.

It is well known that Arnheim was far from the only theoretician to exhibit hostility toward the replacement of silent film by the talkie. In their famous "Statement on Sound," first published in a German translation in 1928 and published the same year in the journal *Close Up* (issues of which Beckett borrowed), Eisenstein, Pudovkin, and Alexandrov make known their position regarding talking pictures, which at that time had not yet been introduced into the Soviet Union. The declaration aims at giving a warning about the "incorrect direction" of the evolution of cinema. For the three authors the combination of sound and image, while promising in itself, threatens to compromise the development of cinematographic art: "Sound is a double-edged invention and its most probable application will be along the line of least resistance, i.e., in the field of the *satisfaction of simple curiosity.*" They are especially concerned about the "unimaginative" use of sound "for 'dramas of high culture' and other photographed presentations of a theatrical order" (Eisenstein, *Writings* 113–14; emphasis in the original).[6] Eisenstein, Pudovkin, and Alexandrov are, however, clearly less negative than Arnheim with regard to sound cinema. Their recommended solution bears the undeniable mark of Eisenstein's theory of contrapuntal montage: "*Only the contrapuntal use* of sound vis-à-vis the visual fragment will open up new possibilities for the development and perfection of montage" (114; emphasis in the original). Clearly, Eisenstein's position[7] is less reticent than Arnheim's; however, he and his co-pamphleteers, exactly like Arnheim, emphasize the importance of the visual in cinematography: "Contemporary cinema [i.e., silent film], operating through visual images, has a powerful effect on the individual and rightfully occupies one of the leading positions in the ranks of the arts" (113).

Another aspect of Beckett's *Film* corresponds remarkably to the theory of cinema proposed by Arnheim and other theorists: the absence of color. This aspect was so self-evident for Beckett that the published screenplay carries no explicit mention of this characteristic, unlike the laconic notice "The film is entirely silent" (163), as if in 1963 it would be impossible to envisage a silent film in color.[8] But it is obviously no accident that Beckett situates the action of *Film* "around 1929," as if he agreed with Walter Benjamin according to whom remarkable phenomena, especially formal ones, occur during periods of transition when a new medium is coming into existence. It is worth noting that Benjamin's essay "The Work of Art in the Age of Mechanical Reproduction" dates from the same year that Beckett became interested in film theorists. It is therefore self-evident for Beckett that *Film* would be made in black and white; by the same token, it is beyond a doubt for Arnheim that color threatens the artistic character of cinema as much as sound does: "What will the color film have to offer when it reaches technical perfection? We know what we shall lose artistically by abandoning the black-and-white film. Will color ever allow us to achieve a similar compositional precision, a similar independence of 'reality'?" (154–55/284). Beckett's *Film* constitutes a response, silent of course, to this rhetorical question of the 1930s.

The Close-Up

The third focal point of early cinema theory that is of interest with respect to *Film* is the close-up. This term as such appears only two times in the published text of the screenplay, in the English version at least; these instances can be found in the last part, which takes place in the room and represents in fact more than half of the film according to Beckett's indications in the screenplay: "close up of parrot's eye," "close-up of fish's eye" (167–68; hyphen used inconsistently). To these conspicuous extreme close-ups, the French version adds: "Gros plan des mains crispées dans l'effort" (125), whereas the English has only "straining hands." There are thus only two or three close-ups specified as such; but in fact, the third and final part of *Film* taken as a whole alternates between close-ups, or medium close-ups (mostly called "images" in the scenario), and long or medium shots (it is difficult to establish a firm distinction between these last two terms in a room of limited size like the one where the action of the third part takes place). Hence, frequent close-ups (or medium close-ups): in effect O's (the object's) perception consists of close shots, as will E's (the eye's) perception later on. These shots will often enough be veritable close-ups in each production of *Film* that follows the screenplay on this point. The most frequent example in the text is the "[i]nsistent image of curiously carved headrest" of the rocking chair (167), mentioned more than five times in the short screenplay. However, the most remarkable close-up, a shot that is undeniably the pivotal point of Beckett's only exclusively cinematographic work, is the "very first image (face only, against ground of tattered wall)" of E that appears at the end of the film (169). In the version directed by Alan Schneider, with Beckett present to oversee the production and to counsel the team, there is, at first, not a close-up in the strict sense at this moment, but a medium shot (cut at half-length) followed by a close-up after a reverse shot of O. This American version of *Film* is, moreover, framed by a very particular and pronounced use of the technique of the close-up, since it begins and ends with a single, screen-filling eye that opens and closes.[9] It is a very striking effect, and an extremely rare close-up in the history of cinema, even if it is compared quite often to the sliced eyeball in Luis Buñuel's *Un chien andalou,* which is nevertheless filmed very differently.[10] In short, the use of the close-up in *Film* is not only relatively frequent, but this technique plays a determining role because it is most often applied to the gaze and the eye, especially E's. His look expresses in effect "acute *intentness*" (169; italics in text), which has a profound effect on O and the other characters: hence, the final close-up in the screenplay reveals the sense of the gaze of the camera in *Film* and represents the paroxysm of O's anguished experience.

The close-up occupies an equally prominent place in the theory of cinema at the end of the 1920s and the beginning of the 1930s, as the very title of the journal *Close Up* demonstrates. *Close Up* is still today the best-known journal of the period in the British world and perhaps even in the Anglo-Saxon sphere. During this period close-ups were in effect quite generally seen as the shots that were most characteristic of the new art. Pudovkin, for example, writes in 1926, in a book first published in English in 1929:

> [T]he more clearly our investigating glance examines an object, the more details we perceive and the more limited and sectional becomes our view. [...] The particular, the detail, will always be a synonym of intensification. It is upon this that the strength of the film depends, that its characteristic speciality is the possibility of giving a clear, especially vivid representation of detail. The power of filmic representation lies in the fact that, by means of the camera, it continually strives to penetrate as deeply as possible, to the mid-point of every image. The camera, as it were, forces itself, ever striving, into the profoundest deeps of life; it strives thither to penetrate, whither the average spectator never reaches as he glances casually around him. (90–91)

For Pudovkin, the camera is a force that penetrates into the depth of life, in its "profoundest deeps": these terms might seem for us an apt description of both the technical and the dramatic structure of the astonishing screenplay that is *Film*.

During the same period, other authors of theoretical texts, as much as if not more than Pudovkin, make the close-up one of the essential characteristics, or even the characteristic par excellence, of cinema. Arnheim states: "The true virtue of the delimited image appears from the 'close-up'" (79/88). A few years earlier, Béla Balász, an author of Hungarian origin who wrote his theoretical works in German, devotes a chapter to the close-up in each of his two books on cinema theory. In 1924, he insists that the close-up is what makes cinema a new art form and emphasizes that in a good film the decisive moment is never shown in a long shot (83). To which Beckett replies, less dogmatically but nevertheless approvingly: "close-up of fish's eye," before finally revealing the face of the actor who plays the leading role.

Stereoscopic/Monoscopic Film

Some specific topics that were debated in early cinema theory do not seem to be reconsidered in Beckett's *Film,* for instance (Eisensteinian) montage (cf. Antoine-Dunne). A subject that is much less often mentioned today is, however, surprisingly foregrounded and merits a brief discussion: it is the theme of monoscopy as it appears in the final images. The supposed eventual evolution of cinema toward the *stereoscopic* film is a recurring subject in writings on cinematography in the 1920s and 1930s. The fact that the main character in *Film* wears a patch over his left eye can of course be interpreted in different ways (the photos O looks at in his rocking chair suggest he lost an eye in World War I); but it is clear from a cinematographic angle, which is obviously pertinent in the case of *Film,* that the single eye also hints at the single camera lens, a device that brings about the need to produce by other means the depth of field that stereoscopic vision allows. In this case, for once, the evolution of cinema did not proceed in the direction predicted by early film theorists, for whom sound, color, and stereoscopic cinema were in general considered as inevitable if, for some, regrettable, developments. Cinema has remained monoscopic, and Beckett alludes to this characteristic, which received little theoretical attention after the early period of film theory. The eye that follows the actor, the relentless eye of an enigmatic viewer—a viewer like the one in the movie theater, pushed by his scopic desire—an eye that follows the character up to the room where he believes he is able to escape all observation and to isolate himself from the common visual desire, that eye does not only coincide with the *character* who is being pursued. It is thus not only a double who brings on O's anguish, thanks to the monoscopic gaze that alone can reveal "the depths of life"—unlike the gaze of the characters with two eyes who also figure in the beginning of the screenplay. The single eye in *Film* is indeed also the eye of the new art to which the camera, that cinematographic engine that is so deliberately monoscopic in *Film,* has given birth. The themes of cinematography and self-perception are thus closely linked in *Film,* to instill into the cinema viewer that to want to *see* (a person, or perhaps a movie) is unavoidably to see *oneself* (to the extent possible),[11] and thus to know a reality one thought to have been able to escape, perhaps during the course of a film, by witnessing the arrival of a train in Ciotat station, a love story, or pursuit or fight scenes made in Paris, Hollywood, or Bombay. The camera of *Film* is a cinematographic and monoscopic machine as well as a one-eyed character: as a result, it seems to me, the convergence of *Film* and of modernist film theory of the first decades of cinema stands out only more clearly.

Coda

We can now move on to the conclusion and a brief coda (necessary to avoid making *Film* an overly stereoscopic double of modernist cinema theory). No, I do not believe that Beckett's *Film* is "the greatest Irish film," as Deleuze asserts—in his essay by that title—for the simple reason, apparently, that Beckett was of Irish origin, as was Berkeley. But if Berkeley is a great philosopher, is he also a philosopher with respect to whom one must emphasize that he was *Irish?* That is doubtful, except of course if one ventures to defend the thesis that perception and self-perception are eminently Irish themes. *Film,* the screenplay for which was written in France and the first version of which was filmed in New York, is, in any case, not in the first place a film that clearly foregrounds Irishness, and it does not seem to me to be a true homage to Beckett to call it so, whether jokingly or not (and if there is irony in Deleuze's title—or in his territorializing way of revealing Beckett's intention?—it is certainly not very conspicuous).[12] Beckett's scenario for *Film* is on the contrary a project that reworks early cinema theory, which presented itself as expressly international—even if the first source of inspiration often came from Soviet writings, which were, however, in turn explicitly international in their orientation. *Film* reconnects with a theory that was developed by practitioners and theorists of many countries, fascinated by the possibilities offered by the motion picture camera, but who at the same time ardently wished to transform the first sense of wonderment with this device into an articulate aesthetic position.

Early cinema theory was profoundly modernist, if by modernist we understand an aesthetic that seeks to distance itself from a concern with conformity to external reality and whose preoccupation with form results in a quest centered on the specificity of the medium and the art. In the case of *Film,* it is the specificity of the movie camera, that of the recording instrument whose images are intended to be projected on the big screen, that is indeed at stake. Beckett's master stroke is, obviously, that he anchors the formal search, directed along the lines laid out in the 1920s and 1930s, by adding a philosophical theme closely suited to the media conscious-ness of modernist research (if one forgives him for the fact that the result is perhaps somewhat schematic).[13] That theme is perception by the other and perception by the self that tie us to being, with the self remaining divided as the final images illustrate so insistently. The gaze of God be-comes Christ's becomes the suffering protagonist's, whose gaze requires him to become aware of a self that is not one: the face of "God the Father" "pinned to wall" (167) is in effect replaced later in *Film* by E, with "a big nail [...] visible near left temple" (169), who confronts O. The intricate construction that results from this conjunction of a philosophical theme of the first rank with a modernist media consciousness, even if it is without doubt overly constructed, gains in my opinion by being placed in the con-text of Beckett's use of early film theory and his lasting disposition toward cinematography.

A final nuance should, however, be added to the image of *Film* taking up some of the key elements of modernist cinema theory. Without pretend-ing that this is the only contrast between Beckett's screenplay and early cin-ematographic theory, we must insist on a difference that seems central and very characteristic of Beckett. The beginning of the published screenplay is well known: the Berkeleyan epigraph that *Film* replies to is followed by two reformulations, of which the second is the most notably Beckettian:

Esse est percipi.
   All extraneous perception suppressed, animal, human, divine, self-perception maintains in being.
   Search of non-being in flight from extraneous perception break-ing down in inescapability of self-perception. (163)

The words "breaking down" stand out in this context, just like the curious stumbling block that the *look* functions as in a cinematographic work. The "search of non-being" *fails,* and it fails because of *perception.* It is the gaze that makes the subject conscious of being and thus makes him suffer, as the pursuit of O throughout *Film* shows in such a perhaps obstinate manner.

We should indeed not forget what is at stake in the battle waged by the first theorists of "film as art": for them it is a struggle for emancipation whose objective is to prove that Charlie Chaplin has access to Parnassus, to speak with Eisenstein (*Writings* 29) and his coauthor Sergei Yutkevich.

This battle often takes the form of a hymn to the camera and a song of praise of moving images projected on the big screen. The early theory of cinema celebrates the gaze; it fetes the visual. This first excitement, this celebration is indisputably absent in Beckett. *Film* does not sing praises of the look. Certainly this work, as should be emphasized one last time, is marked by an acute consciousness of techniques available to the cinematographic media; and the conjunction of this use of filmic practices and of the cinematographic theory of the 1920s and 1930s is striking, as I hope to have shown. However, the thematic axis of *Film* makes this work a lament for the gaze, a *lamento* on the eye, an *enueg* of self-perception.

I obviously do not mean to say that *Film* denies the value of cinema in particular, or of so-called visual culture in general: the *lamento* does not in any way concern cinematographic art or visuality as such, and in this the screenplay is therefore not in opposition to the first theories of cinema. Only, the gaze in *Film* is not exclusively formal; the camera is not solely a cinematographic device. It is also the eye that creates being, in an instance of a self that is trying to see the self that is trying not to be seen.[14] *Film* is clearly a *lamento* on this gaze, and the cinematographic aesthetic here gives way on the screen to the theory of self-perception and being. End of the celebration of the gaze. In the face of the suffering that identifies him with a Christ, eyewitness to his own passion, what else is the figure to do but flee before the camera? Finally, what is there to do except for this gesture of O, so characteristic of the Beckettian universe and so *little* characteristic of early cinema theory: "He covers his face with his hands" (128). O and E: "I can't go on, I'll go on," as the Unnamable has it. One is tempted to evoke Œdipus tearing out his eyes once he learns who he is. Œdipus who is looking for himself without knowing it is he, like O with regard to whom the viewer does not know that he is pursuing himself in *Film*.[15] A half-Œdipus, then, blind in a single eye: it is curious to ascertain, thanks to this supplemental interpretation of the single eye of the character, at what point the monoscopic character of the camera combines with the "esse est percipi" revisited by Beckett: with a single eye one sees the world differently— better without a doubt—than with two. Œdipus whose initial Œ, quite unusual in both French and English, unites the O of "object/*objet*" and the E of "eye" to form the Œ of Œdipus and of *œil*. But all this relates to literature, in a sense, and takes us therefore far from the early theories of cinema that constitute the focus of this essay.

Notes

1. Critics of Deleuze's use of Beckett: Schwab 189–219, Lommel 343, Sweeney.

2. Knowlson (212–13) and others following him.

3. Letter of 29 Jan. 1936 (Correspondence with Thomas MacGreevy; this letter erroneously dated 1935). Without a doubt it concerns texts written *by* the authors cited by Beckett, not *about* these authors as Knowlson writes (212). Bair's earlier biography has "by and about" (204), which is followed by Bignell (40), who in 1999 still adheres to Bair's not altogether reliable presentation of the facts of Beckett's interest in cinema.

4. Letter of 6 Feb. [1936] to MacGreevy; the passage is cited partially in Knowlson 213. Surprisingly, Ackerman does not quote this letter in an article in which only few of the forty pages deal with what the title nonetheless calls the "flatness of *Film*."

5. In this essay I cite the text from the frequently reprinted 1957 edition, the 1933 first English edition being very rare. For the 1957 edition, Arnheim reviewed the translation of his book and deleted several sections. I indicate for each citation the page from the 1957 edition followed by the page from the first English edition, the terms of which are occasionally slightly different without affecting the meaning of the quotations I give.

6. The statement signed by the three Soviet authors was published in the October 1928 number of *Close Up*. The journal published another seven texts by Eisenstein spread over nine numbers between May 1929 and June 1933. Cf. Donald et al.

7. Or the author (Eisenstein) and his cosignatories (see Leyda 258). Cf. Pudovkin (171–73, 183–93) for his similar position.

8. Some films of this type were made at the time Beckett wrote his scenario or later by, for example, Paul Morrissey (1960s), Marcel Broodthaers (1970s), and Peter Sellars (1990s).

9. See Schneider 39.

10. E.g., Feshbach 345; Brater was without a doubt the first academic critic to make the comparison (76–77).

11. The place of the viewer in *Film* was discussed in academic criticism from the very first; see, among others, Perlmutter (91), still a very good analysis of *Film,* and Brater (79).

12. The Irish review *Film West* thus unsurprisingly heralds Deleuze as a critic who recognizes the "specifically Irish aspects" of *Film* (Waugh and Daly).

13. Some critics have expressed reservations about *Film's* success from an aesthetic (literary and/or cinematic) perspective (e.g., Perlmutter 83, Gontarski 135–36, and Dodsworth).

14. Beckett's phrase is "For one striving to see one striving not to be seen" (qtd. in Gontarski 129).

15. Note as well that the room is described, although this is of no use to the viewer of *Film,* as being that of the mother of the principal character. Beckett adds, it is true, realistic details that are not linked to the myth of Œdipus. Beckett's words about the room apply perfectly, however, to the case of Œdipus: "There is nothing in this place, this room, that

isn't prepared to trap him" (qtd. in Feshbach 349). The allusion to Œdipus was already briefly evoked in Perlmutter 83, 85.

Works Cited

Ackerman, Alan. "Samuel Beckett's *Spectres du noir:* The Being of Painting and the Flatness of *Film.*" *Comparative Literature* 44 (2003): 399–441.

Antoine-Dunne, Jean M. B. "Beckett and Eisenstein on Light and Contrapuntal Montage." *Samuel Beckett: Endlessness in the year 2000.* Vol. 11 of *SBT/A.* Ed. Angela Moorjani and Carola Veit. Amsterdam: Rodopi, 2001. 315–23.

Arnheim, Rudolf. *Film.* London: Faber, 1933.

———. *Film als Kunst.* Berlin: Rowohlt, 1932.

———. *Film as Art.* 1957. Berkeley: University of California Press, 1983.

Bair, Deirdre. *Samuel Beckett: A Biography.* New York: Harcourt, 1978.

Balász, Béla. "*Der sichtbare Mensch*": *Kritiken und Aufsätze 1922–1926.* Vol. 1 of *Schriften zum Film.* Munich: Hanser, 1982.

Beckett, Samuel. Correspondence with Thomas MacGreevy. Ms. 10402. Trinity College Dublin Library.

———. *Film. Collected Shorter Plays.* London: Faber, 1984. 161–74.

———. *Film. Comédie et actes divers.* Paris: Minuit, 1972. 111–34.

Bignell, Jonathan. "Questions of Authorship: Samuel Beckett and *Film.*" *Writing and Cinema.* Ed. Bignell. Harlow: Longman, 1999. 29–42.

Brater, Enoch. *Beyond Minimalism: Beckett's Late Style in the Theatre.* New York: Oxford University Press, 1987.

Deleuze, Gilles. *Cinema 1: The Movement-Image.* Trans. Hugh Tomlinson and Barbara Habberjam. 1986. Minneapolis: University of Minnesota Press, 1991.

———. "The Greatest Irish Film." Trans. Daniel W. Smith and Michael A. Greco. *Essays Critical and Clinical.* Minneapolis: University of Minnesota Press, 1997. 23–26.

Dodsworth, Martin. "*Film* and the Religion of Art." *Beckett the Shape Changer.* Ed. Katharine Worth. London: Routledge, 1975. 161–82.

Donald, James, Anne Friedberg, and Laura Marcus. *Close Up 1927–1933: Cinema and Modernism.* London: Cassell, 1998.

Eisenstein, Sergei M. *Film Form: Essays in Film Theory.* 1949. Ed. and trans. Jay Leyda. London: Dobson, 1951.

———. *Writings 1922–34.* Vol. 1 of *Selected Works.* Ed. and trans. Richard Taylor. London: BFI, 1988.

Feshbach, Sidney. "Unswamping a Backwater: On Samuel Beckett's *Film.*" *Samuel Beckett and the Arts: Music, Visual Arts, and Non-print Media.* Ed. Lois Oppenheim. New York: Garland, 1999. 333–63.

Gontarski, Stan E. "*Film* and Formal Integrity." *Samuel Beckett: Humanistic Perspectives.* Ed. Morris Beja, Gontarski, and Pierre Astier. [Columbus]: Ohio State University Press, 1983. 129–36.

Knowlson, James. *Damned to Fame: The Life of Samuel Beckett.* New York: Simon, 1996.

Leyda, Jay, ed. *A Premature Celebration of Eisenstein's Centenary.* London: Methuen, 1988.

Lommel, Michael. "Aspekte zur Intermedialität der Wahrnehmung und der Imagination bei Samuel Beckett: Ein Forschungsüberblick." *Kino-/(Ro)Mania: Intermedialität zwischen Film und Literatur.* Ed. Jochen Mecke and Volker Roloff. Tübingen: Stauffenburg, 1999. 323–51.

Perlmutter, Ruth. "Beckett's *Film* and Beckett and Film." *Journal of Modern Literature* 6 (1977): 83–94.

Pudovkin, Vsevolod I. *Film Technique* and *Film Acting.* Ed. and trans. Ivor Montagu. London: Vision, 1968.

Schneider, Alan. "On Directing *Film*." 1972. *The Savage Eye.* Vol. 4 of *SBT/A.* Ed. Catharina Wulf. Amsterdam: Rodopi, 1995. 29–40.

Schwab, Martin. *Unsichtbares–Sichtbar gemacht: Zu Samuel Beckett's* Film. Munich: Fink, 1996.

Sweeney, Kevin W. "Deleuze on Beckett's *Film*." *Film and Philosophy* 4 (1997): 85–94.

Waugh, Katherine, and Fergus Daly. "*Film* by Samuel Beckett." *Film West* 20 (1995): 22–24.

Beckett's Theater

Embodying Alterity

ANNA McMULLAN

T HE NATIONAL AND international celebrations throughout 2006 in honor of the centenary of Samuel Beckett's birth have confirmed his status as a global cultural figure. In a trajectory illustrative of Pascale Casanova's paradigm of the minority writer who leaves the limited literary field of his native country and installs himself in the literary metropole, Beckett left Dublin in 1937 to settle in Paris until his death in 1989. He continually crossed linguistic borders through his wide multilingual reading as a student of modern languages at Trinity College Dublin,[1] his translations of Mexican poetry,[2] his theatrical directing in Germany, and, of course, his bilingual writing and self-translation. This essay will focus on *Eleutheria,* Beckett's first full-length play, written in French in the immediate post–World War II period.[3] I will explore Beckett's embodiment of an ethics and aesthetics of alterity in this play that refuses the boundaries of a familial, national, or cultural world that excludes other histories or nonnormative subject positions.

Beckett's oeuvre can be placed in the context of exilic writing,[4] defined not by the boundaries of place and identity but by their dislocation. His dramatic subjects reproduce the fragments of a particular history, his own and that of his characters, formed through a juxtaposition of Irish and other cultural "appurtenances" (Katz 47), but the temporality and liminal space of performance work against the recuperation of those fragments and layers into the stable and exclusive contours of a normative world, location, or identity. However, Beckett's work also interrogates the power of symbolic, social, or political authority to assert and surveil the mechanisms and hierarchies of self and other, identity, and alterity: to categorize us and them, or like Pozzo in act 1 of *Waiting for Godot,* to decide whose suffering or indeed humanity counts, and whose does not.[5]

If the cultural conservatism of the early decades of the Irish Free State fueled Beckett's embrace of the cosmopolitan climate of Paris, his experience of World War II confirmed the need for a global perspective. On the one hand, Beckett seems to have been very aware that he was moving between distinct "literary fields": his hibernicized self-translation of *En attendant Godot* situates him in an Irish theatrical and historical genealogy that includes Yeats and Synge,[6] and indeed invokes the Irish Famine: "the skull, the skull in Connemara."[7] This passage from Lucky's speech is given in the French text as "la tête en Normandie," evoking the more recent trauma of World War II, and the reference to the death of Voltaire in the French text is replaced by that of Bishop Berkeley in the English-language version. On the one hand, relocating Beckett within French or Irish or English literary or theatrical genealogies can foreground his oeuvre's debts to, and impact on, national traditions. On the other hand, Beckett's work suggests the artifice and exclusions of such national boundaries, as its languages, geographies, historical traces, and literary or cultural references continually traverse them.[8]

Although never broadcast, Beckett's talk for Irish national radio (Radio Telefís Eireann), "The Capital of the Ruins," on the Irish Red Cross Hospital at Saint-Lô, France, virtually destroyed in the war, where he worked from August 1945 to January 1946, reveals his attempts to negotiate between Irish and French (dis)locations and perspectives. He concludes that whatever difficulties or "pains" the Irish project in Normandy encountered "were those inherent in the simple and necessary and yet so unattainable proposition that their way of being we, was not our way and that our way of being they, was not their way" (25). Beckett here recognizes cultural difference but also envisages a way of being "they" in being "we," and "we" in being "they."[9] In *The Philosophy of the Limit,* Drucilla Cornell theorizes a "nonviolative relationship to the Other," drawing on the work of Theodor Adorno, Jacques Derrida, and Emmanuel Levinas. Cornell cites Adorno's "art of disunion that allows things to exist in their difference and in their affinity" (16).

Eleutheria focuses on the failure of the world of the Krap family to accommodate difference in a nonviolative way or to identify with others beyond their own narrow circle. Mme Krap in particular cannot accept the defection of her son Victor, who left the family home two years before the play opens. In the next two acts, the female guardians of the bourgeois home (including Mme Krap's friend, Mme Meck) are counterpointed by two male guardians of social and dramatic norms, the Glazier and the Spectator. *Eleutheria* exposes the increasing epistemological and corporeal violence of the attempts to reintegrate Victor into the conventional middle-class world of the Krap salon during the course of the play.

Eleutheria was written on Beckett's return to Paris after his experiences in the Resistance, time in Roussillon waiting for the end of the war and the liberation of Paris, and aid and reconstruction work in Saint-Lô. Surely it is no coincidence that the play's title is the Greek word for freedom. The play is set in a Parisian postwar middle-class milieu, with specific references to areas of Paris such as Passy, where we are told Victor goes to rummage through dustbins for food. However, Beckett's dramaturgy destabilizes any mimetic location and presents Victor's alienation from his home, his family, and his world in spatial, visual terms through the split set on stage, where the emptiness of Victor's rented room contrasts with the "domesticated and respectable" though cramped space of the Krap salon, ostentatiously furnished in conventional bourgeois manner (5). Other dislocations fracture the world of the play. Peter Boxall has commented on the "subterranean Irish geography" of autobiographical memories of Dublin events and places (such as the Forty Foot bathing place in Sandycove) that haunt the apparently Parisian setting of the play (250). The characters' names are drawn from a mixture of mainly slang English and French with some other language sources: M. Krap, Mme Meck, Dr Piouk, Olga Skunk, Mme Karl. Moreover, the play continually refers to its status as theater.

References to the prompter, the arrival of the Spectator who cites the author "Beckett (*he says Béké*), Samuel" (136), and frequent metatheatrical comments throughout the dialogue foreground the constructed and clichéd theatrical nature of this world. M. Krap notes in act 1 that "From the dramatic point of view, there's no point in my wife's absence" (24), makes references to "keep[ing] the punters amused" (33), and calls for the curtain at the end of act 1 (this turns out to be an announcement of his imminent demise). In act 3 this role of metatheatrical commentator is taken up by the Glazier, who informs Mme Meck that Victor is under the bed "as in Molière's day" (69), and in act 3 by the Spectator, who complains that "we've been somewhat deprived of wit so far" (131).

Beckett was evidently satirizing the idea of a theater of "entertainment and public relaxation" (70) associated with middle-class mores, drawing on a complex genealogy of experimental theater in his efforts.[10] The artifice of the dramatic conventions exposed evokes the artifice of the bourgeois world they parody: there are many references to life as "bluff," "simulacrum," and, in the French text, "comédie."

Victor's alienation from this masquerade of home conveys a bitter critique of the failure of postwar bourgeois society (whether French or Irish) to adequately acknowledge or respond to the traumas of the recent war and the Holocaust. In *Eleutheria,* Beckett presents these ethical issues in immediate sensory or perceptual terms.

Peggy Phelan draws attention to the central role of modes of vision in Beckett's work:

> At the center of Beckett's project is a question about how to see and how to be seen.[...] What is startling about the account of seeing that his work offers is how deeply it touches the consequences of not seeing.[...] Like many artists who came of age after World War II, he was deeply affected by the scandal of ethical blindness underlying the catastrophe of the Holocaust. But he was boldest in exploring the relation between this blindness and the imperative to see that serves as the aesthetic orthodoxy of modernist art. Pozzo in *Godot* and Hamm in *Endgame* dramatize blindness in a theatre of mordant spectacle. We see them not seeing, and in that insight we are made aware of what we cannot and do not see in the scene. (1281)

Eleutheria also focuses on seeing and not seeing, and indeed on visual tricks or traps. From the beginning Beckett splits the audience's viewpoint, since there are two spaces on stage, the main and the marginal action, even though little actually takes place in the marginal action: "Most of the time it is only a question of a site and of a person in stasis" (6). Moreover, the angle from which the audience sees the two spaces shifts between each act, with Victor's room audience left in act 1, and audience right in act 2. In the final act, the bourgeois salon has, perceptually speaking, fallen into the orchestra pit during the change of scene. Modes of perception are self-consciously evoked through the figure of the Glazier with his multiple intertextual resonances, including references to Strindberg's *Dream Play,* Cocteau's *Orphée,* and perhaps Baudelaire's prose poem "Le mauvais vitrier." The Glazier immediately repairs the window through which Victor has thrown his shoe, resealing the hermeticism of the stage space[11] and drawing attention to the boundaries between interior and exterior, the seen and the unseen, like the windows of the set in *Endgame*.

The sense of boundaries in relation to place and time is materialized by the extraordinary image of barbed wire in the Kraps' flat, which, as M. Krap explains, his wife has introduced in order to "keep—yet in a way abolish—our son's favourite places, for we all, Victor, my wife and I, had our favourite places in this house, as far back as my memory reaches, and personally I still have mine[...]. That's only the beginning. The flat will soon be covered in barbed wire" (41–42). The subsequent reference to the surrealist exhibition that inspired this practice disguises the very troubling conjuring of incarceration imagery from the recent past of World War II and the concentration camps. However much this bourgeois family seeks to eliminate experiences or memories that do not immediately concern them, evidence of such persists. Yet Mme Piouk has not seen the barbed wire under the table:

MLLE SKUNK: What's this barbed wire for? (*She points to a thin strip of barbed wire fixed under the edge of the table and running down to the floor.*)
MME PIOUK: Barbed wire?
MLLE SKUNK: (*touching it*) It's got spikes! Look!
Mme Piouk stands up and leans over the table.
MME PIOUK: How it is that I hadn't noticed it?
DR PIOUK: My wife is not very sensitive to the macrocosm.
M. KRAP: But she reacted to the light.
DR PIOUK: That's because she really suffered from it. (40)

Such failure to see indicts the world of the play and poses a challenge to its audience. The borderline between the stage world and the space of the auditorium across the footlights is quite self-consciously foregrounded through the Pirandellian device of the character of the Spectator who enters the stage in act 3 and, in particular, through Victor's approach to the footlights and inarticulate attempts to communicate across it: "*Victor [...] runs to the footlights, wants to say something but can't, makes a helpless gesture, exits, gesticulating wildly. Silence*" (97). These moments of silence or inarticulate stammers contrast with all the verbal explanations offered by others and, indeed, Victor himself during the play. The entire dramatic edifice of the play comments on the inadequacy of existing symbolic systems, visual or verbal, to express "how it is." The one occasion when Victor attempts to confess or clarify his motives occurs between the acts.

This failure of Victor to explain himself is what drives all the other characters, except perhaps his father, to understand, interpret, and seek to "cure" Victor. The Glazier complains that Victor, and therefore the whole play, does not make sense and urges him to: "Explain yourself, no, that's not what I mean, I put it badly. Define yourself, that's it. It's time you defined yourself. You sit there like a kind of [...] how can I put it? Like a kind of oozing pus. Like a kind of sanies, that's it. Get a bit of body for God's sake" (82).[12]

Victor's offstage explanation to Jacques and Marie in between acts 2 and 3 is a source of particular outrage to the Spectator and Glazier, the self-appointed guardians of appropriate behavior in the play: "He's only prepared to explain himself off-stage, and then only to imbeciles" (125). The "explanation" apparently occurred under the influence of alcohol, so neither Victor nor Jacques can recall its essence in words. It is described as "a bit like music" (125).

Victor's resistance to clarity and articulation progressively erodes the ability of the other characters to either see or act. In act 3 the Spectator complains: "It's odd. No sooner am I on stage among you lot than I start to dry up. To lose my resources.[...] Everything has become hazy, blurred, I can't see properly" (132). The characters become infected with lassitude. When her husband, Dr Piouk, goes missing, his wife asks: "What can we do?" The stage directions indicate, "*This passage comes to an abrupt end, as if overcome by a feeling of fatigue and fatuity. Silence. Gestures of helplessness, of indifference. Shrugged shoulders*" (140).

Yet Victor provokes continual efforts to return him to the bosom of his family, and increasingly violent modes of interrogation to transform his resistance into a category that can be understood by rational logic (the Glazier) and might provide some satisfaction and entertainment to the Spectator. When this does not seem to be forthcoming, the Spectator threatens torture and produces Chouchi, the Chinese torturer, an orientalized stereotype of menacing otherness. The idea that torture might be essayed as a form of spectacle as well as clarification comments on the blinkered ethical framework of the world of the play.

That world abounds with threats of violence, from Mme Meck's vision of Mme Krap knocked down by a lorry and covered in blood, to M. Krap's threatened attack on his wife with a razor, to Joseph's attempts to remove Victor, which are immediately stopped by the Glazier's attack on Joseph with a hammer (78). On a macrocosmic scale, Dr Piouk attempts to exterminate the human race through various means, including mass euthanasia using his suicide pill. As the Glazier tries to extract one more effort of explanation, Victor retorts:

> VICTOR: Don't you think this massacre has gone on long enough?
> GLAZIER: Just one more tiny corpse. (156)

The violent corporeal effects of epistemological interrogation will recur as a motif in many of Beckett's plays, especially his last, *What Where* (1983). It is significant that Victor and Jacques prove themselves incapable of violence toward others (123), whereas the "hideous" Dr Piouk is defined as a "man of action" (108). Angela Moorjani comments on Beckett's use of "irony and mock-seriousness to launch an attack on the belief in the efficacy of historical action that had become dogma for existentialists and Marxists alike" (72).[13] For Victor all action involves collusion in the coercive and conflictual norms of the world of the play. *Eleutheria* defines the only ethical, nonviolative option open to Victor as a refusal of the world around him as currently constituted. However, Victor's refusal is also a challenge: "It isn't me you should be interrogating. It's yourselves" (144). The play turns the interrogatory gaze back on its inhabitants and the structures of identity and alterity they surveil so anxiously.

The Spectator urges that if Victor would only explain and define himself in terms that they could understand, he would no longer trouble them, and they would not have to engage with anything or anyone beyond their own circle: "Dead or alive, he belongs to us, he's one of us again. That's all we had to prove. That basically there's only us" (152).

Victor mocks the boundaries that define and delimit this circle of "us" and shield it from unbearable realities:

> Saints, madmen, martyrs, victims of torture—they don't bother you in the least, they are in the natural order of things. They are strangers, you will never be one of them, or at least you hope you won't.[...] You turn away from them. You don't want to think about them.[...] Nothing to do with you. (145)

While the guardians of the play attempt to reintegrate or eliminate Victor, who threatens to disturb the boundaries between "us" and the "strangers" who are simply ignored, strange metamorphoses and slippages of identity occasionally occur. These center on father-son relationships. The protean possibilities of identity to inhabit or metamorphose across particular bodies is suggested by the parallels between Victor and his father: at the end of act 1, Mme Krap calls M. Krap "Victor." But Victor's father seems to have submitted to his lack of freedom in the matriarchal space of the home: "My freedom diminishes daily. Soon I shan't be allowed to open my mouth" (20).[14] The Glazier and his son Michel form a second father-son dyad; indeed, the Glazier is specifically described as resembling M. Krap in appearance (75) and speech (94). The play seems to be investigating various incarnations of subjection and identification in the father-son relationship.

Another son figure evoked in the play is Jesus Christ. Victor lives in the "Impasse de l'Enfant Jesus." The temporal structure of *Eleutheria* over three consecutive days with the third described as "the third day, the great day, when all things must be made plain" (119), refers specifically and ironically to the Resurrection. Victor remains in "limbo" (164), without the triumphant exit out of hell. Dante's infernal iconography is invoked by Victor's father, who insists he is in the ninth circle, that of the treacherous. In canto 33 of the *Inferno*, one of the inhabitants of that circle, Fra Alberigo, explains that "many a time the soul falls down here before Atropos sends it forth.[...] The soul falls headlong into this tank here, and [...] in body appears still living above" (411–13). This image casts another perspective on the references to life in the Krap salon as "simulacrum," a living hell masquerading as everyday reality. It also prefigures the doubleness of the body in much of Beckett's work: irremediably carnal and subject to pain and torture that Victor cannot endure, and also a projection, a dislocated phantasm, since, as Amelia Jones reminds us, "the body is both insistently 'there' and always absent (never fully knowable through vision)" (32).

The title of the play, *Eleutheria,* is evidently ironic, and multilayered.[15] At the end of the play, Victor gives up his attempt at absolute freedom defined as seeing himself dead. He realizes that this is also "du théâtre," and Boxall suggests: "He recognises that he will never break out of the purgatorial circle of the play, as his movement towards negativity relentlessly collapses into an acknowledgement of his ineluctable containment within the cultural and theatrical references which bring the stage that he occupies into being" (256). Beckett moves beyond this impasse of alienation in his subsequent plays by transforming the boundaries of the theatrical space and, in the later work, the boundaries of the body itself.

Beckett's subsequent theater focuses on the self-other relationship, on the one hand, presenting anatomies of domination (from *Endgame* to *What Where*), and, on the other, incarnations of subjectivity and subject-other relations that eschew positions and structures of domination, possession, or exclusion (from the interplay between Estragon and Vladimir in *Waiting for Godot* to Listener and Reader in *Ohio Impromptu*). Embodiment may be what constitutes the human subject in his or her vulnerability,[16] presented acutely in Victor's "emaciated back" turned on humanity at the end of *Eleutheria,* but the possibility of imagining alternative embodiments, which emerges in Beckett's subsequent theater, may also play a role in negotiating the relationship between self and other, affinity and difference.

Notes

1. See Engelberts, Frost, and Maxwell.

2. See Paz.

3. The play was written early in 1947. Beckett withdrew performing rights to the play after the success of *En attendant Godot,* and it was not published until after his death. It has never had a professional production. Beckett's French text was published reluctantly by Édition de Minuit, Paris, in 1995, after an English translation by Michael Brodsky was proposed by Barney Rosset in New York, and was published later in 1995. See Cohn 152. Citations in this essay are from the excellent translation of *Eleutheria* by Wright.

4. See, for example, Hyland and Sammells, who include discussion of Swift, Shaw, Yeats, Beckett, and Joyce.

5. When Pozzo enters in act 1, he considers Vladimir and Estragon to be of the same "species" as himself albeit inferior specimens, but Lucky is relegated to the nonhuman or animal, addressed as "pig" or "hog." Moorjani relates this to Beckett's parody of the pervasive influence of Kojève's reading of the Hegelian master-slave dialectic, where "only the master's self-consciousness partakes of the human" (74).

6. See Dukes 103–12.

7. See Roach 311.

8. Chamberlain notes Beckett's confounding of most library classification systems (18).

9. See Katz, ch. 2.

10. McMillan and Fehsenfeld point out that "there are parodies or allusions from Sophocles, Shakespeare, Molière, Corneille, Shaw, Zola, Ibsen, Hauptmann, Pirandello, Yeats, Symbolism, Surrealism, Artaud, Jarry and Socialist Realism, to name only the most evident" (31). See also the discussion of avant-garde theatrical intertexts in Bradby (11–23) and Engelberts (89–112).

11. Moorjani points out that the Glazier also installs a lock in Victor's room (76).

12. The Édition de Minuit text has, "Prenez un peu de contour, pour l'amour de Dieu" (84).

13. Moorjani reads Beckett's pessimistic assessment of human history as grounded in his "concrete experience of the infliction of unspeakable tyranny and suffering and annihilation." His anti-Hegelian critique of the "domination and violence of inner and outer masters," she argues, matched his "resistance to a world envisaged as split into two opposing camps" (83).

14. *Eleutheria* certainly confirms Mary Bryden's elucidation of the recurrent trope of women in Beckett's early writing, "impeding the access to stasis of the perversely uncommunicative central male" (72).

15. Beckett used the Greek word previously in *Murphy,* in an ironic reference to some turf that was "truly Irish in its eleutheromania, it would not burn behind bars" (130). In *A Beckett Canon,* Ruby Cohn notes that "Beckett hesitated between *Eleutheria* and *L'Eleutheromane* as the title of his first complete play" (152). Peter Boxall also cites the name given to a Bahaman island by "a group of colonists called the Company of Eleuthérian Adventurers, to provide a safe haven for freethinking dissenters from the 17th century religious disputes in Bermuda" (250).

16. See Judith Butler.

Works Cited

Beckett, Samuel. "The Capital of the Ruins." *As the Story Was Told: Uncollected and Late Prose.* London: Calder, 1990. 17–28.

———. *Eleutheria.* Paris: Minuit, 1995.

———. *Eleutheria.* Trans. Barbara Wright. London: Faber, 1996.

———. *Murphy.* London: Calder, 1963.

———. *Waiting for Godot.* London: Faber, 1978.

Boxall, Peter. "Freedom and Cultural Location in *Eleutheria.*" *Beckett versus Beckett.* Vol. 7 of *SBT/A.* Ed. Marius Buning et al. Amsterdam: Rodopi, 1998. 245–58.

Bradby, David. *Beckett: Waiting for Godot.* Cambridge: Cambridge University Press, 2001.

Bryden, Mary. *Women in Samuel Beckett's Prose and Drama: Her Own Other.* Basingstoke, UK: Macmillan, 1993.

Butler, Judith. *Precarious Life: The Powers of Mourning and Violence.* London: Verso, 2004.

Casanova, Pascale. *The World Republic of Letters*. Trans. M. B. DeBevoise. Cambridge, MA: Harvard University Press, 2004.

Chamberlain, Lori. "'The Same Stories': Beckett's Poetics of Translation." *Beckett Translating/Translating Becket*. Ed. Alan Warren Friedman, Charles Rossman, and Dina Sherzer. University Park: Pennsylvania State University Press, 1987. 17–24.

Cohn, Ruby. *A Beckett Canon*. Ann Arbor: University of Michigan Press, 2001.

Cornell, Drucilla. *The Philosophy of the Limit*. New York: Routledge, 1992.

Dante Alighieri. *The Divine Comedy 1: The Inferno*. Italian text with trans. John D. Sinclair. New York: Oxford University Press, 1961.

Dukes, Gerry. "Beckett's Synge Song: The Revised *Godot* Revisited." *Journal of Beckett Studies* 4 (1995): 103–12.

Engelberts, Matthijs. "Victor(ious) Retreats: Beckett's *Eleutheria* and Roger Vitrac's Departure from Surrealism." *Drawing on Beckett*. Ed. Linda Ben-Zvi. Tel Aviv: Assaph, 2003. 89–112.

Engelberts, Matthijs, Everett Frost, with Jane Maxwell, eds. *Notes Diverse Holo: Catalogues of Beckett's Reading Notes and Other Manuscripts at Trinity College Dublin*. Vol. 16 of *SBT/A*. Amsterdam: Rodopi, 2006.

Hyland, Paul, and Neil Sammells. *Irish Writing: Exile and Subversion*. Basingstoke, UK: Macmillan, 1991.

Jones, Amelia. *Body Art: Performing the Subject*. Minneapolis: University of Minnesota Press, 1998.

Katz, Daniel. *Saying I No More: Subjectivity and Consciousness in the Prose of Samuel Beckett*. Evanston, IL: Northwestern University Press, 1999.

McMillan, Dougald, and Martha Fehsenfeld. *Beckett in the Theatre*. London: Calder, 1988.

Moorjani, Angela. "Diogenes Lampoons Alexandre Kojève: Cultural Ghosts in Beckett's Early French Plays." *Drawing on Beckett*. Ed. Linda Ben Zvi. Tel Aviv: Assaph, 69–88.

Paz, Octavio, ed. *Anthology of Mexican Poetry*. Trans. Samuel Beckett. Bloomington: Indiana University Press, 1958.

Phelan, Peggy. "Lessons in Blindness from Samuel Beckett." *PMLA* 119 (2004): 1279–88.

Roach, Joseph. "The Great Hole of History: Liturgical Silence in Beckett, Osofisan, and Parks." *South Atlantic Quarterly* 100 (2001): 307–17.

Beckett's *Posture* in the French Literary Field

JÜRGEN SIESS

F ROM THE BEGINNING of his literary career in France, Samuel Beckett wanted to distinguish himself from other writers, James Joyce on the one hand, Jean-Paul Sartre and the committed writers on the other. In avoiding the mainstream, he set out to find his own solitary path. He could have made the motto of the Sturm und Drang poet and dramatist Jakob Michael Lenz his own: "Ich aber werde dunkel sein und gehe meinen Weg allein" (I however will be dark, by myself I make my way).[1] Drawing on literary pragmatics and the sociology of literature, I examine in this essay the *posture* of the outsider and the ethos of the isolated writer that Beckett himself elaborated. My investigation of this constructed image entails three interrelated figures of the writer: Beckett's position as the empirical author in the French literary field of the 1940s and 1950s; his *posture* on entering the French context (elaborated through his critical discourse); and the functions of implied author and self-narrator within the discursive framework of his early French fiction.

Beckett's Outsider Status in the French Literary Field

From March 1946, when he returned to postwar Paris, and for the next ten years Beckett immersed himself in the French language and culture. He thus broke with his linguistic and cultural origins and distanced himself from the literary institutions that had published his early works (Casanova 65, 260). Whatever he might say or think about the given situation, the Anglo-Irish Beckett, who until then was known only to insiders, looked for a rapprochement with French literary institutions. In other words, he looked for a way into a literary world in which his status as an outsider left him few alternatives: he could either join one of the existing groups, or he could try to create his own niche. Beckett chose the second option, which he pursued with an aesthetic radicalism for which he would become famous. In the immediate postwar years, Beckett was to challenge the Parisian *république des lettres,* a literary community made up of movements, such as surrealism and existentialism, and their leading figures, André Breton and Jean-Paul Sartre.

Beckett adopted the *posture* (in the meaning given this term by Alain Viala) of the exceptional writer who lays claim to a unique aesthetic project. Viala defines authorial *posture* as the distinctive manner in which authors position themselves in the literary field of their times. Enacting the role of author in relation to an audience, he further reminds us, involves both social and textual self-presentation (Molinié and Viala 216–17). In a certain sense, Beckett tried to establish a one-man avant-garde that seemed to allow him to remain outside the literary institutions. From the standpoint of Bourdieu's influential views on the rules that govern artistic activity, however, writers cannot position themselves outside the literary field: "the artist who produces a work is himself produced, at the heart of the field of production, by all those who contribute to his 'discovery' and to his consecration as a 'known' and recognized artist—critics, writers of prefaces, booksellers, etc." (238). For Bourdieu, the literary field is characterized by forces acting on everyone who enters it, and at the same time by competitive struggles that aim to preserve or to transform this energetic field (323).

Looking for an opportunity to be recognized in the French context, Beckett paradoxically pretended to remain an outsider. As Jacques Dubois maintains, writers who attempt to position themselves outside the literary field are not uncommon, as they are "torn between two temptations, either to overrate or overemphasize [their] role, or to doubt whether [their] activity is significant or not—insofar as it is unproductive and not really acknowledged" (106). What distinguishes Beckett's attitude and behavior is that he endows the second temptation with the meaning of a fundamental principle, insisting upon the status of the deliberately decentered artist unwilling to make the least concession either to the demands of the institution or to prevailing aesthetic doctrine. The only motivation Beckett would recognize was the need to write.

At the time Beckett chose to immerse himself in the French language, the newly established existentialists were in competition with the well-established surrealists. Indeed, Sartre intended to wrest the first rank from the surrealists to bestow it on his own movement. This project underlies *Qu'est-ce que la littérature?* (*What Is Literature?*), Sartre's programmatic essay published in 1948. Beckett's image of the author contrasts strikingly with this representation of the author that Sartre proposes: the profession of the writer requiring social responsibility and taking sides (281, 344); writers committing themselves, which in 1947–1948 meant coming to the defense of the proletariat (332) and restoring dignity to language (341). In Sartre's view, isolated writers can limit themselves to a merely critical, subversive task, whereas literary praxis must be first of all constructive (349). As Anna Boschetti notes, Sartre saw literature as an intrinsically revolutionary activity in opposition to *art pur* (245–46).

Beckett, as is well known, did not subscribe to this program. He intended to call language into question, if not to subvert it, telling Maurice Nadeau in 1951 that he had started to write in order to do the opposite of what Joyce had done. Joyce had faith in the omnipotence of language, Beckett told him, but "[il] a montré du même coup la vanité du langage. Le cri, le hurlement, le glou-glou de la gorge, le borborygme sont aussi des langages, et qui ne mentent pas" (at the same time [Joyce] has shown the vanity of language. The scream, the howl, the gurgling in the throat, the rumbling noise, too, are forms of language, and they don't lie) (qtd. in Nadeau 365–66). Furthermore, calling into question literature as a constructive praxis, Beckett responded to Nadeau's statement about his advancing further into rarefied realms: "Non pas plus loin... Plus bas, encore un peu plus bas. [...] Une bouche, seulement une bouche, qui parlerait, qui dirait des paroles sans suite" (No not further on... Lower down, always lower down. [...] A mouth, only a talking mouth, uttering words without sense) (qtd. in Nadeau 365). With such comments, he implicitly distinguished himself from the figure of the committed writer.

Devising a New Position in the Literary Field: The Artist of Failure

There are, of course, many more instances in which Beckett characterizes his own status, or "experience," as that "of a non-knower, a no-can-er," as he told Israel Shenker in a much-quoted 1956 interview (qtd. in Graver and Federman 148). Some years later (1961) he told Gabriel d'Aubarède that he considered the belief in knowledge, logic, and ontology to be the wrong track and even to be a folly: "*Molloy* and the others came to me the day I became aware of my own folly. Only then did I begin to write the things I feel" (qtd. in Graver and Federman 217). In calling into question knowledge and logic, he places value on his feelings, his inner life, especially its "dark side" (see Knowlson 319).

Beckett's specific image of the writer was first elaborated through his critical discourse. One of the major figures in his reflections on literature and art is the solitary, who isolates himself so that he can concentrate on his inner life and its depths. Yet this image is not free from contradictions. In an interview with John Barber on 5 April 1986, Beckett said he had "to leave 'a stain upon the silence,' and remind men of the eternal truths of life and death" (qtd. in Fletcher 76). Here we find the most modest minimalism side by side with the pretension to have a voice similar to that of a prophet. However, such references to his readers are rare, as he tends to valorize the writer who isolates himself from the realm of communication and publicity. Beckett's solipsistic stance in his critical discourse leaves little space for audience response. His discomfort with interviews, moreover, can be understood by the lack of control he as the interviewee would have over an interaction that may place him in a one-down position and force him to respond to fixed questions. Indeed, an interview can put him doubly at risk: in relation to the interviewer and in relation to the public that may consider some of the utterances recorded in the interview as the author's programmatic statements. Such an involvement was what Beckett strongly and continuously refused.

Beckett was to relate his art of unknowingness to willed impoverishment and failure. In a 1973 conversation, he told Charles Juliet that for him there was no hope left of finding an answer or a solution: "Il faut se tenir là où il n'y a ni pronom, ni solution, ni réaction, ni prise de position possibles" (You have to stay where there's no pronoun left, no solution, no reaction, no point of view) (qtd. in Juliet 49). The only concession he was inclined to make was to search for an adequate *way* to fail in a world without meaning, in the face of an existence without hope: "peut-être n'y a-t-il que de fausses routes. Mais il faut trouver la mauvaise route qui vous convient" (perhaps there are only wrong tracks. But you have to find the wrong one that suits you best) (qtd. in Juliet 38). The artist who necessarily fails and who accepts his failure is placed in the foreground. Yet with this image Beckett draws the portrait of an artist who impoverishes himself voluntarily. When in 1968 he spoke to Ludovic Janvier about the turning point after the war, he added that on moving back to his apartment after the Liberation, he began to write in French "avec le désir de m'appauvrir encore plus. C'est ça le vrai mobile" (wishing to impoverish myself even more. That's the real impulse) (qtd. in Janvier 18). For Beckett, writing in French implied the impoverishment that a second language represents for writers who are adept at tapping into the riches of their first.[2] Reviewing *Molloy* in 1951, Gaëtan Picon already speculated that Beckett's choice of the French language is related to his vow of *pauvreté* (poverty) and *dépouillement* (bareness).

When Beckett presents images associated with his own role, or when he deals with models supposed to be imitated, he does not refer to the field of literature, but to the field of art. In the late 1940s, the model he presents is Bram van Velde, a painter living exclusively for his art, making concessions neither to the expectations of the public nor to the dominant conception of the Artist and of Art. As Anthony Cronin pertinently observed, this discourse does not pretend to contribute something to art criticism, but allows Beckett to clarify his own aims: he seems to have "merged his own position with that of van Velde" (397). Reflecting on the painter, Beckett considers his willingness to confront the "ultimate penury" as the condition of the artist's work (*Three Dialogues* 143).

The solitary, the autonomous, and the impoverished artist are traditional figures, of course, much celebrated throughout the nineteenth century. For instance, Verlaine's praise for the outcast status of the *poète maudit* was reinforced by portraying himself as a poor man among the poor. (See his prose poem "Mon Testament.") Nevertheless, while describing himself as a defiant outcast, he aimed at writing highly crafted poetry. In his sociological examination of the cultural field, Bourdieu considers Verlaine the leading figure of the *décadents,* the literary *bohème* of the late nineteenth century (372–73). And as Anne Atik recalls, Verlaine was among Beckett's favorite poets (52). On the other hand, in adopting the traditional postures of the solitary and autonomous artist who lives for his art alone far removed from the literary market, Beckett radicalized this position by assuming the tension between his impulse to write and his doubt about finding meaning in his writing: he thus emphasized the notion of the *artiste raté* doomed to fail and made of this necessary failure his distinctive feature.

Beckett's artistic *posture* both builds on traditional figures of the artist and distinguishes itself from them. The autonomous writer/artist doomed to fail and indifferent to success allows him to create a new position in the literary field by extending the artist as a *poète maudit,* maligned, bereft, and defiant toward society, and emphasizing the *artiste raté.* Paradoxically, while he pretended to stay outside the field, Beckett could position himself within it by inventing this unclaimed position in postwar French culture.

Beckett's Mediated Entry into the Literary Field

In reality, however, in his behavior and social relations, the potential French author Samuel Beckett consistently relied on the help of others to gain access to the literary and the theatrical field. Beckett's success beginning with the publication of *Molloy* and the performance of *En attendant Godot* in the early fifties is owing to a specific combination of forces involving at the same time cultural institutions (publishing houses, literary magazines, radio, theater) and the individual (the potential author). The opportunity to be recognized as a writer who paradoxically intended to remain an outsider was offered to Beckett by an *avant-gardiste* within the institution, the young publisher Jérôme Lindon. Lindon activated a network of critics and succeeded in obtaining an immediate legitimization of his authors: "subverting the rules of the literary game [...] he in the proper sense 'creates' a certain number of writers; and, principal among them, Samuel Beckett" (Simonin 389). The attribute "auteur-Minuit" designates "a young writer (around 30), of provincial or foreign origin, and in any case not belonging to the Parisian literary milieu" (394). Beckett's retreat from the market (the business and the vanities) was used by his publisher as a means of promotion: the retreat delivered "the proof that the artist and his work are authentic" (390). The writer who preferred the isolation to visibility and social distinction is an image in the sense of an illusion, a stereotype that in the end serves institutional (i.e., economic) aims.

Angela Moorjani has determined that at the time of Minuit's publication of *Molloy* in 1951, Lindon rallied at least twenty-five of the most important critics to review the book. Without such concerted action, it is most unlikely that so many reviewers would write on a novel by a largely unknown author. The French *Murphy,* for instance, when it was published by Bordas in 1947, was met with silence and sold so few copies that Bordas was not interested in publishing more Beckett. In his memoir, Maurice Nadeau explains that it was in response to a phone call by the poet and resistance fighter Tristan Tzara that he took up the novel of this unknown (363–64). Nadeau's review in *Combat* of 12 April 1951 was one of the first to recognize *Molloy* as an *événement*. Robert Kanters, on the other hand, who was one of the few dissenting voices in the chorus of praise for Beckett's novel, points out at the beginning of his review that Minuit sent the novel to reviewers with a description of the author as one of the "plus grands écrivains contemporains" (greatest contemporary writers) (Moorjani). There was then both a publicity machine and the social capital of the literary field behind *Molloy*'s success. From Beckett's biographers we know, in addition, to what extent the image of the isolated writer hides an important part of the actual situation: the helping hands and the numerous intermediaries who devoted themselves to the promotion of the artist, among them Suzanne Dumesnil, Maurice Nadeau, Roger Blin, Jean-Marie Serreau, and Michel Polac (who produced a shortened radio version of *Godot* as early as February 1952).

The Textual Postures of Self-Narrator and Implied Author

I now turn to the question of the extent to which Beckett's authorial *posture* can be discerned in his early fictional texts in French at the time he was first elaborating his position through the discourse of criticism and interview. The fictional works that Beckett wrote in French—from *La fin* and *Premier amour* to *L'innommable*—"served as a liberating elixir for Beckett," in Ruby Cohn's view (133). As they make use of first-person narration, Beckett had to take into account a set of generic and discursive constraints and opportunities. How does he exploit these tacit rules? First-person narratives actually offer the possibility of occupying an elevated point of view, as seen, for example, in Denis Diderot's *Jacques le fataliste et son maître* and Marcel Proust's *Recherche*. The *I* nevertheless tends to concentrate on its peculiar history and its intimate self, the egocentrism of the narrator becoming the distinctive narrative element. At the same time, self-narration allows the elaboration of an addressed text and an interaction linking the *I* and *you*. In *Molloy*, the novel I will be concentrating on, the first-person narrator interacts with the *you* by trying to maintain or to recapture the dominant position that he considers his due. Thus, he may appeal to the other as well as mock him or ascribe to him a position of inferiority.

Although Beckett's first-person discourse may at first sight appear monological, it is characterized by an exchange between three different pairs of interlocutors: (1) the narrator and addressee, (2) the implied author and reader, and (3) the empirical author and his potential readers. In order to understand the functions the speaker is endowed with, we have to distinguish carefully between the implied author and the narrator and to discern the functions that each one fulfills. The implied author remains in the background rather than becoming a distinct figure. He may be considered as the invisible hand capable of guiding the narrator.

Molloy is in two parts, with Molloy narrating the first part, and Moran the second. The latter's narrative is supposed to report on his search for Molloy, but it actually drifts toward a self-confession. Moran's discourse shows an instability similar to that of the first part "signed" by Molloy (Abbott 109). In Molloy's narrative, as well, two stories are intertwined or, more precisely, compete with each other. The first story concerns Molloy's "journey" to his mother, with whom he has a strong, troubling relationship; the second story (a commissioned text) deals with Molloy's life. The first-person narrator in part 1 is thus divided by inner tensions. On the one hand, Molloy claims to tell a story of his own making: "Moi je voudrais maintenant parler des choses qui me restent, faire mes adieux, finir de mourir" (7)/"What I'd like now is to speak of the things that are left, say my goodbyes, finish dying" (7). On the other hand, his writing is subordinated to the will of the figure who commissions it, whom he does not know directly, but only through the subordinate who visits him:

> Cet homme qui vient chaque semaine [...] me donne un peu d'argent et enlève les feuilles. Tant de feuilles, tant d'argent. Oui, je travaille maintenant, un peu comme autrefois, seulement je ne sais plus travailler. [...] Oui, ils sont plusieurs, paraît-il. Mais c'est toujours le même qui vient. [...] Quand je n'ai rien fait il ne me donne rien, il me gronde. Cependant je ne travaille pas pour l'argent. (7)
> There's this man who comes every week. [...] He gives me money and takes away the pages. So many pages, so much money. Yes, I work now, a little like I used to, except that I don't know how to

work any more. [...] Yes, there's more than one, apparently. But it's always the same one that comes. [...] When I've done nothing he gives me nothing, he scolds me. Yet I don't work for money. (7)[3]

Molloy's own project and wish to say his good-byes is followed by the statement "They don't want that," which can be taken as a critical remark addressed indirectly to the commissioning group ("there is more than one, apparently" [7]). Such messages of resentment appear at various points in the narrative.

Paradoxically, then, Molloy wants to write and, at the same time, is writing against his will. Moreover, the chore imposed on him is in competition with the project he would like to pursue. At the beginning of his text, the project he alludes to consists in speaking of the things left: thus he seems to try one last time to achieve what he has not been able to achieve. More precisely, what still matters is the discourse he wishes to elaborate on his own account, the story of the "unreal journey" to his mother (16). What he is expected to do, though, and what he does only against his will, is to write the story of his life and feelings. Thus two different, contradictory projects are at stake, two narrations, corresponding to two divergent interests. From the start the failure of the project that is dear to him becomes clear. What in Molloy's eyes constitutes an opening is marked by strong negations: "I don't know" is repeated six times in the opening paragraph, appearing alongside "I've forgotten" (two times) and "I haven't much will left." Moreover, he acknowledges a crucial lack that calls into question his desire to write: "I've forgotten how to spell too, and half the words" (7–8). The would-be writer, who wants to elaborate his own text, portrays himself as having lost the indispensable means of his activity.

Molloy nevertheless insists on his project and its starting point: "I began at the beginning, like an old ballocks, can you imagine that? Here's my beginning. Because they're keeping it apparently. I took a lot of trouble with it. Here it is" (8). The "beginning" of the story he intended to write has been criticized by those who have authority over him: "he told me I'd begun all wrong" (8). The first words of his actual beginning are "This time, then once more I think, then perhaps a last time, then I think it'll be over, with that world too. [...] A little more and you'll go blind. [...] You go dumb as well and sounds fade" (8). "This time" opens a sequence in which the *I* claims to become an author independent of the will of the institutional authority. However, this beginning, although valorized by the narrator, contains strong utterances that cast doubt on the meaning he ascribes to his writing: "What business has innocence here?" (10); "you would do better, at least no worse, to obliterate texts than to blacken margins" (13); or "This should all be re-written in the pluperfect" (16).

Molloy pits his wish to invent a story of his own against the institutional authority's will. The deliverance from the pressure the latter exerts is suggested when the *I* refers to its *ground,* its depth, the capacity to invent, which is linked to the unconscious: "deep down is my dwelling, oh not deepest down, somewhere between the mud and the scum" (14). He tells of two characters, A and C, that are part of his own narrative project, the story of his journey. Toward the end of his narrative, however, it appears that he is unable to write a coherent story, to establish himself as a writing subject fully involved in his act and using all available means to complete it. The problem lies in his initial inability to make a choice: either to deliver the commissioned text as best he can or to dedicate himself entirely and at all costs to his own project. Instead, Molloy remains trapped by the tension created by two simultaneous claims. It is difficult to determine to what extent the failure is due to an external condition or to an internal incapacity.

A similar ambivalence characterizes the position the first-person narrator adopts with respect to his addressees: the *you*–institutional authority and the *you*-narratee. The self-narrating Molloy pretends on the one hand that he does not need an interlocutor, that he is writing for himself as if he were a diarist, expecting nevertheless to be recognized by the narratee. On the other hand, he is irritated by the pressure that the addressee exerts upon him, reacting against him and occasionally offending or even insulting him. The narrator's resentment against the institutional group on whom he is dependent seems to be transferred to the narratee. A vulgar utterance such as "allez-vous faire foutre" (fuck you; 103)—translated into the less vulgar "damn the bit of it" (76)—implies that the narrator does not care about the reaction of the addressee and that his independence prevails at the expense of the other's expectations. Even if it is at times difficult to determine who is the addressee, we can infer that the positive role is reserved for the narrator, whereas the negative role is ascribed to the addressee and that Molloy maintains his claim not to need an audience.

Molloy's Ethos

Molloy tries to create both the image of the solitary, independent narrator-writer and the image of a potential writer whom the institution puts under pressure and who nevertheless strives to complete his own writing project. The text, however, shows the illusion of such autonomy and the failure of *I*-Molloy to become a writing subject. In other words, the text is centered on failure. On this (thematic) level, the first-person narrator appears as submissive to the power of the institution while trying to impose the ethos of an autonomous self. On the discursive level, the narration presents the image of an *I* failing to become a writing subject. The narrator appears as a failure, an *artiste raté*. Molloy also claims autonomy in his relationship with the addressees, even though the narration shows his actual dependence on them. The text reveals the failure of Molloy's self-positioning with respect to the institution as well as to his audience. In the intratextual dimension, behind the narrator, we perceive the figure of the implied author as the one who is capable of staging the narrator-writer who fails. The implied author ironically denounces the failure of the narrator.

This failure, however, is somewhat diminished by the contrast between Molloy's narration and the report written by Moran in part 2. This second, complementary narrator appears as a mediocre man who is devoted to an institution, a caricature that enhances the portrayal of Molloy. Through the confrontation of the two narrators' images and through the staging directed by the implied author, Molloy is valorized despite his negative characteristics. It shows an artist involved in contradictions that he is unable to resolve but that are inherent to the conditions under which he is working. In this image, the principal difficulty for the artist is how to reconcile external demands and internal dispositions.

The implied author also stages Molloy's relationship with the audience as a failure. The narrator is confronted with the necessity of establishing a relationship with the other. He paradoxically needs him to be recognized as solitary and unique. The implied author thus benefits from Molloy's failure through the staging of this very failure. The ethos of the narrator as *artiste raté* serves to enhance his image. He appears as the one who masters the failing narration; he proposes and even organizes the failure, thus producing a unique and completed text. And here is where the intratextual postures of narrator and implied author join the empirical author's positioning in the literary field as analyzed earlier in this essay.

If I have introduced a more critical perception of Beckett, I do not forget that he, eluding the literary "vanity fair," was perfectly aware of a risk of another sort that he was running when he ostentatiously chose the retreat: to succumb to the narcissism so many writers are subject to. Franz Schubert, he said in a conversation with Avigdor Arikha and Anne Atik, was the model that allowed him to elude this trap. The composer was not aware of any positive response, and this, in Beckett's view, is the ultimate distinction (Atik 133): "If you notice the echo you are done for" (Si on se rend compte de l'écho, on est fichu).

Notes

I am grateful to Angela Moorjani for her pertinent remarks and suggestions.

1. My translation. Subsequent parenthetical translations from the French are by myself and the editors, unless otherwise noted.

2. As Nathalie Léger observes, Beckett in his conception of a learned and an impoverished language is indebted to Giambattista Vico (53).

3. In the interest of space, subsequent quotations are mostly from the English *Molloy*, although I have worked from the French.

Works Cited

Abbott, H. Porter. *The Fiction of Samuel Beckett: Form and Effect.* Berkeley: University of California Press, 1973.

Atik, Anne. *Comment c'était: souvenirs sur Samuel Beckett.* Paris: Seuil, 2003.

Beckett, Samuel. *Molloy.* Paris: Minuit–Coll. double, 1994.

———. *Molloy. Malone Dies. The Unnamable.* London: Calder, 1966.

———. *Three Dialogues. Disjecta.* Ed. Ruby Cohn. New York: Grove, 1983. 138–45.

Boschetti, Anna. *Sartre et "Les Temps modernes": une entreprise intellectuelle.* Paris: Minuit, 1985.

Bourdieu, Pierre. *Les règles de l'art: genèse et structure du champ littéraire.* Paris: Seuil, 1992.

Casanova, Pascale. *La république mondiale des lettres.* Paris: Seuil, 1999.

Cohn, Ruby. *A Beckett Canon.* Ann Arbor: University of Michigan Press, 2005.

Cronin, Anthony. *Samuel Beckett: The Last Modernist.* New York: Da Capo, 1999.

Dubois, Jacques. *L'institution de la littérature.* Brussels: Labor, 1978.

Fletcher, John. *About Beckett: The Playwright and the Work.* London: Faber, 2003.

Graver, Lawrence, and Raymond Federman. *Samuel Beckett: The Critical Heritage.* London: Routledge, 1979.

Janvier, Ludovic. *Beckett.* Paris: Seuil, 1969.

Juliet, Charles. *Rencontre avec Samuel Beckett.* [Montpellier]: Fata Morgana, 1986.

Kanters, Robert. "Autant en emporte le vent." *L'Age Nouveau* 62 (1951): 68–70.

Knowlson, James. *Damned to Fame: The Life of Samuel Beckett.* New York: Simon, 1996.

Léger, Nathalie. *Les vies silencieuses de Samuel Beckett.* Paris: Allia, 2006.

Molinié, Georges, and Alain Viala. *Approches de la réception.* Paris: PUF, 1993.

Moorjani, Angela. "Reading Beckett's *Molloy* in the French Context." MLA Convention. Washington, DC. 30 Dec. 2000.

Nadeau, Maurice. *Grâces leur soient rendues: mémoires littéraires.* Paris: Albin Michel, 1990.

Picon, Gaëtan. "Héritier de Joyce, l'Irlandais Samuel Beckett a choisi la langue française." *Samedi soir* 12 May 1951.

Sartre, Jean-Paul. *Qu'est-ce que la littérature?* Paris: Gallimard–Idées, 1948.

Simonin, Anne. *Les éditions de Minuit, 1942–1955: le devoir d'insoumission.* Paris: IMEC, 1994.

The Spear of Telephus in *Krapp's Last Tape*

IRIT DEGANI-RAZ

T HE MYTHICAL FIGURE Telephus, son of Heracles, was the king of the Mysians. When his kingdom was attacked by the Greeks mistakenly landing in Mysia on their way to the Trojan War, he was wounded by Achilles' spear. When the wound would not heal, Telephus consulted an oracle and was told: "He that wounded shall heal"; and indeed the same spear that wounded became the instrument of his healing. The spear of Telephus has since served as a cultural metaphor for the abstract idea of wounding and healing embedded in the same entity. In the opening paragraph of his essay *Proust,* Beckett uses the spear of Telephus as a metaphor for the dualistic structure of Proust's work: "In Proust each spear may be the spear of Telephus," and especially the dualistic nature of time: "that double-headed monster of damnation and salvation" (1).

This essay aims to examine the function of the tape recorder in *Krapp's Last Tape,*[1] which is commonly regarded as Beckett's most Proustian/anti-Proustian play.[2] The picture of old Krapp listening to the moments of his own past emerging from the spools of tape has become a powerful visual image of the human longing for time lost and the failure to reclaim it. The present essay argues that the function of the tape recorder in the play is shaped by what might be described as a modern version of the spear of Telephus. Whereas in the original myth the wound precedes its healing, that is, "He that wounded shall heal," the modern one develops in the opposite direction, that is, "it that healed shall wound." In other words, I attempt to show that the tape recorder, which can be grasped as an extension of human memory and as such as encompassing the promise of healing human longing for a paradise that has been lost,[3] inverts and reveals itself to be a damaging tool capable not only of distorting memory but even of corrupting the original event itself. Moreover, I suggest that this inversion is presented in the play as a result of self-destructive aspects of this technology in particular, and of the very perception of knowledge that underlies technological progress in general. The modern version of the spear of Telephus is used in the article as a central scaffold in order to suggest a new reading of the play that illuminates its ethical aspect.

The ideational skeleton of the first part of my discussion draws on the structure of enlightenment that emerges from Horkheimer and Adorno's *Dialectic of Enlightenment* and its critique of instrumental reason.[4] The task these thinkers set themselves in their work was the discovery of why the Enlightenment, which was initially accompanied by expectations of leading to increased happiness for humankind, instead eventuated in quite the opposite: "why mankind, instead of entering into a truly human condition, is sinking into a new kind of barbarism" (xi). Horkheimer and Adorno's analysis, which attempts to trace the source of human misery and suffering experienced during the twentieth century—the disaster of fascism, the relapse into barbarism, mass murder, and genocide—exposes the destructive tendencies within the rational progress of the modern West.[5] Reason, they claim, has become irrational. This thesis concerning the destructive aspect of progress can be described in terms of a wound inherent in the entity that heals and, in this restricted sense, can be described as a modern version of the spear of Telephus.

In their explanation of how reason has become irrational, Horkheimer and Adorno fundamentally challenge a common optimistic vision held by intellectuals in which the application of reason aims at the establishment of human sovereignty over nature, and the achievement of social freedom embodies the promise of promoting human welfare. Horkheimer and Adorno claim that, in fact, reason itself has become entangled in blind domination, and it is that blind domination which is the source of today's calamity. They indicate in this context a process in which what started as humankind's mastery of nature has been paid for by humans' progressive alienation from nature, eventuating in a radical disjuncture between human beings qua subjects and nature as object that is subordinated to their will: "Men pay for the increase of their power with alienation from that over which they exercise their power. Enlightenment behaves towards things as a dictator towards men. He knows them in so far as he can manipulate them. The man of science knows things in so far as he can make them. In this way their potentiality is turned to his own ends" (9).

The fundamental intention to dominate nature, consequently, led to the rise and domination of a kind of unreflective rationality, whose concept of nature involves its conversion into manipulable material. This kind of rationality thereby fails to recognize the particular qualities of the object to which it is applied. As a consequence, utility becomes the Enlightenment's criterion for judging acts and ideas, as Held succinctly explains in his *Introduction to Critical Theory*:

> The specific categories under which nature is subsumed depend on a view as to how it can be used. Nature is useful. The concept of "useful" follows almost naturally from the enlightenment perspective. Nature is not valuable in and for itself and, therefore, if it is to have significance, it must serve the ends and purposes of another (human beings and/or God). Utility becomes, as Hegel noted, the ethic of the enlightenment. Acts and ideas are judged according to their usefulness which is assessed in terms of their consequences for some goal or aim. (153)[6]

Horkheimer and Adorno call such reason that is reduced to instrumentalism "instrumental reason." Instrumental reason, they claim, leads not only to blind domination of outward nature but also to the domination of nature within human beings and to human beings' domination of other human beings: "What men want to learn from nature is how to use it in order to wholly dominate it and other men. That is the only aim" (4). It is important to emphasize that Horkheimer and Adorno do not say that enlightenment is a bad thing but, rather, their critique of enlightenment "is intended to prepare the way for a positive notion of enlightenment which will release it from entanglement in blind domination" (xvi).

I am proposing, then, that the reversion of reason from that which was once liberating to that which is repressive—stemming from self-destructive elements of enlightenment—can be described in terms of the reversed spear of Telephus. The homology exists in two intimately connected senses: as a wound that is an integral part of the entity that heals, and the order in which the healing and wounding are effected. This structure of progress, that contains the seeds of its reversal, and the intellectual history

Horkheimer and Adorno trace concerning the relationships between power and rationality in Western thought are central to my discussion of the spear of Telephus in *Krapp's Last Tape*. Of particular interest is the emphasis they place on technology as the essence of instrumental rationality.

A clear manifestation of the regressive aspect of progress (the reversed spear of Telephus effect) in the play is Krapp's relation with his own past that is wound up in the spools of the tape itself. The tape recorder, which has the ability to capture moments of Krapp's past and embodies the promise of healing his longing for a lost paradise, is at the same time that which turns Krapp's past into an object of control and manipulation by Krapp himself. The sound-recording technology enables Krapp time and again to evoke the memory of what seems to be the most significant and valuable moments of his entire life, to remember them in detail, and in a sense even to relive them. Yet at the same time, it is also the apparatus that separates Krapp from his previous experiences and his old egos, turning them into detached objects over which he exercises the power he gains from the machine. He switches the machine on and off, interrupts the narrative, and imposes on it a new order according to his own will; he mocks the aspirations of his old egos and, in short, manipulates his own alienated past. It can be said that the tape is blindly applied by Krapp without his having any real capacity to reflect on the ends to which it is applied. By turning his own past into an alienated manipulable material, he destroys the substantial tie that connects him to his old selves. Deprived of a past to rely on and a future to anticipate, Krapp is trapped in the present, and at this point his situation is brought to its extreme: total solitude. In his solitude and self-alienation Krapp becomes a representative of a modern human being (in the sense of Horkheimer and Adorno) who, by applying blind domination over nature with no self-reflective thought about its consequence, becomes the victim of the same conditions that constituted him as master: a victim of his own creation.

Another regressive aspect of progress in the play involves the very idea of repeatability that is inherent in recording technology.[7] The tape recorder's capability to repeat the most precious moments is at the same time that which nullifies these moments by depriving them of their uniqueness and values. In order to shed light on the regressive aspect of repeatability, I shall compare the representative power of what I term the "instrumental memory" of the tape recorder to that of Proustian involuntary memory. By naming the memory of the tape instrumental memory, I imply that the self-destructive aspect that is involved with repeatability is tightly connected to the fact that the mechanical device is a product of instrumental reason. It is important to note that the idea of concretizing memory on the spools of a tape so suggestively recalls Proustian voluntary and involuntary memory that Beckett critics have used these terms since the play was first performed to describe the function of this apparatus. Several approaches have been proposed and have contributed significantly to an understanding of this topic.[8] Yet they appear to have neglected what I understand as a central aspect of the play: the implied critique of the instrumental memory of the tape recorder and its ethical implications that can be explicated in terms of Horkheimer and Adorno's critique of instrumental reason. In my approach, involuntary memory serves as a background (as an ideal case of representation) against which the critique of instrumental memory can be identified.[9] The concepts "identity," "duplication," and "repetition" constitute the analytical corpus of the following discussion.

In his analysis of the mechanism of Proust's involuntary memory, Beckett underscores the duplication of total past sensation as a central factor that explains involuntary memory's inherent ability to penetrate the surface of things and expose their true essence:[10]

> If by some miracle of analogy the central impression of a past sensation recurs as an immediate stimuli which can be *instinctively* identified by the subject with the model of *duplication* [...], then the total past sensation, not its echo nor its copy, but the sensation itself [...] comes in a rush to engulf the subject in all the beauty of its infallible proportion. [...] *Such participation* [of immediate with past experience] *frees the essential reality that is denied to the contemplative as to the active life.* (54–55; emphasis added)

It is important to stress in this context that in Beckett's analysis the impression of past sensation with the wealth of its colors and perfumes recurs in its "integral purity" (54) in the immediate sensation precisely because it did not pass through the filter of the intelligence (as Beckett emphasizes, the duplication is guaranteed by forgetfulness). This passivity of reason is contrasted by Proust, as is well known, to the act of intellection that is involved in voluntary memory that is "conditioned by the prejudices of the intelligence" (53).[11] However, in *Krapp's Last Tape* the main opposition is between involuntary memory and instrumental memory. Here the passivity of reason is diametrically opposed to the total activity that is involved in the repetition of past sensation by the tape, an act that is tightly intertwined with domination. What is repeated by the tape is not a duplication of the total past sensation but *a reduction* of it to the reproductive capabilities of the machine. These capabilities are conditioned by scientific knowledge that, as Horkheimer and Adorno put it, "makes the dissimilar comparable by reducing it to abstract quantities" (7) that can be manipulated at will. In place of the objective identity of immediate with past experience that exists in the case of involuntary memory, instrumental memory results in a kind of *artificial identity* that involves the imposition of power over nature.[12] Since instrumental reason is not capable of recognizing the particular qualities of the material to which it is applied, the tape recorder (as a product of instrumental reason) does not repeat the original sensation in its own complex uniqueness, but rather creates an instrumental echo of it, a reductive copy that converts the unique into the common, the unrepeatable into the repeatable. It might thus be claimed that whereas involuntary memory is involved with real representation, instrumental memory involves misrepresentation.

While the self-destructive aspect of repeatability (and hence of the tape recorder as a sound-reproduction technology) is indeed relevant to the recorded voices of the many Krapps, it has no relevance as far as the documented events of the past are concerned. After all, what we actually hear are Krapp's own descriptions of the events and not the sounds of the events themselves mediated by the tape recorder. In this sense, the content of the tapes (that describe the events from Krapp's own perspective) instead of misrepresenting the external world (the way the events objectively occurred) allow us a kind of access to Krapp's inner world: the impression of the events on Krapp's senses and their assimilation to his consciousness. Since Krapp's inner world is the only reality that is of significance as far as the modification of his personality on the time axis is concerned—as Beckett puts it in *Proust:* "the only world that has reality and significance, the world of our latent consciousness" (3)—it seems, on the face of it, that while the tape recorder is indeed incapable of representing external reality, it does succeed in representing Krapp's inner reality.

I claim, however, that the very use of the recording machine has a distorting effect on Krapp's own descriptions of the events. In his *Proust* essay Beckett describes what he terms Proust's impressionism: "By his impressionism I mean his non-logical statement of phenomena in the order and exactitude of their perception, before they have been distorted into intelligibility of cause and effect" (66). Krapp's situation is anything but impressionistic in this sense; he does not describe the events in the order and exactitude of their perception, but rather as products of a self-reflective mediating consciousness. In other words, Krapp records his own description of the events, totally aware of their representative function in the future, and as such it raises the possibility that he describes them in the way he would like them to be remembered, and not necessarily the way he perceives them. Krapp's attitude here might be compared to that of Proust's grandmother, in an incident in which she had insisted on having her photograph taken so that her beloved grandchild might have at least that poor record of her last years. Beckett indicates that "she had been very particular about her pose and the inclination of her hat, *wishing the photograph to be one of a grandmother and not of a disease*" (30; emphasis added). The same constructivist aspect of a self-aware act of documentation is echoed in Roland Barthes's *Camera Lucida:* "But very often (too often, to my taste) I have been photographed and knew it. Now, *once I feel myself observed by the lens, everything changes: I constitute myself in the process of 'posing,'* I instantaneously make another body for myself, I transform myself in advance into an image" (10–12; emphasis added). It might be claimed that Krapp's records, very much like Barthes's self-aware photography, are constructivist rather than impressionistic.[13] They construct rather than reflect the object.

I would like to suggest, however, that the self-destructive aspect of the tape can be perceived in the extreme if we bear in mind that Krapp seems to be obsessed with documentation. This recognition raises the possibility of distorting the original events themselves. The very idea of documentation, Krapp's awareness that the event is going to be documented, transforms him into one who simultaneously acts out the roles of an actor and a spectator of the drama of his own life. The representing documentation and the represented event are now woven into the same fabric in such a way that they cannot be separated from each other. As a result, the object of documentation is modified. Krapp's actions—in what is supposed to be the original documented events—are nullified of their authentic values. An illustration of such a type of distortion can be found in Italo Calvino's

Invisible Cities. The ancients built the city Valdrada, Calvino tells us, on the shores of a lake:

> Thus the traveler, arriving, sees two cities: one erect above the lake and the other reflected, upside-down.[...] Valdrada's inhabitants know that each of their actions is, at once, that action and its mirror-image [...]. Even when lovers twist their naked bodies, skin against skin [...] even when murderers plunge the knife into the black veins of the neck [...] *it is not so much their copulating or murdering that matters as the copulating or murdering of the images, limpid and cold in the mirror.* (43–44; emphasis added)

This inherent possibility of depriving events of their authenticity, which is found in any situation in which the awareness of documentation precedes the event itself, intensifies the self-destructive potential of the tape recorder. In this case we do not just have a misrepresentation of external events, but rather a situation in which the central condition of the very possibility of representation—the originality of the object of representation—is undermined.

These various aspects of the reversed spear of Telephus of the tape recorder, I maintain, illustrate most of all the internal relations between technology, utilitarian ethics, and power. It is the radical separation between subject and object, humanity and nature, underlying the scientific-technological thinking, that legitimizes Krapp's treatment of his own past as an object of control and manipulation. Guided by his wants and passions, Krapp finds the usefulness of his totalitarian activity more important than the context within which it is applied, and as a result he remains indifferent both to the values of his past and to the ends of his activity. In this respect Beckett's description of Proust's human beings as victims of their own blind will seems perfectly suitable for Krapp and yet obtains new meaning when ascribed to him: "And so in a sense are Proust's men and women, whose will is blind and hard, but never self-conscious, never abolished in the pure perception of a pure subject. They are victims of their volition, active with a grotesque predetermined activity, within the narrow limits of an impure world" (69).

One might consequently claim that the tape recorder, which illustrates the interrelations between technology, ethics of utility, and power, is the most incompetent instrument for capturing the pure essence of one's own past. This apparatus's incompetence to resurrect the past nevertheless converts the function of the tape in the play from a literal one to a symbolic one; rather than representing reality by the power of its mechanism, it functions as a negative symbol that refers to that which it is not. The only way to present those inexpressible and untouchable moments of Krapp's life with their pure human values is by using negative symbols that evoke their absence.[14] This functioning of the tape recorder as a symbol of that which it is not is exemplified in Krapp's bending over the machine and embracing it when he recalls the memory of the girl in the boat. The deepest longings and aspirations of a human being are evoked here by that in which they are most absent—a cold, inhuman machine.[15] By this transformation of the operation of the tape from literal to symbolic, the tape's failure to represent reality in positive terms is countered by its success in conjuring it up by negative ones. In other words, since Beckett does not share Proust's optimistic vision of the inherent ability of involuntary memory to reveal the real, he instead works through its negation, a kind of instrumental memory whose inability to provide access to essential reality is inherent in its very structure.

My central claim, then, is that it is the imaginative play's illustration of what an instrumental damaged memory is like that allows intimations of a possible undamaged memory to show through, a kind of fleeting glimpse of the elusive figure of essential reality. Over and above that, it is the imaginative play's illustration of what a damaged ethics is like—the reversed spear of Telephus aspects of the tape recorder—that allows the silhouette of a possible undamaged ethics, one that is free from considerations of utility and is more sensitive to moral values, to show through. Using the tape recorder as a negative symbol is, thus, Beckett's way to include in his work what is beyond the limits of representation. This subtle evocation of a possible humanistic ethics (in the sense that acts are assessed according to moral values and human justice) is reflected in the atmosphere of the play that Beckett describes as tender and lyrical—"A woman's tone goes through the entire play, returning always, a lyrical tone. . . . Krapp feels tenderness and frustration for the feminine beings" (qtd. in Knowlson, *Damned* 442)—and is contrasted to its elements of power and domination. It is this contrast that charges the play with its dramatic tension.

Finally, the way Beckett shapes the function of the tape recorder in the play (the reversed spear of Telephus) is in fact a manifestation of his ethical stance as an artist who, on the one hand, is fascinated by the possibilities opened up for humankind at large and for his artistic work in particular by new technological innovations, and yet, on the other hand, feels obliged to expose technology's latent self-destructive elements. Daniel Albright indicates in *Beckett and Aesthetics* that "Beckett in some sense wanted to be uneasy about technology. Just as Krapp struggles to find the right passage of tape, and eventually throws away a tape in disgust, so Beckett [...] refuses to take advantage of what the medium can do well, preferring the effortful, the recalcitrant, even the incorrect" (1). Albright explains Beckett's uneasiness in terms of Beckett's way "to foreground the medium, to thrust it in the spectator's face, by showing its inadequacy, its refusal to be wrenched to any good artistic purpose" (1). I suggest an understanding of Beckett's "uneasiness" about technology in the light of his recognition of its regressive aspects. The structure of the reversed spear of Telephus that is embedded in *Krapp's Last Tape* can be seen in this respect as the act of an artist who incorporates technology into his work as a means of artistic innovation, while at the same time using its characteristic capabilities to criticize the very technology itself, by transforming its covert regressive elements into overt ones.

Notes

1. Though most Beckett critics have underscored his innovation in using technology to evoke the passage of time, few have placed technology as the focal point of their work. A notable exception is Albright's analysis of *Krapp Last Tape* in *Beckett and Aesthetics*.

2. Many Beckett critics have emphasized Proustian echoes in Krapp. For example, as early as 1973 Cohn writes: "Unlike Proust's Marcel, Krapp does not have to depend on involuntary memory for lost time. He can find it on the spools of tape, methodically numbered, titled, and catalogued" (165); and Brater notes: "Proustian memory is literally made concrete, permanent, and concise in a series of recording sessions designed for future broadcast" (9).

3. I use the term "Paradise" in the sense that Beckett defines it in *Proust:* "[...] the only Paradise that is not the dream of a madman, the Paradise that has been lost" (55).

4. Jarvis underscores that "Adorno and Horkheimer do not use the term enlightenment primarily to designate a historical period running from Descartes to Kant. Instead they use it to refer to a series of related intellectual and practical operations which are presented as demythologizing, secularizing or disenchanting some mythical, religious or magical representation of the world" (24).

5. For example, in their study of "elements of anti-Semitism," which is concerned with "the actual reversion of enlightened civilization to barbarism" (Horkheimer and Adorno xi),

they show that self-destruction has always been a characteristic of rationalism and in more specific terms that the "irrationalism" of anti-Semitism "is deduced from the nature of the dominant *ratio* itself, and the world which corresponds to its image" (xvii).

6. Held emphasizes that Adorno and Horkheimer's study of the structure of enlightenment is indebted to Hegel: "Particularly, Hegel's claim that there is an internal relationship between enlightenment, an ethic of utility and terror (especially the Terror of the French Revolution) is paralleled in their own discussion of the relationship between scientific consciousness (based on instrumental reason), pragmatism and ethical decision-ism, and barbarism (especially the barbarism of totalitarianism)" (151).

7. For a complementary discussion of the illusory character of reproduction, see Albright 85–86. Albright's discussion draws on an earlier essay of Adorno ("Curves of the Needle" [1928]).

8. For example, Knowlson shows that the "mechanisation of the process of memory" works against the revelations of involuntary memory (*Light and Darkness* 20); and Oppen-heim writes: "Although Krapp seeks not to obliterate but, rather, to reify the perception of self, what Proust immortalized as 'voluntary' and 'involuntary memory' are the dramatized operative modes" (145). See also note 2.

9. I describe involuntary memory as an ideal case of representation since Beckett, as is well known, does not share Proust's possibility of access to essential reality provided by involuntary memory. See in this context Wood's analysis.

10. As Wood indicates, Beckett's analysis of Proust's work is constructed on a philo-sophical "geometry" that consists of two planes: one is the surface, the conceptual prison of language; and the other is that in which things can be seen in their true essence.

11. As Beckett explains in *Proust:* "The most trivial experience—he [Proust] says in effect—is encrusted with elements that logically are not related to it and have consequently been rejected by our intelligence" (55).

12. In this context see Jarvis's discussion on what Adorno calls "identity thinking" (165–68).

13. It might be interesting to refer in this context to McMillan and Fehsenfeld's note: "In working with Marcel Mihalovici on the text for his opera *Krapp,* Beckett acknowledged that Krapp's recordings were like a photograph album evoking memories of central mo-ments of his past" (327).

14. That Beckett works in this play with oppositions is explicitly manifested in the Manichaean elements associated with the dichotomy of spirit and flesh: light/dark; black/white. For a detailed description of Manichaean elements in *Krapp's Last Tape,* see McMillan and Fehsenfeld 245–52. These oppositions, I suggest, serve as cues for the spectator of the more implicit opposition: the function of tape recorder as a negative symbol that evokes its absent positive counterpart. This opposition on the symbolic level suggests a likeness with the transposition between negative and positive form in Picasso's collages. See, in this con-text, Krauss's discussion (33–34).

15. It is interesting to note that Albright provides a detailed analysis of the tape recorder's operation as "a mechanical sex partner" and in this sense suggests a literal interpretation of Krapp's relation with the machine. Yet he concludes his discussion by indicating that "no matter how faithfully the machine reiterates Krapp's old spiels, it is still a warped, unreal thing, a plot-contrivance, a 'stage-image,' more than a credible piece of technology" (91).

Works Cited

Albright, Daniel. *Beckett and Aesthetics.* Cambridge: Cambridge University Press, 2003.

Barthes, Roland. *Camera Lucida: Reflections on Photography.* Trans. Howard Richard. London: Fontana Paperback, 1984.

Beckett, Samuel. *Collected Shorter Plays.* New York: Grove, 1984.

———. *Proust. The Collected Works of Samuel Beckett.* New York: Grove, 1970.

Brater, Enoch. *Beyond Minimalism: Beckett's Late Style in the Theater.* Oxford: Oxford University Press, 1987.

Calvino, Italo. *Invisible Cities.* Trans. William Weaver. London: Pan Books, 1979.

Cohn, Ruby. *Back to Beckett.* Princeton, NJ: Princeton University Press, 1973.

Held, David. *Introduction to Critical Theory: Horkheimer to Habermas.* Berkeley: University of California Press, 1980.

Horkheimer, Max, and Theodor W. Adorno. *Dialectic of Enlightenment.* Trans. John Cumming. London: Lane, 1973.

Jarvis, Simon. *Adorno: A Critical Introduction.* New York: Routledge, 1988.

Knowlson, James. *Damned to Fame: The Life of Samuel Beckett.* London: Bloomsbury, 1996.

———. *Light and Darkness in the Theatre of Samuel Beckett.* London: Turret, 1972.

Krauss, Rosalind. *The Originality of the Avant-Garde and Other Modernist Myths.* Cambridge, MA: MIT Press, 1986. 23–40.

McMillan, Dougald, and Martha Fehsenfeld. *Beckett in the Theatre.* London: Calder, 1988.

Oppenheim, Lois. *The Painted Word: Beckett's Dialogue with Art.* Ann Arbor: University of Michigan Press, 2000.

Wood, Rupert. "An Endgame of Aesthetics: Beckett as Essayist." *The Cambridge Companion to Beckett.* Ed. John Pilling. Cambridge: Cambridge University Press, 1994. 1–16.

Re-Figuring the Stage Body through the Mechanical Re-Production of Memory

ANTONIA RODRÍGUEZ-GAGO

S AMUEL BECKETT'S *Krapp's Last Tape* has been read in numerous ways, most often as a parody of Proust's ideas on the workings of involuntary memory, demonstrating the impossibility of recovering the past, even when memories have been mechanically archived on magnetic tape; or as a paradigm of the Cartesian dualism analyzed through binary images of mind/body, spirit/flesh, change/changelessness. In this essay I will discuss the play from a different point of view: the relationship established between the stage figure of Krapp and the recorded voice of memory, particularly the process of the protagonist's creation, that is, how Beckett re-figures in performance the protagonist's body through the mechanical reproduction of memory. According to Stanton B. Garner, "bodied spatiality is at the heart of dramatic presentation, for it is through the actor's corporeal presence under the spectator's gaze that the dramatic text actualizes itself in the field of performance" (1). This general statement that can be applied to all plays in performance is modified and extended by Beckett in *Krapp's Last Tape* to include an incorporeal recorded voice of memory that, together with Krapp the corporeal presence, become the dual protagonists of the play. As Andrew Head observes, "The inclusion of recorded speech as a significant and meaningful protagonist in this confessional drama adds a technological dimension" and originates the problematic relationship between a stage body and a talking machine, or "between live and (what has become known as) mediatized performance" (2).

Actors and stage directors who have worked with Beckett frequently repeat that he paid minute attention to the creation of the physical stage image and dealt with the stage body as if it were "the raw materials of the painter or sculptor, in the service of a systematic exploration of all possible relationships between the body and movement, the body and space, the body and objects, the body and light and the body and words" (Chabert 23). In *Krapp's Last Tape* the performance focuses on the physical actions of Krapp—his posture, movements, gestures—and on the relationships he establishes with props. His moments of agitation are followed by almost total stillness. Immobility is stressed when Krapp listens to his tapes, his body becoming a portrait of memory or, in Jeanette Malkin's words, a "posture of memory" (37).

Beckett places Krapp's staged body in confrontation with his taped voice of memory, and the dramatic tension in the play is generated by the coincidences and the disparities between these two entities. Krapp's initial routines with objects are only delaying tactics, which lead him to his main "addiction": listening to his tapes. It is through Krapp's attentive listening to memories he has long forgotten that the play's action moves forward and that the physical presence of the central character undergoes different metamorphoses.

Beckett's fascination with recorded sound has been well documented, ever since Clas Zilliacus's seminal book, *Beckett and Broadcasting,* of 1976. Beckett became aware of the existence of tape recorders in a visit to the BBC in the 1950s. According to Martin Esslin, in 1958 Beckett wrote to Donald McWhinnie telling him that he had written a stage monologue for Pat Magee and asked him "for operating instructions for a tape recorder since he had to be sure how it worked" (qtd. in Zilliacus 203). Beckett's dramatic use of technology in *Krapp's Last Tape* was quite an innovation at the time, as was his creation of a recorded voice as one of the play's two characters. Working on this play, Beckett discovered how recorded, disembodied voices could create dramatic tension. The separation of voice and body in *Krapp's Last Tape* offered new ways of simultaneously presenting different moments in the life of a single protagonist, and of showing different levels of contrasting inner experiences, a technique he would use in his later TV and stage plays. The recorded voice of Krapp is the first embodiment in sound of the "dead voices" of memory that haunt Didi and Gogo, in *Waiting for Godot,* and torture Joe in the TV play *Eh Joe.* The difference is that Krapp seeks and wants to hear his "dead" voice of memory, whereas Joe struggles "to throttle" the dead voices that sound in his mind. It can also be argued that Joe, isolating himself in his room, creates the conditions for the female voice to speak, and he practices his "mental thuggee" for company.

By contrast, in *Krapp's Last Tape,* the mechanically reproduced memories provide examples of the changes that have occurred in Krapp's life and background for his present situation. This situation has been wonderfully summarized by Ruby Cohn as that of "an old man looking back regretfully upon a life in which he sacrificed love to artistic ambition" (238). Artistic ambition is the key theme of the "memorable equinox" episode, and love is central in the love affair with the girl in the punt, a scene Krapp plays three times, each time listening with increased attention. Old Krapp's failure to achieve artistic ambition and keep love constitute the central thematic pivots around which the play evolves, and they provide the most climactic moments of the recorded memories. Since he is a recipient of the voices of memory presented as external to the stage body, Krapp becomes a clear predecessor of the disembodied head/protagonist of *That Time* who is also a recipient of recorded voices of memory, which, in that play, seem to sound of their own accord from different points of the stage, and from different moments of the protagonist's past.

If memory, external to the body, is central to the action of *Krapp's Last Tape,* so is forgetting. As I have argued elsewhere, "forgetting is [...] an important part of the act of remembering" (113), for the gaps left by memory are always replaced by inventions. Thus Beckett's characters use forgetting and misremembering in a creative, active way. Recollections are never to be trusted; it becomes evident that his storytellers misremember, contradict themselves, hesitate, pause, and often give different versions of the same story. This occurs more frequently in his later plays, in which older characters not only have bad memories but also are "visual and aural embodiments of obsessive memories" (Rodríguez-Gago, 114). Krapp's solution to avoid the problems of misremembering is to record his autobiography on tapes, thus arming himself against forgetting—hoping that in old age, when memory fails, he can always turn to his tape recorder in order to remember crucial moments of his past archived there. The play's central irony is that time erodes even recorded memory, and neither thirty-nine-year-old nor sixty-nine-year-old Krapp can recognize or identify himself with "that young whelp" (13) or "that stupid bastard" (17) presented by the voices of memory. Audiences, however, are able to recognize the common features and routines shared by the onstage protagonist and his past taped selves. All Krapps are addicted to bananas and drinking, are "hesitating" storytellers, and look at their past with a mixture of nostalgia, regret, and disbelief.

It is tempting to read *Krapp's Last Tape* (following Drew Leder's interesting article on the body in medical practice) as a "tale of two bodies: the Cartesian corpse and the lived body" (117), the body as machine and the experiencing body. "The lived body," that of old Krapp, as an "intending being [...] a being in relation with that which is other: other people, other things, an environment" (123), contrasts with "the Cartesian corpse," thirty-nine-year-old Krapp, the body as machine, which is derided and dissected on old Krapp's table, and which, nevertheless, exerts fascination and power over the stage figure. This Manichaean reading, however, is prevented by the visible process of integration and mingling of contrasting elements that affect all aspects of the play. For instance, black and white colors appear together in costume and objects, and in the light and darkness emblems that constitute the play's central imagery and that are visually embodied in its setting. It is evident that the play's central action is not one of separating but of trying to understand and reconcile opposing elements, and this tendency affects not only the material properties but, most significantly, the central character(s). The stage body and the memory voice are two sides, past and present, of the same dramatic persona, Krapp, presented as both "perceiver and perceived, intentional and material" (Leder 124).

In the Schiller Theater Notebook Beckett underlines the importance of integrating opposing images in this play. He notes, for instance, eighteen moments of "explicit integration light dark" (132). This process of integration at work in the play seems to question the Manichaean vision. Therefore, I share Sue Wilson's point that "The Manichaean presence is signalled in *Krapp's Last Tape* so that Krapp may be seen to offend against its ethical and intellectual strictures" (131). The play in this view is a critique of its protagonist's useless Manichaean and metaphysical obsessions shown specifically through the young Krapp's recorded voice. Old Krapp does not seem to be worried about the intellectual problems of "separating the grain from the husks" or light from darkness; his only aim seems to be recuperating, or reliving, emotional moments of his past ("to be there again") aided by his recorded tapes in which his younger voice is archived.

Old Krapp is an experiencing body more disillusioned than his younger self and does not seem to believe in the power of the intellect over the senses, of mind over body. This becomes explicit when he records his summary of the present year, where the artistic ambition of young Krapp is derided: "Just been listening to that stupid bastard I took myself for thirty years ago, hard to believe I was ever as bad as that" (17). The play's dramatic tension, which is initially created by the antagonism between man/machine and body/voice, is constantly modified by Krapp's reactions to the recorded voice, and by divergences between narrated and acted experiences.

While listening to past events narrated by the taped voice, the audience simultaneously witnesses how these recorded events affect the stage figure. Old Krapp's musings, exclamations, curses, gestures, movements, and other bodily actions prove how the stage body is visually re-figured by his memory voice, and how the mechanically reproduced memory carries the play's action forward. The following are a few examples to illustrate this point.

Krapp's Last Tape opens with its protagonist involved in a moment of intense thinking. Beckett emphasizes this moment by adding new stage directions in his revised text for the Schiller Theater: "KRAPP sits with both hands on table. He *remains a* good *moment motionless,* staring before him. He shudders, *looks at his watch,* grunts, puts it back in his pocket and returns to his first attitude" (RT 3; additions in roman). After turning back to his immobile, sculptural posture for a few more seconds, he gets up, paces to and fro, and starts his routine of eating bananas. In order to remember, Krapp—like Didi in *Godot*—needs to move. Apparently, this method works, for Krapp suddenly *"throws banana backstage, and goes with all speed he can muster backstage right into darkness"* (RT 3). His senses seem to take him back to the past more faithfully than his intellect; his pacing and the taste of his bananas have helped him to remember the year of the tape to which he wants to listen. He immediately runs to his cubbyhole to find his tapes and his memory machine before he forgets, prompted by his need to relive a specific moment of his past experience: young Krapp with the girl in the punt. In other words, "To be there again" he needs his tape recorder, the machine that takes him back to his past. According to Beckett, Krapp has forty-five tapes he has been recording every birthday, beginning at "24 years of age" (Notebook 53). He selects on this occasion box three, spool five (*Krapp* 11), where thirty-nine-year-old Krapp has recorded the most important events of his past year.

On stage we see old Krapp handling the containers of his memory with loving care, like Winnie handles her possessions in *Happy Days*. He even tries to personalize his tapes, addressing them as "the little rascal!" (10) or "the little scoundrel!" (11). His discontinuous movements and his "happy smiles" while reading the content of his tapes seem also a model for Winnie, another character trapped by daily routines with objects and words. When sitting at the table, Krapp is visible only from his waist up, like Winnie in the first act of *Happy Days*. However, Beckett does not repeat himself exactly but presents variations on similar situations, as it is clear by the way he deals with the stage body (male and female) and with memory and forgetting in both plays. Winnie, who like Krapp has a bad memory, fills the gaps left by memory with inventions and improvisations. Krapp, on the other hand, does not have to invent or improvise his memories; he has them archived, recorded on magnetic tapes that he can reproduce at random according to his present wishes and needs. Paradoxically, Krapp's taped memory is not better, more "objective," or more reliable than Winnie's fragmented evocations. His recorded memories are distorted by continuous hesitations, pauses, and interruptions that undermine their meaning and place doubts on the truth of the narrated events. Old Krapp pretends he does not recognize himself in "that stupid bastard" he was thirty years ago and laughs at his aspirations and resolutions, but his routines with objects, his gestures, and his recording the most significant events of the past year on his birthdays show the connection between the two Krapps, the recorded voice and the stage figure.

Krapp's physical aspect, costume, gesture, and movement are precisely described by Beckett's stage directions: "*Rusty black narrow trousers too short for him. Rusty black sleeveless waistcoat, four capacious pockets. Heavy silver watch and chain. Grimy white shirt open at neck, no collar. Surprising pair of dirty white boots* [...]. *White face. Purple nose. Disordered grey hair. Unshaven.*" His physical limitations are also underlined. Krapp is "*very near-sighted*" and "*hard of hearing.*" Perhaps to emphasize decay and the importance of sound in this play, the protagonist has a "*cracked voice*" and "*distinctive intonation.*" Also related to sound and old age is Krapp's "*laborious walk,*" which is always accompanied by the sound of his heavy breathing (*Krapp* 9). Other bodily sounds that play a central part in the play are coughing, salivating, cursing, and murmuring. We are made aware of Krapp's physical limitations through his interaction with the ledger, tapes, and tape recorder. These actions and sounds stress the materiality and the presence of the stage body.

In her interesting article on Beckett's use of the human body onstage, Katherine M. Gray argues that "we are made aware of the material body by its transgressions into playing space, [...] the material body sweats, salivates, drools, spits, coughs, belches, weeps, sneezes, hiccoughs, tears, urinates, bleeds." She suggests that the "material body processes can, to an extent, be scripted as 'action' so that the production of matter activates the play world's response to its appearance, but generally the material body's evidence is unwelcome to the conventional stage" (8). Following Gray, it can be argued that old Krapp's physical decay and unconventional behavior are embodied in sound. We can hear old Krapp belching and coughing offstage, in his drinking rounds, and cursing and swearing when he is irritated by young Krapp's intellectual ambitions.

However, Krapp's physical actions in the play go beyond bodily sounds. They are often the result of reaction to the mechanical voice of himself on tape, which causes him to engage in discontinuous motions. Discontinuity is often related in Beckett to defective memory. In the play, for instance, moments of agitation are usually followed by moments of almost total inactivity, and these contrasting actions, or postures of the body, provide dramatic tension. Beckett establishes old Krapp's two basic postures: one of motionless listening and the other of agitated listening. In the Schiller Theater revised text he stresses Krapp's initial immobile posture: "KRAPP *sits with both hands on the table. He remains a good moment motionless, staring before him*" (RT 3). This posture of memory is explained by the author as follows: "At curtain up he is thinking of the story of the boat and trying to remember which year it was (how old he was)" (Notebook 49). This can be important information for the actor playing Krapp, but in performance one sees a still silent figure staring at us, and it is impossible to guess what he is thinking. Krapp's immobile posture of intense thinking, however, is repeated with variations at the opening and closing of the play, and in other moments of intense listening. This immobile posture of the body is always related to moments of forgetting. Krapp's fight against forgetting is usually followed by movement and by his business with objects. One could say that an act of forgetting opens the play, starts the action, and moves it forward, leading thus to the progressive re-figuring of the stage body: from sitting immobile at his table, to standing, to walking to and fro, to recording, to sitting again listening at his table.

Forgetting is a feature throughout the play. Once he has found the tape he wants to listen to, Krapp has to make further efforts to remember the episode he wants to hear and turns for help to the entries in his old ledger. His expressions of surprise, when he reads these entries, the shrugging of his shoulders, and his repeated puzzlement and brooding show Krapp's inability to remember his past through his annotations:

(*He peers at ledger, reads entry at foot page.*) Mother at rest at last.... Hm... The black ball... (*He raises his head, stares blankly front. Puzzled.*) Black ball?... (He peers again at ledger, reads.) The dark nurse... (*He raises his head, broods, peers again at ledger, reads.*) Slight improvement in bowel condition... Hm.... Memorable... what? (*He peers closer.*) Equinox, memorable equinox. (*He raises his head, stares blankly front. Puzzled.*) Memorable equinox?... (*Pause. He shrugs his shoulders, peers again at ledger, reads.*) Farewell to—(*he turns page*)—love. (11)

A gesture, "he turns the page," and the sound of the word *love* help Krapp to remember, and he immediately switches on his taped voice. "*He raises his head, broods, bends over machine, switches on and assumes listening posture, i.e. leaning forward, elbows on table, hand cupping ear towards machine, face front*" (11).

Krapp adopts this listening posture, his body bent over the tape recorder, almost touching it, indicating his interest and readiness to receive his voice of memory. An image of union between the protagonist's body and his memory machine—the rememberer and the remembered—is thus visually established. Listening to his recorded voices also provides entertainment for Krapp and helps him relive past moments of intense emotion and avoid his present boredom. Depressed at the prospect of celebrating yet another birthday, "the awful occasion," and lamenting his decaying physical condition, Krapp turns to his tapes, trying to find in them some meaning for his present troubles, or perhaps some moments of emotional gratification. His recorded voice, however, brings back wanted as well as unwanted memories. Krapp reacts to the former by adopting a posture of "*motionlessness listening,*" and to the latter with one of *agitated listening*, described by Beckett as "*agitation listening*" (Notebook 45). These contrasting postures of the body, which are repeated with variations during Krapp's acts of listening, serve to illustrate how the stage body is constantly re-figured through the mechanical reproduction of his voice of memory. Krapp's act of "intellectual transgression" (Notebook 141) occurs mainly in the reported episodes, especially in the "memorable equinox" section where images of light and darkness multiply. The "intellectual" process of mingling the opposites, which is mainly narrated by the taped voice of young Krapp, is echoed visually by a mixture of dirty white and black colors, and by the progressive physical union between the stage body and his recorded voice, leading perhaps to old Krapp's acceptance of his past intellectual and emotional decisions: "Ah well, maybe he was right. (*Pause.*) Maybe he was right" (18).

In this last section, I will focus on some moments of intellectual and sensual mingling that lead to the reconciliation between the stage figure and his voice of memory. It is in these moments when Krapp's body posture changes from motionlessness to agitated listening. In one of the first reported episodes, "Mother at rest at last," the contrasting images of black and white that move the narration forward are related to objects (blinds up and down), to people ("white and starch" nurse pushing a black hooded perambulator), and to actions, thirty-nine-year-old Krapp giving a black ball to a white dog: "the form here is that of a mingling" (Notebook 141), an act of sacrificing sense to spirit resulting in a paradigmatic moment of intellectual transgression. During this episode, Krapp listens with attention, switching the tape off only twice, the first time intrigued by the word "viduity," and the second to brood over the girl's eyes. The meaning of words he has forgotten and women's eyes are the focus of his nostalgic musings. The narrating voice describes this year as one of "profound gloom" until "that memorable night in March, at the end of the jetty" when he had his "vision at last" (15), and it is this vision mainly that he wants to record for the future. During the "memorable equinox" episode, Krapp is in a situation of agitated listening and progressive anger, showing his disgust and disagreement with the narrated story: "*KRAPP curses, switches off, winds tape forward, switches on again*" (16). Furious with his memory voice, Krapp switches the tape off and on, and winds it forward several times during the narration, thus undermining its meaning and its relevance for the present listener, though, paradoxically, the spectators are more intrigued by the content of the tape, which they cannot understand given its constant interruptions. This constant stopping and starting indicates also what Krapp is really interested in listening to. He now knows what has happened with his young aspirations and resolutions, and so he curses at and derides them. The only moment he wants to recover of that year is the scene with the girl in the punt. Constant interruptions function dramatically as delaying tactics to postpone the listening of this climactic episode.

Krapp's relationships with several women are evoked in the recorded and in the live performance. Krapp seems to have had "affairs" with many different types of women, but he can only remember their eyes. Words and eyes are the focus of his nostalgic musings. Old Krapp pays a tribute to the women's eyes, whenever they are mentioned, by switching the tape off and brooding about them for some seconds. Women's eyes provide moments of sensual and spiritual union often related in the play to images of light and darkness. The first narrated event providing one of these moments of union, evoked by the recorded voice, is young Krapp's affair with Bianca (white), a woman he had lived with in Kedar (black) Street, when he was in his twenties. "Not much about her," he says, "apart from a tribute to her eyes. Very warm. I suddenly saw them again. (*Pause.*) Incomparable!" (12–13). Old Krapp—whose life, Beckett reminds us, is "drowned in dreams" (Notebook 241)—cuts the narration and broods over these incomparable eyes. The second woman young Krapp evokes is a nursemaid "all white and starch," pushing "a big black hooded perambulator," who had eyes "like [...] chrysolite!" (14–15). For young Krapp, women's eyes seem to be only mirrors in which he can see himself, or just beautiful objects of aesthetic contemplation. Only in the climactic episode with the girl in the punt do eyes figure more prominently, not only as mirrors but also as passages through which body and soul could perhaps be integrated, as can be inferred from this fragment: "I asked her to look at me and after a few moments—(*Pause.*)—after a few moments she did, but the eyes just slits because of the glare. I bent over her to get them in the shadow and they opened. (*Pause. Low.*) Let me in. (*Pause.*)" (17).

At this point old Krapp's body starts bending over the tape recorder, and he ends this movement by almost embracing the machine, in a posture of "motionlessness listening," as if wanting to relive this moment and be again with the girl in the punt "drifting among the flags." Memory, experience, and desire are aurally and visually mingled at this point. Before starting his live recording, Krapp muses again over that girl's eyes: "The eyes she had! (*Broods, realizes he is recording, silence, switches off, broods. Finally.*) Everything there, everything, all the—(*Realizes this is not being recorded, switches on.*) Everything there, everything on this old muckball, all the light and dark and famine and feasting of... (*hesitates*)... the ages!" (18).

Krapp is paralyzed for several seconds brooding at this moment of union, dreaming perhaps of his past lost love, and wants to record his present feelings for a future listener. The importance of this episode in the play, however, is quite clear from the start when old Krapp struggles with his memory in order to remember the year when it was recorded. This is also the only episode he listens to repeatedly, allowing his recorded voice to momentarily take over live performance, reducing the stage figure to immobility and silence.

In a letter to Alan Schneider of 21 November 1958, Beckett talks about Magee's performance of these last moments. He is positively surprised by "the kind of personal relationship that developed" in the production "between Krapp and the machine," and mentions one scene when this relationship became especially interesting: "At the very end when 'I lay down across her etc.' comes for the third time, the head comes down on the table and remains down until 'here I end etc.,' on which it comes up and the eyes staring front till the end" (qtd. in Harmon 50). Romantic old Krapp ("drowned in dreams") seems to believe that a moment of intense passion is superior and more lasting than the fire of the intellect that replaced it. This conclusion is undermined by the final image of the play with Krapp motionless staring before him, his "last tape" left running silently. The physical confrontation between a stage body and a talking machine reproducing his voice of memory ends with Krapp and the tape recorder, body and voice achieving a moment of almost perfect union, past memories momentarily inscribed on the present stage body.

Krapp's Last Tape, perhaps "the most influential dramatic monologue of the 20th century" (Egoyan 14), shows, among many other things, that the past cannot be recovered voluntarily even when previously recorded on tapes and carefully archived in boxes, for memories are always contaminated by the present rememberer, and words and images lose their meanings in time and change with different situations. What can be represented is a stage body reacting to and being re-figured by the mechanical reproduction of his voice of memory. In this respect, the play was ahead of its time.

Works Cited

Beckett, Samuel. *Krapp's Last Tape*. 1958. London: Faber, 1969. (Abbreviated *Krapp*.)

———. *Krapp's Last Tape*. Revised text. 1969. Knowlson 1–10. (Abbreviated RT.)

———. Production Notebook for *Das letzte Band*, Schiller-Theater-Werkstatt, Berlin, 1969. Knowlson 39–248. (Abbreviated Notebook.)

Chabert, Pierre. "The Body in Beckett's Theatre." *Journal of Beckett Studies* 8 (1982): 23–28.

Cohn, Ruby. *A Beckett Canon*. Ann Arbor: University of Michigan Press, 2001.

Egoyan, Atom. "Memories Are Made of Hiss: Remember the Good Old Pre-digital Days?" *Guardian* 7 Feb. 2002: 14.

Garner, Stanton B., Jr. *Bodied Spaces: Phenomenology and Performance in Contemporary Drama*. Ithaca, NY: Cornell University Press, 1994.

Gray, Katherine M. "Troubling the Body: Towards a Theory of Beckett's Use of the Human Body on Stage." *Journal of Beckett Studies* 5 (1996): 1–17.

Harmon, Maurice, ed. *No Author Better Served: The Correspondence of Samuel Beckett and Alan Schneider*. Cambridge, MA: Harvard University Press, 1998.

Head, Andrew. "'. . . I wouldn't want them back' Issues of Process and Technology in a Recent Production of *Krapp's Last Tape*." *Studies in Theatre and Performance* 25 (2005): 1–8.

Knowlson, James, ed. *Krapp's Last Tape*. Vol. 3 of *The Theatrical Notebooks of Samuel Beckett*. London: Faber, 1996.

Leder, Drew. "A Tale of Two Bodies: The Cartesian Corpse and the Lived Body." *Body and Flesh: A Philosophical Reader*. Ed. Don Welton. Oxford: Blackwell, 1998. 117–29.

Malkin, Jeanette R. *Memory Theatre and Postmodern Drama*. Ann Arbor: University of Michigan Press, 1999.

Rodríguez-Gago, Antonia. "The Embodiment of Memory (and Forgetting) in Beckett's Late Women Plays." *Drawing on Beckett: Portraits, Performances, and Cultural Contexts*. Ed. Linda Ben-Zvi. Tel Aviv: Assaph, 2003. 113–26.

Wilson, Sue. "*Krapp's Last Tape* and the Mania of Manichaeism." *Pastiches Parodies and Other Imitations*. Vol. 12 of *SBT/A*. Ed. Marius Buning, Matthijs Engelberts, and Sjef Houppermans. Amsterdam: Rodopi, 2002. 131–44.

Zilliacus, Clas. *Beckett and Broadcasting*. Abo: Abo Akademi, 1976.

Part III

ECHOING BECKETT

Words and Music, . . . but the clouds. . . , and Yeats's "The Tower"

MINAKO OKAMURO

WORDS AND MUSIC (1962) contains no direct reference to William Butler Yeats, but some hints of the poet and his works can be found in its language. The radio play has three characters, if we can call them "characters": Words called Joe, Music called Bob, and their master, Croak. At the beginning, Croak requests forgiveness from Words and Music for his belated arrival, saying: "Be friends! [*Pause.*] I am late, forgive. [*Pause.*] The face. [*Pause.*] On the stairs. [*Pause.*] Forgive. [*Pause.*] Joe" (*CDW* 287). Addressing Bob, he continues, "Forgive. [*Pause.*] In the tower. [*Pause.*] The face" (288). Although there are no specific details about "the stairs" and "the tower," the words could be references to Yeats's two collections of poems entitled *The Winding Stair and Other Poems* (1933) and *The Tower* (1928), respectively, the former containing a series of poems entitled "Words for Music Perhaps,"[1] and the latter containing the poem "The Tower." The "face" also reminds us of the woman's face in . . . *but the clouds*. . . (1977), where the woman actually quotes from "The Tower."

This essay aims to demonstrate that *Words and Music* as well as . . . *but the clouds*. . . were written under the influence of Yeats and to answer the questions: why is the scene located in the tower in *Words and Music,* and why does the woman in . . . *but the clouds*. . . quote from Yeats's poem?

Yeats's Influence in *Words and Music*

Croak gives Words and Music the themes of "love" and "age" for their composition of a speech and a tune. In response to his request, Words

217

tries to express "love" by saying: "Arise then and go now the manifest unanswerable—" (*CDW* 288). This is a "garbled quotation" (Fletcher and Fletcher 157) from the first line of Yeats's poem "The Lake Isle of Innisfree," which reads: "I will *arise and go now,* and go to Innisfree." Croak tries to reconcile Words and Music to each other by commanding them to create a song of "love" and "age" in cooperation, but in vain, since words and music are in discord with each other: verbal versus nonverbal, logical versus illogical, rational versus irrational. Although Words is uncertain enough of the reliability of language to say, "What? [*Pause. Very rhetorical.*] Is love the word? [*Pause. Do.*] Is soul the word? [*Pause. Do.*] Do we mean love, when we say love? [*Pause. Do.*] Soul, when we say soul?" (289), all it can do is to utter words. The only way Words and Music collaborate with each other is to *sing a song*. Therefore, when the words are accompanied by the music, Words tries to sing:

> Age is when to a man
> Huddled o'er the ingle
> Shivering for the hag
> To put the pan in the bed
> And bring the toddy
> *She comes in the ashes*
> *Who loved could not be won*
> *Or won not loved*
> Or some other trouble
> Comes in the ashes
> Like in that old light
> The face in the ashes
> That old starlight
> On the earth again. (*CDW* 131; emphasis added)

After the song, Croak murmurs, "The face" repeatedly, conjuring up an image similar to the one that appears in *...but the clouds....* The expressions in the song, "She comes in the ashes / Who loved could not be won / Or won not loved" interestingly echo, "Does the imagination dwell the most / Upon a woman won or woman lost?" in "The Tower" (*CP* 222). This similarity suggests a strong relation between *Words and Music* and Yeats's poem. Then why does the woman in *Words and Music* appear in the ashes? The symbolic meaning of "The Tower" can serve as a clue to help us answer this question.

"The Tower" is a poem about the imagination of an old poet and the evocation of the dead. It is divided into three parts. The first part sets up a dissonance between the "absurdity" of old age and an "excited, passionate, fantastical imagination." Because of the absurdity, the speaker must "choose Plato and Plotinus for a friend" instead of his Muse "until imagination, ear and eye, / Can be content with argument and deal / In abstract things" (*CP* 219). The discord, however, becomes modified in the second part, as Daniel Albright observes. He writes, "in fact the imagination gains its strength from the man's incompetence, wretchedness, destitution, and frustration. Old age, then, far from disqualifying the poet, enhances his power; and the imagination, not abstract reason, is the faculty that turns poverty into plenty, that sustains the young, the old, and the dead" (633). Despite the initial discordance, old age and imagination thus come to be reconciled to each other. Then at the end of part 2, in which the speaker calls up the dead, he writes:

> Old lecher with a love on every wind,
> Bring up out of that deep considering mind
> All that you have discovered in the grave,
> For it is certain that you have
> Reckoned up every unforeknown, unseeing
> Plunge, lured by a softening eye,
> Or by a touch or a sigh,
> Into the labyrinth of another's being. (*CP* 222)

The third part refers to the pride of the old poet; the pride of "the hour / When the swan must fix his eye / Upon a fading gleam / Float out upon a long / Last reach of glittering stream / And there sing his last song" (*CP* 223). The last stanza reads:

> Now shall I make my soul,
> Compelling it to study
> In a learned school
> Till the wreck of body,
> Slow decay of blood,

Testy delirium
Or dull decrepitude,
Or what worse evil come—
The death of friends, or death
Of every brilliant eye
That made a catch in the breath—
Seem *but the clouds of the sky*
When the horizon fades;
Or a bird's sleepy cry
Among the deepening shades. (*CP* 224–25; emphasis added)

In Thomas R. Whitaker's analysis of the last twelve lines he points out, "The poem has moved to the acceptance of death, and to the creation of death in that acceptance. The horrible splendor of desire—the creative and destructive, illuminating and blinding power of the imagination—here attains its final ethereal harmony: "a bird's sleepy cry / Among the deepening shades" (202–03). The quietness of the end of the poem indeed depicts the "final ethereal harmony" as Whitaker observes. In order to understand the precise meaning of the harmony, it would be worth considering the title of the poem.

The title, "The Tower," is regarded as Yeats's reference to the tower called Thoor Ballylee, where he lived with his wife, George. Albright asserts: "In his early work, he depended on symbols with a predetermined, transcendental meaning, such as the Rose; but his later symbols, such as the tower, are not so much donors of meaning as receivers of it" (633). However, the tower is as significant a symbol as is the rose in an alchemical sense because, as *A Dictionary of Alchemical Imagery* explains, a tower is "a synonym for the athanor or philosophical furnace. Illustrations of the furnace frequently resemble the turret or tower of a castle. According to *The Golden Tract* the glass vessel in which the brother and sister lovers (Sol and Luna) are captured is 'situated in a strong tower, and surrounded with a gentle continuous fire' (*HM* [*Hermetic Museum*], I: 47)" (Abraham 203–04). In the process of alchemical transmutation that occurs in the tower, "such opposite states and qualities as sulphur and mercury, hot and cold, dry and moist, fixed and volatile, spirit and body, form and matter, active and receptive, and male and female are reconciled of their differences and united" (Abraham 35). This union of the substances, or the reconciliation of opposites called a "chemical wedding," is the goal of alchemy.

Yeats himself mentions the symbolic meaning of the tower in his notes for his *The Winding Stair and Other Poems* as follows: "In this book and elsewhere I have used towers, and one tower in particular, as symbols and have compared their winding stairs to the philosophical gyres, but it is hardly necessary to interpret what comes from the main track of thought and expression. Shelley uses towers constantly as symbols, and there are gyres in Swedenborg, and in Thomas Aquinas and certain classical authors" (*VP* 831). Yeats thus identifies the winding stairs in the tower with the "philosophical gyres," which embody the key concept of the occult philosophy Yeats developed in *A Vision*. Yeats's gyres are two whirling, interlocking cones. Notably, the double cones oppose each other, one expanding as the other contracts. Therefore, the tower can be the magical place where the discord between old age and imagination, and the boundary between the dead and the living, can vanish.

William T. Gorski points out: "In 'The Tower' (1926), Yeats invokes the alchemical union of Sol and Luna for bardic inspiration: 'O may the sun and moonlight seem / One inextricable beam, / For if I triumph I must make men mad' (*VP* 441)" (171). The speaker of the poem might have dreamed of the alchemical union with the lost woman. Can we apply this thinking to Croak and ask, does Croak desire that as well?

The Face in the Alchemical Ashes

Now let us return to the question: why does the woman in *Words and Music* appear in the ashes? *The Dictionary of Alchemical Imagery* defines "ash" as

> that which remains after the calcinations (conversion to a fine white powder through heat) of the base metal; the philosophical earth which remains in the bottom of the vessel when the volatile matter of the [Philosopher's] Stone ascends into the alembic. *Ash is the incorruptible substance left in the alembic after the matter of the Stone has been subjected to the purgatorial fire.* The ash can no longer be set on fire, and is, psychologically speaking, free from the turmoil of the passions. It is a synonym for the white stage of the opus, the albedo, when the dead, blackened body or bodies (of united sulphur and argent vive) have been whitened and purified by the refining fire (i.e. the mercurial water). (Abraham 12; emphasis added)

Thus, ash is another important symbol of alchemy. Ash is all that is left in the bottom of the vessel after the matter of the philosopher's stone is burned in the purgatorial fire.[2] Beckett seems to have known the symbolic meaning of Yeats's tower. It can be presumed that in *Words and Music* Croak tries to unite the two things in discord with each other, words and music, in an alchemical process of transmutation in the tower. Only when they seem to be united in singing does the woman appear in the ashes. At first, she is described rather grotesquely by Words in the image of a corpse: "[the lips]...tight, a gleam of tooth biting on the under, no coral, no swell, whereas normally...." (*CDW* 132). In the following part of Words's description, however, her face and body miraculously revive: "the brows uncloud, the lips part and the eyes...[*Pause.*]...the brows uncloud, the nostrils dilate, the lips part and the eyes...[*Pause.*]...a little colour comes back into the cheeks and the eyes...[*Reverently.*]...open. [*Pause.*] Then down a little way..." (*CDW* 293). In the alchemical transmutation, the matter of the Stone must die once to be renovated and reborn in a new, pure form. Yet this resurrection of the woman does not please Croak. At the end of the play, despite Words's attempt to sing a song with the music suggested by Music, Croak lets his club fall and impatiently leaves them to their song:

> Then down a little way
> Through the trash
> Towards where
> All dark no begging
> No giving no words
> No sense no need
> Through the scum
> Down a little way
> To whence one glimpse
> Of that wellhead. (*CDW* 133–34)

This song evokes a sexual image, as the word *wellhead* could imply the genitals.[3] Croak's act of letting his club fall could bear a sexual implication, too. The reason he leaves is then obvious. He cannot tolerate the increased discrepancy between the youth of the resurrected woman and his own decrepit body. We might recall that it was the elderly Yeats who was obsessed with the possibility of sexual impotence. He underwent the "Steinach operation" at Beaumont House Hospital, 5 April 1934, which is "a simple vasectomy, intended to increase and contain the production of male hormone, thus arresting the ageing process and restoring sexual vitality" (Foster 496). The operation was so successful that Yeats wrote in his letter to Harold Macmillan: "That operation has almost made me a young man" (qtd. in Foster 499). According to Yeats's biographer, since Macmillan was not an intimate friend, "Dublin was soon revealing the story" (Foster 499). As Beckett was in London for most of 1934 (Knowlson 186) and spent his August vacation in Dublin, he probably heard the story. However, while the operation made Yeats almost "a young man," alchemy in *Words and Music* cannot transmute Croak's old age into youth. In this sense, *Words and Music* can be regarded as a bitter parody of Yeats's success.

Yet this radio play may not only be a parody of Yeats's sexual recovery. Angela Moorjani interestingly relates the woman's transformation in *Words and Music* to the Gaelic myth of the Cailleac Beare: "In the Celtic myth, if the young hero responds to the advances of the old hag, she is transformed into a young woman who helps him to accede to power. It is striking that this version appears in Beckett's 1962 radio play, *Words and Music,* where the old hag or sphinx dissolves into a beautiful woman in whose eyes lies the answer to life's enigma" (104–05).[4] Yeats had, famously, recovered the Cailleac Bheara (the Crone of Beare), who appears in the traditional Gaelic aislings, "when he incorporates the transformation from ancient hag to young queen into his allegory of Ireland" (Cullingford 67). There is a twist, however, as "Yeats's version of the Cailleac demands not sex but [...] death." Cullingford goes on to explain: "Mother Ireland may have had many suitors, but she never satisfied them physically: 'With all the lovers that brought me their love I never set out the bed for any' ([Yeats] *VPL* 226). Like the Queen of Heaven she is a Virgin Mother and demands virgin martyrs; like the woman of the courtly tradition she is unobtainable" (67).

In this context, too, Beckett seems to have created the figure of Croak as a caricature of Yeats, for although the woman in *Words and Music,* like the Cailleac Beare, is transformed from a grotesque corpse into a beautiful woman, she is "unobtainable" for Croak, not because of her virginity but owing to Croak's impotence.[5]

Yet Beckett's rather positive attitude toward Yeats can be seen in *Words and Music*'s "wellhead" motif. The word "wellhead" in the song basically means a "source." The song's plunging movement "down a little way /

Through the trash [...] Down a little way / To whence one glimpse / Of that wellhead" evokes both the "The Tower's" "plunge" into "the labyrinth of another's being" and the descent into "the foul rag-and-bone shop of the heart" in the last stanza of Yeats's poem, "The Circus Animals' Desertion" included in *Last Poems* (1939):[6]

> Those masterful images because complete
> Grew in pure mind but out of what began?
> A mound of refuse or the sweepings of a street,
> Old kettles, old bottles, and a broken can,
> Old iron, old bones, old rags, that raving slut
> Who keeps the till. Now that my ladder's gone
> I must lie down where all the ladders start
> In the foul rag-and-bone shop of the heart. (*CP* 392)

Albright observes the "anti-mythological movement" in this poem and asserts: "In this poem Yeats's myth of his identity, so carefully formulated through his career, breaks down into naked self-expression" (840). The similarity of the song in *Words and Music* to this poem seems to depict Beckett's increasing sympathy with the elderly Yeats who pursued the source of imagination without ostentation. "[T]he foul rag-and-bone shop of the heart" precisely echoes "My temptation is quiet. / Here at life's end / Neither loose imagination, / Nor the mill of the mind / Consuming its rag and bone, / Can make the truth known" (*CP* 346) in Yeats's "An Acre of Grass" (1938). Hiroshi Izubuchi points out that the "mill" evokes an image of an alembic, a vessel in the alchemical furnace, that is, a tower, and the "alembic of the mind" means the purification of the mind (81). Beckett may have realized the importance of alchemical ideas for Yeats when he wrote *Words and Music,* though he caricatured and criticized the poet and gave the bitter ending to the radio play.

... *but the clouds* ... and Yeats

Words and Music seems to have been developed into ... *but the clouds...,* but the latter television play displays not sarcasm or criticism but deep sympathy with Yeats.

In …*but the clouds*… Beckett employs three kinds of camera shots: a near shot, from behind, of a man called M, who is sitting on an invisible stool bowed over an invisible table; a long shot of a circular, lit space, which is either empty or with M 1; and a close-up of a woman's face reduced as far as possible to eyes and mouth. In the long-shot sequence, M 1 in hat and greatcoat comes from the shadow designated "West, roads" into the lit space, stands facing sideways and proceeds east to the closet in shadow, emerges from there in robe and skullcap, and disappears toward his sanctum in North shadow. M in the near shot, wearing a light gray robe and a skullcap, is supposed to be M 1 in the sanctum in North. According to the stage directions, a camera is fixed at the position to shoot the whole lit area.

The narration by V, which is M's own voice, precedes the pictures. V's lines consist of two different temporalities, as Enoch Brater points out: "Words and image represent two separate grammatical dimensions of time as delivered here, words speak in the past tense, pictures and stage directions in the more luminous present" (*Beyond Minimalism* 99). Whereas V narrates in the past tense what he used to do, "When I thought of her it was always night. I came in—" (*CDW* 419), he sometimes comments on the pictures: "No, that's not right," "Right," "Let us now distinguish three cases" (*CDW* 419–22), and so on, and makes the scenes repeat to confirm the details: "Let us now run through it again" (*CDW* 421). Brater analyzes the relationship among M, M 1, and V as follows:

> Whenever M 1 goes to the closet, the sanctum, or out the door, he bleeds into darkness, negative space, "where none could see me." The irony here is that M 1 effectively becomes M when he crouches in his so-called invisible sanctum: that is where we discover him imagining his story at the beginning of the play, and that is where we see him going when he disappears into the "north shadow." He is not alone after all. Unknown to him, the television camera has become an unseen voyeur, recording for the viewer a *"near shot from behind."* (99)

The audience of the program is indeed the "voyeur" of M in his private sanctum. Because V, however, is highly conscious of television technology, he seems to be a director, directing the scenes through the television camera lens and commenting on the pictures while directing.

Or, more precisely, V is directing M's imagination or recollection in his head and is watching it through the lens. The camera eye is therefore not objective but subjective, as in Beckett's *Film,* where the camera eye, E, turns out to be "the pursuing perceiver" who, in Beckett's words, "is not extraneous but self" (*CDW* 323). The reason V is invisible is that V is not an object being seen but a subject seeing the scenes. In this sense, V is the voyeur of his own inner vision, and the audience is also forced to be the voyeur of M's mind, watching M's mind through V's eye without being aware.

V describes the action of M 1 in the sanctum, which is presumably being recollected by M, as follows: "Then crouching there, in my little sanctum, in the dark, where none could see me, I began to beg, of her, to appear, to me. Such had long been my use and wont. No sound, a begging of the mind, to her, to appear, to me. Deep down into the dead of night, until I wearied, and ceased. Or of course until— " (*CDW* 420). It seems that M used to beg a deceased woman to appear in his "sanctum." V distinguishes four possible results. One: she appeared but soon disappeared. Two: she appeared and lingered "with those unseeing eyes I so begged when alive to look at me." Three: she appeared and, after a moment, quotes inaudibly from Yeats's poem "The Tower": "…clouds…but the clouds…of the sky.…" Yet, in most cases—"in the proportion say of nine hundred and ninety-nine to one, or nine hundred and ninety-eight to two"—he begged in vain (*CDW* 421). This ritual could be regarded as a séance enacted by M to evoke the woman's spirit and the appearance of her face as a materialization of her spirit. V explains: "For had she never once appeared, all that time, would I have, could I have, gone on begging, all that time? Not just vanished within my little sanctum and busied myself with something else [...]? Until the time came, with break of day, to issue forth again, shed robe and skull, resume my hat and greatcoat, and issue forth again, to walk the roads" (420).

V now tries to reproduce the image of the woman. He might be seen as a medium who artificially materializes the woman's spirit, using modern optical technology. At this moment, the audience is not only the voyeur of M's mind but also the involuntary sitter at the internalized séance. Part of the reason the woman quotes from Yeats's poem might lie in this séance-like feature of the play because the séance was of great importance for Yeats. He was fascinated by mediums and their materialization of spirits as well as their automatic writing, and actually wrote a séance play called *The Words upon the Window-Pane.*

Both Yeats and Beckett pursued words and images that would come from without or the unconscious. V repeatedly tries to reproduce the image of the woman probably because of his subtle hope that she might appear involuntarily when he "wearied, and ceased" (*CDW* 421) after the repetition. Yeats, in "The Tower," attempts to conjure up ghosts; by adopting a part of the poem as a title of his play, Beckett demonstrates his own interest in seeing and talking to ghosts, and acknowledges the influence of Yeats.

The woman's appearance beautifully echoes the following part of "The Tower":

> And further add to that
> That, being dead, we rise,
> Dream and so create
> Translunar Paradise.
> I have prepared my peace
> With learned Italian things
> And the proud stones of Greece,
> Poet's imaginings
> And memories of love,
> Memories of the words of women,
> All those things whereof
> Man makes a superhuman
> Mirror-resembling dream. (*CP* 223–24)

V's evocation of the woman in ...*but the clouds*... might be an attempt to prepare his peace with "memories of love" and "memories of the words of women." In 1977, when the BBC broadcast Beckett's three plays *Not I, Ghost Trio,* and ...*but the clouds*... in a group, Beckett gave the program the collective title "Shades," which was supposedly named after the last word of "The Tower." "Shades," of course, can also mean "ghosts."

Conclusion

Brater observes: "Beckett's ambivalence in dealing with Yeats, which begins in parody and ends in eloquence, also reveals a Beckett who not only comes to terms with that romanticism, but who finally accepts and embraces it" ("Intertextuality" 40).

At the end of *...but the clouds...,* the woman's face appears without V's direction. This ending might suggest Beckett's acceptance not only of Yeats's romanticism but also of his interest in the occult, which Beckett did not fully embrace while writing the earlier *Words and Music.* Dreaming the unity of the dead and the living, Beckett now seems to be hearing a bird's sleepy cry among the deepening shades.

Notes

I would like to express my gratitude to the editors for their helpful suggestions.

1. Katharine Worth points out the similarity of the titles, *Words for Music Perhaps* and *Words and Music* (259).

2. In this sense, the tower is also an analogy of purgatory, which has important implications for Yeats and Beckett.

3. Ruby Cohn reminds us that "[Clas] Zilliacus was the first to realize that Joe's prose describes a postcoital woman" (269).

4. It is important to consider that the wellhead is glimpsed by looking into the woman's eyes that have just opened, thereby echoing the motif of the eyes in the boat scene in *Krapp's Last Tape.* In both instances sexual and ontological meanings overlap. The "wellhead" could also imply "the source of life," as Moorjani suggests (105).

5. Beckett did not just make fun of the Irish literary master. In "Recent Irish Poetry," his 1934 attack on the leading Celtic Twilighters, he sharply criticized Yeats for using the Gaelic math of the Cailleac (*Disjecta* 71). Rina Kim, for example, holds that in *Murphy* (1938) Beckett ridicules Yeats's *Cathleen ni Houlihan,* with its echoes of the Cailleac Beare, in the character of Miss Counihan. In general, Kim relates Beckett's grotesque female characters in his early fiction to his resistance to the Irish Free State, and she argues that "by ridiculing Yeats's personification of Ireland, the young Beckett undermines the Catholic State's policies as regards religious, social, cultural and political issues" (65).

6. I thank Stanley Gontarski for suggesting the "rag-and-bone shop of the heart" analogy with Beckett's lines.

Works Cited

Abraham, Lyndy. *A Dictionary of Alchemical Imagery.* Cambridge: Cambridge University Press, 1998.

Albright, Daniel. Notes. *W. B. Yeats: The Poems.* Ed. Albright. London: Dent, 1994.

Beckett, Samuel. *The Complete Dramatic Works.* London: Faber, 1986. (Abbreviated *CDW.*)

————. *Disjecta: Miscellaneous Writings and a Dramatic Fragment*. Ed. Ruby Cohn. New York: Grove, 1984.

Brater, Enoch. *Beyond Minimalism: Beckett's Late Style in the Theatre*. Oxford: Oxford University Press, 1987.

————. "Intertextuality." *Palgrave Advances in Samuel Beckett Studies*. Ed. Lois Oppenheim. Houndmills, UK: Palgrave Macmillan, 2004. 30–44.

Cohn, Ruby. *A Beckett Canon*. Ann Arbor: University of Michigan Press, 2005.

Cullingford, Elizabeth. *Gender and History in Yeats's Love Poetry*. New York: Cambridge University Press, 1993.

Fletcher, Beryl S., John Fletcher, et al. *A Student's Guide to the Plays of Samuel Beckett*. London: Faber, 1978.

Foster, R. F. *The Arch-Poet 1915–1939*. Oxford: Oxford University Press, 2003. Vol. 2 of *W. B. Yeats: A Life*. 2 vols. 1997–2003.

Gorski, William T. *Yeats and Alchemy*. Albany: State University of New York Press, 1996.

Izubuchi, Hiroshi. "Kieta Hashigo" ("The Vanished Ladder"). *Yeats to no Taiwa (Dialogue with Yeats.)* Tokyo: Misuzu Shobo, 2000. 78–90.

Kim, Rina. "Severing Connections with Ireland: Women and the Irish Free State in Beckett's Writing." *Historicising Beckett/Issues of Performance*. Vol. 15 of *SBT/A*. Ed. Marius Buning et al. Amsterdam: Rodopi, 2005. 57–69.

Knowlson, James. *Damned to Fame: The Life of Samuel Beckett*. London: Bloomsbury, 1996.

Moorjani, Angela. *Abysmal Games in the Novels of Samuel Beckett*. Chapel Hill: University of North Carolina Press, 1982.

Whitaker, Thomas R. *Swan and Shadow: Yeats's Dialogue with History*. Washington, DC: Catholic University of America Press, 1989.

Worth, Katharine. *The Irish Drama of Europe from Yeats to Beckett*. 1978. London: Athlone, 1986.

Yeats, William Butler. *The Collected Plays of W. B. Yeats*. 1934. Dublin: Macmillan, 1952. (Abbreviated *CPL*.)

————. *The Collected Poems of W. B. Yeats*. Dublin: Macmillan, 1933. (Abbreviated *CP*.)

————. *The Variorum Edition of the Plays*. Ed. Russel K. Alspach and Catherine C. Alspach. New York: Macmillan, 1966. (Abbreviated *VPL*.)

————. *The Variorum Edition of the Poems of W. B. Yeats*. Ed. Peter Allt and Russell K. Alspach. New York: Macmillan, 1957. (Abbreviated *VP*.)

Beckett—Feldman—Johns

CATHERINE LAWS

A NUMBER OF MORTON Feldman's late works (*Elemental Procedures, Neither, Words and Music,* and *For Samuel Beckett*) draw on the work of Samuel Beckett, and the text of *Neither* was written by him at Feldman's request. Much of Feldman's late work is also strongly influenced by the crosshatch paintings of Jasper Johns, and crosshatching first appeared in one section of Johns's *Untitled,* 1972, which subsequently formed the basis of his contribution to *Foirades/Fizzles,* a joint venture with Beckett. In no sense did these three ever truly collaborate. However, a triangle of association and influence is apparent.

This essay seeks to make connections between some past work of my own on Beckett and Feldman, and Steven Johnson's work on the influence of Johns upon Feldman, completing the triangle with a consideration of the little-discussed book project of Beckett and Johns. I am interested in the use of pattern and repetition in relation to reference, memory, and meaning in these works; in how Feldman's and Johns's approaches to these processes relate to Beckett's, and, inevitably, in the extent to which these effects can be translated between art forms.

Feldman—Beckett

Feldman's most substantial response to a Beckett text is his one-act opera for a single soprano and orchestra, *Neither* (1977). I have written about this piece elsewhere and so will only briefly summarize the main points in order to be able to make subsequent connections. The text was sent to Feldman by Beckett in 1976. Beckett's "Neither" is hardly a typical libretto; it is short and abstract, lacking concrete references, narrative, or drama, and evoking nothing more substantial than oscillatory motion. The sense is of a dislocated *betweenness:* ghostly movement back and forth, as if in search of the self. But such absolute presence remains beyond reach; the central position from which self-knowledge might be attained cannot be found (if it exists at all). Feldman described his reaction to the text as follows: "I'm reading it. There's something peculiar. I can't catch it. Finally I see that every line is really the same thought said in another way. And yet the continuity acts as if something else is happening. Nothing else is happening" (*Essays* 185).

Rather than "setting" the text in any traditional sense, Feldman renders this single insubstantial idea in musical terms. He ignores the conventions of opera and has no interest in ensuring that the words are audible; for much of the opera the soprano remains in her highest register but is expected to sing pianissimo, and the textual rhythms are obscured by isolating individual words or even syllables. As in most of Feldman's output, lyricism without melody, the unmediated contemplation of sound, and the avoidance of dramaticism through the use of understated dynamics are all evident. Similarly typical is his treatment of form as a length of time with minimal divisions; the piece is extended without any sense of causality or organic continuity.

Metrically, the alternation of even and uneven time signatures, or the continual alteration of time signatures around a mean of 2/4, contributes to the unsteady sense of motion to and fro, or of the effect of movement in and out across a central position. However, while much of the material within the bars is repetitious, the note lengths (or those of the intervening rests) vary fractionally, such that regular metrical patterns are implied but ultimately avoided. Most of *Neither* is composed of layers of iterations that *almost* form pulses or regular patterns, creating the *effect* of periodicity without true regularity (see figure 1). Straight rhythmic repetition occurs only when the orchestration and/or pitch is changing; the more the material remains the same in terms of pitch and orchestration, the more likely it is that its rhythmic character or its positioning within the bar will be altered slightly. Overall, the treatment of meter and rhythm creates the impression of music in search of a regularity, as if a common denominator, some unlocatable mean pulse, lies beneath the various layers.

The pitch material is similarly treated. For example, much of the music is chordal, generally built from three-note chromatic clusters. These either remain in semitonal intervals or are transposed into wide intervals of minor

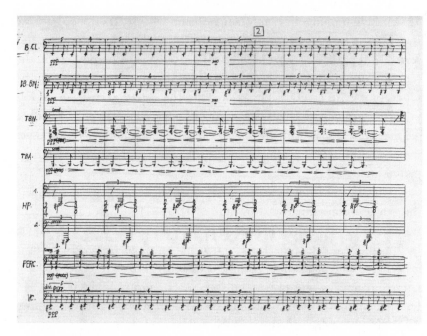

FIGURE I. Extract from Morton Feldman, *Neither*. Reproduced by permission of Universal Edition (London) Ltd.

ninths and/or major sevenths. Thus, while the pitch classes remain constant, the effect is of intervallic expansion and contraction. An independent pulse will then be formed by the iteration of each chord at a different point in the bar, or, if the chords are sustained simultaneously, by the various peaks of the crescendos and diminuendos of each instrument. Effectively, we are presented with several types of motion to and fro, in and out; in addition to the rhythmic oscillations and the expansion and contraction of the intervallic shapes, a range of different chordal iterations are possible: different (but intervallically related) pitch clusters alternated within the line of one instrument, the swinging of intervallically related material between different instruments within the same instrumental group, and the passing back and forth of exactly the same material (in pitch and interval) between instruments of contrasting types (see figure 2, where chords of sevenths and ninths are swung back and forth between pairs of instruments, one from the strings and one from the winds). Each musical parameter is thereby established within a limited range of articulations and constantly reorganized into different permutations; Feldman once wrote: "Essentially I am working with three notes and [. . .] other notes are like shadows of

FIGURE 2. Extract from Morton Feldman, *Neither*. Reproduced by permission of Universal Edition (London) Ltd.

the basic notes" (*Essays* 169). The effect is of ceaseless movement back and forth through contexts that shift by minute degrees.

Feldman seems to play with notions of presence and absence. Mostly he uses three three-note chords at a time, often adding a further pair of semitones so as to use all pitch classes but one. Thus the frustrated attempt to fill the chromatic spectrum seems to correspond to the rhythmic effect of the attempt to find a central pulse. The exclusion of a single pitch class is unlikely to be aurally detectable, but when we *are* presented with all twelve pitch classes, the final pitch is often in an unusual range and/or orchestration, indicating its presence through its very separation from the main texture. Moreover, the missing note is often presented in the soprano line. The soprano and orchestra therefore exist in mutually supportive roles, each fixing its own presence in terms of a lack or an absence in the other, and yet neither is stable. The internal reflection of material through contextual variation and juxtaposition suggests an endless process within which everything shadows everything else. Just as Beckett's text maps the endless searching that it describes, so the near patterning and near symmetries of Feldman's music perform that same process.

Feldman—Johns

While other artists—Philip Guston and Mark Rothko in particular—provided more long-term inspiration, Jasper Johns became an important figure for Feldman in his later life. Feldman listed Johns among those visual artists he regarded as his "graduate school" (*Give My Regards* 115), and in the middle to late 1970s he became particularly interested in Johns's use of crosshatching—works comprising simple, abstract hatching patterns without hierarchical structure.

The influence of Johns upon Feldman has been explored by Steven Johnson, who notes Feldman's comments, in "Crippled Symmetry" (*Essays* 124–37), on the similarities between Johns's crosshatch patterns from 1972 onward and those of Anatolian rugs, which Feldman collected. These rug makers work sequentially, folding completed sections underneath such that the pattern is not copied directly but is reproduced from memory, unlike in Persian rug making, where the whole rug is laid out. Thus the patterns tend to be almost symmetrical, but tiny differences result from the inaccuracies of memory; Feldman notes that this made him reconsider his understanding of symmetry and asymmetry (*Essays* 124). The technique of abrash—dyeing the yarn in small quantities—also causes minor variations in the depth of color across the rugs; the link to the almost symmetries of rhythm, pitch, and orchestration in *Neither* and other Feldman works of the late 1970s is clear.

Johnson discusses Johns's *Scent* (1974), which arranges crosshatching across three panels of differently treated canvas. A sense of direction is introduced through the change in materials, but additionally no bundle of crosshatching can touch another of the same color, and each of the three panels is subdivided into three more vertical sections wherein the first subpanel of each main panel reproduces the final subpanel of the preceding one, thereby suggesting a cylindrical quality. As Johnson says, we are presented with a "surface that is simultaneously simple and complex, simultaneously improvisational and carefully ordered" (219), and our attention is directed "away from surface content toward the process of perception" (220).

Johnson analyzes Feldman's *Why Patterns?* (1978, for flute, piano, and glockenspiel) in relation to Johns's crosshatching, showing how some of the music is systematized and some more intuitive. He suggests that, just as Johns limits contrast through the restriction to a narrow field of marks and colors, Feldman creates an equivalent surface through "isolated, single-attack events" (231) and harmonic uniformity (involving very few chord types). Similarly, Johnson equates Feldman's use of isorhythmic organization with Johns's means of hiding system within apparently more random events (235). There is not room here for more detail, but overall, despite the very different content of the works, the approach to *almost* patterning—of near systems continually disrupted by more arbitrary and intuitive disruptions—relates closely to the effects of *Neither*. The dense orchestral texture of *Neither*, and hence the approach to harmonic space, is in contrast to the sparseness of *Why Patterns?*, but the material is nevertheless generated from similar closed fields and constitutes similar sequences of singular attacks (here orchestrated across a number of instruments). This combines with the use of rhythm and instrumentation to create a comparable process of endless recontextualization that invokes the process of its own perception and understanding as part of its subject.

Beckett—Johns

Beckett's interest in visual art, along with its influence on his work, is now quite well documented (Oppenheim esp. 136; Knowlson 195–97, 378,

588–89; Jones), but the project with Johns is unusual. Johns was apparently hesitant about working with a writer (Field 99), and the project is almost unique in his output. Beckett of course worked with actors and directors on his stage works and allowed a number of artists to illustrate his texts (Wechsler; Oppenheim 162), but these processes always followed the completion of the writing: in no sense were the texts conceived or developed as part of a process of collaboration. This is also true of the Beckett-Johns book; the French versions of Beckett's texts had already been published, and the work cannot be considered truly collaborative. However, the scale and integration of the work is more substantial than in comparable projects of either artist. Moreover, the text-image relationships are complex and suggestive: the images do not "illustrate" the texts in the ordinary sense but instead act as parallel works, reflecting aspects of the texts, formally and in terms of content, while also spiraling off in their own directions.

The project was suggested by Véra Lindsay in the early 1970s.[1] Beckett suggested making a special edition of *Waiting for Godot,* but Johns wanted to work with new material: "I had imagined [. . .] that he would have a sentence or part of a sentence, some really fragmentary structure that he would have saved. Beckett said he had things like that in French [. . .]. He started sending me these pieces. Of course they were not fragments in the way I had thought about them, they were very polished" (Wechsler). This implies that Johns was more open to collaboration; his preference for incomplete fragments suggests that he wanted the writing and images to grow together. However, Beckett did not want to create new pieces specially and sent Johns English translations of five of his eight *Foirades.*[2]

Beckett and Johns met a few more times in Paris but discussed only the basic layout—Beckett left it to Johns to integrate the images and did not see the etchings until the book was nearly finished (Wechsler). The result was a special edition, *Foirades/Fizzles,* containing five Beckett texts, each in both French and English, with thirty-three etchings by Johns placed around the texts.[3]

Beckett's Texts

The word "fizzle" connotes failure or a fiasco—fizzling out, sputtering, or hissing—but its early meaning was to break wind without noise, and the French also refers to a wet fart: these were Beckett's preferred meanings.

Beckett wrote to James Knowlson that the texts were written in the 1960s, after *How It Is* (Knowlson and Pilling 132), but Ruby Cohn shows that the French original of "He is barehead" appears in an earlier manuscript. This implies a much earlier date (1953 or 1954), and Cohn suggests that three more texts were probably completed earlier than Beckett remembered, between 1955 and 1959 (212, 242). Either way, the pieces remained unpublished until the 1970s. Eyal Amiran argues that Beckett's decision not to publish immediately is significant (177); certainly, while echoing many of Beckett's previous preoccupations—birth and death, the relationship between body and mind, the difficulty of establishing a sense of self, the telling of stories, journeying, the difficulty of beginning and ending, sound and silence—the texts are shorter and more fragmented than previously, and some are less completely bound up with a rhetoric of failure.

Following on from the end of the *Trilogy*, the subjects have bodies that are often useless and decaying. They are barely characters, and the difficulty of establishing a stable first or third person persists; *I*s and *he*s are often confused—explicitly in "I gave up before birth" and "Old earth" but also implicitly in "Horn came always," where the implication grows that the pseudocouple of narrator and subject might be one and the same.

Elements of narrative are still apparent in the *Fizzles*, but following the logic of the texts in order to make sense of the situations tends to lead nowhere. One is drawn into piecing together the stories—mirroring the subjects' attempts to make sense of their circumstances—but without success. The texts vary in tone, the negativity of "I gave up before birth" contrasting somewhat with the allegorical progression (however faltering) of "He is barehead"; a number of the texts seem to move beyond the absolute negativity of the end of the *Trilogy* or of *How It Is* and *Texts for Nothing* while still struggling with the problematics of Being, knowledge, and selfhood.

Memory is central to the workings of the *Fizzles*. The figures themselves are, like all Beckett characters, concerned with how to tell stories, which involves the struggle to remember in the face of the unreliability of memory and hence the difficulty of establishing a coherent, stable sense of self. At the same time, intertextual memory is significant. The characters, settings, and situations of the *Fizzles*, such as they are, recall and look forward to other Beckett texts both explicitly and more subtly,[4] and the writing itself also echoes and anticipates, in terms of both specific phrases and structural features. Calling the pieces *Fizzles* suggests pointlessness and incompletion, but the intertextual echoes undermine the implied rejection: Beckett simultaneously derogates and disowns the texts while embedding them fully within his output.

The concentrated style of "Closed place," with its truncated, percussive sentences, is in apparent contrast to the accumulative clauses of the continuous, single-sentence forms of "I gave up before birth" and "Afar a bird." However, the impact is actually very similar; in both the sense is of the difficulty of telling an effective story, of trying to pin down words that will give an accurate representation, and of trying to generate a full sense of self through the accumulation of short statements. The other *Fizzles* used by Johns are less extreme in style, but again the effects are similar; the sentences of "He is barehead" and "Old earth" lack hierarchical structure, instead comprising (sometimes quite long) chains of short phrases separated by commas, implying a determination to move on but the difficulty of doing so. The opening of "Horn came always" pushes more toward the short sentences of "Closed place," but as the text progresses this concision gives way to longer sentences, again made up of short phrases separated by commas. Once more, though, the effect is of spurts of language accumulating into narration; the writing mimics the faltering storytelling and, at times, the stumbling and groping physical movement described: "ambulation as verbal exploration," as Ruby Cohn puts it (213). It also propels the reader onward while simultaneously frustrating expectations; one is caught in the momentum of the text without achieving progress. Additionally, as with all Beckett texts, there are numerous echoes of phrases from other philosophers, artists, and writers (especially Dante), along with odd half-remembered turns of phrase and figures of speech. Thus the texts perform the act of trying to form coherent stories, and the processes of rewording and revising their own textual memories are a conscious part of this.

Johns's Use of the Texts

John's plan, as can be seen from some of his trial proofs, was to integrate the images among Beckett's words (Cuno, *Foirades/Fizzles* pl. 66–69). However, on receiving polished texts rather than fragments he decided to place etchings around the texts and to use both the French and English versions (Field 99). Most of the etchings derive from his *Untitled*, 1972 (figure 3); only the large etched numbers that precede each pair of texts have no relationship to this work. *Untitled,* 1972, comprises four panels. The first contains an abstract crosshatch pattern of short lines in orange, green, and purple on a white background (and it is interesting to note that it was here, in the work that formed the basis for the collaboration with Beckett, that Johns first used the crosshatching that influenced Feldman). The second and third make use of a flagstone pattern, while the fourth comprises wax casts of body parts (face, buttock, torso, feet, leg, and knee, plus one cast of a hand and foot on top of a black sock on a fragment of wooden floorboards) attached to wooden boards of differing lengths screwed onto the canvas.

For the Beckett book, Johns's prints are all in black and white except for the frontispiece and endpiece. The book includes several different cycles of images adapted from *Untitled,* 1972. The double-page etchings that lie between the French and English versions of each text use different combinations of panels; for four of the five spreads Johns works through the consecutive pairings of the panels, starting with the final panel paired with the first (i.e., DA, AB, BC, CD), but because there are five texts he needs five spreads, and for the first of these he produced an etching that comprises the French and English names of the body parts of the casts panel. As Richard Field explains, through a process of overlaying and reversing in copperplate printing, "the image showed darker English words over the burnished French on the left, and darker French words over the burnished English words on the right [...]. Johns had mimicked the process of translation in a way that suggested a lingering presence of the original language. And he equated that act of translation with the specific action of reading this book of French and English texts" (103).

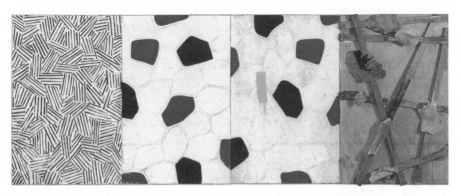

FIGURE 3. Jasper Johns, *Untitled, 1972,* © Jasper Johns/VAGA, New York/DACS, London, 2006.

Elsewhere, Johns names the body parts, either replacing the actual images and labeling empty shapes, or as etchings in their own right; either way he suggests the arbitrary quality of linguistic signs, highlighting the fact that two different (French and English) words can attempt to represent the same image, but that neither is an adequate means of identifying the thing itself, echoing one of Beckett's preoccupations. Johns's use elsewhere of the same empty white shapes without labels implies that visual representation is similarly problematic; the shapes retain the formal connection to the body part but lose all characterization. As Walter Strauss says, Johns shows "how the dismembered language of words can find its reflection, its echo, its 'embodiment,' in the dismembered language of the etching tool" (23).

Overall, Johns's fragmented body images provide the most concrete connection to the texts.[5] Beyond this, Johns makes no attempt to "illustrate" the texts in any conventional manner (just as Feldman makes no real attempt to "set" Beckett's text). Instead, the connection lies more in the approach to materials and their patterning, and in the focus upon the processes of perceiving and understanding.

Returning to Johns's source for the book—*Untitled*, 1972—the contrast between the abstract panels and the body parts seems quite odd, even arbitrary. Structurally, the inclusion of two panels of flagstones in the middle of the picture is also surprising. However, clear formal relationships are apparent in the size of the body parts in relation to the flagstones and in the diagonal placing of the wooden slats compared with the crosshatchings. The two flagstone panels use different media—the left panel is silk set in glossy paint, whereas the right uses an encaustic surface; again we see Johns's interest in shifting only the medium. The panels are not always fully discrete; the border between the two flagstone panels remains intact, but in several other places elements spill very slightly over the panel borders: Johns introduces a subtle element of continuity at the otherwise most disjunctive points. As with Johnson's analysis of *Scent*, then, it is possible to see how quite systematized elements combine with other apparently intuitive decisions.

These relationships are retained in the Beckett book, but the experience changes as the different elements appear more often and in different contexts through the cycles; in a different way from Beckett, Johns explores the idea that a work is always to an extent a residual fragment of others. Additionally, as with Beckett, Johns's etchings both echo and anticipate many of his other pieces. The crosshatching reappears not just in *Scent* but in many subsequent works,[6] while the flagstone motif was first used in

1967, in *Harlem Lights,* and casts of body fragments in *Target with Plaster Casts* (1955). Also as with Beckett, this becomes significant; despite the apparently abstract nature of the imagery, any motif "has a history of associations accumulated from its use in previous works" (Bernstein 143).

Additionally, the crosshatching and the flagstone motifs were both essentially "found" by Johns, glimpsed on car journeys (Crichton 59; Cuno, "Voices and Mirrors" 204). Here, what seems to interest Johns is that these apparently abstract images actually derive from a concrete world. The image is not created by the artist but is selected, and the remembered event is so fleeting that it is bound to be unreliable in some respects; there is a deliberate confusion of subjectivity and objectivity. As Derval Tubridy suggests, "*Foirades/Fizzles* is a book formed by quotation, translation and contamination" (105).

Memory and the Self

Johns's images also allude to other artists. The crosshatching appears to be the most abstract of motifs, but direct links to both Pablo Picasso and Jackson Pollock are apparent, along with looser, more general allusions to other twentieth-century painting (Hindry 227; Krauss 97; Cuno, "Voices and Mirrors" 211). Thus Johns, like Beckett, explores memory both within the works (through internal relationships) and without (in the use of found visual objects and the recollection of other artworks, his own and those of others). But for neither can the process of memory be pure or absolute—remembering always involves forgetting—and hence the process of remembering is one of constant re-creation.

Above all, this exploration of memory is an exploration of the self. Early in their careers, Beckett and Johns appeared similarly determined to remove themselves from their art, with Beckett claiming to know nothing about his characters and Johns stating, "I have attempted to develop my thinking in such a way that the work I've done is not me" (Raynor 145). However, a more complex picture emerges in the later work of each. Additionally, both artists face the paradox that the more they pare down and abstract their work, the more identifiable it becomes. Through this approach to materials, then, as well as through their processes of allusion and the tangible attempt to form and re-form meaning from past experiences, these works do start to trace the possibility of a self—a self that remembers and forgets, makes connections between ideas and forms, and attempts to ascribe significance to those ideas. However, this is a self that is provisional and never fully formed; a tentative self in the constant process of re-creation, lacking true authority or full presence. In both, "technique is not merely an instrument to convey a reality which exists independent of and prior to that technique, but is directly linked to the signification of the work itself": their work "conflates meaning with manifestation" (Tubridy 105).

Returning to Feldman, I would argue something similar. Feldman's work might seem even more removed from the world than that of Beckett or Johns; in comparison, even their subtle allusions seem quite concrete. Feldman, too, seemed concerned early on to remove himself from his work, to let sounds "be themselves." However, the works of the mid-1970s create complex perceptual effects through their internal structures and the use of processes that constantly evade pure repetition, presenting fractionally changing materials in ever-different contexts and hence paradoxically giving the simultaneous impression of progression and reiteration. As with Beckett and Johns, the particularity of Feldman's world becomes more recognizable the more pared down his materials, and hence the retreading of similar paths in different contexts from one work to another becomes equally apparent.[7] Additionally, his use of apparently contradictory compositional processes, both systematic and intuitive, becomes part of the process of mapping a tentative journey toward the possibility of individuation. Johnson suggests that Johns and Feldman fuse different elements in modernist art (245), but these elements are not truly fused or united. Neither, though, is Feldman, Beckett, or Johns reasserting modernist techniques, holding them up for ironic contemplation, or involving themselves in some empty play of signifiers (as might be implied in a more simplistic postmodern reading). Instead, through this juxtaposition of different techniques each artist acknowledges that the attempt to articulate a sense of self is dependent upon memory, and that remembering involves a perpetual re-creation of the self and of fragments of other selves that become as much self as other.

Collaboration?

The Beckett-Johns book and the Beckett-Feldman works were, for all three, rare instances of artistic partnership and can barely be called collaborations.

Instead, this way of working allowed each artist to retain autonomy, and the nature of their work is such that no significant changes in approach were required.

My concern has been to outline artistic parallels, but it is equally important to recognize that the works differ greatly in content, meaning, and, in some ways, approach. In particular, inevitable differences result from the forms and materials; the exploration of the self as constituted in language is a very different thing to visual representation or the patterning of musical sounds in time. Additionally, each is concerned with the ways in which their deployment of materials becomes a part of their meaning; differences in materials are therefore constitutive of differences in significance and effect.

Each of the works, however, does help to shed light on the others. Furthermore, it is interesting to note that each artist to some extent fights the characteristics of his form. Beckett's breakdown of language and narrative effects the increasing musicality of his texts but also constitutes an increasingly specific visual aesthetic through his problematization of representation (Oppenheim 2–4). Johns is dealing with an atemporal art form, yet his concern with perception is absolutely bound up with processes of time, memory, and change. Feldman, conversely, is working within the purest art of time, but his very use of harmonic space and rhythmic patterning to explore memory pushes toward an aesthetic that has important spatial qualities and complex time-space relationships. In this sense, then, the parallels and differences between the works of all three are revealing in terms of the possibilities and boundaries of their respective arts.

Notes

1. The year was 1972 or 1973, depending on which source one believes; Jessica Prinz (480) gives 1973, but Lois Oppenheim (221 n. 75) and Judith Wechsler give 1972.

2. Most of the *Foirades* (the French originals of the *Fizzles*) were first published individually in Minuit, in 1972 and 1973 (Ackerley and Gontarski 200). The collection *"Pour finir encore" et autres foirades* appeared in 1976, followed by the English version.

3. Johns reordered the *Fizzles* he used as follows: "I gave up before birth," "He is barehead," "Old earth," "Closed place," "Horn came always." The 250 copies of the book were handmade, bound in handmade paper and boxed in linen, with an internal lining of color lithographs by Johns. Johns and Beckett signed each copy.

4. The questlike character of some of the texts echoes Beckett's early novels, though the uncertainty of the progress, the goal, and ultimately the subjects themselves is increased.

Murphy reappears in "He is barehead," while other elements evoke *Molloy* and *Malone Dies*. As with other Beckett texts, I/you/he confusions abound, and it is sometimes hard to discern whether one character is a reincarnation of another. Both "He is barehead" and "Closed place" directly anticipate *The Lost Ones*. There are other specific examples, but overall the very absence of characters, locations, or narrative conventions connects the texts in myriad ways to other Beckett works.

5. Only in "He is barehead" are more specific connections implied (with the leg images). Additionally, as Roberta Bernstein suggests, here the flagstone imagery evokes the walls along which the subject gropes his way (145). There are other vague connections in the use of light and dark, and some of the abstracted body-part shapes can, if one wishes, be seen as representing other objects from the texts: bones, or the torch, for example.

6. In *Four Panels from Untitled*, 1972, and *Untitled*, 1975, and with heavier brushwork in a number of other works, including *Corpse and Mirror* (1974), *The Dutch Wives* (1975), the *Cicada Dancers on a Plane*, and *Tantric Detail* pictures (from 1979), and *Between the Clock and the Bed* (1981). Crosshatching also appears in *End Paper* (1976), a title that suggests a relationship to Beckett's *Endgame*.

7. I would suggest that in *Triadic Memories,* in particular, an exploration of his relationship to past composers, is implicit in Feldman's study of sonic memory within the context of the triad—a context that cannot retain its independence from past usage.

Works Cited

Ackerley, C. J., and S. E. Gontarski. *The Grove Companion to Samuel Beckett*. New York: Grove, 2004.

Amiran, Eyal. *Wandering and Home: Beckett's Metaphysical Narrative*. University Park: Pennsylvania State University Press, 1993.

Beckett, Samuel. *Fizzles*. With etchings by Jasper Johns. London: Petersburg, 1976.

———. *"For to end yet again" and Other Fizzles*. London: Calder, 1976.

———. "Neither." *The Complete Short Prose 1929–1989*. Ed. S. E. Gontarski. New York: Grove, 1995. 258.

———. *"Pour finir encore" et autres foirades*. Paris: Minuit, 1976.

Bernstein, Roberta. "Johns and Beckett: *Fizzles/Foirades*." *Print Collector's Newsletter* 5 (1976): 141–45.

Cohn, Ruby. *A Beckett Canon*. Ann Arbor: University of Michigan Press, 2001.

Crichton, Michael. *Jasper Johns*. New York: Abrams, 1977.

Cuno, James, ed. *Foirades/Fizzles: Echo and Illusion in the Arts of Jasper Johns*. Los Angeles: Wight Art Gallery, 1987.

———. "Voices and Mirrors/Echoes and Allusions: Jasper Johns's *Untitled*, 1972." *Foirades/Fizzles: Echo and Illusion in the Arts of Jasper Johns*. Ed. James Cuno. Los Angeles: Wight Art Gallery, 1987. 201–34.

Feldman, Morton. *Essays*. Ed. Walter Zimmerman. Kerpen, Germany: Beginner Press, 1985.

———. *Give My Regards to Eighth Street: Collected Writings of Morton Feldman*. Ed. B. H. Friedman. Cambridge, MA: Exact Change, 2000.

———. *Neither*. London: Universal, 1977.

Field, Richard S. "The Making of Foirades/Fizzles." *Foirades/Fizzles: Echo and Illusion in the Arts of Jasper Johns*. Ed. James Cuno. Los Angeles: Wight Art Gallery, 1987. 99–126.

Hindry, Ann. "Conversation with Jasper Johns/Conversation avec Jasper Johns." Varnedoe 227–34.

Johnson, Steven. "Jasper Johns and Morton Feldman: What Patterns?" *The New York Schools of Music and Visual Arts*. Ed. Steven Johnson. New York: Routledge, 2002. 217–47.

Jones, Alan. "Beckett and His Friends: A Writer among Artists." *Arts Magazine* 66 (1991): 27–28.

Knowlson, James. *Damned to Fame: The Life of Samuel Beckett*. London: Bloomsbury, 1996.

Knowlson, James, and John Pilling. *Frescoes of the Skull: The Later Prose and Drama of Samuel Beckett*. London: Calder, 1979.

Krauss, Rosalind. "Jasper Johns: The Functions of Irony." October 2 (1976): 91–99.

Laws, Catherine. "Morton Feldman's *Neither*." *Samuel Beckett and Music*. Ed. Mary Bryden. Oxford: Clarendon, 1998. 57–86.

Oppenheim, Lois. *The Painted Word: Samuel Beckett's Dialogue with Art*. Ann Arbor: University of Michigan Press, 2000.

Prinz, Jessica. "Foirades/Fizzles/Beckett/Johns." *Contemporary Literature 21* (1980): 480–510.

Raynor, Vivien. "Jasper Johns: 'I have attempted to develop my thinking in such a way that the work I've done is not me.'" Varnedoe 142–46.

Strauss, Walter A. "*Disjecta membra:* Essays in Fragmentation: Samuel Beckett and Jasper Johns." *Dalhousie French Studies* 31 (1995): 11–27.

Tubridy, Derval. "Quotation, Translation and Contamination in the Third Fizzle of Samuel Beckett's and Jasper Johns' *Foirades/Fizzles*." *Imprimatur* 1 (1996): 101–08.

Varnedoe, Kirk, ed. *Jasper Johns: Interviews and Writings*. New York: Museum of Modern Art, 1997.

Wechsler, Judith. "Illustrating Samuel Beckett." *Art Journal*. Winter, 1993. *Find Articles*. 25 Aug. 2004. http://www.findarticles.com/p/articles/mi_m0425/is_n4_v52/ai_14970137.

Ontological Fear and Anxiety in the Theater of Beckett, Betsuyaku, and Pinter

MARIKO HORI TANAKA

I N *HAPPY DAYS*, Julie Campbell writes, "Beckett encourages us to face our fears: our fears of death, of life, of suffering, of all those things we repress and deny in ourselves" (171). Although Winnie makes efforts to hide her anxieties and offer optimistic words to herself and her husband, she conveys a lurking fear of the time when "words fail" (147) and there is "nothing more to say" (152). Her fear of silence evokes similar fears in the audience. Her ontological anxiety, however, is not only felt through silence but also depicted visually onstage: her body sinking into the ground under the control of an unseen force that seems to be burying her. Although Winnie expects that at one point the earth will "yield" (151) and "crack" (152) so that she can fly up to the air, this does not happen.

In his lecture at Trinity College Dublin on 5 April 2006, Terry Eagleton linked Beckett's response to ontological anxiety to an Irish tradition of negative theology and the sense of nonidentity that is "a characteristic of the art after Auschwitz." Such anxiety, coming out of the recognition that the identity of self is problematic and that negativity is all around us, can become a creative force as well as a subject for Beckett and post-Beckettian writers including Minoru Betsuyaku and Harold Pinter. Both younger playwrights, influenced by Beckett yet struggling to find ways to break away from him, similarly create characters with ontological and war-related fears and use these fears to "encourage us to face our fears." Indeed, Betsuyaku, one of the most popular contemporary Japanese playwrights,[1] has written that for him Beckett's antitheatrical staging expressions continue to be valid for representing the ontological situation of modern humanity (*Beckett* 204).

In this essay I analyze visual, hence theatrical, devices—particularly experiments with scenic space and staged torture—as well as the use of language and silence in the theater of Beckett, Betsuyaku, and Pinter that create the sense of insecurity and evoke fears in the spectator's mind.

Insecurity Created through Space and Objects

The three writers, instead of naturalistically representing threatening conditions, allude to them ambiguously or indirectly by the use of non-naturalistic theatrical space to suggest ominous situations. In his essay "Proscenium Arch e no Kaiki" ("The Return to the Proscenium Arch"), Betsuyaku discusses the effects of freeing the stage from naturalistic settings that he finds to be one of the legacies of Beckett's theater. No longer limited by three walls, an object situated at center stage, such as the tree in *Waiting for Godot,* plays a centrifugal role as a "small part" of an "uncharacteristic" and infinitely extending scenic space. Betsuyaku finds such empty space, stretching to the back of the redefined proscenium arch, essential for his own plays; and the telegraph pole, mailbox, or table and chair that he places at center stage are intended to play the same dynamic role as *Godot's* tree. The tree exists to "characterize" the space it is in and to indicate how tiny and insignificant it is in this space, while the infinite space surrounding the tree tries to "extinguish" the meaning and the existence of the tree standing there (273–75). Betsuyaku's objects do the same.

This view of Beckettian space and the objects in it is reflected in the opening stage directions of Betsuyaku's play *Soyosoyo Zoku no Hanran* (*The Revolt of the Breeze Tribe* [1971]):

A stage, which means "nowhere." It looks like a street corner of a town since on center stage there are a telegraph pole, a bus stop, and a bench for people waiting for a bus, but they seem to be laid in a desert. These objects by their withered and stained look show traces of the lives coming and going in the past, but the area surrounding the objects is always so vague and vast that it never follows the traces. [...] For a while, one may try to understand the space as familiar as "a street corner of a town" by reading the concrete meanings out of the precision instruments. But in the next moment, the instruments lose their concrete meanings and begin to assume a new character as grotesque objects surrounded by a strange and unstable space. (7)[2]

For Betsuyaku, every object in the set should be as realistic as possible in order to suggest a specific location of Japanese daily life: a dining room, a park, a neighborhood street, and so forth. In his emphasis on the realistic aspects of his settings, Betsuyaku echoes Pinter, whose plays also demand a "photographically real set" (Cohn 87), specific rooms—a kitchen, basement, or living room—that can be identified with locales such as a British laborer's apartment or a middle-class home. Betsuyaku calls such Pinter settings "actual spaces" (*Serifu* 178), just like his own, though the locales for these two writers are culturally different. Out of such familiar spaces comes an improbable situation: something strange happens or someone unexpected arrives. Betsuyaku appears to be adopting Pinter's "partial realism," which he redefines as the minute depiction of a tiny part of a larger entity. But the information provided is not enough to imagine the whole from the part. And because "the whole" cannot be seen, "we, human beings, constituting that tiny part, feel fear" (Betsuyaku, *Serifu* 63, 179).

Both Betsuyaku and Pinter build anxiety by shattering the semblances of reality they create in their rooms. At times they achieve this effect by purposely blurring the dimensions of the room. In Pinter's *The Homecoming*, for example, the scenic directions indicate that "the back wall, which contained the door, has been removed" (21). Even when a room looks claustrophobic, it is related to the world beyond it, where unseen powers lurk or from which someone arrives to threaten the people inside. Both playwrights obliterate the border between the inside and the outside, so that the characters are simultaneously placed in an infinite and a culturally specific space. Such melding of realistic detail and infinite space is a time-honored artistic and literary device whose effects depend in part on the strategy of defamiliarization, "intensified by the most realistic of settings" (Kane 134). Betsuyaku explains his focus from the most recognizably local to the most unknowable by means of the story of the blind men and the elephant: "Blind men attempted to find out what a huge elephant was by touching its parts, saying 'it's a fan or a pillar, or a wall,'" but they could not understand what an elephant was ("Sorekara" 265). Similarly, through "the most realistic of settings" in Betsuyaku's and Pinter's plays, the audience becomes aware that the world is something ungraspable and inscrutable.

Although Beckett's plays look more abstract, symbolic, and culturally nonspecific than those of Betsuyaku and Pinter, each object in his sets should be as realistic as *Godot's* tree. In *Happy Days,* the mound should look as natural as the mound one would imagine in a wasteland. However, while the mound itself may seem familiar, it is placed in a vast space where one can rarely see human beings. In addition, the protagonists, from the beginning of the play, are confined in this improbable set: Winnie sinking into the mound and Willie inhabiting a hole behind her, both symbolically encased in a tomb. The familiar object thus becomes defamiliarized by the space it is in and the way it is used.

To emphasize spatial infinity, the playwrights often use darkness in their works, which creates the sensation of being in a boundless vastness and awakens our fear and terror. Mysterious things can occur in this dark space. John Lahr, referring to *The Birthday Party* (1958), writes, "He [Pinter] throws the set into darkness [...] solidity evaporates. Objects become massive spectres in the dark" (67). Even when in Beckett's early works there is no such darkness, or a play is set in a room confined by walls, unending space is suggested. In *Happy Days,* for example, where the stage is flooded with light, it is obvious that Winnie is in infinite space. Although gray walls surround the room in *Endgame,* we sense this infinite space beyond the walls. Even if we see the walls, their grayness suggests "a gray zone," the room itself becoming "a small part" of an infinite space extended outward. In *Endgame,* when Hamm asks Clov if he is positioned in the center of the room, the question suggests Hamm's unspeakable fear. He sits insecurely, just like *Godot's* tree stands insecurely in infinite space, and lives in his blind world of darkness that the audience is made to experience indirectly by his uncertainty about his precise physical location.

In Beckett's theater, even though the actors' bodies, like objects on-stage, look stable, the situations they are in seem visually unstable, like Winnie's sinking into the ground. The audience watching stable objects onstage become destabilized shares with the characters the fear of being lost or disappearing in infinite space. In his later work, stage darkness often envelops an object or a fragmented body, so that the defamiliarization and unstableness are apparent from the beginning of the play, creating an immediate sense of fear in the audience. Beckett's *Not I* strongly elicits such a fear of instability: the play's protagonist, Mouth, that is, the performer's mouth, is literally fixed as an object and physically stable, but the situation in which it is placed is visually unstable, so that it looks as if it is dangling in infinite space, an effect created by complete darkness. The mouth onstage faintly lit and placed eight feet above the stage is just a tiny little thing in the theater, but when there is nothing to be seen except the mouth surrounded by darkness, the audience focuses exclusively on its movements and rhythms. Under these viewing conditions, the mouth looms larger and larger in the mind of the spectators as they come to share its sufferings. The Auditor (eliminated in some film and stage productions), stands four feet high downstage and may divert the spectators by four brief hand motions, but since the third and fourth gestures are "scarcely perceptible" (375), by the end of the play, there is nothing to interfere with the spectators' direct connection with Mouth.

Anxiety Created by Staged Torture

A second device shared by the three playwrights is the defamiliarized depiction of physical and mental suffering and death. Elaine Scarry cites Winnie as an example of a tortured person trapped in a tiny space who, nevertheless, accepts her situation as the fate of the "aged" (33). She has the willpower to survive. However, in the case of Mouth in *Not I,* the actor playing the role is not only physically bound but also blindfolded so that only her mouth is visible; thus her torturous situation is worse. Billy Whitelaw, who performed Mouth in 1972, admits that at one point during rehearsal she thought, "I can't do it, it's a form of torture, it'll never work" (125). Performing *Not I* was not only physically painful but also psychologically terrifying for her: "The play had touched terrors within me that I have never come to terms with" (131). Whitelaw had to struggle with the terror within her, as well as the terror of being bound and blindfolded, her body inert, while "vomiting" words at high speed. Rieko Suzuki, the Japanese actor who played Mouth in Tokyo in 2002, experienced similar pain: "I always had difficulty speaking in the last part of the performance. One time I was in a panic, having lost my place, but strangely enough I could not make myself stop speaking. I was in the same situation as the character Mouth was in" (my translation).

Although we do not see the body of the speaker in *Not I* except for her mouth and do not know how torturously the blindfolded actor is put into an immovable situation, we are hypnotized by her rapid, breathless speech and panting, rather than the content of the speech, and feel a sensation of ourselves being pulled into the condition both the character Mouth and the actor suffer. Compelled to sense the pain of the speaker physiologically rather than grasp it logically, by the end of the play, we find ourselves hearing the "buzzing" of Mouth, just as she herself hears it in the play.

The kind of disorientation experienced by the performers of *Not I* and, ideally, by its audience resembles the numbing that the body suffers when afflicted beyond the unbearable point of pain in extreme torture. It is known that the experience of torture can induce a state of psychological death, as the sufferer constantly tries to suppress his or her memories, finally losing the will to live. Giorgio Agamben says that in Auschwitz, by accepting death as a human being, one "becomes an improbable and monstrous biological machine, lacking not only all moral conscience, but even sensibility and nervous stimuli" (57). *Not I* is an extreme case of the torture Beckett imposes upon his actor and indirectly upon his audience. Staged torture is often a main theme in his work, repeated in the plays of Betsuyaku and Pinter. They make us in the audience face what we usually avoid facing: the suffering of the tortured in this world.

In 1941 the "arrest and disappearance to a concentration camp of Joyce's friend, unpaid secretary and helper, Paul Léon" triggered Beckett to join the French Resistance (Knowlson 304). During the war, "[m]embers of the Resistance were tortured in secret, the deportation of the Jews and other 'enemies' of Fascism was undertaken in secret and, until the defeat of the Nazis, their fate was also successfully kept from most of those who lived through the war" (Uhlmann 45). It is no wonder that Beckett, after the war, wrote works such as *Play, Catastrophe,* and *What Where,* in which protagonists are tortured. But in his plays, it is never clarified what the criminal should confess, and no information is gained by the torture. In *Play,* three tortured people alternately and everlastingly confess slices of their lives in endless repetition; in *Catastrophe,* Protagonist stands on a black block, never opening his mouth, and lets the assistant do the director/torturer's bidding; in *What Where,* protagonists are by turns taken to a secret place to confess, but it is never clear what they should confess. In *What Where* the torturers become the tortured, and there seems to be no one responsible for the torture. This situation is what Primo Levi discovered in Auschwitz, that is, the "gray zone" where the "'long chain of conjunction between victim and executioner' comes loose, where the oppressed becomes oppressor and the executioner in turn appears as victim" (Agamben 21). Beckett here portrays the inhuman situation where everyone becomes implicated in the nightmare, which evokes the fear in the mind of the spectator watching this torture game onstage.

Betsuyaku similarly shows a kind of torture game in his play *Soshite Dare mo Inakunatta (And Then There Were None;* 1982), a parody of Agatha Christie's *Ten Little Indians.* The ten characters who gather in Betsuyaku's play as the guests of a person named Godot are all sentenced to death by an unknown voice recorded on a gramophone. But they have no idea why they are guilty, although one of them discovers later in the play that they are put to death for crimes they will commit in an afterlife. They are tortured by the unseen voice, similar to the voice in *What Where,* and murdered for no reason. The last victim to be killed, Wargrave, the murderer in Christie's play, is crushed by a one-ton weight that falls from the sky, while the voice condemns him for having intimated that Godot exists. In the play, the torturer is unseen and nonexistent, and there is no one at the end of the play to testify what happened to the guests, the tortured.

The fact that there existed inhuman treatments during the war is often forgotten, Agamben notes, and those tortured "have not returned to tell about it or have returned mute" (33). Betsuyaku's characters, especially in his early works in the 1960s and 1970s, are afflicted with the trauma of war and hunger. They often feel ashamed of having survived and agonize physically and psychologically over their traumatic past. Others who witnessed the hellish sights try to forget the very existence of those who have suffered.

Unlike Beckett, who rarely has his characters die onstage, Betsuyaku fills his works with dead bodies, the result of accidents, murder, starvation, and suicide. Betsuyaku's cynical view of death comes out of his memories of the atomic bombing of Hiroshima and seeing people killed or thrown into jail unjustly after the war for being in antiestablishment movements. In *Soyosoyo Zoku,* a dead body in the form of a stuffed doll falls from the sky. This farcical beginning of the play shocks the audience, who then hear from a passing woman that she saw a dead body two days earlier as if it were nothing special. Later it will be disclosed that people in this town often witness a dead body falling from the sky. The dead are the "Breeze Tribe" who, afflicted with aphasia since ancient times, "have to die of hunger to inform others that they are hungry" (59). But people in the town fail to understand the Breeze Tribe's desperate message. "It is a tragedy that 'one has to die of hunger to show others that one is hungry,'" writes Betsuyaku, "but it is hopeless when even dying of hunger does not suffice to send the message of hunger to the world. And perhaps we are now in that hopeless state" (*Serifu* 131).

At the end of the play, two main characters voluntarily die of hunger. Before journeying into death, one of them addresses the members of the worldwide Breeze Tribe. Singling out the people who are dying of starvation in India and Africa, he announces that he is about to join them in their wordless unhappiness by seeking refuge in their silence. In intermingling the stark reality of starvation still found in the world today with poetic fantasy and farce, Betsuyaku avoids limiting his drama to either tragedy or science-fiction fantasy. An individual and local experience thus becomes a global experience, just as works by Beckett and Pinter, written in their own individual and European contexts, express the postwar experience to be shared by people around the world. Betsuyaku wants his audience to sense something they "have heard of but cannot recall" (*Kotoba* 311), which reminds us of *Godot's* forgetful characters. Just like them, the "forgetful" audience of Betsuyaku's play are "encouraged" to sense the fear and anxiety of dying of starvation they may have witnessed in their past. The experience may have been so uncomfortable and even terrifying that they did not want to recall it, and so with time forgot it.

Pinter resembles Betsuyaku in that he too focuses on the psychology of the postwar generation, who are exposed to the "tyranny in ordinary everyday behavior" (Innes 283). *The Homecoming* is a good example. In this play an expatriate university professor brings his wife home to North London, where, after she takes the place of his mother, she ends up rejecting her husband. The intruder is welcomed here as a sexual object by the men in the family, but it is also suggested that she may control and dominate the family. Unlike the nostalgic and romanticized title, *The Homecoming*, home is a battlefield. The local domestic setting changes from a seeming shelter into a "harsh universe," so that the wife's initiation into the family is as ominous as "the nuclear menace" or "terrorism," in the words of Martin Esslin ("Harold" 33). Pinter, more politically outspoken in his later plays, writes directly of oppression under dictatorship in South American and

Islamic countries but never specifies who does what and where, preferring to generalize situations. An example of such a play is Pinter's *Mountain Language,* which I will discuss in the third part of the essay.

Indirect Effects of Fear through Staged Language and Silence

The ambiguous status of stage language and silence is a third area the three playwrights explore in their attempts to create indirect effects of fear. For Betsuyaku, Beckettian stage language functions like a stage prop; its apparently stable form serves like *Godot's* tree to situate the characters in an infinite space ("Proscenium Arch" 277–78). "Come on, Gogo, return the ball" (*Godot* 14) is Vladimir's line suggesting his fear of having no response, but the language spoken in *Godot* is literally a ball thrown into the air, that is, an object constituting a tiny part of an infinite space. Beckett's characters are speaking just to pass the time and make sure their words are reaching listeners; whether listeners understand their words does not matter to them. Language does not function as a communicative tool, and so "the spectators of Beckett's plays have to think about 'why his characters speak' while spectators in naturalistic plays have to understand 'what the characters say'" (Betsuyaku, "Proscenium Arch" 277).

The inability to communicate by language is even more apparent in Pinter's theater. "Always, in Pinter's world, personal inadequacy expresses itself in an inadequacy to cope with and to use language. The inability to communicate, and to *communicate in the correct terms,* is felt by the characters as a mark of inferiority," Esslin notes ("Language" 46; emphasis in original). Pinter, like Beckett, portrays distrust of language by "fus[ing] spatial fluidity with silence to intensify disorientation and elicit responses to menace and mystery" (Kane 136). The "spatial fluidity" or insecurity is intensified by the "inadequacy" to speak and by the "silence" in Pinter's plays. In *A Slight Ache* (a radio drama broadcast by the BBC in 1959 and first performed on the stage in 1961), a silent old match-seller stands ominously outside the house of a couple. His failure to speak threatens them, causing their own language to assume a desperate incommunicability, prompted by their growing sense of being inferior to the mute old man. The husband eventually becomes completely helpless and submissive to his wife, who, infatuated by her fantasy of the match-seller, leaves the house.

Thus, the silent figure gains power and ruins the lives of the couple. In the radio play the menace he represents is stronger than in the staged version, for the threat of a silent, unnamed fear in daily life becomes more general and pervasive and can be equated to innumerable fears. The silence of the man also emphasizes the feelings of powerlessness in the audience.

In Betsuyaku's play *Match Uri no Shojo* (*The Little Match-Seller*; 1966), a match-seller also appears as an intruder. A woman who used to sell matches when she was little visits an elderly couple and confesses that she is their daughter. Since their daughter was crushed to death under a train, they do not believe her, but because she insists, they accept her as their daughter, although only reluctantly. She then brings inside her brother, who has been waiting outside, and insists that he too is their son. The elderly couple kindly offers him a biscuit. Then, when he helps himself to a second biscuit, his sister angrily accuses him of greediness in a world where others are starving and orders him to apologize to the couple. Confused by her rage, the couple tries to calm her down. Falling to the floor and seemingly turning into the character of Hans Christian Andersen's "The Little Match-Seller," the sister hoarsely recites the ending of Andersen's story before leaving with her brother. Betsuyaku's match-seller is not as menacing a figure as the mute man in Pinter's *A Slight Ache*, but she frightens the couple like a ghost uncannily returning from the past, making them feel guilty for repressing their past. In an instance of the return of the repressed, the sister and brother are identified with the specters of this past that continue to haunt the couple. In his account of the "uncanny," Freud defines it as "something which is familiar and long-established in the mind and which has become alienated from it only through the process of repression [...] something which ought to have remained hidden but has come to light" (241). Betsuyaku is no doubt suggesting parallels with the many who survived the war, but who, because they regard the war as a national disgrace, prefer to forget the many who died, leaving no one to speak for them. But for him, the past cannot be put aside. Using a well-known children's story, he indirectly raises questions for his contemporary Japanese audience, who tend to block out their memories of a disgraceful past. In this play Betsuyaku manages to mesh his political concerns with his incentive to search for "a theatre of the unconscious" (Betsuyaku et al. 26).

After the 1980s, Pinter began to turn his attention to the forcibly silenced people under modern tyrannies. In *Mountain Language*, the wives of the missing husbands in a totalitarian country are banned from speaking their own language. As a result they are deprived entirely of the power of speech. In the final scene, one of the grieving wives, Elderly Woman, visits her son in prison. Despite having permission to speak her own language at this point, she keeps silent. The shock of seeing him so greatly changed by torture leaves her wordless. The despairing silence of this woman and her prisoner son is one of the most shocking scenes in Pinter's theater.

Both Betsuyaku and Pinter advocate that we listen to the inner voices of people, living or dead, who have been reduced to silence. But it was Beckett who first had us listen to the wordless voices of the dead: "All the dead voices / They make a noise like wings. / Like leaves. / Like sand" (*Godot* 58). Among the critics who read Beckett through the historical lenses of World War II, Ronan McDonald writes, "Beckett's skeletal characters and desolate landscape are haunted by the ghosts of Auschwitz" (142). Pinter also suggests "the nuclear menace," and Betsuyaku responds to it by writing "after the Hiroshima syndrome." Although the three playwrights approach silence in different ways, "the refusal of dialogue [. . .] carries the terror," for we sense in it "a withholding of something submerged" (Benston 117). Silence becomes the most terrifying moment for spectators who are made to face what they have repressed in their unconscious.

The theater of Beckett, Betsuyaku, and Pinter, through the use of non-naturalistic space in relation to objects, staged torture, and incommunicative dialogue and terrifying silence, makes us see "something submerged" or "the uncanny" hidden and repressed in our minds. Their theater exposes ontological fears and anxieties in us that invoke insecurity and a recognition that we constitute just a tiny part of the "whole" world, that this world we live in is ungraspable and uncertain, and that anything can happen but cannot be explained. As Vladimir puts it: "Nothing is certain when you're about" (*Godot* 16). It is terrifying that after Auschwitz and after Hiroshima, people still suffer, and those tortured lose their power to survive and testify, becoming the "Breeze Tribe" like the *Muselmann* in Auschwitz destined to experience "an impossibility of speech" (Agamben 164). But their silence can be eloquent, although their language no longer functions as a communicative tool, for from the silence arises a terrifying fear, a threatening menace, or "the uncanny" previously repressed. In the theater of Beckett, Pinter, and Betsuyaku, we are similarly "encouraged to face our fears" that lie within us.

Notes

1. Betsuyaku, born in 1937, lived till the age of eight in Manchuria, where his father worked for the government. In 1958, he entered Waseda University in Tokyo and joined a left-wing student drama group, the Freedom Stage, involved in the unsuccessful protest against the renewal of the security pact between Japan and the United States. Driven to despair, he left Waseda in 1960 and two years later founded the New Freedom Stage (renamed the Waseda Little Theatre in 1966) with Tadashi Suzuki. In 1968, he received the Thirteenth Kishida Playwright Award for his *Match Uri no Shojo* (*The Little Match-Seller*). Dissatisfied with Suzuki's directorial method, he quit the theatre in 1969 and in 1972 formed his own group. One of the most prolific writers in modern Japan, he continues to write plays for his group, as well as for Shingeki (New Theatre) companies, and has won many major drama and literature awards in Japan.

2. The translations of the extracts of Betsuyaku's works are my own.

Works Cited

Agamben, Giorgio. *Remnants of Auschwitz: The Witness and the Archive.* Trans. Daniel Heller-Roazen. New York: Zone Books, 1999.

Beckett, Samuel. *The Complete Dramatic Works.* London: Faber, 1986.

———. *Happy Days. The Complete Dramatic Works* 135–68.

———. *Not I. The Complete Dramatic Works* 373–83.

———. *Waiting for Godot. The Complete Dramatic Works* 7–88.

Benston, Alice N. "Chekhov, Beckett, Pinter: The St(r)ain upon the Silence." Burkman and Kundert-Gibbs 111–24.

Betsuyaku, Minoru. *Beckett to "Ijime"* (*Beckett and "Bullying"*). Tokyo: Iwanami- Shoten, 1987.

———. *Kotoba e no Senjutsu: Betsuyaku Minoru Hyoronshu* (*Tactics of Words: Essays by Minoru Betsuyaku*). Tokyo: Karasu-Shobo, 1972.

———. *Match Uri no Shojo, Zo* (*The Little Match-Seller, Elephant, and Other Plays*). Tokyo: San'ichi-Shobo, 1969.

———. "Proscenium Arch e no Kaiki" ("The Return to the Proscenium Arch"). Betsuyaku, *Soyosoyo Zoku* 271–79.

———. *Serifu no Fukei* (*The Landscape in the Excerpts of Playscripts*). Tokyo: Hakusuisha, 1991.

———. "Sorekara Sonotsugi e" ("Then, to the Next"). Betsuyaku, *Match Uri* 257–74.

———. *Soshite Dare mo Inakunatta* (*And Then There Were None*). *Taro no Yane ni Yuki Furitsumu* (*The Roof of Taro's House Covered with Snow and Other Plays*). By Betsuyaku. Tokyo: San'ichi-Shobo, 1983. 5–108.

————. *Soyosoyo Zoku no Hanran (The Revolt of the Breeze Tribe and Other Plays)*. Tokyo: San'ichi-Shobo, 1971. 5–61.

Betsuyaku, Minoru, et al. "Zadankai: Engeki no Postmodern" ("Discussion on the Postmodern in Theatre"). *Theatre Arts* 1 (1994): 17–36.

Burkman, Katharine H., and John L. Kundert-Gibbs, eds. *Pinter at Sixty*. Bloomington: Indiana University Press, 1993.

Campbell, Julie. "The Entrapment of the Female Body in Beckett's Plays in Relation to Jung's Third Tavistock Lecture." *Historicising Beckett/Issues of Performance*. Vol. 15 of *Samuel Beckett Today/Aujourd'hui (SBT/A)*. Ed. Marius Buning et al. Amsterdam: Rodopi, 2005. 161–72.

Cohn, Ruby. "The World of Harold Pinter." Ganz 78–92.

Esslin, Martin. "Harold Pinter's Theatre of Cruelty." Burkman and Kundert-Gibbs 27–36.

————. "Language and Silence." Ganz 34–59.

Freud, Sigmund. "The Uncanny." Vol. 17 of *The Complete Psychological Works of Sigmund Freud*. Trans. James Strachey et al. London: Hogarth, 1955. 217–52.

Ganz, Arthur, ed. *Pinter: A Collection of Critical Essays*. Englewood Cliffs, NJ: Prentice-Hall, 1972.

Innes, Christopher. *Modern British Drama 1890–1990*. Cambridge: Cambridge University Press, 1992.

Kane, Leslie. *The Language of Silence: On the Unspoken and the Unspeakable in Modern Drama*. Madison: Fairleigh Dickinson University Press, 1984.

Knowlson, James. *Damned to Fame: The Life of Samuel Beckett*. London: Bloomsbury, 1996.

Lahr, John. "Pinter and Chekhov: The Bond of Naturalism." Ganz 60–71.

McDonald, Ronan. *Tragedy and Irish Literature: Synge, O'Casey, Beckett*. New York: Palgrave, 2002.

Pinter, Harold. *The Homecoming*. Vol. 3 of *Complete Works*. New York: Grove, 1978. 19–98.

————. *Mountain Language. Death etc.* New York: Grove, 2005. 5–20.

————. *A Slight Ache*. Vol. 1 of *Complete Works*. New York: Grove, 1976. 167–200.

Scarry, Elaine. *The Body in Pain: The Making and Unmaking of the World*. Oxford: Oxford University Press, 1985.

Suzuki, Rieko. "Shintai wa Kangaeru: Beckett o Enjite" ("Body Thoughts: Performing Beckett"). Aoyama Gakuin University, Tokyo. 29 Nov. 2005.

Uhlmann, Anthony. *Beckett and Poststructuralism*. Cambridge: Cambridge University Press, 1999.

Whitelaw, Billy. *Billy Whitelaw... Who He?* London: Hodder, 1995.

The Midcentury *Godot*

Beckett and Saroyan

MARY BRYDEN

T HE WRITER WILLIAM Saroyan is widely reported to have remarked
that the impact made by *Waiting for Godot* would make it easier for
him and for everyone else to write freely for the theater. The 2006 centenary of Samuel Beckett's birth coincides with the fiftieth anniversary of
the American and Broadway premieres of *Godot,* and it was in the context
of the latter that Saroyan's remark was made. By then, the young Ruby
Cohn was already familiar with the play. She writes, "Having read nothing
by Beckett, I fell in love with his *En attendant Godot* in 1953, when it was
performed at the short-lived Théâtre de Babylone in Paris. That passion
spurred me to read Beckett's few publications, and I continued to read as
he wrote through the decades—magnetized by his unique depth and originality" (1). In honoring Ruby, and in commemorating these two landmark
dates, it seems appropriate, then, to ask: who or what is that midcentury
Godot?

From the distant vantage point of the twenty-first century, *En attendant Godot/Waiting for Godot* is commonly seen as a landmark in theater
history, a startling new exploration not of what theater is but of what it
can do and of what it can give rise to. Mel Gussow, who, being at that time
a master's student, showed his Columbia ID card to gain free admittance
to the 1956 Broadway production, names a series of later playwrights, including Harold Pinter, Tom Stoppard, and Edward Albee, as being "sons
of Beckett" (Gussow 10). This list could, of course, be supplemented with
other sons, daughters, cousins, or affiliates of Beckett who have extended
and expanded the notion of theatricality. The distinctiveness of Beckett,

for Gussow, is that he "redefined the nature of playwriting, freeing it from traditional bonds of length, plot, character development, specificity of atmosphere and stage movement. In his hands, stasis became a dramatic art" (10). Bert Lahr, who played Estragon in that production, later said that his wife had urged him to accept the role, telling him, "I think you should do it. It's a departure" (qtd. in Gussow 19).

That apparently oxymoronic mix, of stasis and departure, continues to intrigue contemporary audiences. Are there also, however, elements of arrival in that departure? Saroyan's remark seems to suggest that he recognized *Godot* as being not only a prequel but also a sequel, a kind of culmination of his and others' efforts and aspirations—in other words, that Beckett had in some sense provided legitimation to a kicking away of erstwhile obstacles to theatrical innovation, obstacles that he and others had been wrestling with for some decades past. This is not to assert that Saroyan was in any way churlish about Beckett's importance. On the contrary, Saroyan was unreservedly generous in his reception of Beckett's work, especially when one considers that, though he and Beckett were of roughly the same age, his own star as a writer and playwright seemed at that time to be on the wane, while that of Beckett was in the ascendant. This essay aims, therefore, to explore that bifocal view of Beckett by looking at him through Saroyan's eyes and noting the extent to which that view contrasts with the often more guarded response of other contemporary commentators.

While William Saroyan contrasts strongly in many respects with Beckett in terms of personality and writerly identity, there are also some significant similarities to be found. Just as Beckett must be seen in relation both to his native Irish context and to his embraced French context, Saroyan was always conscious of a dual identity deriving from being born in California as the son of Armenian immigrants. However, whereas Beckett, shuttling linguistically between English and French, sought out and valued the feeling of strangeness, foreignness, within language, Saroyan struggled to reconcile Armenian and American identities within his experiences of ethnic intolerance. This feeling of being divided never receded, and, when Saroyan died in 1981, half his ashes were interred in California and the other half in Armenia.

While Beckett gravitated to scholarship and excelled in academic attainment, Saroyan was to a large extent self-educated, having dropped out of high school at an early age. Nevertheless, though both Beckett and

Saroyan were writing prose and short stories at an early stage in their careers, it was Saroyan who at first enjoyed greater success with his first book, *The Daring Young Man on the Flying Trapeze and Other Stories*, in 1934. As a young man, Saroyan, like Beckett, appreciated circus-hall and vaudeville entertainment, but he also absorbed as much serious theater as possible, watching *Othello* in Armenian and catching touring Broadway productions whenever he could. He dreamed of revolutionizing American theater, and yet his reception by theater critics was always unpredictable. His 1939 play, *My Heart's in the Highlands,* was written at the request of the director Harold Clurman for the Group Theatre and was duly praised by him. Later that year, the play *The Time of Your Life* was also submitted to Clurman, who rejected it. Subsequently revising his opinion, Clurman tried to retrieve the rights, but they had already been sold. The play went on to win both the annual prize of the New York Drama Critics Circle and the prestigious Pulitzer Prize, which Saroyan declined, feeling that it compromised his artistic integrity.

Waiting for Godot underwent a similarly cautious and self-revisionist response from Harold Clurman. When reviewing the Broadway production during its run, he writes, in the weekly journal the *Nation* of 5 May 1956, in a manner that suggests his own ambivalence: "Even if I did not like the play, I should still admire it. I have my reservations, yet I think it a masterpiece. But should it prove not to be a masterpiece, I should still insist on its importance" (387). A year later, however, having seen *Fin de partie* in Paris, Clurman writes, again in the *Nation,* "Beckett may be accepted as a true poet in the theatre of our time; but because of the flaw in what he believes and the art that expresses it, his is minor art" (555). According to Clurman, the philosophical and aesthetic flaw in Beckett's writing is that "he wants to essentialize [...] the ground patterns of life's course. But life cannot be essentialized, since the substance of life is not in some supposed abstract design or 'secret,' but in the apparent trivia which so many philosophers begin by discarding" (555). It could, of course, be maintained that this is precisely the *opposite* of what Beckett is working toward—it is, after all, scarcely possible to overlook the ways in which "apparent trivia" stake out the basework of *Godot*'s situational ethics—but to hear this point of view so assertively put forward provides a reminder of the dynamism and unpredictability of early *Godot* criticism.

It was this volatility of reactions to the first American productions that provided a dilemma for Goddard Lieberson, president of Columbia

Records, when attempting to secure sleeve notes on *Godot* for the double LP recording he had commissioned of the Broadway production.[1] On 12 June 1956, George Dale, of Columbia's literary department, wrote to Lieberson, mentioning that, owing to the production schedule for the records, the sleeve notes were urgently needed. Dale himself would normally have considered writing these. He was at the time writing liner notes, for example, for the LP recording of Leonard Bernstein's *Candide*. The problem was that Dale was not enthusiastic about *Godot*. A colleague of Dale's in the literary department, Charles Burr, another accomplished liner note writer, had suggested the possibility of Lieberson writing something himself, but it was doubtful whether the president would have time to write anything comprehensive enough in the time available. It was at this point that Lieberson's thoughts turned to his friend William Saroyan. Wiring him the very next day, 13 June, he wrote, "Did you see Waiting for Godot and did you like it? I have recorded the whole thing and would like liner notes by you two or three thousand words. Not much dough probably hundred bucks but needed soon. Wire me collect and don't keep me waiting for Saroyan."[2] Saroyan did not keep Lieberson waiting, wiring back the same day, to say: "Didn't see Godot but read it. Of course I like it very much and of course I will write what you want. Meantime please send Godot recording soon as possible."

This message is, incidentally, a mysterious one. Notwithstanding Saroyan's assertion not to have seen *Godot*, Alan Schneider writes in his memoir *Entrances* that both Tennessee Williams and William Saroyan were present at the opening night of *Waiting for Godot* in Miami on 3 January 1956.[3] On that disastrous evening, he reports, most of the audience left before the end, with the exception of "the diehards or those whom the steak dinner and whiskey had rendered immobile." Nevertheless, he writes, "we wound up with three mild curtain calls, and both Tennessee and William Saroyan standing up in different sections of the audience shouting 'Bravo!'" (*Entrances* 233). Either Schneider misremembered Saroyan's presence, or Saroyan himself overlooked it (the latter possibility seeming unlikely). A third possibility is that Saroyan is discounting the Miami production, since Lieberson's recording was of the Broadway production in which Bert Lahr as Estragon was the only common factor, the rest of the cast having been replaced.[4]

Whatever the case, Lieberson sent Saroyan on 20 June a seven-and-a-half-inch tape of the recording, with a brief for him to comment not only on the play but also on its broader theatrical significance. Saroyan set to work immediately on the essay, despite discovering that the tape was not compatible with his own tape recorder. Just two days later, the piece was ready, and he writes back to Lieberson, "Since you wanted the stuff as quickly as possible, [...] I thought I had better skip the tavern down the road and write the piece [...]. The fee you mentioned constitutes no fee at all, but the hell with that. I'll take what I can get, but I think you ought to ask somebody to ship me an assortment of new Columbia LPs of all kinds" (Saroyan 22 June 1956).

Saroyan's first draft of the text had read, in one continuous sentence, "I've only read it, I haven't seen it, I like it, and I consider it a play pure and simple."[5] The final version of this first line removes the negative statements and retains just three separate, positive declarations: "I have read it. I like it. I consider it a play pure and simple." This is the only significant change made between draft and print. Within the piece, which is some eighteen paragraphs long, Saroyan convincingly assumes the role of a defense attorney, countering those who would object to the play on the grounds of what they deem it to lack (women, form, meaning, and so on). While conceding that the play demands "patience, watchfulness, courtesy, and even affection," Saroyan ends his comments by asserting the innovativeness and importance of the play. Lieberson was exuberantly appreciative of the text. He wired back to Saroyan, "Your essay arrive [*sic*] and it is for me one of the best pieces you have done ever STOP it will for the first time in the record history make the outside of the album as important as the inside STOP letter following." A letter did duly follow on 27 June. Saroyan's *Godot* text had already received some public airing via the well-connected Lieberson, who writes, "I was really terribly excited about it [...]. I carried it with me to lunch the other day since I was having lunch with Stravinsky and got him and his wife excited about it by reading them excerpts. Then I ran into Irene Selznick and Alan Jay Lerner in the same restaurant and read them excerpts." Lieberson managed to double Saroyan's fee to $200 and promised him a generous parcel of LPs.

What, then, did Lieberson find so compelling about the text of these sleeve notes? It is indeed a startling piece of writing, and one that proceeds partly by a notably Beckettian recourse to cancellatory or qualificatory discourse. Just a few months previously, Grove Press had published the English translation of *Molloy*, with its closing lines: "Then I went back into the house and wrote, It is midnight. The rain is beating on the windows.

It was not midnight. It was not raining" (162). When these lines are cited, later in 1956, by Herbert Gold, in a review for the *Nation,* he comments that Beckett here exemplifies not only the problem but also the hope of "telling what he knows through the lie of fiction" (398). By placing in parallel an assertion and its contradiction, the provisionality of writing and the array of possibilities it may induce remain in play.

One of Saroyan's favored rhetorical strategies in the sleeve text is, indeed, to introduce multivocity. By this means, there is a twofold avoidance at work in his critical practice. The first avoidance is a first-person gush of enthusiasm, and the second is a bloodless and impersonal analysis. Rather, using a direct and conversational address, he will frequently quote a criticism of the play and then concede it, counter it, or keep both possibilities in play, thereby undermining the univocal validity of the criticism. Compare Saroyan's statement, "A charge against it is that it is crazy. It is, or it isn't, and one way or the other doesn't matter as much as one may imagine," with a similar remark later in his essay, "Still another charge against it is that it doesn't mean anything, or rather that it means perhaps too many things, none of them clearly defined. Charge dismissed. It means what it means to whoever is watching, listening, or reading. What else could it possibly mean?"

There are further examples like these to be found in the text, but I have highlighted these because they have to do not so much with refutations of irrationality as with suspensions of the imperative or even the hypothesis of rationality. Saroyan's thesis is that an act of art is necessarily an act of madness, the product of someone who is, in his words, "touched," an adjective that has the pleasing double meaning of both affected with sympathy and, more colloquially, affected with insanity. Pursuing the theme, he asserts that those who proclaim a work of art to be "crazy" are usually themselves "quite daft and disorganized, if in a very boring manner, whereas the maker of the work is quite clear-eyed."[6] As well as being clear-eyed, *Waiting for Godot* is powerful for Saroyan both because of the fact that "it certainly isn't comforting, for which thank God. It just is." and also because of what it is not, and this he expresses again in dialogic manner: "The maker could make in another manner. Then, why does he make in a crazy manner? That question is the beginning, of impatient scorn, or of decent study—the beginning of rejection, or of an essay at acceptance."

The crux of that acceptance, for Saroyan, is a taking of the play on its own terms, grueling and aspirin-free as these might be. At the heart of the play's arguments and speculations, Saroyan discerned what he terms a "deathly still" dynamic, which requires the need to accept that "the play is about nothing. All is nothing. All comes to nothing. All is nothing from the beginning. Life is nothing. Death is nothing. Everything is nothing." It might appear from this pullulating rhetoric that Saroyan is attempting to ventriloquize Beckett. In a sense he is, but he is also voicing perceptions that had already formed part of his own earlier writing. In his most famous play, *The Time of Your Life,* people drift in and out of a down-at-heel San Francisco bar. Their conversation ranges over mundanities and over larger questions of survival, purpose, and failed aspirations. Uncertainty and the threat of violence inhabit these spaces, while at the same time passing comfort can be found in drink, in companionship, words, and music. At one point, one of the principal characters, Joe, a habitué of the bar, reflects on the continuum of life and death, giving what might be seen as a verbal rendition of Beckett's play *Breath*: "What? What-not? That means this side, that side. Inhale, exhale. What: birth. What-not: death" (*Time of Your Life* 407).

In 1958, in a dedication attached to a selection of his major works, Saroyan paid tribute to writers who, in his words, had "impelled [him] to write" (*W. S. Reader* v). Among these is the author of the Book of Ecclesiastes. This memorable short book, written in the third century B.C., proceeds in an intriguingly oscillating way through a series of repetitions and variations on the idea that human life is permeated with emptiness. "Vanity of vanities," it proclaims. "All is vanity!" (Eccles. 1.2).[7] Those things to which human beings attach value—knowledge, love, wealth, pleasure—are all illusory, and life is no more than a succession of meaningless events leading to a common death for all. Yet this apparently grim message inhabits a text that reaches out to the reader on multiple levels. The Preacher arouses sympathy and even humor as he tries various remedies to counter the perception of emptiness, only to take a pratfall again as vanity once again looms. The second chapter begins: "I thought to myself, 'Very well, I will try pleasure and see what enjoyment has to offer.' And there it was: vanity again!" (Eccles. 2.1). Throughout these trials, the Preacher manages somehow to retain faith, and does derive and recommend the enjoyment to be gained from wine, love, study, and the pursuit of wisdom.

Ecclesiastes is notable for its exposition of the experiential segments which constitute human activities, activities which, when aggregated and taxonomized, may appear mutually inimical: "a time to kill, and a time to heal; a time to break down, and a time to build up; a time to weep, and a time to laugh," and so on.[8] The title of Saroyan's play, *The Time of Your Life*, is clearly affiliated with this litany of temporality, which can be set side by side with the often-quoted prologue to his own play, from which the following is extracted: "Have no shame in being kindly and gentle, but if the time comes in the time of your life to kill, kill and have no regret. In the time of your life, live—so that in that wondrous time you shall not add to the misery and sorrow of the world, but shall smile to the infinite delight and mystery of it" (376).

Ecclesiastes is an example of a work that may impact on the reader on the basis not of creedal or doctrinal adherence but simply as an engaging grappling with human rhythms and dilemmas, the procession of moments that string out to form the passage from womb to tomb. Beckett was, of course, very familiar with its resonance. Among other textual echoes, the narrator of *Dream of Fair to Middling Women* adverts to, and subverts, Ecclesiastes in saying, "The dead fart, says the Preacher, vanity of vanities, and the quick whistle" (146). Saroyan recognized similar preoccupations to his own in *Waiting for Godot*, and, in his essay on the play, he writes of how Ecclesiastes translates into other shapes and manifestations within ongoing literary experimentation: "The play itself [*Godot*] is in fact a chapter in the contemporary Bible of course, as all true and new works are. The gospel so to say according to Samuel Beckett, and good enough. Whoever wrote Ecclesiastes put it only a little differently."

A rapprochement between the oeuvre of Beckett and that of Saroyan may be achieved only on a restricted and carefully delineated basis. Those attached to the sparsity of late Beckett will undoubtedly find some of Saroyan's late writing extravagantly overwrought. Nevertheless, Saroyan's work does contain elements and impulses that illustrate why he should have been so responsive to Beckett's writing. In particular, contrary to those critics who considered the landscape of waiting to be an inappropriate context for a theatrical event, Saroyan engaged with it as the basic currency of life. In *The Time of Your Life*, Joe responds to questions about his life from Mary, an Anglo-Irish girl, by saying, "It doesn't make any difference who you are or what you do, twenty-three and a half hours of the twenty-four are spent *waiting*. [...] That goes on for days and days, and weeks and months and years, and years, and the first thing you know *all* the years are dead. All the minutes are dead. Yourself are dead. There's nothing to wait for any more" (401).

The waiting can be rendered more leaden, or more acute, by the questions it elicits, to which there are no answers. Saroyan includes some of these in his essay on *Godot*: "Is wretched waiting for the inevitable the reward we have run so swiftly to seize, when all along we believed it would be something better? Is that all our reward is? In terms of this simple play, [...] it is, of course." He goes on to discuss how waiting may take different forms, and how human beings resort to short-term strategies to vary the waiting experience. Nevertheless, the play, he asserts, does not ingratiate itself, endear itself. As he defines it negatively: "*Waiting for Godot* is not instantly irresistible."

The viewers Saroyan had in mind as candidates for resistance to the play would include those, it seems, who remain attached to the notion of recipe or formula, and those troubled by the absence of women, the absence of murders of relatives or rivals, or the absence of movie adaptation potential, all of which absences Saroyan discusses. It is this latter absence—the play's dissociation from marketable and bankable extension—that is strongly endorsed by the essay's commissioner, Goddard Lieberson. This was, after all, a time when commercial concerns were a powerful restraining force in American theater. Musical comedies from the Gershwins or Rodgers and Hammerstein could be relied upon for success, and serious or experimental drama had found few regular outlets since the dissolution of the Group Theatre in 1941. It should be remembered that one of Lieberson's great successes as an entrepreneur derived from offsetting Columbia's highly profitable recording streams—the Broadway musicals such as *My Fair Lady* or *West Side Story*—with the less profitable but, in Lieberson's eyes, equally important recording projects such as the spoken word, original cast series of which *Godot* was a part.[9] Hence, Lieberson ends his letter to Saroyan acknowledging the *Godot* essay with the following terse but revelatory words: "Thanks again for doing it not only so quickly, but so well. I guess what I didn't say was that I think the piece is a whole critique of the New York theater in all of its avarice, mendacity—you fill in the rest...." Lieberson censors himself with that final ellipsis, but it is in an important sense an acknowledgment not only of the ways in which *Godot* goes out into inhospitable terrain to set up new theatrical paradigms but also of the ways in which it offered fresh hope to other writers who feared, or had become casualties of, the consequences of theatrical innovation or challenge.

This was a terrain all too familiar to Saroyan, and, though he considered himself to have resisted the temptations of compromise, he recognized their potency. He indicates this in the penultimate paragraph of his *Godot* notes, where he hails the play not so much as a theatrical thunderbolt but as an emancipation of allied impulses that other committed playwrights had experienced and then sublimated. Hence, Saroyan writes of *Godot,* "It is an important play because it [...] suggests to cleverer and more skillful playwrights a little of the enormity they have denied themselves through expert adjustment to reality and the market."

By the time he wrote the *Godot* essay, as I suggested earlier, Saroyan's career was far from prosperous. He continued to write prolifically, but on the whole, his postwar works never reached the receptive audience that had greeted those of the prewar period. Some of the later plays, such as *The Slaughter of the Innocents* (1958), were largely overlooked, and some among those now archived at Stanford University were never performed at all, partly because they were felt by some to be overly sentimental, or too tied to the specificities of the Great Depression era. Despite comparisons later made with the work of writers such as Beckett, Eugène Ionesco, or Arthur Adamov, interest in Saroyan's work declined. Nevertheless, he made no concessions to an altered readership. In an essay written just before his essay on *Godot,* and entitled "A Writer's Declaration," Saroyan declares uncompromisingly, "Nothing that I wrote was written to order, on assignment, or for money [...]. If an editor liked a story as I had written it, he could buy it. If he wanted parts of it written over, I did not do that work. Nobody did it. [...] I have never been subsidized, I have never accepted money connected with a literary prize or award, I have never been endowed, and I have never received a grant or fellowship" (490).

Saroyan's oeuvre is extensive, and inevitably there are unevennesses in quality. Some of his best work, however—among which the play *The Time of Your Life* should in my view be counted—continues to resonate for modern audiences. In the recent American Conservatory Theater (ACT) production of *The Time of Your Life,* the director Tina Landau reported that she had found the play to be "an amazing tapestry, a kind of postmodern collage," and "more musical and hallucinatory than a linear narrative play." As "a pure ensemble play in which a society of people live, work, and play together," it functions, she says, "like a piece of music, and has to flow" (qtd. in Berson).[10] Those descriptions—tapestry, collage, ensemble—indicate the multiplicity and variability of tone within the play. Saroyan's writing tends to the elastic and expansive, whereas Beckett's tends to the pared-down and contractive. But perhaps because of their straddling of more culture than one, their ability to view bifocally or multifocally, both writers are able to refrain from the creation of synthesis, and to retain differing flows in play without seeking to channel them unilaterally. Saroyan also discerns unevennesses in Beckett's work, but this is no obstacle to his enthusiasm. He writes, "I do not mean this unkindly, but it isn't very likely in my opinion that Samuel Beckett will write a better play. I don't know how he wrote this one, but I'm glad he did. It's really quite bad, but that's beside the point." He adds, in the closing words of the essay: "It also happens to be great."

Lieberson's prediction had been that Saroyan's sleeve notes would render the outside of the album as important as the recording inside. Both have now receded into relative obscurity, after five ensuing decades of ongoing Beckett criticism. There is a strong argument for this historic recording to be rereleased in a modern digital format. Whatever the case, Saroyan's resonant acclaim of the play not only contrasts strongly with the circumspect responses of many of his contemporaries but also anticipates the status and longevity that *Godot* would later enjoy.

Notes

Quotations from William Saroyan's letters to Goddard Lieberson reproduced with kind permission from Peter Lieberson and from the Trustees of Leeland Stanford Junior University.

1. The two-record album was released in 1956 in the Columbia Masterworks series (ref. 02L238). The album producer was Goddard Lieberson, and the total playing time amounts to just over 1 hour and 45 minutes. It incorporates some musical sounds composed by Lieberson, himself an accomplished musician and composer. He describes them on the sleeve notes as "invented sounds of a more or less abstract nature."

2. Correspondence cited in this essay is from the Music Archives, Yale University, ms. 69.

3. This information is repeated in a footnote in Harmon 8.

4. Tom Ewell (Vladimir) was replaced by E. G. Marshall, Jack Smart (Pozzo) by Kurt Kasznar, Charles Weidman/Arthur Malet (Lucky) by Alvin Epstein, and Jimmy Oster (Boy) by Luchino Solito De Solis.

5. Held in the Yale correspondence collection cited earlier.

6. Cf. Beckett's 1955 advice to Schneider when the latter was rehearsing the play: "[Pozzo] is a hypomaniac and the only way to play him is to play him mad. The difficulty always experienced by actors with this role [...] results I think from their efforts to clarify it" (Letter 27 Dec. 1955, qtd. in Harmon 6).

7. This and subsequent quotations from Ecclesiastes are from *The Jerusalem Bible*.

8. Cf. the words of Sweeney in Saroyan's 1939 play *Sweeney in the Trees* (its title borrowed from Flann O'Brien's original and discarded title for the novel *At Swim-Two-Birds*): "The cackle of laughter is not absent from any object of this world or from any event of this life. [...] And in the laughter itself is every variation of delight and grief" (172).

9. Other recorded performances that could be cited in this connection include the original company of Edward Albee's *Who's Afraid of Virginia Woolf* and the "Don Juan in Hell" sequence from Shaw's *Man and Superman* (the 1952 production starring Charles Boyer, Charles Laughton, Cedric Hardwick and Agnes Moorhead).

10. The ACT Web site, http://act-sf.org (Path: Publications; Past Articles; "A Valentine to San Francisco"), describes the 2004 production.

Works Cited

Beckett, Samuel. *Dream of Fair to Middling Women.* London: Calder, 1993.

———. *Molloy.* London: Picador, 1979.

Berson, Misha. "In the Time of Your Life—Live." *Seattle Times* 25 Mar. 2004. 23 July 2006 <http://act-sf.org>. Path: Publications; Past Articles; "A Valentine to San Francisco."

Cohn, Ruby. *A Beckett Canon.* Ann Arbor: University of Michigan Press, 2001.

Clurman, Harold. "Theatre." *Nation* 5 May 1956: 387, 390; 22 June 1957: 554–55.

Gold, Herbert. "Beckett: Style and Desire." *Nation* 10 Nov. 1956: 397–99.

Gussow, Mel. *Conversations with and about Beckett.* New York: Grove, 1996.

Harmon, Maurice, ed. *No Author Better Served: The Correspondence of Samuel Beckett and Alan Schneider.* Cambridge, MA: Harvard University Press, 1998.

The Jerusalem Bible. Ed. Alexander Jones. London: Darton, 1968.

Lieberson, Goddard. Correspondence with William Saroyan. Music Archives. Ms 69. Yale University, New Haven, CT.

Saroyan, William. Correspondence with Goddard Lieberson. Music Archives. Ms.69. Yale University, New Haven, CT.

———. Liner notes. *Waiting for Godot.* By Samuel Beckett. 1956 Broadway Production. Two LPs. Columbia Masterworks (ref. 02L238), 1956.

———. *Sweeney in the Trees. The Beautiful People and Two Other Plays.* New York: Harcourt, 1941. 101–210.

———. *The Time of Your Life. The William Saroyan Reader* 375–450.

———. *The William Saroyan Reader.* New York: Braziller, 1958.

———. "A Writer's Declaration." *The William Saroyan Reader* 490–98.

Schneider, Alan. *Entrances: An American Director's Journey.* New York: Limelight, 1987.

Beckett, McLuhan, and Television

The Medium, the Message, and "the Mess"

LINDA BEN-ZVI

SOCIOLOGIST MANUEL CASTELLS's sweeping three-volume study, *The Information Age*, begins with the assertion: "Our societies are increasingly structured around the bipolar opposition of the Net and the Self" (1: 3). The Net, a term covering the ever-expanding networked communication media, he defines as fluid and constantly changing, while the Self is in a constant search for some fixity or surety now that primary markers of identity—sexual, religious, ethnic, territorial—are no longer clearly delineated or self-evident. This bipolarity has given rise to a condition Castells describes as "structural schizophrenia," in which "patterns of social communication become increasingly under stress" (1: 3).

Although Samuel Beckett died in the late 1980s, just at the dawn of the period Castells surveys, when the information highway was still little more than a two-lane road, his writing already reflected this bipolarity and resultant social and personal schizophrenia. Beckett's earliest fictional narrator, Belacqua Shuah, in *Dream of Fair to Middling Women,* may call for "The facts—let us have facts, facts, plenty of facts" (32), but his narrative illustrates that the more he knows the less he understands and can tell about himself or the world. Under a deluge of details, the very scaffolding of the fictional form collapses, burying with it—Beckett makes clear—the belief that information can act as a clarifying agent. In 1949, two years before Marshall McLuhan published his first media study, *The Mechanical Bride,* Beckett had already written a play that staged the impending confrontation between the new technology and the individual: Lucky, in *Waiting for Godot,* caught in "a net," suffering from informational overload, spewing out

271

facts and regurgitating the words and ideas of others, his thinking reduced to performance-on-demand, with accompanying dance steps, ending, finally, in silence. The image, no less than the play itself, illustrated Beckett's awareness that all fact-based systems (like the one he had observed close up in Vichy France), and like the languages on which they are built, have the potential to entrap and render mute those caught in their "net."

That does not mean that Beckett avoided technology. His post-*Godot* stage works are filled with it: magnetic tapes and tape recorder in *Krapp's Last Tape;* unseen recording devices in *Footfalls, That Time, Rockaby, Catastrophe,* and *What Where;* light sources as stand-ins for absent physical presences in *Play* and *Breath;* and gadgets and objects of all sorts to aid, vex, and perplex his characters. Of his thirty-three dramatic works, six were written for radio, one for film, and five for television, and he took keen interest in all phases of their production.[1] They are among his most experimental creations, avant-garde even by today's standards, breaking the conventions of the designated medium just as his stage plays reshaped the contours and possibilities of theater.

My focus in this essay is on Beckett's television drama, a topic that has received particular attention of late, thanks to the research of Eckart Voigts-Virchow, Gilles Deleuze, Graley Herren, and, particularly, Daniel Albright.[2] In *Beckett and Aesthetics,* Albright argues that while Beckett, like surrealist artists, is "doting on technique" (2), he does so not to show technology's potential and power but, rather, its "muteness, incompetence, non-feasance of transmission" (3), the medium allowed "to dwindle before the stress that Beckett places on it" (2). I agree that Beckett uses technology to indict itself—just as he uses language to reveal its own paucity—creating a technology of the unworkable just as he committed himself at the beginning of his career to write "a literature of the unword" (Beckett, Letter 172).[3] But it does not necessarily follow, as Albright claims, that Beckett totally evacuates human presence in these plays, that his characters are only "flimsy, jury-rigged theatrical conveniences, all dreck and bricolage" (25): *Ghost Trio* "just a game with superimposed rectangles—the visual system [...] detaching itself from every human meaning" (136); *Eh Joe* "the flimsy pattern of dark and light dots on the screen" (129). The television plays display Beckett's usual decrepits: those that Deleuze calls "the exhaustive, the dried up, the extenuated and the dissipated"(12), and Beckett describes as "falling to bits" (qtd. in Shenker 148). However, just as these disintegrating, enervated figures are almost never completely vanquished from his stage plays, they are never completely obliterated by technological means in his television works. Beckett understood the possibilities the medium afforded him and took full advantage of its technology to create "a syntax of weakness" (Harvey 135–36) in which form would not impose itself as "a sign of strength" (136) but would allow "the dustman" (137), his fictive creature, to be visible and perceivable, although just barely.

As my title indicates, I will discuss Beckett's television drama through the work of Marshall McLuhan, one of the early media theoreticians, who wrote at precisely the time Beckett began his own technological explorations, when television was in its infancy and few realized either its potential or its power. Certain McLuhan theories provide useful ways of approaching Beckett's television work and assessing his praxis. They also illustrate how well Beckett read the technological environment of his own time and instinctively understood the world in wait just around the millennial bend.

McLuhan on Beckett

Marshall McLuhan is a name up to now absent from Beckett studies, and it is not difficult to understand why. If ever there were two men diametrically opposed in temperament, philosophy, creative output, and just about everything else, it was the self-contained, publicity-shy, precise, inner-seeking, minimalist Beckett and the 1960s media guru–cum–pop icon McLuhan, a man given to bumper sticker slogans and metaphoric riffs, whose penchant for showmanship finally led him to be more embraced on the Johnny Carson show, in Woody Allen's *Annie Hall*, and the pages of *Playboy* magazine than in academe. As Castells puts it, McLuhan was "the great visionary who revolutionized thinking in communications in spite of his unrestrained use of hyperbole" (1: 329). Done in by the nearly total commodification and cannibalism of his theories by the popular culture he championed, and by serious critiques of his works that pointed out inconsistencies and distortions, he disappeared from critical attention after his death in 1980. However, in the past ten years McLuhan has enjoyed something of a revival, interest fueled by a growing awareness that many of his "messages" about the television medium, seen as excessive or crackbrained (the old style) in the 1960s, may have, in fact, been correct. Some of these ideas have relevance to Beckett's television work.

McLuhan had a penchant for overarching schema, but unlike Castells his were based not on economic or behavioral data but on the modernist literary trinity he revered: Pound, Yeats, and—most important—Joyce. While his student Hugh Kenner[4] went on to add Beckett's name to that hallowed list, McLuhan did not. As his biographer Philip Marchand explains: "It was an unspoken article of faith with McLuhan that all great artists were really Catholic, either overtly or in their secret sympathies. Those who could not, by any stretch of imagination or conjecture, be termed Catholic, like Milton or Samuel Beckett, were hopeless cases" (106). And worse. When the Canadian sculptor Sorel Etrog, a close McLuhan friend and Beckett admirer (he illustrated Beckett's *Imagination Dead Imagine* for publisher John Calder), once suggested that the two men might have things in common, "McLuhan, who regarded the absolute godlessness of Beckett's work with something approaching horror, grew so red in the face that one of his veins stood out" (Marchand 286).

Despite this antipathy, there are interesting and surprising Beckett citings in McLuhan's studies. For example, Beckett's name appears in the introduction to the second edition of his groundbreaking book *Understanding Media* (1964) in a passage as general, elliptical, and slippery as is most of his writing: "The existential philosophy, as well as the Theater of the Absurd, represents anti-environments that point to the critical pressures of the new electric environments. Jean-Paul Sartre, as much as Samuel Becket and Arthur Miller, has declared the futility of blueprints and classified data and 'jobs' as a way out" (xi). When he writes of "anti-environments," McLuhan refers to his theory that each technological innovation creates a new environment growing out of the one it replaces: talkies supplanting silent films, television built on radio. Those who live in the present are generally incapable of understanding, identifying, or analyzing such new environments, since they are absorbed within them and cannot find the necessary position of objective distance that would allow critique. "Environments are invisible. Their ground rules, pervasive structure and overall pattern elude easy perception," he argues (McLuhan and Fiore 84–85). Although the present affords no glimpse of itself, it does provide a retrospective look at what it replaced, the nature of the earlier medium now apparent as the content of the new form. McLuhan claims that people "look at the present through a rear view mirror" (McLuhan and Fiore 75), not in horror, like Walter Benjamin's angel of history, but rather in denial, a mark of "some essential numbing of consciousness such as occurs under stress and shock conditions" (*Understanding Media* 265). That is, all but artists. They have, he often repeats, "the resources and temerity to live in immediate contact with the environment of their age" (*Media* 87).

His example is Joyce, on whom McLuhan patterns his own writing style and whom he continually refers to as "the artist of this century who gave the most careful attention to the impact on language and art of all technical development in the means of communication" (*Media* 80). In the case of Beckett, McLuhan believes that instead of engaging with the environment of his time as Joyce did, trying to tease people into some perception of new media that affect their lives, he chose instead to focus on the negative and alienating effects, not the possibilities. This position is close to what Albright expresses when he writes, "Aloof, eremitical, Beckett wrote about technology as if it were somebody else's environment" (1). However, McLuhan assumes Beckett denied the sway of technology as many other intellectuals did, whereas Albright argues, and I concur, that Beckett cleverly used technology and media for his own purposes.

McLuhan expands his comments on Beckett in a section of *Understanding Media* entitled "Wheel, Bicycle, and Airplane," which traces progressively more complex forms of technology. Directly borrowing Kenner's argument set forth in his seminal study *Samuel Beckett,* published three years earlier, McLuhan writes that Beckett's use of the bicycle is "the prime symbol of the Cartesian mind in its acrobatic relation of mind and body in precarious imbalance" (166), describing Beckett's unsteady cycler as a clown "who mimes the acrobat in an elaborate drama of incompetence," his bicycle "the sign and symbol of specialist futility in the present electric age, when we must all interact and react, using all our faculties at once" (166). Extending his metaphor, he equates this bicycler/clown with Humpty-Dumpty, who cannot be put back together again because those who try have "no unified vision of the whole, they are helpless" (166)—what McLuhan sees as Beckett's central message and his failure. In contrast, he credits Joyce, who, in his "a-stone-aging" *Finnegans Wake,* had the ability of "recovering a unity of plastic and iconic space, and *is* putting Humpty–Dumpty back together again" (166).

What is interesting in this discussion is how closely McLuhan follows Beckett's own positioning of himself vis-à-vis Joyce. Beckett, too, called Joyce "a synthesizer," who "wanted to put everything, the whole of human culture, into one or two books." Himself he described as "an analyzer. I take away all the accidentals because I want to come down to the bedrock of the essentials, the archetypal" (qtd. in Knowlson and Knowlson 47, 49). McLuhan was also correct about Beckett's denial of any "unified vision of the whole," and his recognition of human "helplessness" and the impossibility of "horses and men"—or technology—to repair the broken, little man on the ground, or return him to his wall and his smug certainty that aid will come should he begin to totter.

The Medium Is the Message

McLuhan's most famous—and infamous—aphorism, "the medium is the message," was interpreted by writers such as Rebecca West to mean that content was no longer important, and they attacked what they took as "the tacit approval of emptiness which is the core of McLuhanism" (West 18). McLuhan denied this reductive interpretation, arguing that "societies have always been shaped more by the nature of the media by which men communicate than by the content of communication" (McLuhan and Fiore 88), and must be made aware of this condition. McLuhan's intention is similar to what Albright cites as Beckett's strategy: "Beckett saw much more clearly than most of his contemporaries that art resists the models imposed on it; and so, instead of imposing purposes and templates upon art, he experimented with the notion that an artistic medium itself might be made to speak, if approached with a sort of intelligent humility" (2). Most early critics of McLuhan assumed that what the speaking medium would tell, in McLuhan terms, would be of its own power and potential. However, contemporary media theorist Cecelia Tichi suggests that he may have been a less vociferous supporter than anxious observer of the media he described (184). As McLuhan explained in a television interview as early as 1966: "Many people seem to think that if you talk about something recent, you're in favor of it. The exact opposite is true in my case. Anything I talk about is almost certainly something I'm resolutely against. And it seems to me the best way to oppose it is to understand it. And then you know where to turn off the buttons" (qtd. in Benedetti and DeHart 70). The idea of a medium whose content would be the nature of that medium is consistent with Beckett's approach in his stage and media plays, in which he foregrounds the apparatus of the medium by revealing its trappings, conventions, and artifice.

Media Cool and Hot

For McLuhan, cool and hot media were differentiated mainly by their means of transmission and their effects on viewers. The television image, he noted, was created by a "light through" process, similar to that in which light shines through stained glass, creating mosaic patterns that observers must reassemble, while film and photography are "light on" media, the illumination bouncing off but not interacting with, or changing, the contours of the already fixed, predetermined images. Television of the 1960s was also low definition, its borders imprecise, its images blurry, its means of transmission billions of dots per second from which the viewer "accepts only a few dozen each instant, from which to make an image" (*Understanding Media* 273). Film, by contrast, was high definition, offering detailed information, its images clear, crisp, bright, and fixed. Not a process like television, it is a product, pictures presented in frames, not fragments, unaltered and unalterable by transmission or reception, requiring nothing of viewers except to observe what is projected from behind them and superimposed on a screen in front. "The TV image is not a *still* shot," he argued; rather, it is "a ceaselessly forming contour of things limned by the scanning-finger. The resulting plastic contour [. . .] has the quality of sculpture and icon, rather than of picture" (*Understanding Media* 272–73). Television for him was cool, like jazz: open, seductive, drawing viewers to its unfinished form. Film was hot—big band music—polished, complete, needing no active responses from audiences.

I have found no record indicating McLuhan's awareness of Beckett's media plays; perhaps his antipathy to the writer muted his interest. He certainly could have read of these works in Kenner's studies, which by 1973 included analyses of all the radio plays and the television play *Eh Joe*. Had he done so, he might have recognized that far from denying the possibilities the electronic age provided, Beckett marshaled media not, as Joyce did, to show the plasticity of the whole but rather to reveal its fractures and fissures. McLuhan might also have noted that Beckett built these works on a few of his own central tenets:

1. that a new medium might be delineated by calling attention to the old medium it supplants;
2. that the medium is the central message conveyed by a media work;

3. that the low-density, blurred images of television can create a heightened, evocative power involving viewers and suggesting levels of exploration beyond surface reality.

Beckett through McLuhan

Film (1964) is a good example of a medium speaking itself. It also illustrates McLuhan's notion that a present environment can be understood by using the past medium as the content of the present technology, now reified as art. A "talkie," filmed in 1964, *Film* is set in 1929, the era of silent film,[5] shot in 35mm black and white, twenty-two minutes long (the usual length of a silent film), and is silent, except for one telling "Shhh," an auditory joke to indicate that the film could speak if it wanted to. The completed work demonstrates that Beckett was struggling against the seduction of modern cinema, which, as McLuhan noted, is more about action than reaction, fixed rather than fluid, predicated on linear narratives not random sequences, creating a finished product rather than a process for viewers to puzzle over and complete. Beckett's solution was to return to the early, silent form, allowing him to jettison color, sound, and camera work that foist a sense of reality in modern film. By so doing, he both offers an homage to silent film and points to the traps and snares of the present technological environment. Although the results were striking, there were numerous production problems (Knowlson 523; Schneider 63–94) that probably led Beckett to turn to television, a newer technology, one less expensive, less time-consuming, and more congenial to his intimate explorations of being.

Eh Joe (1965) and *Ghost Trio* (1975) have their roots in *Film,* the natural order McLuhan pointed out, presenting progressively more nebulous images, typical of the "cool" TV medium. Thematically, the three are examples of what Kenner calls "the man in the room" (13–78) motif, Joe resembling O, the protagonist in *Film,* but more passive, the focus now on reaction, not action. Whereas *Film* was virtually silent, *Eh Joe* talks with a vengeance. V (Woman's Voice) is the audible pursuer; presumably a spurned lover, she prods Joe about his betrayals, isolation, and—most dramatically—the suicide of the woman who took her place. In her revenge tale, she is abetted by the camera. In the pauses between sections of her monologue, it moves closer in nine four-inch increments, until virtually flush with Joe's face, revealing his responses to her relentless voice and painful recriminations.

As McLuhan argued, the TV medium is best suited for close-ups that capture the complex nuances of feeling. In this play Joe says nothing; his face says it all. At the same time, the steady progression of the camera accomplishes what McLuhan described: it draws the viewer into Joe's inner world from which "a dead voice in his head" (qtd. in Harmon 201) emanates.[6] Albright assumes that the intrusive camera destroys any empathetic relation between character and viewer, Joe's face losing both its corporeality and humanity: "open him up and find a TV receiver" (129). In fact, in several letters to Alan Schneider—who was about to direct the play in America with George Rose—Beckett takes pains to humanize Joe, requesting that Schneider add a "smile at very end when voice stops (having done it again),"a sign that "he 'wins' again" (qtd. in Harmon 198, 202). In terms of the model of the television medium that McLuhan suggested, the proximity of this final shot, with its blurred, fluid image, illustrates how television, that "peephole art,"[7] can be employed to create intimacy, by allowing a man in a room to be seen by another person sitting in a room, seeing what the figure is feeling.[8] V's repeated word "imagine," added by Beckett in a late typescript (Ackerley and Gontarski 164), also prods viewers to recreate in their own minds the suicide scene V relates in such detail. Rather than machine routing Joe or Joe reduced to machine, as Albright claims, Beckett makes Joe and his conscience visually and audibly palpable and communicative, through his manipulations of the camera and recorded voice, employing the seductive nature of the medium.

In *Eh Joe,* part of the power of the work is created by V's monologue, spoken with "plenty of venom" (qtd. in Harmon 198), addressed to Joe but overheard by the television audience. In *Ghost Trio,* V (Female Voice) is not a spurned lover in the head but a mechanical voice in the machine itself, some sort of director, producer, or prompter, her words spoken—at least initially—not to the televised figure in the play but to the viewers in front of their TVs, Beckett's most direct foregrounding of medium as message. To point to the technology at work, he playfully has V repeat her first three opening sentences, suggesting that some glitch in the mechanical reproduction may have occurred, the disembodied, recorded voice perhaps stuck, prompting the viewer to want to check the equipment. However, V quickly forestalls such manipulations. "Keep that sound down," she demands, ironically pointing to the viewer's possibility of controlling or even ending reception—a potential McLuhan often emphasized—weighted against V's attempt to wield power and punish deviation. The same struggle is replicated within the play between F (Figure) and V, who also attempts to control his movements. Both parallel plots, if they can be called that, hearken back to Castells's description of technology versus self.

In Part 1 of *Ghost Trio*'s three sections—Pre-action, Action, and Reaction—after assigning names to the interchangeable rectangular gray forms V describes and then reinscribes within the confines of the constructed chamber, she finally introduces the inhabitant of the space: "sole sign of life a seated figure" (*Plays* 449), the sibilants breathing life into F, frozen until she speaks him into being. Unlike in *Film* and *Eh Joe*, where the men had dimensionality and bodily contours, here, as the title indicates, F is spectral, reminiscent of McLuhan's description of the ultimate TV image: "sculpture and icon, rather than of picture."

Again the camera is a palpable presence, but used in more complex and subtle ways than in *Eh Joe*. In addition to demarcated moves backward and forward from A, the furthest remove; B, middle zone; and C, nearest shot of F, stool, and door, the text also calls for unlettered shots: an angle from above focusing on F's head, hands, and the cassette he is holding; another in part 3 establishing F's perspective as viewing subject as well as perceived object; and a close-up of a mirror reflecting nothing. These numerous positions destabilize the patterning Beckett initially establishes, exposing the medium by foregrounding the ways it functions, not in some regulated, understandable fashion but capriciously, pointing to the inherent instability of all mechanical reproduction, the limits of those, like V, who stand invisible behind the scenes and direct its use, or the acquiescence of those who watch unquestioningly at home.

This same sense of technology run amok is reinforced by V's failing attempts to control F. In part 1 she brings him to life, and in part 2 specifies the actions he will execute. He plays it as she says it. However, when he makes an unscheduled, and presumably self-determined, stop in front of the mirror, V's surprised "Ah!" seems to give voice to her loss of control as much as to F's awareness of self; and her next command, "now to door," is her attempt to regain authority, as she did in the opening section in relation to the viewers. However, when F instead goes to his stool, V's words "Stop" and then "Repeat"—her last audible commands before lapsing into silence—mark either her defeat or irrelevance for the upcoming section, Re-peat, or F's failure, as actor, to get the prompt right. Either way the medium is exposed.

An even more intriguing manipulation of technology creating similar ambiguity and calling attention to the medium concerns the play's music: the largo movement of Beethoven's Piano Trio, op. 70 no. 1, known as "The Ghost." As Catherine Laws suggests, Beckett uses the music "in the same way as he does other elements of the play, positing them provisionally only in order to undermine their stability as their constructedness is revealed" (202). In her close analysis of the excerpts played, she shows Beckett's manipulations of the score, for example, beginning with second parts of sections, and "rearranging the temporal order of some extracts" (208). These alterations, easily missed by one unfamiliar with the music, raise questions about what the television audience actually hears. In a draft of the play, Beckett noted that there is to be "heard" and "unheard" music (Maier 272–73), an indication that F and the audiences are not hearing the full work, pointing once again to the "constructedness" of all musical accompaniment in media.

Beckett not only undermines the integrity of the music in the play but also calls into question its source. In radio, film, and television, music is usually ancillary to plot and action, providing punctuation that determines and directs the emotional responses of audiences. Its source or mechanical means of reproduction is rarely indicated; if music is doing its job, it is supposed to go unnoticed. Not so in *Ghost Trio*. Beckett's directions indicate a clear correlation between the level of the sound and the movement of the camera in relation to the implied object of transmission, the cassette. At position B faint music is audible, at C it rises, and in close-up it is further heightened. However, at A, the furthest remove from F and the cassette, it is inaudible. But not always. At the crucial end of part 2, after F breaks his ambulatory cycle and returns to his stool rather than to the door as V commands, the directions indicate, "Faint music audible for first time at A. It grows louder. 5 seconds" (*Plays* 251). Just as he revealed the randomness of the camera angles, Beckett points to the arbitrariness of the sound/object relationship he had initially constructed and undermines the viewer's surety that the music is in fact emanating from the small, battery-operated cassette that F holds but never turns on or off.

Beckett uses the music as one more way of pointing to technological indeterminacy, thereby foregrounding the medium as content. The ostensible plot of *Ghost Trio* concerns a tryst—its earlier title—F awaiting the visit of a woman whose failure to appear is announced by a young boy at the end of part 3, a variation of *Waiting for Godot* reduced to the intimate confines of the television screen. Were music used in a traditional fashion, it would rise and fall depending on the vicissitudes of the tryst story. By the end of the play, however, when the boy leaves, the last swelling notes of the largo point less to the woman's failure to arrive than to F's transformation from spectral ghost to actor in the play. Beckett creates this reversal and embodiment in the final shots, as the camera moves from A to a close-up of F who slowly lifts his head and gazes face front for the first time in the play. It then moves back to A revealing F's full seated body, relaxed and upright. His hands, which had held the cassette clawlike, are now crossed in repose, marking the end of his performance.[9] The last image on the screen is of a faint smile darting across F's face, similar to the one Beckett required at the conclusion of *Eh Joe* (and would use seven years later in *Catastrophe*), perhaps again indicating that the figure "has won," that he has not been vanquished by the medium that sought to control and objectify him, or that what the television play ultimately seeks to reveal is that it is a television play.

By the intertwining and ghosting of the figure observed and the observer— the-man-in-the-room seen by men and women in their own rooms—Beckett calls into question viewers' easy manipulations by television, of which McLuhan warned, and forces them to confront its power and seduction, and at the same time provides a corrective similar to the one McLuhan suggests: "the best way to oppose [a medium] is to understand it. And then you know where to turn off the buttons." However, in Beckett's world, it is never that easy. Technology stilled or media "outed" cannot put an end to "this buzzing confusion" (qtd. in Driver 218) inherent in "the mess" (219) of existence. That remains. The "*viral* endemic, chronic, alarming presence of the medium [...] dissolution of TV into life, the dissolution of life into TV," that Baudrillard describes (qtd. in Brooker and Brooker 77), is not its source but rather its symptom. What technology can do is to provide one more way of calling attention to "the mess" by allowing chaos into art, but not trying to quell or explain it, Beckett's way of "failing better" in the contemporary world.

Notes

A longer version of this essay, titled "Beckett and Television: In a Different Context," appeared in a special issue of *Modern Drama* 49.4 (Winter 2006).

1. For Beckett's work in radio, see Esslin 214; in film, see Knowlson 521–24 and Schneider 63–94; and in television, see Knowlson 538 and Fehsenfeld 360–66.

2. For earlier discussions of Beckett's plays for specific media, see Ben-Zvi ("Media Plays"), Gidal, and Kalb.

3. For a discussion of Beckett's method of using language to critique itself, see Ben-Zvi ("Beckett, Mauthner").

4. Marchand discusses the relationship between Kenner and McLuhan, quoting McLuhan as saying, "I have fed Kenner too much off my plate" (106).

5. For an excellent discussion of *Film* as a "silent film," see Brater 74–84. See also Engelberts's essay in this volume.

6. Jack MacGowran called *Eh Joe* "the most grueling 22 minutes I have ever had in my life" and described the camera as "really photographing the mind" (qtd. in Knowlson 538).

7. Beckett's description, in conversation with the author, Paris, July 1985.

8. In the 2006 Atom Egoyan stage production of *Eh Joe* in Dublin, a giant screen was used to project the face of Michael Gambon, the actor playing Joe, who listened to the taped voice of Penelope Wilton as V, sent out to the audience over two large speakers placed on either side of the proscenium. The impact was equally strong and may point to the way that, more and more, live theater approximates television.

9. For an interesting discussion of Beckett's manipulation of hands in his plays, see Haynes and Knowlson 75–77.

Works Cited

Ackerley, C. J., and S. E. Gontarski, eds. *The Grove Companion to Samuel Beckett.* New York: Grove, 2004.

Albright, Daniel. *Beckett and Aesthetics.* London: Cambridge University Press, 2003.

Beckett, Samuel. *The Collected Shorter Plays.* New York: Grove, 1984. (Abbreviated *Plays.*)

———. *Dream of Fair to Middling Women.* Ed. Eoin O'Brien and Edith Fournier. New York: Arcade, 1992.

———. *Film.* New York: Grove, 1969.

———. Letter to Axel Kaun, 9 July 1937. Trans. Martin Esslin. *Disjecta.* Ed. Ruby Cohn. London: Calder, 1983. 170–73.

Benedetti, Paul, and Nancy DeHart, eds. *On McLuhan: Forward through the Rearview Mirror.* Cambridge, MA: MIT Press, 1997.

Ben-Zvi, Linda. "Samuel Beckett, Fritz Mauthner, and the Limits of Language." *PMLA* 95 (1980): 183–200.

———. "Samuel Beckett's Media Plays." *Modern Drama* 28 (1985): 22–37.

Brater, Enoch. *Beyond Minimalism: Beckett's Late Style in the Theater.* New York: Oxford University Press, 1987.

Brooker, Peter, and Will Brooker, eds. *Postmodern After-Images.* London: Arnold, 1997.

Castells, Manuel. *The Information Age: Economy, Society and Culture.* 3 vols. London: Blackwell, 1996–98.

Deleuze, Gilles. "The Exhausted." Trans. Anthony Uhlmann. *SubStance* 24.3 (1995): 3–28.

Driver, Tom. "Beckett by the Madeleine." Graver and Federman 217–23.

Esslin, Martin. "Telling It How It Is: Beckett and the Mass Media." *The World of Samuel Beckett.* Ed. Joseph Smith. Baltimore: Johns Hopkins University Press, 1991. 204–16.

Fehsenfeld, Martha. "Beckett's Late Works: An Appraisal." *Modern Drama* 35 (1982): 355–62.

Gidal, Peter. *Understanding Beckett.* London: Macmillan, 1986.

Graver, Lawrence, and Raymond Federman, eds. *Samuel Beckett: The Critical Heritage.* London: Routledge, 1979.

Harmon, Maurice, ed. *No Author Better Served: The Correspondence of Samuel Beckett and Alan Schneider.* Cambridge, MA: Harvard University Press, 1998.

Harvey, Lawrence E. "Conversations with Beckett, 1961–62." Knowlson and Knowlson 133–37.

Haynes, John, and James Knowlson. *Images of Beckett.* Cambridge: Cambridge University Press, 2003.

Kalb, Jonathan. "The Mediated Quixote: The Radio and Television Plays, and *Film.*" *The Cambridge Companion to Beckett.* Ed. John Pilling. Cambridge: Cambridge University Press, 1994. 124–44.

Kenner, Hugh. *Samuel Beckett.* Berkeley: University of California Press, 1968.

Knowlson, James. *Damned to Fame: The Life of Samuel Beckett.* London: Bloomsbury, 1996.

Knowlson, James, and Elizabeth Knowlson, eds. *Beckett Remembering Remembering Beckett.* London: Bloomsbury, 2006.

Laws, Catherine. "Beethoven's Haunting of Beckett's *Ghost Trio.*" *Drawing on Beckett: Portraits, Performances, and Cultural Contexts.* Ed. Linda Ben-Zvi. Tel Aviv: Assaph, 2003. 197–213.

Maier, Michael. "*Geisertrio:* Beethoven's Music in Samuel Beckett's *Ghost Trio.*" *Samuel Beckett: Endlessness in the Year 2000.* Vol. 11 of *SBT/A.* Ed. Angela Moorjani and Carola Veit. Amsterdam: Rodopi, 2001. 267–78.

Marchand, Philip. *Marshall McLuhan: The Medium and the Messenger.* Cambridge, MA: MIT Press, 1998.

McLuhan, Marshall. *Media Research, Technology, Art, Communication.* Ed. Michel A. Moos. Amsterdam: Overseas, 1997.

———. *Understanding Media: The Extensions of Man.* New York: Signet, 1964.

McLuhan, Marshall, and Quentin Fiore. *The Medium Is the Massage.* New York: Bantam, 1987.

Schneider, Alan. "On Directing *Film.*" *Film.* By Samuel Beckett. New York: Grove, 1969. 63–94.

Shenker, Israel. Interview with Samuel Beckett (1956). Graver and Federman 46–49.

Tichi, Cecelia. *Electronic Hearth: Creating an American Television Culture.* New York: Oxford University Press, 1991.

West, Rebecca. *McLuhan and the Future of Literature.* London: English Assoc., 1969.

Beckett and Caryl Churchill along the Möbius Strip

ELIN DIAMOND

We cannot know and we cannot be known.

—Samuel Beckett

"WHERE NOW? WHO now? When now?" So begins *The Unnamable* by the very namable Samuel Beckett whose centenary was celebrated in settings around the world. It is my task in this essay to imagine "who now?"—whose plays might be seen to be lurking in his distinctive precincts. Every serious dramatist since *Waiting for Godot* has had to contend with that play's challenges, and while Harold Pinter always gets the nod as Beckett's inheritor, I turn here to Caryl Churchill, a writer thirty-two years Beckett's junior, yet whose career as a dramatist already spans almost a half century. Born in 1938 in London, raised in Montreal, Churchill wrote her first play at Oxford in the late 1950s and later settled in London with her husband and three sons. Writing alone and in collaboration, Churchill has authored more than forty-five plays for radio, stage, and television; and while publicly reticent about the meaning of her plays, she has attracted, not unlike Beckett, a loyal cohort of outstanding directors who aver that directing her works produces unique imaginative and theatrical challenges. Yet, in aesthetic vision and underlying philosophy these two writers, especially if represented by their most famous plays, Beckett's *Waiting for Godot* and *Endgame* and Churchill's *Cloud Nine* and *Top Girls,* could not seem more different. Churchill shies away from Beckett's metaphysical comedy (Hamm's "We're not beginning to...to...mean something?" [*Endgame* 32]) and seems to have little interest in Beckett's

285

art of impoverishment and failure, or in creating characters resembling his deracinated, near-sexless, sometimes bodiless beings. Instead, Churchill gives us distinctly if eccentrically rendered historical worlds and situations that generate comedy by laying bare the social and political ideologies—particularly gender ideologies—that discipline and derail the actions and desires of her characters. Indeed, I have called Churchill's *Cloud Nine* and *Top Girls,* with their innovative gender- and time-bending forms, "feminist satire" ("Feeling Global").

But artistic careers, when they are long and complex, continually demand new critical framing. Speaking about Proust, though he might as well have been speaking for himself, Churchill, and all writers, Beckett noted: "The aspirations of yesterday were valid for yesterday's ego, not for to-day's" (*Proust* 3). Playwrights and their characters—invented egos all—change, revert, change again. Beckett's career, after the benefit of three accomplished literary biographies and the revelation of his writing notebooks, is given a shape that we would not have understood at the time of his death. Not only do we distinguish between the early Joyce-influenced fiction in English and the postwar novels and plays in French, we are seeing new interconnections between and among them, and while the *dramaticules* of the 1970s and 1980s seem to be stagings of the deepest implications of the early French fiction, the later fiction has moved from the rhetoric of many voices to hermetic zones that the late plays refract through increasing abstraction. The critical frame will change again and again as Beckett's apparently sui generis work is rethought with and against other texts and artifacts in the receding twentieth century.

Not quite seventy, Churchill will continue to write plays and so demand different points of entry from her critics. Among British dramatists of Churchill's generation—Pam Gems, David Hare, John McGrath, and Howard Brenton—existential anguish was replaced by an insistence that the human struggle in a fragmented post–World War II world had historical causes and possibly historical (socialist) remedies. Yet, from her earliest radio plays Churchill presented "the historical" with unsentimental precision, writing dialogue that was emotional but also impersonal and ambiguous, belying motive, never presenting a finished or even a coherent personal story.[1] Furthermore, in the 1990s Churchill seemed to turn from her comfort zone of feminist satire to dramatize a kind of psychic and social dislocation propelled by dialogue that ran the gamut from explosive antisemantic lyricism (*The Skriker*) to cool abstraction (*Hotel*). Beckett's

Hamm curses Clov with "infinite emptiness [...] all around you" (*Endgame* 36), and this seems an appropriate descriptor for the barely recognizable social locales of Churchill's later plays. Her characters range from the merely human to the mythical and paranormal (a Vampire and Archangel in *Mad Forest*), a host of fairy-tale goblins (*The Skriker*), as though she were seeking surrogate responders to register the pain of contemporary reality. For Churchill, globalization has produced a world dominated by economic forces as impersonal and unknowable as the "they" who beat Gogo or the "they" who torture Clov with promises of beauty and order. Churchill's characters have always been lonely, even on a stage full of people, but recently their isolation has a metallic Beckettian taste.

With this "turn" in Churchill, other career-long links to Beckett, perhaps always lurking, become accessible. I am certainly not describing influence. Stubborn individuality of purpose has defined Churchill's career no less than Beckett's. Both are dark and precise poets of a suffering that is comically and self-consciously inflected. Both locate the human subject in interstices, not positivities, in the gaps where meaning beckons but will not congeal. Beckett's typical utterer is generally a barely gendered figure in greatcoat or shapeless wrap, who can never say "it all" yet never stops trying. Churchill's typical utterer is a woman, sometimes pregnant, sometimes old, but never fully revealed to or connected to those around her. Ruby Cohn suggests that Beckett and Churchill can be linked through the ways in which "their theater awaken[s] an emotional response to the individual.² This is shrewdly put. There are no "individuals" in view—certainly not Beckett's feeble agents whose stuttering pronominals oscillate across tenses, creating and unraveling all props to individuality; and certainly not Churchill's characters, so disciplined by social ideologies or absorbed by inarticulable desires, or, since *Top Girls,* speaking over each other's lines, such that individual voices overlap and turn dialogue into sound-and-rhythm scores. The "emotional response to the individual" lies in the perspective of the viewer. The variously fragmented worlds of Beckett and Churchill stimulate and frustrate our own dreams of psychic unity and coherence—of beauty and order.

Churchill used the image of a Möbius strip as an emblem of the temporal and spatial illogic in her play *Traps* (1977). The trick of the Möbius strip (as we see when one of the characters actually makes one) is that what appears to be two separate surfaces constitutes in fact a single continuous plane. Yet to the eye, the strip, like Churchill's play, is an "impossible object," its surfaces discontinuous and irreconcilable (Churchill, *Plays 1*: 71). The Möbius strip is, I think, an appropriate figure for Beckett and Churchill. To put them together creates an impossible object, but one that implies, in ways not readily perceptible, zones of connection along the twisted strip. In what follows I identify three zones of connection: concern with form, with mothers, and with God.

Morphing

Beckett's pronouncement about form in Joyce's *Work in Progress*—"here form *is* content, content *is* form"—stands with Pound's "make it new" and Eliot's "fragments I have shored against my ruins"—as one of the key pronouncements of modernist aesthetics.[3] David Pattie, in a recent assessment, notes that Beckett's writing can be seen to epitomize the deliberate formal strangeness that is a central concern of modernism. Critics in the modernist vein, Pattie argues, view Beckett's characters as "stripped of all social restraints and encumbrances," engaged in a heroic, often comic struggle for meaning against cosmic indifference and darkening mortality (227). And yet, Pattie points out, Beckett's oeuvre (especially the fiction) has been annexed to the postmodernist canon, critics finding equally prescient evidence of the aporias, the constitutive undecidabilities of a language universe in which human struggle is merely a fictive effect. Pattie wisely refuses such strict oppositions. Clearly Beckett's oeuvre bursts any barriers between the two critical camps, flowing through and over both with a mocking roar.

Churchill's work also resists obvious categorization. If for Beckett and his peers a world in fragments implied an absent totality, in the 1970s the possibility of totality was not even thinkable. Yet, while a generation after Beckett, in a cultural moment generally identified as postmodern, Churchill was raised on modernist classics. Penning her first post-*Godot* play as early as 1958, she inherits the innovations of postnuclear absurdism and takes historical and psychic fragmentation as a given. Perhaps, then, it is not surprising that while sharing her peers' commitment to socialist-feminist alternatives to conservative capitalism (a point of view that grew sharper when the Thatcher era began in 1979), Churchill was equally drawn, not unlike Beckett, to extreme mental states—"lovesickness [and] schizophrenia" (Thurman 54)—which inspired two of her best radio plays,

Schreber's Nervous Illness and *Not Not Not Not Not Enough Oxygen* (1971)—
both with Beckettian echoes. The former, based on the memoirs of Daniel
Paul Schreber, a judge and schizophrenic who believed that God was transforming him into a woman, featured a voice with the rigorous self-consciousness of Beckett's French narrators, for example, Moran:

> Early one morning, perhaps in June, three attendants appeared in
> my cell with a suitcase and told me I was leaving the asylum. Since
> they were only fleeting-improvised-men I did not think it worth
> asking where the journey was to lead, and in any case I could not
> fare worse than I had in Flechsig's asylum. I never saw him again.
> (Churchill, *Schreber* 69)

> It was in August, in September at the latest, that I was ordered
> home. It was spring when I got there, I will not be more precise. I
> had therefore been all winter on the way.
> Anyone else would have lain down in the now, firmly resolved
> never to rise again. Not I. I used to think that men would never get
> the better of me. I still think I am cleverer than things. (*Molloy* 165)

Churchill's voice of female panic from this period is a closer indicator
of voices to come. In *Not Not Not Not Not Enough Oxygen,* a play set in a
smoky, hellish urban future of "the Londons," Vivian registers the horror
of her ecological disaster through a detail of barely remembered vanity,
recalling Beckett's long-suffering Winnie and Beckett's style of narrational
self-interruption:

> VIVIAN: I remember I remember birds but bigger than that, it shows
> I'm not so young not so young as I—well I am thirty thirty had
> you thought? But what's youth youth youth these days? (44)

> WINNIE: Ah well, natural laws, natural laws, I suppose it's like every-
> thing else, it all depends on the creature you happen to be. All I can
> say is for my part is that for me they are not what they were when
> I was young and...foolish and...[...]...beautiful...possibly
> lovely...in a way...to look at. (*Happy Days* 34)

Waiting for Godot signaled the death of King Ibsen, as Ruby Cohn
once put it. *Godot* displaced the storytelling pleasures of theater and the

predictable hierarchies of plot and character with extended acts of waiting that utterly reordered the formal resources of the stage. Character, speech, movement, space, and time, released from logical plotting, were re-sorted into small or large structural units that were not *about* waiting but rather *did* the waiting.

Throughout her career Churchill has made form a large part of the content of her plays, in constantly inventive ways. Speaking of Joyce, Beckett offered an extreme reading of the form = content doctrine: "When the sense is sleep, the words go to sleep. [...] When the sense is dancing, the words dance" ("Dante" 27); and: "Dante's [Purgatory] is conical and consequently implies culmination. Mr Joyce's is spherical and excludes culmination" ("Dante" 33). In Churchill's *Blue Heart* (1997), a dramatic diptych, the anguish of waiting for one's heart's desire is dramatized as a constant and precise "reset" of lines and actions, so that we see and see again, indeed almost two dozen times, gestures and words from the play's beginning and midsections. Form itself becomes the voice of this witty play, suggesting that with respect to an object of desire people endlessly repeat the same gestures and words. The arrival of an enormous bird (an echo of surrealism), of killers who shoot everyone, and of rampaging children do nothing to change the command to reset and begin again. In the second play, *Blue Kettle,* in which a young man, Derek, tries to scam elderly women into believing he is the son they gave up for adoption, what could be a cruelly comic dissection of maternal longing in the manner of Joe Orton becomes an arcane language game, where nouns, verbs, and adjectives are replaced by the word "blue" or "kettle." Here the linguistic props to individuality drop away; language and being are severed. This is not a case of words raving away by themselves, as in Beckett's *Not I.* Here words-turned-nonsense are spoken in the mundane syntax of naturalistic dialogue:

MOTHER: Blue you was a little blue you liked buses.
DEREK: Did I blue to blue a bus?
MOTHER: You kettle buses and you kettle golden syrup.
DEREK: Did I blue to be golden syrup? (60).

As the spectator works, with increasing difficulty, to plug back in the words replaced by "blue" and "kettle," the form-content relation becomes clear: a play about substitution and loss is enacted at the formal level by substitution and loss in conventional syntax.

Twenty years before *Blue Heart*, Churchill's *Traps* created a unique theatrical conundrum, an uncompromising experiment in formal elements. Only the jigsaw puzzle and the clock that tells real time orient the audience to an action that Churchill, as noted earlier, glosses as a Möbius strip. Clock time advances, but dramatic time slips back or skips ahead unpredictably. The relationships and erotic tension of a group of people in a commune are, in their specificity, not unusual, but one stage encounter, internally logical, cannot be placed in sequence with another. One character is described as having died but emerges "later" without comment. There is no offstage or fantasized Godot or hammering Hamm calling the shots. Instead, refracting Beckett's innovations through her own concerns, Churchill's stage is stripped of tired mimetic conventions like plots and expectations and becomes what she calls an "impossible object," where illogical events "can happen on stage, but there is no other reality for them" (*Traps* 71). *Traps* like *Blue Heart* ran for the briefest of periods and will be remembered as interesting but minor experiments. Yet with such plays Churchill encounters Beckett on their relational Möbius strip, her plays exploring a form-content equation as rigorous as that of any other playwright since Beckett himself.

Maternal

Beckett's scathing satiric treatment of sexuality in the early fiction, the mockery of adultery in *Play* and of conjugality in *Endgame* and *Happy Days*, seem to have little to do with the exuberant gender send-ups in *Cloud Nine* and *Top Girls*, plays that established Churchill's international reputation. The serious fun of these plays was to mock femininity and masculinity as absurd yet historically entrenched constructions. Here, too, dramatic form was not merely toyed with but turned on its head. History, for Churchill, should never be grasped as a linear narrative but rather apprehended in temporal loops; hence in *Cloud Nine* her characters age 25 years while dramatic time jumps 100 years. In *Top Girls* famous women from many historical periods meet to celebrate the present-time promotion of Marlene, a female monster of corporate greed, the kind of woman Churchill loves to pillory. But Churchill and Beckett gesture toward each other across tropes of, as James Knowlson puts it, Beckett's "long-standing interest in abnormal psychology" (544), and Churchill's early "obsession" with "mental states [...] lovesickness, schizophrenia and so on" (Thurman 54). For both playwrights, the figure for this deep psychic disturbance is often an ancient female who carries the weight of both maternity and childhood: the pacing female figure of *Footfalls* and the old mothers in Churchill's *Owners, Fen,* and, in a curious gender key, *The Skriker.* As I have written elsewhere, Beckett's *Footfalls* is a harrowing exploration of maternal engulfment. For May, "revolving it all" in her poor mind, Beckett provides an unusually specific gloss: a remark made by C. J. Jung in a lecture Beckett attended. Jung spoke of the tragedy of a young girl who died but who had never really been born. In her obsessive pacing and in her inability to produce a story or an identity that allows her to separate herself from the womb/voice of her mother, May performs not being born. For Beckett the death that is birth redounds to the mother: "Yes, I'd have a mother, I'd have a tomb [...] here are my tomb and mother" (*Texts for Nothing* 119).[4]

Typically Churchill socializes and historicizes this maternal engulfment. In the opening scene of *Fen* (1983), a Japanese businessman articulates, for the first time on a Churchill stage, the voice of transnational corporate greed, and immediately after, we see stooped women, potato picking down a field, an immemorial image of sweated labor. It is intriguing to juxtapose the image of May pacing and the Fen women picking row after row, left to right, right to left. May is in the grips of inexpressible psychic obsession, the women in the grips of seemingly unchangeable economic conditions. As in Beckett's *Footfalls,* the Fen women are daughters and mothers who have produced daughters, and all are caught in the same cycle of despair. Val's back-and-forth affair with Frank, leaving her children to join him, leaving him to rejoin her children, is transacted onstage not in the crafted canters of Gogo and Didi but in quieter repetitions that, like May's pacing, point to an obsession that is beyond individual control:

> VAL: I was frightened.
> FRANK: When?
> VAL: When I left you.
> FRANK: I was frightened when you came back. (19)

In scene 14, generations of women in Val's family celebrate the ninetieth birthday of great-grandmother Ivy, whose memories of a long laboring life are expressed with a self-conscious bleakness that Beckettians will recognize: "IVY. Sometimes I think I was never there" (17). This is Hamm's avowal: "I was never there. [...] Absent, always. It all happened without me" (*Endgame* 74). Rehearsing *Footfalls* with Beckett in 1976, Billie Whitelaw once asked, "Am I dead?" and Beckett replied, "Let's just say you're not quite there" (qtd. in Kalb 235). Near the end of *Footfalls*, May tells a story in which she claims she was never there, and in the play's final moments the lights fade to reveal "*No trace of May*" (49).

Beckett's characters are often presented in a half-lit state, seemingly hovering between life and death. In *Fen*, Churchill utterly drops the convention that speaking actors play characters who are alive. Beckett's witty reply to Whitelaw, "Let's just say you're not there," might serve as the caption for the final moments of *Fen*. After Frank axes Val to death and shoves her in a cupboard, she walks out again (the night I saw the play, two people in the audience screamed), and suddenly her habitual monosyllables explode into a frenzied monologue in which she sees and ventriloquizes the dead. For the Fen women, life is a deathlike repetition, but the "afterlife," according to Val, is chaotic, full of visions, voices, and perturbation. Churchill mocks the stage as a perpetual "here" as, one by one, the Fen women arrive "there," in Val's death-space, to achieve a kind of emotional release.

The maternal in Churchill is never sentimental but rather a powerful source of symbolic and material information. Beckett excoriates maternity, often comically, for launching the nonsense of human existence. For Churchill maternity becomes a symptom zone of social disaster—capitalism in *Owners*, the desecration of the planet in *The Skriker*, the banality of evil in the all-out war of *Far Away* where "children under five" are hunted for destruction. In *The Skriker*, the eponymous figure is an ancient fairy and voice of a wounded earth, but at least one of her guises is that of a devouring mother. Manipulating the desire of two young women, Lily and Josie, the Skriker especially hungers for the pregnant Lily's baby. One of the most chilling moments in *The Skriker* is the description of Lily's fetus in utero, seen magically by the Skriker in imitation of the technology of electron microscopes: "Look at it floating in the dark with its pretty empty head upside down, not knowing what's waiting for it. It's been so busy doubling doubling and now it's just hovering nicely decorating itself with hair and toenails" (15–16). When Lily gives up her child to join the Skriker in order to, she hopes, prevent more natural disaster, she returns a hundred years later to find her own issue deformed and howling her rage at an ancestor who failed to stop the planet's destruction.

Under drastic social conditions, maternity itself becomes a source of harm or violence. Older women are liars (the Skriker, Harper in *Far Away*) or crazy (Ivy in *Fen*), and children are abused (Lily's baby in *The* Skriker, Angie by Becky in *Fen,* and all "children under five" in *Far Away*). In *Not I* (1972), the first of Beckett's three brief "woman-plays," as Ruby Cohn calls them (361), Mouth obsessively returns to the disaster of her birth: "tiny little thing…out before its time [...] no love…spared that" (22). In *Owners* (also in 1972), a black comedy about real estate dealings, babies and aged women are both fodder for destruction. In the course of *Owners,* one infant is exchanged for tenancy in a corrupt real estate scheme, and another infant is burned alive in an insurance-fraud arson of the same property. The old grandmother of the renting family is usually benignly ignored onstage, comically tipping over when no one is looking. In a later scene she lies in hospital on life support when her son Alec, without explanation, disconnects her drip, remarking, "There. That saves a lot of bother" (48). Beckett's Hamm, with Nell "bottled" and possibly dead, could not have put it better.

Godsounds

Beckett called himself a God-haunted man and demonstrated in almost every line he wrote that scripture was, as he put it, a "mythology with which he was perfectly familiar" (qtd. in Bryden 35). Bryden notes that Beckett used Old and New Testament passages never to enshrine or venerate but to generate ironic meanings (35). Churchill follows this well-trodden modernist path. In *Owners,* Marion's capitalist religion is sanctioned with the old Protestant hymn "Onward Christian Soldiers," and in *Cloud Nine* Christian platitudes are constantly yoked to colonial oppression. But in her later plays scripture is invoked not ironically but as a discourse of passion and rage. To the Skriker's "damaged" cross-wired syntax of rhymes, puns, Joycean portmanteaus, references to consumer and popular culture, and British fairy lore, Churchill adds the sounds of a thundering deity. Skriker delivers her opening monologue in the guise of a homeless woman, sitting in a ratty chair that bursts through the stage floor and is lifted hydraulically above the audience at whom she shouts her almost incomprehensible speech. The opening is a jangled redaction of "Tom Tit Tot," the English version of the folktale "Rumpelstiltskin," and contains ominous puns on two British nuclear reactors, Dungeoness and Sizewell ("dungeonesse under the castle"; "Never marry a king size well beloved" 1),⁵ as well as fairy lore about changeling babies ("Put my hand to the baby and scissors seizures seize you sizzle" 2); of enchantment run amok ("Don't get this ointment disappointment in your eyes I say to the mortal middlewife" 3), but in the penultimate section, in her "damaged" rhetoric, Skriker turns to the human neglect of the natural (fairy) world: "They used to leave cream in a sorcerer's apprentice. Gave the brownie a pair of trousers to wear have you gone? Now they hate us and hurt hurtle faster and master. They poison me in my rivers of blood poisoning makes my arm swelter" (4), to which the Skriker's response is biblical vengeance: "We'll follow you on the dark road at nightingale blowing (4–5)—or unscrambled: "... on the dark road at night in gale blowing" echoing the "whirlwind" and "storm" of the Lord who "revengeth" the crimes of Nineveh (Nahum 1.1–15). Then comes the last section:

> Revengeance is gold mine, sweet. Fe fi fo
> fumbledown cottage pie crust my heart and hope
> to die. My mother she killed me and put me in
> pies for sale away and home and awayday. Peck
> out her eyes have it. I'll give you three wishy
> washy. An open grave must be fed up you go like
> dust in the sunlight of heart. Gobble gobble says
> the turkey turnkey key to my heart, gobbledegook
> de gook is after you. Ready or not here we come
> quick or dead of night night sleep tightarse. (5)

The simple idiom "revenge is sweet" is collapsed into the impreca-
tion from Romans 12.19 "Vengeance is mine, saith the Lord, I will repay."
Added to this is the association of "mine" with "gold," and the three meanings convey a malevolence that the audience can sense if not fully comprehend. That children are killed and put in pies is old folklore, but the dust
of destruction has biblical echoes, as does the last line in which a game of
hide-and-seek—"ready or not here we come"—is attached to the phrase
"quick or dead." In Acts 10.42 and in the Apostles' Creed, the Son of God
is named the judge of all humanity, quick (alive) or dead. Yet the apoca-
lyptic reference is immediately juxtaposed with the tender bedtime wish,
"night night sleep tight," which is mocked in turn by the comic vulgarity
"tightarse." Beckett's Hamm uses biblical hyperbole to upbraid his story's

beggar: "But what in God's name do you imagine? That the earth will awake in Spring? [...] That there's manna in heaven still for imbeciles like you?" (*Endgame* 53). Forty years later Churchill uses the flattest sarcasm to excise even the assumption that human beings live in relation to a renovating natural world: "MAN/SKRIKER. It was always possible to think whatever your personal problem, there's always nature. Spring will return even if it's without me. Nobody loves me but at least it's a sunny day. This has been a comfort to people as long as they've existed. But it's not available any more. Sorry. Nobody loves me and the sun's going to kill me" (43–44).

In her last play, *A Number*, Churchill's Salter literally plays God. Having botched the rearing of his son, Bernard, Salter clones him, puts the original into foster care, and begins again, rearing Bernard 2 as his "real" son. Salter has a way of referring to the batch that produced B2 as "things" and attaches the word "thing" as well to one of the few references to the mother of the first Bernard. (The maternal function is, of course, eliminated by the cloning.) Salter is one who adds salt to food, or perhaps to wounds, but the name is also a homonym for the earliest and most impassioned book of the Old Testament, the Book of Psalms, known in the Protestant tradition as the Psalter. If there is one insistent rhetorical figure in the Psalter, it is the cry for help: "hearken unto the voice of my cry" (Psalms 5.2); "Attend unto my cry" (17.1); "In my distress I called upon the Lord and cried unto my God" (18.7); "My God, my God why hast thou forsaken me? why art thou so far from helping me, and from the words of my roaring? / O my God, I cry in the daytime, but thou hearest not; and in the night season, and am not silent" (22.1–2). In a scene between the now middle-aged Salter and the grown and clearly deranged Bernard 1, the latter reminds his father that he shouted in the night, but you "you never came, nobody ever came":

B1: again and again and again, every night I'd be
SALTER: no
B1: so you didn't hear?
SALTER: no but you can't have
B1: yes I was shouting, are you telling me you didn't
SALTER: no of course I didn't
B1: you didn't
SALTER: no
B1: you weren't sitting there listing to me shouting
SALTER: no (*Number* 31)

But in a later scene Salter gives up godlike denial, admitting that he was indeed sitting there, drink in hand, listening and not responding to the shouting of his son.

Eventually B1 kills B2 and himself. At the end of the play, Salter encounters Michael Black, a clone, one of "a number," who has escaped the imperative to "be" (B1 or B2) in Salter's male family. The name Michael derives from the Hebrew root meaning "who is like God?" and his surname directly opposes the white of salt, which is perhaps why, when Salter commands Michael to speak of himself, none of his statements, from the innocuous to the troubled, satisfy Salter's criterion for individuality. Salter wants suffering, a demand rooted in the Judeo-Christian view of existence. If Michael finds joy in belonging to "a number" like himself, and to a head of lettuce with which he shares 30 percent of his genes, the play does not abandon Salter's query. What is the individual? On the one hand, new technologies of reproduction are part of vast global systems that reduce human beings to, as Hamm puts it, "a little bit of grit in the middle of the steppe" (36). On the other hand, Hamm continues "to play," and Michael too finds pleasure in a walk in the park. Here Churchill and Beckett nod to one another in passing along the Möbius strip.

Notes

1. Betty's final monologue in *Cloud* Nine is the rare exception.
2. E-mail to the author, 23 July 2006.
3. Beckett's line is from "Dante...Bruno. Vico..Joyce" 27; the Pound line is the title of his 1935 book of essays, and the Eliot line is from *The Waste Land* of 1922.
4. See Diamond, "Feminist Readings" 53–59.
5. I am indebted to Derek Attridge's unpublished essay, "From *Finnegans Wake* to *The Skriker*," for pointing out the names of these British nuclear reactors.

Works Cited

Beckett, Samuel. "Dante...Bruno. Vico..Joyce." *Disjecta*. Ed. Ruby Cohn. London: Calder, 1983. 19–34.

———. *Endgame*. New York: Grove, 1958.

———. *Footfalls. Ends and Odds*. New York: Grove, 1976.

———. *Happy Days*. New York, Grove, 1961.

————. *Molloy. Three Novels by Samuel Beckett*. New York: Grove, 1958.

————. *Not I. Ends and Odds*. New York: Grove, 1976.

————. *Proust*. New York: Grove, 1957.

————. *Stories and Texts for Nothing*. New York: Grove, 1967.

Bryden, Mary. *Samuel Beckett and the Idea of God*. New York: St. Martin's, 1998.

Churchill, Caryl. *Blue Kettle. Blue Heart*. New York: TCG, 1997.

————. *Fen*. London: Methuen, 1983.

————. *Not Not Not Not Not Enough Oxygen. Shorts*.

————. *A Number*. New York: TCG, 2003.

————. *Owners. Plays* 1.

————. *Plays* 1. London: Methuen, 1985.

————. *Schreber's Nervous Illness. Shorts*.

————. *Shorts*. London: Hern, 1990.

————. *The Skriker*. London: Hern, 1994.

————. *Traps. Plays* 1.

Cohn, Ruby. *A Beckett Canon*. Ann Arbor: University of Michigan Press, 2001.

Diamond, Elin. "Feeling Global." *A Companion to Modern British and Irish Drama: 1880–2005*. Ed. Mary Luckhurst. Oxford: Blackwell, 2006.

————. "Feminist Readings of Beckett." Oppenheim 45–67.

Kalb, Jonathan. *Beckett in Performance*. Cambridge: Cambridge University Press, 1989.

Knowlson, James. *Damned to Fame: The Life of Samuel Beckett*. New York: Simon, 1996.

Oppenheim, Lois, ed. *Palgrave Advances in Samuel Beckett Studies*. London: Palgrave, 2004.

Pattie, David. "Beckett and Bibliography." Oppenheim 226–46.

Thurman, Judith. "Caryl Churchill." *Ms. Magazine* May 1982: 52–57.

Beckett and Paul Auster

Fathers and Sons and the Creativity of Misreading

JULIE CAMPBELL

MORTON FELDMAN ONCE declared: "I never liked anyone else's approach to Beckett" (qtd. in Albright 149). This statement makes a good starting point for my exploration of Paul Auster's creative misreading of Samuel Beckett, whose presence can be strongly sensed in the American writer's work. In this essay I focus both on the ties binding Auster to the literary father who influenced his development as a writer and on the family bonds, especially the bond (or, more pertinently, the lack of one) between father and son that both writers explore with poetic intensity. I draw on Harold Bloom's anxiety of influence and the misreadings resulting from it and Donald Winnicott's potential space of cultural creativity to derive the notion of creative misreading. This melding of the two influential thinkers will guide my investigation of the conflicted relationships between literary and family generations. I am particularly interested in the overlapping of potential spaces, Auster's with Beckett's and mine with both writers': approaching Bloom by way of Winnicott permits me to creatively (mis)read Auster via Beckett and Beckett via Auster.

From the Anxiety of Influence to Creative Misreading

Born in New Jersey in 1947, Paul Auster came into the world the year Beckett was writing *Molloy*. After completing his M.A. at Columbia University in 1970, he spent several years in Paris, meeting Beckett for the first time and "leading a hand to mouth existence" supporting himself as a translator, reviewer, and essayist (Auster, *Invention* 53). On his return to New York in 1974, he published the first of his five books of poetry, *Unearth,* continuing his career as a translator and essayist. At this time he felt he was a disappointment to his own father—another Sam—to whom "it made no sense [...] that he had produced a poet for a son" (53). He corresponded with Beckett and suggested translating his poetry from the late thirties, but Beckett declined, as he felt "only he could do the translations—and he didn't feel up to the task" (Auster, Editor's Note vii). *The New York Trilogy,* Auster's trilogy of experimental detective novels, was completed in 1987, earning him considerable critical acclaim. His most recent novel, *Brooklyn Follies,* appeared in 2005.

As the general editor of the Grove centenary edition of Beckett, Auster describes reading Beckett as "an experience unequaled anywhere in the universe of words" (Editor's Note viii). Recognizing the "tremendous hold" Beckett has had on him, he writes in *The Red Notebook,* "the influence of Beckett was so strong that I couldn't see my way beyond it" (105). This eloquent admission of an anxiety of influence leads him to "twist" another writer's work "into something I'm familiar with" (111), evoking a Bloomian "swerving" (more on this later). Akin to Winnicott, however, Auster emphasizes the creativity of misreading, which he facilitates in his own texts by leaving, as he writes, "enough room in the prose for the readers to inhabit it," and declaring, "The text is no more than a springboard for the [reader's] imagination" (*Red Notebook* 111, 140).

Before investigating Auster's response to the "tremendous hold" Beckett had on him, let me examine the divergent ways Bloom and Winnicott envisage the relation between writers and their forerunners. Bloom asserts in *The Anxiety of Influence* that on first discovering poetry, writers experience it as being both within and outside themselves: poetic "self-recognition" necessarily involves responding to other poets (25–26). For Bloom, this awareness of the source of poetry outside oneself results in the "dread of threatened autonomy forever" (26). Because of the anxieties artists feel about their own belatedness, they will misread their precursors, Bloom claims, "so as to clear imaginative space for themselves" (5). For him, for instance, a writer "swerves away" from precursors or completes them "to retain their terms but to mean them in another sense" (14). There are no readings for Bloom other than misreadings.

Bloom's account of how a poet comes into existence parallels Winnicott's description of a child's discovery of the world in the potential space between me and not-me. For Winnicott, an object a child plays with is at the same time subjective and objective: it exists in objective reality but is simultaneously as if created by the child (*Playing* 64). The child's relationship with a transitional object, such as a blanket or a stuffed toy, is analogous to an adult's creative response to a cultural object. While watching a play, for instance, each of us brings to the interaction "a unique style of attempting to unite inner and outer realities" (Schwartz 61) and, in Winnicott's words, "each one of us will create the play" (*Home* 133). This creative response to the potential space of the text involves for Winnicott both self-recognition and cross-identification, that is, the recognition of the other beyond the self, in which "the sharp line between me and not-me is blurred" (*Playing* 139).

Unlike Bloom, Winnicott downplays the "anxiety" involved in the acquisition of culture and self-knowledge through others: "The interplay between originality and the acceptance of tradition as the basis of inventiveness seems to me just one example, and a very exciting one, of the interplay between separateness and union" (*Playing* 99). When Bloom writes about the budding poet, "The poem is *within* him, yet he experiences the shame and splendor of *being found by* poems—great poems—*outside* him" (26), he places "shame" first, whereas Winnicott would put the stress on the "splendor," the excitement and the enriching nature of this "self-recognition."

Reconsidered in the light of Winnicott's theories of creativity and the interplay between separateness and interdependence, Bloom's misreading loses some of its sting. Bloom defines a "strong misreading" as "a profound act of reading that is a kind of falling in love with a literary work. That reading is likely to be idiosyncratic, and it is almost certain to be ambivalent" (xxiii). Drawing on Winnicott, I would suggest that the reader "fall[s] in love" with certain texts because there is a recognition that impels creative involvement. Consequently, the "swerve," "completion and antithesis," "purgation," and other strategies authors use, which Bloom sees as driven by anxiety (14–15), Winnicott would evaluate as positive, creative, and exciting, and as part of the necessary development and growth of the artist. Accordingly, a "misreading" by a would-be successor can turn into an act of creation of the forerunner's work.

Agreeing that in the act of "misreading," whether anxiety-driven or not, artists can create the works of their predecessors, Bloom and Auster both quote Kierkegaard's maxim: "He who is willing to work gives birth to his own father" (Bloom 26, 56; Auster, *Invention* 68). In his early prose fiction Auster is not only "twisting" Beckett's work in a different direction but also filling in many of the gaps in Beckett's work, giving substance to what lacks substance. He writes eloquently on the subject of gaps in a text: "The mind won't allow these things to remain blank; it fills in the details itself, it creates images based on its own memories and experiences—which is why [...] stories resonate so deeply inside us. The [reader] becomes an active participant in the story." In other words, Auster is using his literary father's work as "a springboard for the imagination" (*Red Notebook* 140). In the Winnicottian sense, the text is the potential space between the self and the other—the play area where the forerunner's work is reimagined by his successor. Eventually, Auster can be seen to be "giv[ing] birth" to his literary father through his creative misreading.

There is a fascinating complexity to the interweaving of self and other that Auster brings about as a creative misreader of Beckett's worlds. Beckett can be clearly recognized as a literary father in several works: his remarkable memoir after his father's death, *The Invention of Solitude* (1982), the fiction of the eighties—*The New York Trilogy, In the Country of Last Things, Moon Palace*—and *The Music of Chance* (1990). These works include a sparseness and an abstract quality that plunge us into an atmosphere reminiscent of the kind we meet in a Beckett text. But the Beckettian themes of aloneness, of life lived at the margins, of deprivation and hunger are reimagined through Auster's own voice, his own specific situations: an inward journey into the psyche exploring an identity displaced from the world of competition, consumerism, and the struggle to make a living and a "success" out of life. The reader has a strong sense of entering Auster's potential space, involving not only the interrelation of his imaginary world and reality but also the interconnection of his fictional world with Beckett's.

The claustrophobic confinement of *Malone Dies*, for instance, is reshaped and transformed in *The New York Trilogy*, in which both the sparseness and the father and son theme bring Beckett to mind quite forcefully. In the trilogy's first volume, *The City of Glass*, the protagonist Quinn (a name that evokes both *Murphy* and *Watt*) chooses to shut himself up alone in a darkening room, a situation not unlike Malone's in *Malone Dies*. And there is the sad story of Peter Stillman, locked up by his father in a dark room for most of his childhood. In *Ghosts*, the second volume, the character White hires Blue to watch Black, who sits in his room endlessly writing. Identities merge: both Blue and Black spend much of the narrative confined in their respective rooms, each watching the other; Black and White, we discover, are the same person. Expected to write a report as is Moran in *Molloy*, Blue begins to identify with Black in a way that recalls Moran's growing resemblance to Molloy. Blue also brings to mind Watt, as he is described as moving "along the surface of things" (143), while words begin to become detached from the things they are supposed to name. Yet Auster also veers away from Beckett: the setting is New York, and the literary references are to American writers, predominantly Henry David Thoreau, as well as Nathaniel Hawthorne, Walt Whitman, Edgar Allan Poe, and Raymond Chandler, among others.

Swerving and completing, agonistically or not, are inevitable, as Auster both retains and changes his precursor's terms. In taking elements from Beckett's works, Auster resituates them in specifically American contemporary settings, fleshing out for his audience what is abstract and condensed in Beckett. In introducing more detail and a more familiar illusion of reality, Auster nevertheless avoids any straightforward compliance with realist conventions. One example is his adoption of the constant motif of things running out, so prevalent in *Endgame*. This motif is central to *In the Country of Last Things*, which begins with the words: "These are the last things. [...] One by one they disappear and never come back" (1), and is revisited in *Moon Palace*, where, as the apartment gets emptier and emptier, the narrator speaks of how the external emptiness is echoed by a sense of his identity vanishing, alongside his belongings: "I could follow the progress of my own dismemberment. Piece by piece, I could watch myself disappear" (24).

Clearly, there is cross-identification in Auster's creative response to Beckett. He describes Beckett's style as "so distinctive that it resists all attempts at imitation" (Editor's Note viii). Avoiding imitation, Auster reconfigures Beckett's style to invigorate his own. The reason Auster gives for becoming a translator of French poetry helps to explain his interrelationship with Beckett: "I was driven by a need to appropriate these works, to make them a part of my own world" (*Red Notebook* 101).

Yet prior to the creative reimaginings of Auster's mature work of the 1980s, an earlier work shows the dangers a strong precursor can have for a successor. *Laurel and Hardy Go to Heaven* was one of three plays written during a six-month stay in Berkeley, California, in 1976. Although Auster considered them "hardly more than spare, minimalist exercises" (*Hand to Mouth* 101), John Bernard Myers decided to stage the Laurel and Hardy reworking of *Waiting for Godot*. It was not a success. Auster's play is a two-hander, with the dialogue of the two characters full of the kind of comedy and pathos, the trivial and the serious, and the scatological and the philosophical "blathering" (Beckett, *Godot* 66) that we associate with Didi and Gogo. Punishment is one significant theme, among others, that the two plays share. We do not know why the characters are building a wall in *Laurel and Hardy Go to Heaven*, but it appears that they are being forced to build it anew every day by unnamed persecutors. Still, unlike *Godot*, this is a play in which something happens: a wall is built. Although not a slavish reproduction, this early work nevertheless clearly manifests the need, conscious or not, to write a play like Beckett, or more particularly, to work through (or play with) the influence of *Godot*. This early and none-too-expert stab at "doing Beckett" is a far less creative "misreading" than other examples of Auster's responses to his forerunner.

It is only when *Laurel and Hardy Go to Heaven* is looked at again from the new perspective provided by *The Music of Chance* (1990) that this "spare minimalist exercise" (101) begins to gain an identity of its own. The play has been refashioned, resurfacing within the novel form and working on its own terms. There is a stronger "swerve" away from Beckett's influence: the abstractions have been brought down to earth, filled out, and to some extent made explicable. *Godot* can still be glimpsed, however, in the over-riding concern with punishment and redemption and the mystery at the core of the work. When Gogo and Didi discuss salvation in *Godot,* and Didi's suggestion, "Suppose we repented," is met with Gogo's questions, "Repented what?" [...] "Our being born?" (11), this exchange is unsettling within the bleak atmosphere of the play. When the same themes, which go so far in creating that strangely fascinating sense of threat in *Godot,* resurface in *The Music of Chance,* they retain their power. Pozzi and Nashe, the novel's two main characters, are forced to build a wall to settle a gambling debt. The repayment of this debt by building the wall is associated in Nashe's mind with punishment as well as redemption. Flower, along with Stone—one of the paternal and godlike controlling figures of the novel— envisages the wall they have ordered built to be "a memorial to itself [...], a symphony of resurrected stones, and every day it will sing a dirge for the past we carry within us." To which Nashe adds, "A Wailing Wall" (*Music* 86). These religious associations are joined to the wall's utilitarian purpose to "teach the culprits a lesson" (105). But what are Pozzi and Nashe being punished for? In order to shed some light on these questions, I will consider the theme of the absent father in Auster's work and the intermingling of this theme with his debt to Beckett.

Fathers and Sons

To return now to the notion of a successor giving birth to a precursor's work, I will focus on the extent to which Auster's creative misreadings of his literary father can serve to produce new insights into Beckett's texts. The topic I will probe is the father-son relation as it obsessively recurs in both their works. Auster's preoccupation with the absent father, the guilt and shame that attach to his absence, and the need for some kind of punishment to somehow redeem this "crime" on the part of the "victim" clearly have implications for Beckett's work. Both Nashe and Pozzi suffer from their fathers' absence—Nashe had not seen his in more than thirty years; Pozzi recalls meeting his father only twice in his life—and they are dismayed by their fathers' attempts to amend what cannot be "amended" by giving or leaving them money (*Music* 2–3, 40). Auster's own absent father had indeed left him such a legacy, the money coming at a time of great distress for Auster, and he writes of how "my father's death saved my life" and "in some sense, all the novels I've written have come out of that money my father gave me" (*Red Notebook* 132). In *The Invention of Solitude,* written directly after his father's death, Auster tell us about his own father's absence: "Even before his death he had been absent, and long ago the people closest to him had learned to accept this absence, to treat it as the fundamental quality of his being" (6). There is much in this portrait of his father that reminds me of my own. Auster's words "You do not stop hungering after your father's love, even after you grow up" (19) affect me deeply, as these feelings are associated with a sense of failure, loss, and need for authentication. I would take the statement further to suggest that this hunger does not stop, even after your father's death. "From the beginning, it seems," Auster recognizes, "I was looking for my father. Looking frantically for anyone who resembles him" (*Invention* 21). It is the death of his father that impels Auster to write his memoir in an attempt to give his father substance in defiance of the invisible quality of his existence.

In his novel *Moon Palace* (1989), the expelled protagonist Fogg is on a quest for both a father figure and his own autonomy. His homeless existence in New York's Central Park strongly recalls Beckett's narrators wandering the streets of Dublin in search of a home. When the uncle with whom he lived leaves on tour, Fogg wears his suit to mitigate the anxiety of his absence, explaining that he "managed to stay in spiritual contact with him by wearing [his uncle's] suit" (15). It is clear that Fogg is comforted by the love of his uncle, as the suit "swaddles" him (15). It is interesting that such a maternal image is evoked for a father figure: it resembles, moreover, a Winnicottian transitional object that children create to diminish their separation anxiety. But when his uncle dies, this comfort is no longer available, and the suit is discarded, now "worn through" and "abandoned" (25). After his uncle's death, Fogg is eventually evicted from his apartment; the hunger and aloneness he suffers, both before his eviction and out on the streets, appear like a penance he must endure as a result of being abandoned and unloved.

When read in the light of Auster's recurring theme of a father's absence, my own reading of Beckett's four novellas, "First Love," "The Expelled," "The Calmative," and "The End," shifts in focus. Another creative misreader has entered the potential space. This approach encourages me to "see" certain aspects more sharply and assign them greater significance. For instance, in the last part of Beckett's fourth novella, "The End," the narrator recalls an evening with his father: "I was with my father on a height, he held my hand. I would have liked him to draw me close with a gesture of protective love, but his mind was on other things" (92). This "vision," which comes toward the end of the narrator's life, eloquently conveys the need for the comfort and assurance of "protective love," but this desire is thwarted. The father is absent, thinking of other things, and this sense of the absence of the father and of the father's love can be strongly felt throughout the four narratives.

"First Love" begins by recounting the death of the narrator's father. Irretrievably deprived of his father's protection, the narrator is evicted from his house. What does his father mean to him? It is difficult to say with any precision. The father is the one "who wanted me in the house," unlike the unnamed others (11). The father defends his son: "leave him alone, he's not disturbing anyone" (11). But is this love? The narrator muses, "Perhaps he merely pitied me" (11). "The Expelled" similarly begins with the narrator's expulsion from the house he has lived in since childhood. But this time there is a stronger sense of punishment; he fears he will be beaten; he imagines "they" will be watching his "chastisement" (34). In both stories, the father leaves the son some money, as happened to Auster and his characters

Fogg and Nashe. But the narrators of "First Love" and "The Expelled" seem to disregard this inheritance; what matters is the fact that they are forced to leave home. In thinking of the use Fogg made of his uncle's suit to better bear his absence, we can read the "travelling costume" that the narrator of "First Love" puts on and that he lists with precision, "shoes, socks, trousers, shirt, coat, greatcoat and hat" (12–13), as serving a similar purpose. In the sense of a transitional object, his costume substitutes for the loss of the father's protection and reduces the anxiety of his expulsion. His hat, "the one my father gave me" (19), is certainly important to him, and he never parts with it. And yet in "The Expelled," the hat's ability to comfort is questioned, as his father's gift of the hat resonates with resentment rather than the love of the father toward the son: "I have often wondered if my father's purpose was not to humiliate me, if he was not jealous of me who was young and handsome, fresh at least, while he was already old and bloated and purple" (35). The hat is mocked by his childhood peers, so his father's suggested aim of humiliation succeeds. Despite the trials the hat imposes on him, the narrator declares, "when my father died I could have got rid of this hat, there was nothing more to prevent it. But I could not" (35). Here the desire for the father's love is doubled by father-son rivalry and the conflictual anxiety of influence between generations. In "The Calmative" the narrator wears his father's "long green greatcoat," but it is described as a "great dead weight, with no warmth to it" (55). Instead of substituting for the father's protection, these garments represent the crushing and punishing influence of the absent father.

In *Moon Palace,* absent fathers and three generations are among the elements of Beckett's *Endgame* that Auster creatively reworked in his novel. Fogg, who has never known his father at this stage of the narrative, takes a job looking after a man who, unbeknownst to him, is his grandfather. Effing (a name that recalls *Watt*) is an invalid, in a wheelchair, and apparently blind, although Fogg cannot be sure. His resemblance to Hamm is clear in his appearance and in his uncontrolled "selfishness and arrogance" (108). In a position like Clov's, Fogg sees for Effing, pushing him around in his wheelchair and suffering "a considerable amount of abuse" (109). He listens to his story, a story that seems at least in part invention. These are useful examples of Auster's technique of borrowing while "twisting" and "completing" the original situation: he fills it out and gives it a concreteness and credibility, while still retaining a strange and unsettling atmosphere. *Endgame* is there, but as a "springboard." Auster takes it on an imaginative flight: Effing and Fogg are not confined to a room like Hamm and Clov; their walks take them all over New York, and Fogg describes what he sees with a vividness and detail that would seem to form a part of his apprenticeship as a writer. Clov's far more curt descriptions in *Endgame,* such as "Zero" (13); "It's the same" (25), and "Grey" (26), would not appease Effing's need to know the exact description of the objects they pass on their walks. Where *Endgame* is sparse and bleak, with a single minimalist stage set where "something," never clearly expressed, "is taking its course" (17), *Moon Palace* is full of detail, descriptions, embedded stories, rich in changing situations, journeys, inheritances, a father found and lost, love and the loss of love. The references to Beckett's work encourage us to read the novel with the play in mind, and this increases the sense of its fullness and richness, its exuberance.

Similarly, reading Beckett "through" Auster opens up *Endgame* in a direction I have not paid much attention to before: the fear of loss of self through the numbing sameness of day after day, but also the loss of self-worth through lack of love. The three generations are immured together, and the absence of love, father for son, can be seen as increasing the sense of incarceration and punishment. Hamm can say to Clov, "I was a father to you" (29), but this seems related to his concern that Clov is suffering sufficiently at his hands (14). Hamm calls his father, Nagg, "Accursed progenitor" and "Accursed fornicator" (15). Fatherhood is not revered but is treated like a crime. Hamm curses his father, but his father, in return for a cruelty from his son, recalls how he ignored him when he was "a tiny boy, and [was] frightened, in the dark" (38). This is what this reading brings out most forcefully: the absence of love, and the repetition of this absence, and the cruelty and the suffering that result. As Nagg tells Hamm, "Yes, I hope I'll live till then, to hear you calling me like when you were a tiny boy, and were frightened, in the dark, and I was your only hope" (38–39). He hopes for the repetition of a past cruelty, yet another repetition in a play full of repetitions. It is again the absence of that "gesture of protective love" that is narrated so poignantly in "The End." It encourages some pity for Hamm. Clov, another "victim" of the absence of love, wonders why he never refuses to do what Hamm asks (32): "Why do I always obey you?" (48). The cycle of suffering seems endless, as Clov realizes: "I say to myself—sometimes, Clov, you must learn to suffer better than that if you want them to weary of punishing you—" (51). Among the many echoes of *Endgame* in Auster's work is Nashe's sharing of Clov's hope of redemption through suffering in *The Music of Chance* by building the wall for his "fathers," Flower and Stone. Nashe's "crime" seems to be the absence of his father from his life; his punishment is welcomed as a penance for the lack of his father's love.

There are bleak moments such as these for Fogg in *Moon Palace* as well, but they are counterbalanced by joys and achievements. And Auster creates a crucial "swerve." The end is there in the beginning of the novel, as it is in *Endgame*—"The end is there in the beginning and yet you go on" (45)—but the end of the novel promises a new beginning: on the penultimate page Fogg can say: "This is where I start [...] this is where my life begins" (306). *Endgame* leaves us with an ending that seems only to promise the repetition of the same: an end that never comes, and no new beginning. The ending of Auster's novel suggests hope for the future, a movement beyond the deadening cycle of repetition. Here we have Bloom's idea of completion by antithesis enacted. But if we move beyond Bloom, if we bring into the picture the "potential" of Winnicott's "space," a potential to create ourselves and the way we interact with the world, as against either compliance or an agonistic conflict with an authoritative precursor, the positive and creative nature of Auster's response to Beckett can be seen clearly as driven less by anxiety than by creativity.

One of the things Auster must have recognized in Beckett is the absence of fathers, even when their presence is formidable, and the indelible effects the father can have upon a son when that "gesture of protective love" is unforthcoming. You do not stop yearning for this gesture, even after your father's death, as Beckett realized. In *Company* the comforting presence of "your father's shade" is there (19), and the "loved, trusted face" is recalled (23), bringing to mind Kierkegaard's belief that "he who is willing to work gives birth to his own father." Bloom is skeptical (56), but it seems to me a good maxim, and like *Moon Palace* achieves a movement that breaks out of the cycle of repetition. We create our own misreadings and in doing so create others' imagined worlds and ourselves. The son "giv[ing] birth to his own father" can be misread, creatively, as the son giving birth to himself. Auster, it can be suggested, has moved beyond both the anxiety of inheritance and the compliance involved in uncreative repetition.

In terms of Auster's creative life, Beckett has the role of a father figure. But Auster has had many fathers, many influences. In this, too, he takes after Beckett, whose literary fathers are everywhere in evidence in his work, alongside the creative misreadings he bestows on them. Auster emphasizes their significance: "That's why," he explains, that "The Book of Memory" (the second half of *The Invention of Solitude*) "is filled with so many references and quotations, in order to pay homage to all the others inside me" (*Red Notebook* 144). Auster is proud of the "dozens of authors" (144) who have gone toward making him the writer that he is. He has found his way beyond Beckett and, refreshingly, is happy to acknowledge the legacy—of Beckett and of others—in his work. It is a positive, productive inheritance, which, alongside the inheritance from his father, "all the novels [he has] written have come out of" (*Red Notebook* 132).

Works Cited

Albright, Daniel. *Beckett and Aesthetics*. Cambridge: Cambridge University Press, 2003.

Auster, Paul. Editor's Note. *Samuel Beckett: The Grove Centenary Edition*. Vol. 1. New York: Grove, 2006. vii–viii. 4 vols.

———. *Hand to Mouth*. London: Faber, 1998.

———. *In the Country of Last Things*. 1987. London: Faber, 1990.

———. *The Invention of Solitude*. 1982. London: Faber, 1989.

———. *Moon Palace*. 1989. London: Faber, 1990.

———. *The Music of Chance*. 1990. London: Faber, 1992.

———. *The New York Trilogy*. 1987. London: Faber, 1999.

———. *The Red Notebook*. London: Faber, 1996.

Beckett, Samuel. *The Beckett Trilogy: Molloy; Malone Dies; The Unnamable*. 1959. London: Pan, 1979.

———. *Company*. London: Calder, 1980.

———. *Endgame*. 1958. London: Faber, 1985.

———. *The Expelled and Other Novellas*. Harmondsworth: Penguin, 1983.

———. *Waiting for Godot*. 1956. London: Faber, 1978.

———. *Watt*. London: John Calder, 1963.

Bloom, Harold. *The Anxiety of Influence: A Theory of Poetry*. 2nd ed. Oxford: Oxford University Press, 1996.

Schwartz, Murray M. "Where Is Literature?" *Transitional Objects and Potential Spaces: Literary Uses of D. W. Winnicott*. Ed. Peter L. Rudnytsky. New York: Columbia University Press, 1993. 50–62.

Winnicott, D. W. *Home Is Where We Start From: Essays by a Psychoanalyst*. 1986. Harmondsworth: Penguin, 1987.

———. *Playing and Reality*. London: Tavistock, 1971.

Staging Sam

Beckett as Dramatic Character

HERSH ZEIFMAN

O N 3 JANUARY 1956, *Waiting for Godot* had its now notorious American premiere at the Coconut Grove Playhouse in Miami. The critical (and, more important, audience) response was mostly baffled and dismissive: the play was viewed as incomprehensible, an Irish/Gallic hoax. When *Godot* opened on Broadway later that spring, its producers were so desperate for an audience that they were reduced to advertising for "seventy thousand intellectuals" (Knowlson 350); only intellectuals, it seems, could appreciate such an abstruse and deeply enigmatic work.

Flash forward fifty years, to a winter evening in 2005. I'm ensconced, as usual, in front of the TV, mindlessly watching one of my favorite programs, the medical series *House*. In this particular episode, the mother of a critically ill patient whose time is running out refuses to approve a risky surgical procedure for her son until she gets an opinion from the Centers for Disease Control. The CDC apparently takes its own sweet time responding to such requests; as one of the show's doctors dryly comments, "Godot would be faster" ("Poison"). *House* is broadcast—and that's *broad*cast, not "narrowcast" on public television or specialty cable—on Fox, one of the major American television networks and thus not, I hasten to point out, a normal haven for intellectuals. Later that same evening, I finished a mass-market paperback novel, Michael Fredrickson's *A Cinderella Affidavit*, a legal thriller without even a trace of intellectual pretension or merit. At the novel's conclusion, Matthew Boer, its disillusioned protagonist, decides to stop practicing law; one of his partners, Ira Teitelbaum, tries to dissuade him: "'It won't be the same old shop without you,' said

311

Ira, his voice softer. Matthew forced himself to smile. 'We used to be together at the top of the Trifle Tower, Ira. But I was respectable in those days. Now they wouldn't even let me up.' Ira laughed. 'Goddamn English majors'" (447). Significantly, the novel doesn't even bother to identify its *Godot* quote, assuming, rightly or wrongly, that such identification is no longer required.

At the risk of exposing in public my appalling taste for schlock, I relate these anecdotes in order to illustrate how pervasive *Waiting for Godot* has become in the culture at large—and not just for English majors. For a play whose title character famously fails to appear, *Godot* now appears everywhere. He's in recent dramatic "offshoots" such as John Griffin's *Godot Has Left the Building*, Brendan Gall's *Alias Godot*, Geoff Sobelle and Trey Lyford's *All Wear Bowlers*; in *New Yorker* cartoons, including Alex Gregory's "Beckett on Ice," in which two "tramps," wearing ice skates, stand forlornly in the center of a rink; even in mass-market greeting cards (I was once sent a birthday card in which a line-drawn birthday boy, wearing a paper hat and holding a red balloon, sits patiently at a streamer-bedecked table; the caption beneath him reads, in a deft bilingual pun, "Waiting for Gateau").

In a remarkably short period of time, then, this formerly bewildering and impenetrable intellectual puzzle of a play has become a classic: familiar and iconic. And so has its author. It should, therefore, come as no surprise that interest in and admiration for Beckett's work have extended from the writing to the writer himself. Witness, for example, the many biographies published both before and after Beckett's death, capped by James Knowlson's magisterial *Damned to Fame*. Even more indicative of this embrace of Beckett's art and life is the number of plays in the past few years in which Beckett appears as an onstage character—three of which are the subject of this essay.

The most mainstream of these plays, and in some ways the least successful, is Michael Hastings's *Calico*, which opened in London's West End in the spring of 2004. Beckett is only a supporting character in *Calico;* the play's primary focus is on James Joyce and his family, particularly his mentally disturbed daughter, Lucia, whose existence Hastings claims has been "vapourized" (Note 9). Hastings is revisiting familiar territory here: in the introduction to his play *Tom and Viv* (1984), which shines a harsh spotlight on the marriage of T. S. Eliot and his mentally disturbed first wife, Vivienne Haigh-Wood, he describes Viv as "that painted shadow in the background [...], Stalinized into cultural obscurity" (32). *Calico,* like *Tom and Viv,* is Hastings's attempt to reposition a marginalized female figure by placing her at the center of his play, thus giving her a voice. Lucia's psychotic behavior, the play argues, stemmed from the tensions within a deeply dysfunctional, perhaps incestuous, family. And it is into this family, in the Paris of 1928, that the twenty-two-year-old Sam Beckett gingerly steps.

In the play Lucia is madly in love with Beckett—and for once the cliché is literally true: her unrequited love was indeed a kind of madness. She fantasizes that she and Sam are married and the proud parents of three sons, living an idyllic life in Galway, where in his spare time her school-teacher husband "wrote novels about landed Protestants" (70). It's hard to imagine a more unlikely bourgeois scenario for Beckett, and yet, in his desire to help, he reluctantly participates in Lucia's fantasy—an act, Hastings writes, of "astonishing compassion" (Note 11).

In his biography of Joyce, Richard Ellmann states that both Joyce and Beckett were "addicted to silences" (648); it is this essential silence of Beckett's character that Hastings captures most believably in *Calico.* Thus, Joyce refers to Sam in the play as "Mr Beckett of less words" (121); Nora Joyce notes his "loud ability to say nothing at all" (112); and Lucia calls him her "silent enigmatic Sam" (118). But it is not simply a matter of how the other characters see him; Hastings sees him this way as well, and so, of necessity, do we. Scene after scene features Sam lurking quietly in the background, a silent witness to the family romance being enacted in front of him. And in two revealing conversations in the second act of the play— first with Nora and then with Lucia—Sam manages to engage in a genuine dialogue in which he never once opens his mouth (111–12, 119).

If only he had remained silent throughout, however, for it's when Sam speaks that *Calico* goes seriously wrong. "Beckett's mind," Ellmann notes, "had a subtlety and strangeness that attracted Joyce as it attracted, in an-other way, his daughter" (648). Yet there is little evidence of that subtlety in *Calico*'s dramatic portrait of Beckett. Everything Sam says in the play is bland and predictable; there is nothing truly eccentric—truly *Beckettian*— in Hastings's Beckett. He is reduced, instead, to a plot device: an Irish version of the Gentleman Caller in *The Glass Menagerie.* (Williams's Gen-tleman Caller may be named O'Connor, but he's finally as all-American as public speaking courses and chewing gum.) With enormous tenderness Sam first supports Lucia's delusion and then, because he must, destroys it.

But there is no recognizable flutter of a heartbeat behind this facade of a character—only a dry and lifeless stock figure who happens to bear the name of a famous writer, a man of few (unexceptional) words spoken with a slight Irish brogue.

The Beckett we encounter in Canadian Sean Dixon's play *Sam's Last Dance* (1997), on the other hand, is anything but dry and lifeless. Well, maybe technically lifeless: the play's opening image is of Sam's *"pale face in a tight spotlight.* [. . .] *All around there is darkness, though from the spill we can see he is standing in a confined space. It is actually as if he is lying on his back, and we are watching him from above"* (1). Sam will return to this "sarcophagus" (5) throughout the play, but he is not in fact dead; we find him instead in that liminal space which he later describes as "[t]he moment between stirring still and stop" (4). Like all the contemporary playwrights under discussion in this essay, Dixon has done his homework, thoroughly researching both Beckett's life (Knowlson should sue for a share of the play's royalties) and, more significantly, his art: there are direct or indirect allusions to at least a dozen Beckett works in the play. "Here I am at last," Sam announces. "Alone at last" (2). And yet Sam is not alone; "to one on his back in the dark" (11) comes company. The nature of that company, and what it implies about his "aloneness," is the subject of Dixon's play.

The character who accompanies Sam during the course of the play is *"a dead ringer for an older Buster Keaton"* (3), the star of Beckett's *Film*—one Stone Face confronting another. Unlike Hastings, Dixon doesn't attempt to capture the "real" Beckett—whatever chimera that might be—in his play. All we can ever truly know is the public persona, this solitary figure struggling brilliantly to both invade and evade the nothingness that surrounds him, a persona Dixon uses as a springboard to dramatize two interrelated aspects of Beckett's aloneness. "We have some unfinished business, you and I" (6), Buster informs Sam. Since *Film* was, according to Buster, "a piece of shit" (6), he has come to offer Sam a second chance: their next collaboration should be "[a] show called 'Show'" (16). Sam is intrigued: to write, for once in his life, a work about what he terms "moreness" (24). And so, in *"a landscape casually reminiscent of the setting for 'Waiting for Godot'"* but lit now by the sun instead of the moon (22), Sam creates a show fairly bursting with "moreness": a World War II action film in which he gets to sing and dance, leap from bridges, blow up a Nazi train, and save all the great paintings of Europe. This show-within-the-play is deliberately contrived and often silly, but it raises a poignant issue: the psychic toll on Beckett in choosing to create—even if there was no true choice—a body of work that continually strives for "lessness," that explores so relentlessly the darkness of human existence, that measures with harrowing precision the exact confines of his aloneness. Beckett has given his public a great gift, but at what cost?

Buster knows the cost—but that's because Buster, Dixon indicates, is to be played by a woman with a French accent; "[y]ou look like my wife...Suzanne," Sam informs him (5). Here is the personal, as opposed to the artistic, side of Beckett's perceived aloneness; the more he disappeared into the "Vanishing Point" of his writing, the more Suzanne felt shut out. "[A]ll the written evidence," she laments, "shows that he is alone. / Not two...anymore, just one" (32). Only by impersonating Buster, by appearing with Sam in his show, can Suzanne leave her "mark" on him. In their shared derring-do adventures, the pair thus becomes a kind of hyperactive Gogo and Didi—no waiting required; Beckett may have banned cross-gender casting in *Godot,* but not in Suzanne's revisionist fantasy. "This is what I wanted," she confesses to her husband. "To be inside the work. Walking among the words of your work. [...] I could have been a face in the spotlight. A mouth. A pair of eyes. The sound of a breath. It's the only kind of erotic experience you can have with this man" (25). Sam's last dance—the romantic moment she and Sam share in the play—is in actuality Suzanne's last chance for that erotic experience. Dixon has subtitled the play "an introverted love story"; yet however much she tries to connect with him, Sam is still alone at the end of the play. The final stage direction reads: "*He reaches for her. She disappears. He turns to face out. Looks up. Blackout*" (38).

Suzanne also appears as a character in the play *Burnt Piano* (1999) by the Australian Justin Fleming, but, like Beckett himself, only in a supporting role. The play's protagonist is Karen Idlewild, a bookseller who, as her name suggests, idolizes Beckett—both the man and his writing—with an almost religious fervor. "He is a man unlike every other man" (109), Karen proclaims reverently at the very beginning of the play. According to Suzanne, Karen sees Beckett as a "prophet" and "oracle," a "Christ from out of the desert" (129–30), while her father Pete, himself a writer, accuses her of worshiping Beckett as a "guru" and "patriarch" (166). Karen has been sending Beckett letters her entire life, none of which has been answered. But now, in 1989, after a family tragedy in which one of her two young sons, left briefly alone while she was out running an errand, died in a house fire, she has come to Paris with her father and remaining child in order to meet him in person. After such knowledge—after such pain and loss—what forgiveness? Beckett, Karen claims, is "the only person who can understand" (126), who can explain to her the meaning of her own tragic past.

The work of Beckett's with which Karen especially identifies is *Waiting for Godot;* she was born on 3 January 1953, the date of the first performance of *En attendant Godot* in Paris, and because of this and other coincidences, she considers the play her "star sign" (119). *Burnt Piano* contains numerous quotations—some acknowledged, some not—from Beckett's most famous play. But more significant than these various allusions is the fact that Fleming's play itself, like *Sam's Last Dance,* becomes a kind of alternate version of *Waiting for Godot.* Beckett is Karen's Godot; if only she can meet him, she'll be saved. And so, like Gogo and Didi, she waits, as the act 1 curtain lines emphasize. When her son Jonah collapses at the very end of the act, she phones Emergency Services and informs them: "Yes, I'll wait. J'attends" (144). Composing one final letter to Beckett in act 2, Karen sends Jonah to deliver it—for "in [Beckett's] writing," she reminds us, "it's a child who brings messages" (127). Thus it is Jonah, the boy who was saved (in the belly of a piano) while his brother was "damned," who winds up twice encountering both Sam and his wife, their dialogue hauntingly echoing the form, rhythm, and often exact words of the Boy's meetings with Gogo and Didi in *Waiting for Godot.*

The Sam we see in *Burnt Piano* is, appropriately, most often a ghost, a shadowy figure bathed in a "*mysterious dream-light*" (120). Karen meets him throughout the play, but only in her imagination. And whenever he is *not* a ghost—for example, in the two domestic scenes with Suzanne, who humanizes him—he is simply a frail old man in the last year of his life, who plays the piano and is fond of whiskey and chess. Here is Fleming's point, and the reason Suzanne was included in the play: Beckett is neither God nor Godot, but all too fallibly mortal. Karen has imagined him, as we imagine all our gods; whatever universal truths she sees in his writing are her own creation. As Suzanne tells Jonah: "Monsieur Beckett knows nothing she does not know herself!" (130).

Beckett's writing contains no magic key to unlock life's mysteries or explain away its miseries—as Karen discovers when she finally meets Sam at Suzanne's graveside near the end of the play. Their "conversation," which occupies almost five pages of text, is totally one-sided; remarkably, Sam never utters a single word. "I had long imagined his counsel," Karen later comments. "Instead I was given his silence. [...] Or had I been waiting for his wisdom? And, instead, I found my own illumination" (173). Beckett's writing is only a mirror: the consolation and self-forgiveness Karen learns from him reside, ultimately, within herself.

And so we have three very different versions of Beckett as a dramatic character in three very different plays. In *Calico*, Hastings tries to create a realistic portrait of the young Sam Beckett (before he "became" Beckett, in a sense), but fails dismally, though initially there's a kind of frisson in the sheer novelty of seeing someone purporting to be Sam Beckett on the stage, which soon dissipates as the portrait refuses to come alive. In his introduction to the play, Hastings labels *Calico* "'critical fiction'" (11), but its fiction never rings true and—for the character of Beckett, at least—no critical context is present. We learn next to nothing about Beckett qua Beckett—or, as Lucky would say, quaquaquaqua Beckett; he provides merely a convenient biographical opportunity for Hastings to explore the true interest of his play, Lucia Joyce. Beckett proved useful primarily because, like Mount Everest, he was there.

Sam's Last Dance and *Burnt Piano,* on the other hand, genuinely attempt to engage with Beckett qua Beckett—or, at any rate, with Beckett in his role of writer. In bringing Beckett to theatrical life, all three plays necessarily speculate about the nature of his personality. But while *Calico's* speculation is fueled simply by biography, *Sam's Last Dance* and *Burnt Piano* take a more intriguing (and rewarding) approach: their portraits of Beckett are extrapolated from his writing. The focus of these plays, then, becomes the discovery not so much of the man but of the writer; what kind of man could produce his body of work? Though she's certain she knows the answer, that is Karen Idlewild's question (and quest) in *Burnt Piano.* And it's also the question underlying the dramatic treatment of Beckett in *Sam's Last Dance.* Near the end of the second act of that play, a new character suddenly appears—entering, significantly, from the audience. This figure is dismayed by what he considers the "disconnect" between the writer whose lifework, he believes, was "to illuminate for us—as with—a candle—the unheroic—journey towards frailty and well death" and the fun-loving, singing-and-dancing personality on display in the "Moreness" show. When Sam defends himself by declaring, "There's a difference between my life's work, and my life," the man replies: "I see your point I see your point yes. But I had thought not. I'm afraid I had thought you had embodied it—more or less. I mean that's what a fellow thinks when he looks you in the face: sees all your work, all of it, right there, in your face" (35–36).

This is the face that Dixon and Fleming chose to present in their plays: the face of Beckett the writer. In their desire to explain why his writing is so profoundly meaningful to so many people, both playwrights elected to bring Beckett onto the stage—to let him, in effect, speak for himself. Ironically, however, although their tremendous admiration for him comes through clearly, neither one of them is able to capture Beckett's complex personality. Their reading of the man thus reflects our reading of his texts: it's finally impossible to represent Beckett onstage because the only Beckett that truly exists for us is the one we create by responding to his work. That work becomes a pane of glass ("no symbols where none intended") in which we recognize both ourselves and, through that recognition, the "person" we call Beckett. The portraits of Beckett in Dixon's and Fleming's plays are thus at best only portraits of his imagined public persona; all any of us can do, the plays suggest, is project onto Beckett the man our own individual responses to Beckett the writer. Despite his forays from one side of the footlights to the other, then, the "real" Samuel Beckett remains, in the end, as stubbornly elusive as his most famous creation.

Works Cited

Beckett, Samuel. *Waiting for Godot*. London: Faber, 1965.

Dixon, Sean. *Sam's Last Dance: An Introverted Love Story*. Toronto: Playwrights Union of Canada, 1997.

Ellmann, Richard. *James Joyce*. Rev. ed. Oxford: Oxford University Press, 1983.

Fleming, Justin. *Burnt Piano. Coup d'Etat and Other Plays*. Philadelphia: Xlibris, 2004.

Fredrickson, Michael. *A Cinderella Affidavit*. New York: Doherty, 2000.

Gregory, Alex. "Beckett on Ice." *New Yorker* 3 Apr. 2006.

Hastings, Michael. *Calico*. London: Oberon, 2004.

———. Introduction. *Tom and Viv*. Harmondsworth: Penguin, 1985. 13–50.

———. A note about *Calico. Calico*. 5–13.

Knowlson, James. *Damned to Fame: The Life of Samuel Beckett*. New York: Simon, 1996.

"Poison." Episode 8. *House*. Fox TV. 25 Jan. 2005.

Williams, Tennessee. *The Glass Menagerie*. 1945. London: Methuen, 2000.

Index

Stevens, Wallace, 35
Stirrings Still
 Leibniz's influence in, 114
 "no body is at rest" and, 113
 Walther and, 28
 windows in, 109
Strauss, Walter, 240
structuralism, 71
subjectivity, 45, 73–75
surrealists vs. existentialists, 178, 179
Suzuki, Rieko, 250–251
Swedenborg, Emanuel, 221
Sweeney in the Trees (Saroyan), 270n8

tape recorder in *Krapp's Last Tape*
 as harmful technology, 193–199
 recorded voice of memory vs. Krapp's
  corporeal presence, 202–205
 romanticism and, 147–149
Target with Plaster Casts (Johns), 240–241
technology
 Beckett's uneasiness about, 199
 Beckett's use of, 272
 information overload and, 271–272
 Krapp's tape recorder as harmful
  technology, 193–199
 parodied in *Waiting for Godot*, 271–272
 run amok in *Ghost Trio*, 280
 utilitarian ethics, power, and, 197–198
Telephus, spear of, 190–191, 198–199
 reversal of, 192
television
 Beckett's plays for, 272. *See* Deleuze
  vs. film as media, 277–278
 "peephole art," 279
theory. *See* McLuhan, Marshall
temporality, 266
 See also time
Ten Little Indians (Christie), 252
Tennyson, Alfred, 142
testimony, 54–57, 62–65
Text, 42, 48
Texts for Nothing
 heteronymy in, 57–59, 62
 the mother and, 292
 narrative testimony in, 62–65
 reflections on, 37, 42, 44, 45–46, 52
 trauma, testimony, and shame in, 55–57
That Time, 42–43, 204

theatereality, 5, 125
theatrical space
 cosmic significance and, 131, 134
 darkness and, 125, 130–131, 134–135, 249
 infinity and, 247, 249–250
 instability and, 130, 135, 249–250
 influence of Maeterlinck on, 131
 nonnaturalistic, 134–135, 246–249
theatrum dei, 125, 127–130
theatrum mentis, 125, 126–127, 130
theatrum mundi, 125–126
Theodicy (Leibniz), 118n6
"The Return of the Proscenium Arch"
 ("Proscenium Arch e no Kaiki")
 (Betsuyaku), 247, 254
The Revolt of the Breeze Tribe (*Soyosoyo Zoku
 no Hanran*) (Betsuyaku), 247–248,
 252–253
Thomas Aquinas, 221
Thoor Ballylee, 220
Three Dialogues, 54, 75, 137n7
Tichi, Cecelia, 276
Tiepolo, Giovanni Battista (Residenz
 Würzburg), 27, *27*, 28
Tiepolo ceiling, 28, 30
time, 97, 225, 266
Time and Free Will (Bergson), 93, 95, 104
The Time of Your Life (Saroyan), 261, 265,
 266, 268
Tintoretto, Jacopo, 134
tomb figure of Bishop von Hohenlohe
 (Bamberg Cathedral), *29*
tormentor-tormented
 in Beckett's theater, 250–252
 in Betsuyaku's plays, 252
 instability of and reversal of roles, 127, 252
 spotlight and urn figures in *Play*, 124,
  125–127, 135
 in *Texts for Nothing* and *The Unnamable*,
  59–62, 64
Tokyo conference (Borderless Beckett,
 2006), 6
Tom and Viv (Hastings), 312–313
Top Girls (Churchill), 285, 286, 291
torture and anxiety, 250–254
Tour, Georges de la, 134
"The Tower" (Yeats), 146, 217, 218–221, 226, 227
tower, symbolism of, 220–221, 224, 228n2
trace, subjective, 73